# The Resilience of the Old Regime

In *The Resilience of the Old Regime*, David Art reevaluates the so-called first wave of democratization in Western Europe through the lens of authoritarian resilience. He argues that non-democrats succeeded to a very large degree in managing, diverting, disrupting, and repressing democratic movements until the end of World War I. This was true both in states that political scientists have long considered either full democracies or democratic vanguards (such as the UK and Sweden) as well as in others (such as Germany and Italy) that appeared to be democratizing. He challenges both the Whiggish view that democracy in the West moved progressively forward and the influential theory that the threats of revolution explain democratization. Drawing on extensive historical sources and data, Art recasts European political development from 1832 to 1919 as a period in which competitive oligarchies and competitive authoritarian regimes predominated.

David Art is Professor of Political Science at Tufts University. He is the author of *The Politics of the Nazi Past in Germany and Austria* (Cambridge University Press, 2006) and *Inside the Radical Right* (Cambridge University Press, 2011) and is a faculty affiliate at the Minda de Gunzburg Center for European Studies at Harvard University.

# The Resilience of the Old Regime

*Paths Around Democracy in Europe, 1832–1919*

**DAVID ART**

*Tufts University*

Shaftesbury Road, Cambridge CB2 8EA, United Kingdom

One Liberty Plaza, 20th Floor, New York, NY 10006, USA

477 Williamstown Road, Port Melbourne, VIC 3207, Australia

314–321, 3rd Floor, Plot 3, Splendor Forum, Jasola District Centre, New Delhi – 110025, India

Cambridge University Press is part of Cambridge University Press & Assessment, a department of the University of Cambridge.

We share the University's mission to contribute to society through the pursuit of education, learning and research at the highest international levels of excellence.

www.cambridge.org
Information on this title: www.cambridge.org/9781009710718
DOI: 10.1017/9781009710695

© David Art 2026

This publication is in copyright. Subject to statutory exception and to the provisions of relevant collective licensing agreements, no reproduction of any part may take place without the written permission of Cambridge University Press & Assessment.

When citing this work, please include a reference to the
DOI 10.1017/9781009710695

First published 2026

*A catalogue record for this publication is available from the British Library*

Library of Congress Cataloging-in-Publication Data
NAMES: Art, David, 1972– author
TITLE: The resilience of the old regime : paths around democracy in Europe, 1832–1919 / David Art, Tufts University, Massachusetts.
DESCRIPTION: Cambridge ; New York, NY : Cambridge University Press, 2026. | Includes bibliographical references.
IDENTIFIERS: LCCN 2025034006 | ISBN 9781009710725 hardback | ISBN 9781009710718 paperback | ISBN 9781009710695 ebook
SUBJECTS: LCSH: Democratization – Europe – History – 19th century | Democratization – Europe – History – 20th century | Authoritarianism – Europe – History – 19th century | Authoritarianism – Europe – History – 20th century | Europe – Politics and government – 1815–1871 | Europe – Politics and government – 1871–1918
CLASSIFICATION: LCC D363 .A78 2026
LC record available at https://lccn.loc.gov/2025034006

ISBN 978-1-009-71072-5 Hardback
ISBN 978-1-009-71071-8 Paperback

Cambridge University Press & Assessment has no responsibility for the persistence or accuracy of URLs for external or third-party internet websites referred to in this publication and does not guarantee that any content on such websites is, or will remain, accurate or appropriate.

For EU product safety concerns, contact us at Calle de José Abascal, 56, 1°, 28003 Madrid, Spain, or email eugpsr@cambridge.org.

*To Matilda*

# Contents

| | | |
|---|---|---|
| *Acknowledgments* | | *page* ix |
| 1 | The First Wave and the Study of Democracy | 1 |
| 2 | Paths Around Democracy in Europe | 20 |
| 3 | Crafting Competitive Oligarchy in the United Kingdom | 45 |
| 4 | The European Origins of Competitive Authoritarianism | 91 |
| 5 | Wilhelmine Germany and Edwardian England | 127 |
| 6 | Authoritarian Resilience in Northern Europe | 176 |
| 7 | From Competitive Oligarchy to Competitive Authoritarianism in Italy | 205 |
| 8 | War and Democratization in Europe | 250 |
| 9 | Conclusion | 290 |
| *Index* | | 301 |

# Acknowledgments

Writing this book over the last decade has reminded me why we continue to refer to the production of knowledge in a specific field as a discipline. Without the unflagging enthusiasm and curiosity of my students at Tufts University, I could not have mustered the discipline to complete a research project that I first imagined as an undergraduate. I would like to thank, in particular, Anika Ades, Richard Ammerman, David Attewell, Alexandra Blackman, Andrew Chen, Brendan Hartnett, and Summer Maxwell for their important contributions to this book.

I am indebted to the organizers and participants at the following venues where I had the opportunity to present parts of the argument: Arizona State University, Brandeis University, Boston University, Harvard University, University of Cyprus, Rutgers University, and the University of Zurich. I am grateful to Tufts University, which supported my research through a Faculty Research Award Grant as well as a book workshop cosponsored by the University of Massachusetts and facilitated by my department chair, Nimah Mazaheri. This book benefitted enormously from the careful comments of leaders in the field who attended that workshop: Amel Ahmed, Sheri Berman, Michael Bernhard, Steve Hanson, and Daniel Ziblatt were each extraordinarily generous with their time. I would also like to thank Mark Beissinger, Eva Bellin, Daniele Caramani, Antonis Ellinas, Shamiran Mako, and Michail Moutselos for their contributions.

I am grateful to Robert Dreesen at Cambridge University Press for his confidence in this book and for soliciting two excellent anonymous reviews, both of whom went to extraordinary length to engage with my arguments, point out the flaws, and suggest remedies. I hope that they – and all the other students and scholars noted earlier – see how much of their advice I have incorporated, and how much their effort improved the book.

My family deserves the biggest thank you of all. My amazing wife, Julija, has supported me lovingly and unreservedly through this venture, as she has through every other one since we met as two students in Slovenia. My parents are both prolific authors who continue to read my work as if it were a fourth-grade essay. Suzanne Art's books on history have been read by tens of thousands of students, and Robert Art is one of the intellectual founders of the modern field of security studies. Their love of learning is reflected on every page of this book. My daughter Matilda has been watching me write this book since she was born and would have surely preferred one on large cats or horses. Nevertheless, I devote this book to her.

# I

# The First Wave and the Study of Democracy

Several years before the outbreak of World War I (WWI), James Bryce began an exhaustive empirical study of democracy, or what he termed "popular government." As a member of parliament from 1880 to 1907, Bryce had participated in some of the great debates about political reform in Edwardian Britain. As a professor at Oxford, he had written *The American Commonwealth* that analyzed American political institutions by reproducing the travels of Alexis de Tocqueville a half century earlier.[1] As British Ambassador to the United States from 1907 to 1913, he witnessed how the egalitarianism that Tocqueville identified in the 1830s as the core of American democracy had been transformed into an economic oligarchy. All these experiences left Bryce increasingly unsatisfied with, as he put it, the "references, usually vague and disconnected, to history and to events happening in other countries" that masqueraded as empirical knowledge about democracy. He wondered if "something might be done to provide a solid basis for argument and judgment by examining a certain number of popular governments in their actual working, comparing them with one another, and setting forth the various merits and defects that belonged to each."[2]

He then literally traveled around the world, conducting fieldwork in New Zealand, Australia, Canada, Switzerland, France, and the United States in search of, as he put it, "Facts, Facts, Facts!" Published in 1921, his 700-page *Modern Democracies* was a synthesis of his life's work.

---

[1] James Bryce, *The American Commonwealth*, 3 vols. (London: Macmillan, 1888).
[2] James Bryce, *Modern Democracies*, 1 vol. (New York: The Macmillan Company, 1921), vii.

Two facts, in particular, emerged from his research. First, there had been an undeniable proliferation of democracies worldwide over his lifetime. Whereas "a century ago there was in the Old World only one tiny spot in which the working of democracy could be studied," Bryce finds that "there are now more than one hundred representative assemblies at work all over the earth legislating for self-governing communities."[3] The second was that democracy had become recognized as the proverbial "only game in town":

> A not less significant change has been the universal acceptance of democracy as the normal and natural form of government. Seventy years ago, as those who are now old can well remember, the approaching rise of the masses to power was regarded by the educated classes of Europe as a menace to order and prosperity. Thus, the word Democracy awakened dislike and fear. Now it is a word of praise. Popular power is welcomed, extolled, worshipped. The few whom it repels or alarms rarely avow their sentiments. Men have almost ceased to study its phenomena because they now seem to have become part of the established order of things. The old question – What is the best form of government? – is almost obsolete because the center of interest has been shifting. It is not the nature of democracy, nor even the variety of the shapes it wears, that are to-day in debate, but rather the purposes to which it may be turned, the social and economic changes it may be used to affect.[4]

The rise of authoritarianism in many European states within several years of the publication of *Modern Democracies* made it clear that democracy had not, in fact, become "part of the established order of things." Other regime types – from competitive authoritarianism to totalitarianism – emerged as alternatives to liberal democracy in the 1920s and 1930s. Writing in 1938, Bryce's longtime friend and fellow academic A. Lawrence Lowell admitted that "reading *Modern Democracies* a score of years after it was written, one is impressed by how far from the direction then expected the political currents of the world have run."[5] And yet that democratic heritage still mattered when Lowell interpreted the ominous geopolitical trends of the time; he pointed out that of the four revisionist powers of Germany, Italy, Japan, and the Soviet Union, "none of them had enjoyed a successful democracy."[6] In the aftermath of World War II (WWII), there was

---

[3] Ibid., 3–4. Bryce is referring to Switzerland as the "one tiny spot in which the working of democracy could be studied."
[4] Ibid., 4.
[5] A. Lawrence Lowell, "The Evolution of Democracy." *Foreign Affairs* 17, 1 (October 1938), 27.
[6] Ibid., 31.

arguably no more urgent question in comparative politics than why Great Britain, France, and several other smaller European states had democratized before WWI, while others – particularly Germany – had failed. Many canonical works in democratization emerged from this comparison as both modernization theorists and their critics mined nineteenth- and early twentieth-century European history for empirical illustrations of their theories.[7] Writing at another highpoint of democratic optimism forty years later, Samuel Huntington renamed the territory that Bryce had covered in *Modern Democracies* as the "first wave" of democratization. This concept has become widespread in the literature, even though Huntington's overriding concern was the "third wave" of democratization that began in the early 1970s.[8]

The first wave is more than an academic construct: It is an integral chapter in the stories that European democracies tell themselves. The common element in these narratives of democratization is that today's consolidated democracy is the product of a stepwise progression of democratic achievements beginning centuries ago. This is the history that one learns in high school, the history one finds on the websites of national parliaments, and the history politicians rely on for ceremonial occasions. Typical of the latter are remarks by British Prime Minister Gordon Brown in 2007 who perceived "a golden thread which runs through British history" extending from a "long-ago day in Runnymede in 1215 when arbitrary power was fully challenged with the Magna Carta, on to the first bill of rights in 1689 where Britain became the first country where parliament asserted power over the king, to the democratic reform acts."[9]

One might be tempted to dismiss such rosy narratives in Great Britain as the legacy of Whig history, which Herbert Butterfield famously defined as "the tendency of many historians to write on the side of Protestants

---

[7] These include Seymour Martin Lipset, *Political Man* (Garden City: Doubleday, 1959); Barrington Moore, *Social Origins of Dictatorship and Democracy* (Boston: Beacon Press, 1966); Robert Dahl, *Polyarchy: Participation and Opposition* (New Haven: Yale University Press, 1971); Gregory Luebbert, *Liberal, Fascism, and Social Democracy: Social Classes and the Political Origins of Regimes in Interwar Europe* (New York: Oxford University Press, 1988); Dietrich Rueschemeyer, Evelyne Huber Stephens and John D. Stephens, *Capitalist Development and Democracy* (Chicago: University of Chicago Press, 1992); Ruth Berins Collier, *Paths toward Democracy: The Working Class and Elites in Western Europe and South America* (New York: Cambridge University Press, 1999).
[8] Samuel Huntington, *The Third Wave: Democratization in the Late Twentieth Century* (Norman: University of Oklahoma Press, 1991).
[9] "Full Text of Gordon Brown's Speech," *The Guardian*, February 27, 2007.

and Whigs, to praise revolutions provided they have been successful, to emphasize certain principles of progress in the past and to produce a story which is the ratification if not the glorification of the present."[10] But such stories are hardly confined to the UK. Sweden has embraced a national narrative that "stresses the heritage of a free and politically active farming class, economic egalitarianism, and a responsive state."[11] That Sweden was one of the least democratic states in Europe prior to WWI, and that its regime more closely resembled Prussia's rather than England's for most of the "first wave," has little salience in Swedish historical memory. In Denmark, a conservative government, with a strong push from the radical right Danish People's Party, established a committee "for the purpose of drawing up a democracy canon" in 2006. The goal, according to Prime Minister Anders Fogh Rasmussen, was to "highlight Danish and international historical philosophical trends and political texts that have had a special impact on the development of fundamental freedoms and democracy in Denmark."[12] The final product was a Whiggish document that told "a rather nice story of Danish Democracy" with the central message that the "Danes have preferred reform to revolution."[13]

These narratives are preferable to the jingoistic ones that predominated in Europe a century earlier. They also contain important elements of truth; some moments of political liberalization deserve to be commemorated, if not celebrated. Yet we should recognize historical mythmaking when we see it, and these narratives of democratization that politicians embrace are not consistent with the historical record. The intellectual problem, however, is that political scientists still have a view of the first wave that largely follows Bryce in focusing on its democratic features, and most literature on the period – both classic and contemporary – is still concerned primarily with explaining the emergence of democracy against the backdrop of royal absolutism. According to Daniel Ziblatt, for example, the triumph of democracy in Western Europe "occurred in the reactionary shadow that followed the French Revolution, facing new and not entirely understood economic

---

[10] Herbert Butterfield, *The Whig Interpretation of History* (New York: W. W. Norton, 1965), 2.
[11] Erik Bengtsson, "The Swedish Sonderweg in Question." *Past and Present* 244, 1 (August 2019), 123–161.
[12] Danish Democracy Canon, Danish Ministry of Education, 2008.
[13] Jeppe Nevers, "A History of Democracy beyond National Narratives." *Geschichte und Gesellschaft* 44, 3 (July–September 2018), 422.

dislocations and absent the certainty of carrying out the reforms with the democratic transition playbook in hand." As such, he continues, "the relative *success* of democratic reforms in late-nineteenth century Europe should strike contemporary political scientists as nearly an unfathomable puzzle."[14]

Judging from the volume of research within the last two decades, the puzzle remains unresolved. Daron Acemoglu and James Robinson helped jumpstart the debate about the origins of European democracy with their article "Why Did the West Extend the Franchise" and their extension of the argument in *Economic Origins of Dictatorship and Democracy* (2006). The authors used both the 1832 and 1867 Reform Acts in Great Britain to illustrate that the old regime only extends the franchise under the threat of revolution.[15] Both advocates and critics of the political economy approach reexamined nineteenth and early twentieth-century European history for further illustrative examples.[16] The result has been a rebirth of the field of European political development as scholars use the first wave to generate and test specific theories about democratization.[17]

---

[14] Daniel Ziblatt, "How Did Europe Democratize?" *World Politics* 58 (2006), 311.

[15] Daron Acemoglu and James Robinson, "Why Did the West Extend the Franchise? Democracy, Inequality, and Growth in Historical Perspective." *Quarterly Journal of Economics* 115 (2000), 1167–1199.

[16] Daron Acemoglu and James Robinson, *Economic Origins of Dictatorship and Democracy* (New York: Cambridge University Press, 2006); Carlos Boix, *Democracy and Redistribution* (New York: Cambridge University Press, 2003); Ben Ansell and David Samuels, *Inequality and Democratization: An Elite-Competition Approach* (New York: Cambridge University Press, 2015); Giovanni Capoccia and Daniel Ziblatt, eds., "The Historical Turn in Democratization Studies," Special Issue of *Comparative Political Studies* 43, 8/9 (August 2010).

[17] Amel Ahmed, *Democracy and the Politics of Electoral System Choice: Engineering Electoral Dominance* (New York: Cambridge University Press, 2013); David Bateman, *Disenfranchising Democracy: Constructing the Electorate in the United States, the United Kingdom, and France* (New York: Cambridge University Press, 2018); Sheri Berman, *Democracy and Dictatorship in Europe: From the Ancien Regime to the Present Day* (New York: Oxford University Press, 2019); Stephen Hanson, *Post-Imperial Democracies: Ideology and Party Formation in Third Republic France, Weimar Germany, and Post-Soviet Russia* (New York: Cambridge University Press, 2010); Isabella Mares, *From Open Secrets to Secret Voting: Democratic Electoral Reforms and Voter Autonomy* (New York: Cambridge University Press, 2015); Dawn Teele, *Forging the Franchise: The Political Origins of the Women's Vote* (Princeton: Princeton University Press, 2018); Kurt Weyland, *Making Waves: Democratic Contention in Europe and Latin America since the Revolutions of 1848* (New York: Cambridge University Press, 2014); Daniel Ziblatt, *Conservative Parties and the Birth of Democracy* (New York: Cambridge University Press, 2017).

## 1.1 A RIPPLE, NOT A WAVE

But what about authoritarianism? Bryce's count of democracies before WWI included only seven countries: Australia, Canada, France, New Zealand, the United States, the United Kingdom, and Switzerland.[18] Nondemocratic regimes were the norm in pre-WWI Europe, but most of the literature on European political development is devoted to explaining democratic exceptionalism.

The goal of this book is to reduce this asymmetry by asking a different macro-question about the first wave. The puzzle is not that democracy was so successful over this period, but that the transition to some form of mass politics in the birthplace of both the Enlightenment and industrial revolutions produced so few democratic successes. If there was indeed a democratic first wave, it was an extraordinarily small one. And if this is true, then it is not the democratic achievements of the first wave, but rather the successful blocking strategies of the old regime that deserve our attention today.

Other scholars have made similar arguments before. Writing in 1980, Arno Mayer noted that "the conventional wisdom is still that Europe broke out of its *ancien régime* and approached or crossed the threshold of modernity well before 1914."[19] He challenged this view in *The Persistence of the Old Regime* and concluded that "down to 1914, the 'steel frame' of Europe's political societies continued to be heavily feudal and nobilitarian." Mayer continued that "in spite of vast national and constitutional variations, there were significant family resemblances among all the regimes" and speculated that "perhaps this affinity was rooted first and foremost in the enduring importance of landed interests and of rural society throughout Europe."[20] For Mayer, then, the endurance of authoritarianism was ultimately explained by the persistence of feudalistic class relations in otherwise industrializing societies, which were in turn, per Marxist theory, the result of the existing factors of production.

Mayer is correct that the landed elite retained far more power in pre-WWI Europe than most historians had assumed. Yet to ascribe this endurance primarily to material forces obscures the success of the old regime in

---

[18] Bryce did not analyze the British case in *Modern Democracies* on the grounds that he could not serve as an impartial judge of his own country's democratic institutions. It seems an odd defense today but it did limit the book to under 1,000 pages.
[19] Arno Mayer, *The Persistence of the Old Regime* (New York: Pantheon, 1981), 5.
[20] Ibid., 186.

springing back into shape in the face of enormous challenges. Resilience is more accurate than persistence, for what is most remarkable about the endurance of authoritarianism in Western Europe is how creative – and indeed how successful – old regime elites were in avoiding the system of one-person, one-vote. Consider that it took democratic reformers nearly a century to enact the program that 60,000 English citizens demanded on August 16, 1819, and that the Chartists – the largest working-class movement in British history – mobilized for universal suffrage in the 1840s. The rise of socialism on the continent similarly challenged the old regime, for one of the major demands of socialist parties everywhere was universal and equal manhood suffrage. The old regime proved resilient here as well, for nowhere in Europe did socialist pressure lead to full democratization before WWI. The few genuine cases of democratization in Europe also created an additional challenge to authoritarians, for democratic reformers could point to existing democratic systems as models. Swedish reformers, for example, could draw inspiration from Norway (1898) and Denmark (1901), and all of Europe after 1875 could look toward France. The old regime was resilient in that it, by and large, found paths around democracy before the transformations caused by WWI.

These authoritarian features of European political development have become clearer to scholars in recent years. One of the central lessons Sheri Berman draws from the European past is that "achieving consolidated liberal democracy easily or quickly is extremely unusual," noting further that "even the cases most often heralded as having done so had far more trouble and took much longer than most observers recognize."[21] For Ziblatt too, the first wave was an "age defined not only by democratization but also by conservative counter-movements."[22] Amel Ahmed shows that nineteenth-century European elites who feared democracy designed a myriad of "exclusionary safeguards" into their electoral systems to preserve their power.[23] David Bateman demonstrates that the first wave in the United States, Great Britain, and France was marked by nearly simultaneous enfranchisements and disenfranchisements. The short-lived French Second Republic (1848–1851), for example, retracted the universal suffrage it had proclaimed only two years earlier and committed "among the largest single disenfranchisements by an otherwise democratic regime in world history" with its Electoral Law of May 31,

---

[21] Sheri Berman, *Democracy and Dictatorship in Europe: From the Ancien Regime to the Present Day* (New York: Oxford University Press, 2019), 384.
[22] Ziblatt, *Conservative Parties and the Birth of Democracy*, 5.
[23] Ahmed, *Electoral System Choice*, 2013.

1850, that cut the electorate from ten to seven million.[24] But it is in fact an older work – Robert Goldstein's *Political Repression in 19th Century Europe* published in 1983 – that comes closest to my own argument.[25] Goldstein writes:

> The highly systematized, institutionalized, day-to-day, and non-violent nature of most class-biased suffrage systems made them both extraordinarily effective instruments of political repression and extremely easy to underestimate in historical retrospect. Most political scientists and historians are well aware that such systems were widespread in nineteenth-century Europe. However, they generally tend to point this out once or twice in passing, even in lengthy studies dealing with European politics and social history (because the discrimination was so institutionalized and was rarely manifested in spectacular incidents), without analyzing the impact that suffrage restrictions had on the basic nature of European political development during the era.[26]

One line of thinking holds that such suffrage restrictions were part of a broader set of counter-majoritarian institutions – such as unelected upper legislative chambers, plural voting, and militaries outside of civilian control – that served democracy's long-term interests by reassuring old regime elites that they would still hold disproportionate influence under the new system.[27] I reach the opposite conclusion and agree with Ziblatt that "rather than 'way stations' on the path to fuller democracy, counter-majoritarian institutions may be permanent detours."[28] To take one example, the 1866 reforms in Sweden that were deeply counter-majoritarian have often been described as "society preserving" and an important step in preparing the old regime elite for future democratization. Yet it is equally plausible to ask: "Why did [1866] become a roadblock against further reform, allowing Sweden to become one of the least democratic countries in Western Europe, rather than a stepping-stone for reformism?"[29]

By taking a "glass half empty" approach to first-wave democratization, some unappreciated features of European political development

---

[24] Bateman, *Disenfranchising Democracy*, 283.
[25] Robert Goldstein, *Political Repression in 19th Century Europe* (Totowa: Barnes and Noble Books, 1983).
[26] Ibid., 334.
[27] Barry Weingast, Susan Alberts and Chris Warshaw, "Democratization and Counter-majoritarian Institutions: The Role of Power and Constitutional Design in Self-Enforcing Democracy," in Tom Ginsburg, ed., *Comparative Constitutional Design* (New York: Cambridge University Press, 2012).
[28] Ziblatt, *Conservative Parties*, 366.
[29] Bengtsson, "Swedish Sonderweg," 160.

come into sharper view. There are legions of studies of the European roots of liberal democracy, but few about the European origins of competitive oligarchy and competitive authoritarianism. Competitive oligarchy is no longer common, as the idea of explicitly limiting the right to vote along class, ethnic, or gender lines is no longer considered consistent with the practice of elections themselves. It was, however, in nineteenth- and even early twentieth-century Western Europe. Competitive oligarchies were underpinned by a liberal ideology that viewed the vote not as a right but as a privilege based on "capacity." We often forget that "liberal democracy" is a twentieth-century invention, and that many of the leading liberal politicians and intellectuals viewed universal suffrage as a threat to civilization, as a "menace and order to prosperity" according to Bryce. During the entirety of the first wave, elites constructed, or fought desperately to preserve, counter-majoritarian institutions to secure their positions. Up until the eve of WWI, they had been relatively successful overall, leading to the conclusion that competitive oligarchy might well have persisted longer had it not been for an exogenous event of extraordinary magnitude.

Competitive authoritarianism, by contrast, is widespread today, leading some to conclude that it is a new form of regime type. The scholars who introduced the term take this position: Steven Levitsky and Lucan Way claim that competitive authoritarianism was an unintended consequence of the end of Cold War.[30] No longer able to count on anti-communism or anti-capitalism to receive foreign aid, they argue, autocracies around the world introduced elections and democratic reforms largely in the interests of preserving ties with the only surviving superpower, one that had rediscovered its zeal for democracy promotion. Some of these regimes democratized, but most either reverted to authoritarianism or achieved a competitive authoritarian equilibrium.

This book demonstrates that competitive authoritarianism is not historically bounded, as Levitsky and Way argue, and that its portability across time is one of its most underappreciated strengths as a regime category. I argue that competitive authoritarianism was designed to stabilize monarchies/empires in Europe, first in Bonapartist France and then in

---

[30] Steven Levitsky and Lucan Way, *Competitive Authoritarianism: Hybrid Regimes after the Cold War* (New York: Cambridge University Press, 2010). They define competitive authoritarianism as follows: "Competitive authoritarian regimes are civilian regimes in which formal democratic institutions exist, but in which incumbents' abuse of the state places them at a significant advantage vis-à-vis their opponents (5)."

Imperial Germany. Both states combined universal suffrage and regular elections with counter-majoritarian institutions and electoral manipulation. Neither could really be described as a "halfway house" on the way to full democracy, as they survived intact for nearly two and five decades, respectively. An investigation of European political development before WWI offers further evidence that competitive authoritarianism is neither historically bounded nor necessarily unstable.[31]

Overall, the fact of democratic consolidation in most of contemporary Europe should not blind us to the old regime's success in preserving non-majoritarian institutions or harnessing universal suffrage to its own advantage. Karl Polanyi, commenting on the entirely unrelated matter of the Tudor's attempts to stem the enclosure movement in seventeenth-century Britain, puts the issue better than I can. Whereas economic liberals, whom Polanyi was arguing against, claimed that the eventual triumph of the enclosure movement demonstrated the futility of state action against market forces, Polanyi stresses that this is the wrong point to draw. "Why should the ultimate victory of a trend be taken as proof of the ineffectiveness of the efforts to slow down its progress? And why should the purpose of these measures not be seen precisely in that which they achieved, i.e., in the slowing down of the rate of change?"[32]

If this reading of the first wave is more plausible than its alternatives, four theoretical implications follow. The first is that modernization theory fails to explain the very cases that generated it. Modernization theory was a product of the early cold war, and social scientists studied European history for examples of economic development – which was conceived as liberal economic development – that ushered in *political* liberalization. The United Kingdom offered an excellent example as the first state to industrialize, to produce a middle class, and to include that class into the decision-making apparatus of the state. That this story of political development was quintessentially Whiggish was not viewed as problematic by proponents of the theory. However, if Great Britain, Belgium,

---

[31] For the current debate on the stability of competitive authoritarianism, see: Michael Bernard, Amanda Edgell and Staffan Lindberg, "Institutionalizing Electoral Uncertainty and Authoritarian Regime Survival." *European Journal of Political Research* 59 (2020), 465–487; Amanda B. Edgell, Valeriya Mechkova, David Altman, Michael Bernhard and Staffan I. Lindberg, "When and Where Do elections matter? A Global Test of the Democratization by Elections Hypothesis, 1900–2010." *Democratization* 25 (2017), 422–444. https://doi.org/10.1080/13510347.2017.1369964
[32] Karl Polanyi, *The Great Transformation* (Boston: Beacon Press, 1944), 39.

and the Netherlands are better understood as cases of competitive oligarchy rather than vanguard democracies, the democratizing power of the middle class during the first wave needs serious revision.[33]

A second implication is that another prominent theory of democratization – that elites only agree to redistribution (through democracy) given a credible threat of revolution – also fails to capture the major elements of the first wave. I will show that in case after case – including the ones identified by proponents of the theory – the key decision-makers either did not perceive there to be a revolutionary situation, or that they reacted through repression rather than concession. The more interesting point is not that the threat of revolution hypothesis finds little empirical support, but *why* it does not. My answer is that the old regime developed new forces of coercion – specifically the police – to deal with potential insurrections. The police have not featured prominently in studies of European political development, despite the fact that the first modern police force was created in London in 1829 to deal not only with crime but also with political unrest. The nationalization of policing in the UK occurred during a major period of Chartist agitation, and by 1867 the domestic police were large enough to control any crowd of demonstrators. Police were even more important in the French Second Empire (1851–1870), where they not only monitored public opinion but were also expected to "manage elections" and produce Bonapartist victories. Police, in short, were an integral and underappreciated part of the old regime.

A third implication is that partial democracy is neither a halfway house on the road to full democracy nor a temporary respite from authoritarianism. This claim would have been much more provocative – arguably even heretical – during the crest of the "transitology paradigm." Huntington asserted in 1991 that "the experience of a third wave strongly suggests that liberalized authoritarianism is not a stable equilibrium; the halfway house does not stand."[34] Three decades later, Jason Brownlee's claim that partial democracy is less "a way station, than a way of life" looks closer to

---

[33] For a recent and compelling critique of modernization theory based on cases in Latin America (including several "first wave" cases), see Scott Mainwaring and Aníbal Pérez-Liñán, *Democracies and Dictatorships in Latin America: Emergence, Survival, and Fall* (New York: Cambridge University Press, 2013). See also Nimah Mazaheri and Steve Monroe, "'No Arab Bourgeoisie, No Democracy?' The Entrepreneurial Middle Class and Democratic Attitudes since the Arab Spring." *Comparative Politics* 50, July (2018), 523–550; Bryn Rosenfeld, *The Autocratic Middle Class* (Princeton: Princeton University Press, 2021).

[34] Huntington, *The Third Wave*, 137.

TABLE 1.1 *Date of female suffrage versus year of democratic transition*

| Country | Year of female suffrage[a] | Year of full democratization[b] |
| --- | --- | --- |
| Norway | 1913 | 1898 |
| Denmark | 1915 | 1915 |
| Netherlands | 1919 | 1917 |
| Sweden | 1919 | 1918 |
| Germany | 1928 | 1919 |
| United Kingdom | 1928 | 1918 |
| France | 1946 | 1875 |
| Italy | 1946 | 1912 |
| Belgium | 1948 | 1918 |
| Switzerland | 1971 | 1848 |

[a] From Pamela Paxton, "Women's Suffrage in the Measurement of Democracy: Problems of Operationalization." Studies in Comparative International Development 35 (September 2000), 92–111.
[b] From Ruth Collier, *Path's Toward Democracy*.

the mark.[35] One of the major changes in the field of comparative politics has been the (re)discovery of nondemocratic regimes as worthy of study in themselves. The long nineteenth century in Europe offers a wide array of variations on authoritarianism that this book has only started to uncover.

Fourth, a revised survey of the first wave reveals that international war played a much greater role in the democratization of Europe than most analyses suggest. The wave metaphor implies that WWI was the culmination of a long process, a time in which many states made a final transition to democracy. On closer inspection, however, WWI was transformative rather than incremental. It was only in the context of an international war of previously unimaginable carnage that a group of supposed first-wave democratizers adopted universal suffrage and/or abolished their counter-majoritarian institutions.

Before developing these arguments, we should note up front that there are two other compelling challenges to the conventional view of democratization in Europe. First, one could argue that no state in Europe was democratic until all adult women could vote (see Table 1.1). Since there were several states in the world where women could vote before WWI, it is impossible to argue that the West was somehow incapable of enfranchising women at this point in its historical development. Women were demanding, and in the case of some radical suffragette movements in

---

[35] Jason Brownlee, *Authoritarianism in an Age of Democratization* (New York: Cambridge University Press, 2007), 16–17.

Britain, fighting for the vote on the eve of WWI. Second, one can also plausibly argue that democratization and colonialism were not compatible, and thus democracy only truly arrived after decolonization in the two decades following WWII. Even then, the persistence of systemic racism and highly restrictive citizenship policies still undercut democratic quality in former colonizers, as they do in the United States. Hopefully scholars will follow Michael Hanford's lead in pursuing this foundational critique of the West's democratic heritage.[36] This book is less ambitious by accepting a much lower standard for democracy and demonstrating that much of Europe failed to meet even that.

## 1.2 HISTORIOGRAPHY AND THE FIRST WAVE

This book uses mostly qualitative data.[37] Much of it is primary source, but the bulk of the evidence comes from secondary sources. This raises an immediate methodological issue, for as Marcus Kreuzer notes "political scientists commonly draw on history but often do not read actual historians carefully."[38] His concerns echo those of Ian Lustick, who warns political scientists that "the work of historians is not understood to be, and cannot legitimately be treated by others as, an unproblematic background narrative from which theoretically neutral data can be elicited for the framing of problems and the testing of theories."[39] Many political scientists would surely concede this point, yet most still appear

---

[36] Michael Hanford, *The Spectre of Race: How Discrimination Haunts Western Democracy* (Princeton: Princeton University Press, 2018). Hanford's observation that "surprisingly little scholarship exists within comparative politics on the impact of slave regimes within nominally democratic societies and their political institutions" also holds for democracies with colonies (14).

[37] Cross-national statistical data for this period is both incomplete and unreliable. This is not surprising, as the mass collection of political, economic, and social data was a product of the behavioral revolution of the 1950s. It is a substantial issue, however, given that some of the most influential treatments of the first wave involve complex economic models whose implications are difficult to assess without high-quality data. To take one example, Boix's central concept of asset specificity has proven difficult to operationalize in the context of late nineteenth-century Europe (Ansell and Samuels, *Inequality and Democratization*, 2011). Put simply, it is tough to recreate the figures that the state did not collect itself or failed to do so with any regularity or accuracy.

[38] Marcus Kreuzer, "Historical Knowledge and Quantitative Analysis: The Case of the Origins of Proportional Representation." *American Political Science Review* 104, 2 (May 2010), 369.

[39] Ian Lustick, "History, Historiography, and Political Science: Multiple Historical Records and the Problem of Selection Bias." *American Political Science Review* 90, 3 (September 1996), 604.

to operate under the assumption that an actual historical record exists and that historians are in the business of reconstructing the facts, much as survey researchers are in the business of capturing the state of public opinion. Political scientists are generally quite attuned to the methodological strengths and limitations of survey research, but they often fail to make such distinctions among historical works.

For example, take the case of the political regime of "liberal Italy" from unification in 1861 to the fascist seizure of power in 1922. The first histories of this period were written either by liberals, who praised the regime's progressive achievements, or by communists, who were the victims of its repression. After the fall of the fascist regime, the histories of liberal Italy increasingly presented it as an authoritarian precursor to the totalitarian state. Several decades after that, a "revisionist" history of liberal Italy began to appear, which was not hagiographic but nonetheless insisted that the regime had some positive democratic elements. Understanding the historiography of the British "age of reform," the Second Empire of Louis Napoleon Bonaparte, or Wilhelmine Germany involves reaching a similar command of competing ideological and methodological perspectives that have shifted over time. In other words, political scientists need to uncover and make transparent the historiography of a period as a preliminary step in "reading history carefully." It was not shocking that modernization theorists in the 1950s drew on Whig histories, or that Marxist academics in the 1960s relied on a "history from below," but political scientists need to recognize how a wholesale embrace of one historiographical perspective influences the specific evidence they then use to test their hypotheses. With very few exceptions, political scientists have ignored this basic advice.

Reading carefully also means avoiding the temptation of cherry-picking historical evidence to conform to theoretical predictions. This practice takes at least two different forms. First, political scientists often choose a few words of historical text (usually the bits that support their argument) and leave out other relevant material contained in the same text. One prominent example of this is the invocation of Lord Grey's statement on the First Reform Bill of 1832: "The Principal of my Reform is to prevent the necessity of revolution. I am reforming to preserve, not to overthrow." Less often noted is what Grey said several breaths later: "there is no one more dedicated against annual parliaments, universal suffrage, and the [secret] ballot, than I am."[40] Although the second

---

[40] Earl Grey, Speech in House of Commons, November 1830. Parliamentary Debates, i.613.

statement is consistent with the first, leaving it out renders Grey more of an enlightened reformer and less a defender of the old order.

A second form of cherry-picking is selecting on the dependent variable. Here again the case of the First Reform Bill is illustrative. Many scholars have argued that the public agitation that accompanied the bill's passage through the parliamentary system explains its ultimate success. As I argue in Chapter 3, the balance of evidence does not support this view. But the more general problem is that all the cases in which public agitation leads not to reform but to repression are left out. The snuffing out of the Luddite uprisings, the Peterloo massacre, the passage of the notorious "Six Acts," and the crushing of the Chartists are often excluded from an "age of reform" focused on the two reforms of 1832 and 1867.

A final practice that political scientists should avoid is taking quotes of politicians at face value. This would seem obvious were it not for the fact that some prominent academics have suggested the opposite. According to Adam Przeworski, "the strongest evidence in favour of the argument that suffrage was extended to the poor under the threat of revolution," he writes, comes "not from the events themselves but from voices of the historical protagonists." "These voices were often so explicit," he claims, "that one does not need to impute the motivations."[41] I do not share this assumption. There are a host of reasons why elites would knowingly exaggerate the threat of unrest, the most important being that it added an additional argument to a policy that they supported for other goals. Invoking the threat of mass social unrest is also a classic rhetorical strategy that both proponents and opponents of democratization have used across time and space. Thus, while elites may talk a lot about revolution during periods of institutional change, there are good reasons for making a serious effort to place their claims in historical context.

## 1.3 GOALS AND OUTLINE

To recap: My objective is to simultaneously challenge two central frameworks for understanding the first wave – gradualism and threat of revolution – while also explaining how scholars coalesced around these two paradigms. Revising conventional understandings of the first wave is critical for any future work in democratization that draws upon this period. Rather than considering the nondemocratic features of the first wave as

---

[41] Adam Przeworski, "Conquered or Granted? A History of Suffrage Extensions." *British Journal of Political Science* 39, 2 (April 2009), 311.

relics of the old regime, as simple barriers to would-be democratizers, I place authoritarian resilience at the center of analysis and uncover the multiple mechanisms – institutional, ideational, and repressive – that the opponents of democracy deployed – with considerable success – across Europe before WWI.

Chapter 2 provides a synthetic review of a century of scholarship on the first wave and distills three central narratives of political development: gradualist, revolutionary, and "special" (for Germany). The seminal contribution of Robert Dahl to the field of democratization – and to European political development – is explained. It demonstrates how different data sets provide completely different interpretations of the period. Whereas Polity IV largely supports a gradualist narrative of development, V-Dem contends there was far less democratization over time and significant authoritarian resilience. The chapter closes with a snapshot of European regimes on the eve of WWI to demonstrate how far most were from democracy: only Norway and Denmark (not the cases that Bryce noted) meet the Dahlian criteria upon which most contemporary views of democracy are based.[42]

Chapter 3 argues that political elites during the English "age of reform" were far less concerned with the gradual fostering of democracy than with the defense of competitive oligarchy. Synthesizing the extensive literature on the First and Second Great Reform Acts, it shows how the Whig view of the period – a view that still largely informs political science research today – overstates both the progressive ideology of reformers and the democratizing effects of the two bills. It also includes two periods that are difficult to fit into a reformist narrative and are subsequently downplayed in most accounts of the English democratization. The first is the several decades of political reaction marked by the crushing of the Luddite movement (1811–1813), the massacre at Peterloo (1819), and the passing of the Six Acts (1819). The second is the repression of the Chartist movement between 1834 and 1848. Both episodes reveal how the British state generally responded to mass protests demanding political change. Rather than conceding to the demands of would-be revolutionaries, the state developed its coercive forces – most notably the police and the Home Office – to meet the new challenge. The chapter also assesses the claim that the threat of revolution explains either of the major franchise expansions, finding that the evidence is at best mixed for 1832 and entirely unconvincing for

---

[42] Robert Dahl, *Polyarchy: Participation and Opposition* (New Haven: Yale University Press, 1971).

1867. In sum, both the traditional Whig story of progressive democratization from above and the labor-inspired view of democratization from below are myths. Even after the Second Great Reform Bill of 1867, political elites still felt they had largely dodged democracy. Great Britain would remain a competitive oligarchy until the end of WWI.

Chapter 4 turns to France between 1848 and 1870. It examines how the first competitive authoritarian regime in Europe – the Second Empire (1851–1870) – emerged from the collapse of Europe's first modern democracy, the French Second Republic (1848–1851). Louis Napoleon tilted the playing field in otherwise competitive elections through legal chicanery and media dominance, and the Bonapartist party he created has a legitimate claim to the mantle of the world's first hegemonic political party. This system was quite stable and was brought down by a disastrous international war and not through internal opposition to it; elections reinforced competitive authoritarianism rather than undermining the regime. Bonapartism was also the model for Europe's second competitive authoritarian regime: Imperial Germany from 1870 to 1918. Bismarck's observation of, and extensive personal experience in, Bonapartist France changed his hitherto arch-reactionary views on universal suffrage and led him to see the electorate as a conservative rather than liberalizing force.

Chapter 5 compares Wilhelmine Germany with Edwardian England and arrives at an unconventional conclusion about their relative stability. There is a scholarly tradition of viewing the Second Reich, particularly after the fall of Bismarck and the political ascension of King Wilhelm II, as so ridden with internal contradictions that it was in near-permanent crisis. More recently, scholars have argued that Germany was in fact democratizing, suggesting again that this major historical case of competitive authoritarianism was volatile. I find instead that the balance of evidence indicates that Imperial Germany is a good case of institutionalized competitive authoritarianism, and that it was Edwardian England rather than Wilhelmine Germany where the most serious threat of regime change existed. I contest two widely held misconceptions: (1) that the UK had transitioned to democracy significantly before the outbreak of WWI and (2) that the landed elite acquiesced in this transition. I argue instead that the UK was not only a prototypical competitive oligarchy before WWI, but that it was in a constitutional crisis and close to civil war. The political dimensions of the "Edwardian Crisis" have been neglected because they were transformed by WWI.

Chapter 6 adopts a cross-national perspective to reassess the overall strength of the first wave of democratization outside of Britain and

France. It argues that four states that scholars have long considered examples of vanguard democracies or "settled cases of democracy" in northern Europe (Belgium, the Netherlands, Denmark, and Sweden) do not really fit this description. Belgium and the Netherlands were clearly competitive oligarchies on the eve of WWI. Denmark was indeed one of the most democratic states in Europe by WWI, but its path there had been marked by periods of militarism and rollbacks of suffrage. Sweden was not a democracy by any measure until after WWI. Chapter 7 turns to Italy (and briefly to Portugal and Spain) to show that the supposedly "liberal" regimes in Southern Europe were not democratic, but rather combined elements of competitive oligarchy and competitive authoritarianism.

The role of international war in the first wave of democratization is the theme of Chapter 8. Scholars have long noted an increase in franchise extensions during wars, and political economists have recently formalized this insight. Still, there is a prevailing view in the literature that international war – particularly WWI – merely hastened the ultimate success of prewar democratization efforts. I argue that international war was not the final straw for the old regime but rather was one of only a small category of exogenous events capable of dislodging a resilient system of competitive oligarchy. Chapter 9 reflects on the three major mechanisms of authoritarian resilience – ideas, institutions, and repression/cheating – in light of the current debate about the state of liberal democracy in Europe and the United States.

If the conventional view of the first wave needs revision, so too does Bryce's reputation as a Pollyannish democrat who is most remembered for his conclusion that humanity had arrived at a "universal acceptance of democracy as the normal and natural form of government." In fact, Bryce harbored no illusions about the eventual triumph of democracy, and indeed he expressed misgivings about the desirability of democracy itself throughout *Modern Democracies*. He posits no natural tendency among human societies to develop democratic institutions, noting that "as a rule, that which the mass of any people desires is not to govern itself but to be well-governed" and that "most people want good government, not democratic government."[43] He asserts that "popular government has been usually sought and won and valued not as a good thing in itself, but as a means of getting rid of tangible grievances or seeking tangible benefits."[44]

---

[43] Bryce, *Modern Democracies*, Vol. II, 501.
[44] Ibid., Vol. I, 41.

One thing about Bryce is clear: he was not a democrat in the modern meaning of the term. He was a liberal who voted against female suffrage in Great Britain in 1918 on the grounds that women lacked the capacity to make informed political choices because "they do not meet and talk about politics" and "do not read political news in the way men do."[45] With politicians like Bryce representing the leading edge of reform and radicalism against the old regime in many first-wave cases, it is hardly surprising that Europe was far from democracy on the eve of WWI.

[45] Hansard, Lords, Viscount Bryce, December 17, 1917, c. 183.

# 2

# Paths Around Democracy in Europe

The study of European democratization is one of the oldest concerns of modern comparative politics. This chapter introduces three master narratives of political development that a century of research has produced: gradualism, revolution, and German exceptionalism. It then moves to the empirical measure of first-wave European democracies, comparing the Polity IV data set with the V-Dem historical data set. Whereas Polity IV supports an overall gradualist view of democratization, V-Dem points to the overall stability of authoritarianism. A quick survey of European regimes in 1915 introduces the cases that will be covered in the rest of the book and provides a categorization of the nondemocratic regimes of the first wave.

## 2.1 MASTER NARRATIVES OF THE FIRST WAVE

There is a scholarly consensus on four major points about European political development from the French Revolution to the end of World War I: (1) that there was indeed a first wave in Western Europe, (2) that it was, in general, a far more gradual transition from authoritarianism to democracy than in most other places and times (3) that this gradualism was a key component of "successful" democratization in Western Europe and (4) that the gradual path of political development in the paradigmatic case of Great Britain (but also in Sweden, the Netherlands, and several other states) does not fit the cases of France or Germany. Given the historical importance of the latter two, their transitions to mass politics have produced two other master narratives of political development. Though both are often cast as exceptional, France's *revolutionary* trajectory and Germany's *authoritarian endurance* (or *Sonderweg*) represent two alternative pathways of political development in Europe before World War I.

Students of European history will be familiar with the major political protagonists in these narratives: monarchists, conservatives, liberals, radicals, Christian Democrats, and Socialists. With the exception of the latter two groups, none of the other four functioned as modern political parties in the period before World War I. The conservatives' and liberals' organizational weaknesses, however, were in fact a reflection of their political dominance: they did not need strong parties in a competitive oligarchy.

Of central concern is the position of these political forces toward male suffrage. Monarchists were, by definition, opposed to it, though there were monarchies with extremely limited suffrage. Conservatives in most states and at most times were opponents of suffrage extensions, though some, like Otto von Bismarck, supported universal suffrage for authoritarian motives, and others, like Benjamin Disraeli in Britain, occasionally found themselves supporting suffrage extensions for partisan advantage. Liberals generally supported suffrage extensions so long as they were grounded in "political capacity," meaning that liberals often found themselves opponents of universal suffrage.

The three other major political groupings advocated for universal male suffrage. The English radicals – sometimes referred to as democrats – were early advocates of one-man-one-vote. Its early leaders, such as the orator Henry Hunt, were capable of holding mass demonstrations but incapable of exerting any power in parliament. The French republicans fared somewhat better in 1848, but only briefly. Nevertheless, there is a secular and nonsocialist root of democracy in nineteenth-century Europe. The Socialists were proponents of universal suffrage from the beginning, as were, in most cases, the Christian Democrats. Both generally viewed themselves as beneficiaries of genuine suffrage expansions, as their political organizations could mobilize voters better than their competitors. Many suffrage expansions, as we shall see, were not in fact genuine, so Socialists and Christian Democrats not only fought for universal suffrage but also against the counter-majoritarian institutions that liberals and conservatives created to preserve their influence.

### 2.1.1 Gradualism

The gradualist narrative is central both to classic and contemporary accounts of European democratization. Dahl used the term evolutionary rather than gradual, but the argument is similar. Along this path to democracy, according to Dahl, "The old regime is transformed by *evolutionary* processes: the new regime is inaugurated by incumbent leaders, who yield peacefully (more or less) to demands for changes and participate in the inauguration of polyarchy or near polyarchy." Singling out Great Britain and Sweden as two examples of independent nation-states that evolved into polyarchies – the first of his three paths to polyarchy – he claims that this path, or at least "some approximation of this path," constitutes the "commonest sequence among the oldest and most stable polyarchies."[1] He also includes Belgium, Denmark, the Netherlands, Norway, and Switzerland as cases of liberalization preceding inclusiveness, and as states that made a successful transition over the course of decades from competitive oligarchies into polyarchies.

To understand why gradual was better for democratization than the alternatives, consider Dahl's third axiom: "the more the costs of suppression exceed the costs of toleration, the greater the chance for a competitive regime."[2] Dahl frames democratization as a result of political conflict between two players (the government and the opposition) rather than as the triumph of modernity, economic development, the Enlightenment, or some other broad process. He assumes no good intentions on the part of either player in this utility calculation. What matters, ultimately, is that a mutual security guarantee emerges from a government that decides it is less costly to tolerate the opposition than to repress it and an opposition that behaves similarly when it becomes the government.

Dahl then asks: "what circumstances significantly increase the mutual security of the government and oppositions and thereby increase the chances of public contestation and polyarchy?"[3] He claimed that sequences of political development constituted circumstances in their own right, and it is that point that we shall focus on here, and at various points throughout this study. Noting that "a disproportionately large number of the stable high-consensus polyarchies seem to have come about in the first wave, by peaceful evolution within an already existing nation-state,"[4] Dahl proposed a set of causal mechanisms that form the core of the gradualist argument:

---

[1] Dahl, *Polyarchy*, 36.
[2] The third axiom is derived from the first two. Axiom 1: The likelihood that a government will tolerate an opposition increases as the expected costs of toleration decrease. Axiom 2: The likelihood that a government will tolerate an opposition increases as the expected costs of suppression increase. Dahl, *Polyarchy*, 15.
[3] Ibid., 16.
[4] Ibid., 41.

... the rules, the practices, and the culture of competitive politics developed first among a small elite, and the critical transition from nonparty politics to party competition also occurred initially within the restricted group. Although the transition was rarely an easy one, and party conflict was often harsh and bitter, the severity of conflict was restrained by ties of friendship, family, interest, class, and ideology that pervaded the restricted group of notables who dominated the political life of the country. Later, as additional social strata were admitted into politics they were more easily socialized into the norms and practices of competitive politics already developed among the elites, and generally they accepted many if not all of the mutual guarantees evolved over many generations. As a consequence, neither the newer strata nor the incumbents who were threatened with displacement felt that the costs of toleration were so high as to outweigh the costs of repression, particularly since repression would entail the destruction of a well-developed system of mutual security.[5]

There is a close correspondence between Dahl's story of elite learning and the Whig view of history. Again, this narrative is not confined to a generation of British historians but can be found virtually everywhere in Europe. Even Italy – an unlikely case for Whig history – produced notable historians like Benedetto Croce who wrote:

European society was all leaning towards democracy, as the phrase went; it would have been better to say that it was issuing from the guardianship of restricted ruling groups, of the liberal aristocracy that had guided it through the revolutions and into the new state order, and was now forming a more varied and mobile political class of its own, such as was required by the great variety and mobility of interests that needed to be upheld and reconciled. A manifestation, an instrument, of this ceaseless progression was the gradual extension of the franchise, which in almost all the countries in Europe led up to universal suffrage. This in other times had been instituted or made use of from motives of conservation and reaction, and now served the opposite purpose, that of movement and progress.[6]

This gradualist view of the first wave persists in even the most recent and rigorous studies of the period. Ziblatt's cases of "settled" democratization are virtually the same as Dahl's cases of peaceful evolution. Ziblatt claims:

The first path of *settled democratization* was found in Britain, Belgium, the Netherlands, Norway, Sweden, and Denmark. Between 1848 and 1950, democracy is these countries was gradually constructed via a relatively direct path, absent high-profile moments of backsliding, authoritarian detours, or disruptive coups. Though democratization inevitably faced resistance and was always

---

[5] Ibid., 36.
[6] Benedetto Croce, *History of Europe in the Nineteenth Century* (London: George Allen and Unwin Ltd, 1953), 273–274.

precarious, in these countries, political rights and institutional constraints on executives expanded over time *without* confronting complete constitutional breakdown or any serious retrenchment.[7]

I develop three major critiques of the gradualist, or settled, narrative. The first is that of the six cases of settled democratization, only two of them had democratized by 1915 – Denmark and Norway. Sweden was an authoritarian bastion until the end of World War I. Coding the Netherlands as a democracy prior to 1917 is problematic, as is the United Kingdom before 1918. Democratization in general did not appear to be gradual but to come quite late in the first wave. Second, as Ziblatt and Bateman have recognized, the extension of rights also occurred simultaneously with new counter-majoritarian institutions or with the elimination of previous suffrage rights for other groups. Third, many of the most influential historians of gradualism, from Thomas Macaulay in the United Kingdom to Benedetto Croce in Italy, were themselves liberal politicians, and their academic work cannot be neatly separated from their politics. For decades, many political scientists appeared to have uncritically accepted the histories written by liberal hagiologists, in the case of Macaulay, and by liberal apologists, in the case of Croce.

### 2.1.2 Revolutionary

There were few cases of successful political revolutions during the first wave. And arguably the only case of a social revolution, using Theda Skocpol's criteria, was the one with which most textbooks in modern European history begin.[8] France thus marks the revolutionary exception in Western Europe to the gradualist narrative of democratization. For Dahl, France was the archetype of the second path toward democracy whereby "the old regime is transformed by *revolution*: the new regime is inaugurated by revolutionary leaders, who overthrow the old regime and install a polyarchy or near-polyarchy." Clearly, the French case is much more complicated than that and Dahl is forced to abandon his characteristic parsimony by including three different periods in French history as examples of the "collapse or revolutionary displacement of the old regime" sequence (Ib. 1789–1792, 1848, 1870). That both the French Revolution and the Revolution of 1848 ended

---

[7] Ziblatt, *Conservative Parties and the Birth of Democracy*, 10.
[8] Theda Skocpol, *States and Social Revolutions* (New York: Cambridge University Press, 1979).

in a different form of authoritarianism revealed the perils of this path toward polyarchy. "Was this reversal accidental? Probably not, for where peaceful evolution cannot or does not take place and revolution occurs, the legitimacy of the new regime is more likely to be contested. A sudden collapse of the old regime leaves the new without a legacy of legitimacy; a revolutionary inaugural by the new legitimates the use of revolution against itself."[9]

The revolutionary path is not only likely to end in less democracy in the short term: the division of the body politic into revolutionary and counterrevolutionary forces means that future political conflicts will reproduce and solidify that cleavage. French political development in the nineteenth-century is indeed punctuated by key moments – 1848, 1870, and 1898 – when the ideological heirs of the revolution battled the forces of order. The tradition of contentious politics – including the French acceptance of street mobilization as a vital form of political engagement – is another enduring legacy of its revolutionary tradition. At the same time, an exclusionary, ethnic, and organic view of society that identifies revolution with Jacobinism, Marxism, Leninism, Stalinism, or Maoism (depending on the era) has been the defining feature of the French far right. If the Dreyfus affair ultimately marked the triumph of republicanism over counter-revolution, it also produced *Action Française*, an intellectual movement that anticipated the rise of fascism in Italy by twenty years and whose advocates played a major role in the Vichy regime. The National Rally (formerly the National Front) has long drawn on these and other counter-revolutionary forces in French society, so historical conflicts remain very much alive in the early twenty-first century.

Beyond the French case, the concept of "revolutionary threat" – as opposed to an actual revolution – has recently been turned into a Europe-wide explanatory variable for democratization in the United Kingdom, Germany, and the rest of Europe in the nineteenth and twentieth centuries by political economists.[10] The basic insight is old: Marx, Machiavelli, and Aristotle all recognized that leaders were unwilling to make democratic concessions without the serious threat of revolt. For economists, the credible threat of violence provides a compelling solution to the puzzle of why the rich would ever peacefully agree to increases in taxation

---

[9] Dahl, *Polyarchy*, 43.
[10] In addition to the work by Acemoglu and Robinson, see Toke Aidt and Peter Jensen, "Workers of the World, Unite! Franchise Extensions and the Threat of Revolution in Europe, 1820–1938." *European Economic Review* 72, C (2014), 52–75.

and redistribution that follow from suffrage extension.[11] Acemoglu and Robinson's analysis of the first wave of democratization thus centers on the threat of revolution as the central variable. "[M]ost transitions to democracy, both in nineteenth century- and twentieth-century Europe and twentieth-century Latin America," they write, "took place amid significant social turmoil and revolutionary threats."[12]

This claim has produced its own wave of criticism, much of which questions the links between social inequalities and political action at the heart of the redistributive model. This book adds to the voluminous debate about the threat of revolution hypothesis, but in a different way. I find that rather than reacting to potential revolutionary disturbances through political concessions, the state reacted to revolutionary threats by increasing its domestic coercive power. The growth of the modern police, tasked with both controlling crime and monitoring the political climate, occurred through this dynamic. The balance of evidence also shows that state forces only rarely perceived an actual revolutionary threat emanating from political and social disturbances. Interior or Home Ministers routinely dismissed the warnings of panicky magistrates and government informers. Indeed, there are very few cases in European history where social disturbances can be plausibly connected to suffrage expansions. For such a widely cited theory, the threat of revolution hypothesis has little empirical support.

### 2.1.3 Sonderweg

The "Sonderweg" (loosely translated as "special path") is the third master narrative of European political development. It is really a set of claims about German political development, though there have been some attempts to extend it to Italy.[13] The thesis is that Germany was "special" because economic development did not lead to political liberalization as it had elsewhere in Europe.

The Sonderweg thesis has changed markedly over time. Its initial proponents at the turn of the twentieth century praised German resistance to parliamentary democracy. The second iteration of the Sonderweg thesis, however, was decidedly noncelebratory, as it addressed Germany's

---

[11] Allan Meltzer and Scott Richard, "A Rational Theory of the Size of Government." *Journal of Political Economy* 89, 5 (October 1981), 914–927.
[12] Acemoglu and Robinson, "Why did the West Extend the Franchise?" 27.
[13] See, for example, Paul Corner, "The Road to Fascism: An Italian Sonderweg?" *Contemporary European History* 11, 2 (May 2002), 273–275.

democratic breakdown and the rise of Nazism. For a liberal like Ralf Dahrendorf, it is the failure of economic development to transform feudal political and economic institutions as they did elsewhere that emerges as the central question in modern German history. Referring to no state in particular, he writes that:

> There is an experimental attitude that allows anybody to propose new solutions, but rejects any dogmatic claim to truth. There is a liberal doubt that seeks to build fences around those in power, rather than bridges for them. There is a competitive spirit that can lead to progress only when there is a struggle for predominance in every field. There is a conception of liberty that holds that man can be free only where an experimental attitude to knowledge, the competition of social forces, and liberal political institutions are combined. *This conception has never really gained hold in Germany.* Why not? This is the German Question.[14]

Dahrendorf's most important point is that economic development need not lead to political liberalization: rapid economic development can interact with preexisting authority structures to produce something very different. Drawing on Thorstein Veblen, Dahrendorf notes that "compared with its historical precursors in England and France, industrialization in Germany occurred late, quickly, and thoroughly." The result was that "there was not place in these structures for a sizable, politically self-confident bourgeoisie."[15] It was not that there was not a strong bourgeoisie in Wilhelmine Germany; the problem was that it did not behave self-confidently. Not only did it fail to check autocratic power in 1848, but it also became complicit in Bismarck's competitive authoritarian system. The theme of a pathological middle class – one that aped rather than challenged the militarism of the ruling elite – is a recurring one in postwar studies of German political development.[16]

This version of the Sonderweg thesis has been debated by historians since the 1970s. In their critique of the "peculiarities of German history approach," David Blackbourn and Geoff Eley write that "the questions German historians bring to the past originate in a kind of reverse Whiggism."[17] If the question was how Germany had arrived at 1933 (or 1945), then the answer had to involve the "peculiar pattern of German

---

[14] Ralf Dahrendorf, *Society and Democracy in Germany* (New York: W. W. Norton and Co., 1967), 16.
[15] Ibid., 44.
[16] Norbert Elias, *The Germans* (New York: Columbia University Press, 1998).
[17] David Blackbourn and Geoff Eley, *The Peculiarities of German History: Bourgeois Society and Politics in Nineteenth-century Germany* (New York: Oxford University Press, 1984), 44.

ideological, institutional, and political development, stretching back into the previous century."[18] It is this claim of German exceptionalism that Blackbourn and Eley contest most often and forcefully. They do this by rejecting an idealized version of Western development on which the Sonderweg thesis ultimately rests. "Imperial Germany was less 'backward' and more 'modern' – and therefore more positively comparable to say Edwardian Britain – than most historians have been prepared to admit."[19] Their argument draws on a historiography of British political development in which the aristocracy preserved its power and the middle class was coopted into a competitive oligarchy. Blackbourn and Eley search for – and find significant evidence of – a politically active German middle class that did in fact contribute to the economic and political liberalization of Wilhelmine Germany. The historian Margaret Anderson pushes this claim further in *Practicing Democracy* and comes close to recasting Imperial Germany as a rapidly democratizing society on the eve of World War I.[20] Political scientists have embraced a revisionist reading of Imperial Germany as well. Sheri Berman draws upon Blackbourn and Eley to reinterpret Imperial Germany as a "partial confirmation" of modernization theory.[21] Marcus Kreuzer resuscitates the work of several historians who argued that "creeping parliamentarization" was eroding the autocratic basis of Imperial Germany and creating the basis for parliamentary sovereignty.[22] Scholars have thus come to very different readings of German political development that ultimately depend on their position in the Sonderweg debate.

Of the three narratives, this book is most sympathetic to the Sonderweg view. I find that decades of revisionist scholarship have not overturned the verdict that Imperial Germany was a deeply authoritarian state that was showing few real signs of democratization. But there was nothing "special" or uniquely German about the endurance of authoritarianism – Italy and particularly Sweden looked similar to Germany in many respects. Here I agree with one central critique of the Sonderweg thesis: Germany was not "special" because Europe was, on the whole, much less democratic than in both the classic Sonderweg and the gradualist

---

[18] Ibid., 4.
[19] Ibid., 50.
[20] Margaret Anderson, *Practicing Democracy: Elections and Political Culture in Imperial Germany* (Princeton: Princeton University Press, 2000).
[21] Sheri Berman, "Modernization in Historical Perspective: The Case of Imperial Germany." *World Politics* 53, 3 (April 2001), 431–462.
[22] Marcus Kreuzer, "Parliamentarization and the Question of German Exceptionalism: 1867–1918." *Central European History* 36 (2003), 327–357.

paradigms. Put another way, the nondemocratization of Germany over five decades was part of a broader European story of authoritarian resilience. German conservatives used most of the tools in the old regime's playbook. They rigged elections, particularly before 1900. They defended Prussia's three-class suffrage system – which violated the principle of one-person, one-vote – to the end of the Second Reich. They outmaneuvered those leaders who sought to create a cabinet system of government in the 1890s and blocked parliamentarization thereafter. Perhaps the most exceptional feature of the Second Reich was that a monarcho-military alliance acted as a permanent block to democratization to a far greater degree than other European states. In other respects – tilted playing fields, countermajoritarian institutions, the lack of parliamentary sovereignty – the Second Reich had much in common with most other political regimes of the first wave.

## 2.2 MEASURING THE FIRST WAVE

Although Huntington introduced the wave analogy into the study of democratization, he wrote very little about the first wave as his book was focused on the "Third Wave" of democratization. Given the influence this concept has had on the study of European political development, it is nevertheless necessary to begin with it. Huntington writes "The first wave had its roots in the American revolutions. The actual emergence of national democratic institutions, however, is a nineteenth-century phenomenon. In most countries during that century democratic institutions developed gradually and it is, hence, difficult as well as arbitrary to specify a particular date after which a political system could be considered democratic."[23]

And yet Huntington, like most other scholars of democratization, still insisted on trying to pin down the dates of democratic transition. Using the criteria of (1) male suffrage of over 50 percent and (2) an executive responsible to an elected parliament or a popular vote, Huntington claims that the United States began the first wave in 1828. Then: "in the following decades other countries gradually expanded the suffrage, reduced plural voting, introduced the secret ballot, and established the responsibility of prime ministers and cabinets to parliaments."[24] The upshot was that "in the course of a hundred years over thirty countries established at least minimal national democratic institutions."

---

[23] Huntington, *The Third Wave*, 16.
[24] Ibid., 16–17.

### 2.2.1 Minimalist or Dahlian?

The question of *how* minimal matters very much to our understanding of the first wave. Indeed, the entire history of democratization changes if one uses female suffrage as a core requirement. Using the criteria of female suffrage, the scale of the first wave is cut in half and only begins in 1893, rather than 1828 as per Huntington's original formulation.[25] A different replication of the first wave using the requirement of female suffrage similarly concludes that "transitions to minimal democracy are a twentieth-century phenomenon,"[26] a point we will return to later in the chapter.

Different measures of male democracy (patriarchal democracy) produce very different understandings of political transitions in individual countries. Table 2.1 compares two common coding schemes. The first is a minimal definition (Boix), whereby a democracy is a system in which at least 50 percent of adult men can vote in elections and where the executive branch is responsible either to voters or to an elected legislature.[27] The second (Collier) comes closer to contemporary understandings of liberal democracy as a bundle of institutions, including an independent judiciary that enforces the rule of law, a legislative assembly that has

TABLE 2.1 *Minimalist versus Dahlian coding of European democratizations*

| Country | Boix (Min.) | Collier (Dahl) |
|---|---|---|
| Switzerland | 1848 | 1848 |
| France | 1870 | 1875 |
| Norway | 1900 | 1898 |
| United Kingdom | 1885 | 1918 |
| Denmark | 1901 | 1915 |
| Belgium | 1893 | 1918 |
| The Netherlands | 1896 | 1917 |
| Sweden | 1911 | 1918 |
| Germany | 1919 | 1919 |
| Italy | 1919 | 1912 |

---

[25] Pamela Paxton, "Women's Suffrage in the Measurement of Democracy: Problems of Operationalization." *Studies in Comparative International Development* 35, 3 (2000), 92–111.

[26] Renske Doorenspleet, "Reassessing the Three Waves of Democratization." *World Politics* 52, 3 (April 2000), 398–399.

[27] Boix, *Democracy and Redistribution*.

substantial autonomy from the executive, and free and fair elections that meet Dahl's standards for contestation and participation among adult males.[28] Table 2.1 shows that Switzerland (1848), France (1870–1875),[29] and Norway (1898) – all became democratic at the same time according to both measures of democracy. Germany fails to achieve democracy under either coding scheme until 1919.

These discrepancies about the timing of democratic transitions might seem minor but note that they bear directly on the question of how much World War I mattered for regime change. Great Britain's democratic transition was 1883, according to Boix, and 1918, according to Collier. Similarly, the Dutch and Belgian democratic transitions are wartime developments if one uses a Dahlian coding scheme as opposed to a minimalist one, according to which they democratized in the mid 1890s. Finally, Boix dates Italian democratization to 1919, while Collier argues it occurred in 1912.

### 2.2.2 Polity IV vs. V-Dem

The two major datasets that cover the first wave similarly come to different conclusions about the pace and degree of democratization in Europe. Gurr and Eckstein undertook the first systematic effort to code regime types over a long period of time (since 1800) and the data from their "Polity" project first became available in 1975. The researchers were interested in the durability of institutional frameworks (systems of authority) and not strictly speaking in democracy and authoritarianism. Despite many criticisms, the Polity polyarchy score that ranges from −10 (strongly autocratic) to +10 (strongly democratic) has been by far the most widely used indicator of democracy in first-wave cases.[30]

---

[28] Collier, *Paths Toward Democracy*, 24.
[29] The difference is between the proclamation of the Third Republic (1870) and the establishment of the constitution (1875). The year 1877 also has a reasonable claim as the transition to male democracy when Republicans overcame a constitutional crisis and finally defeated the monarchists.
[30] KS Gleditch and MD Ward, "Double-Take: A Reexamination of Democracy and Autocracy in Modern Politics." *Journal of Conflict Resolution* 41, 3 (1997), 361–383. The authors write that: "at the risk of stating the obvious, all polities with a scale score of X are not equivalent. Vastly different temporal, spatial and social contexts support the same democracy and autocracy score." For example, Polity IV suggests that Greece and Norway were equally democratic in 1915 (see Table 1.3). For a more recent critique, see Vanessa A. Boese, "How (Not) to Measure Democracy." *International Area Studies Review* 22, (2019), 2.

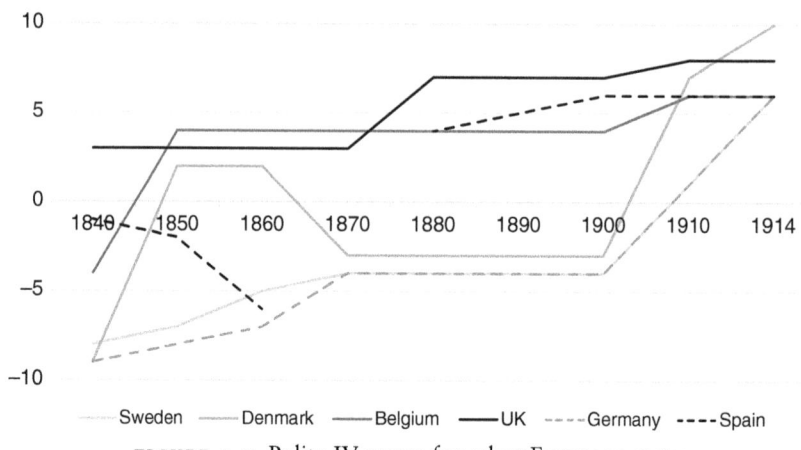
FIGURE 2.1 Polity IV scores for select European states

Polity IV is a very Whiggish data set. Every single state in Europe is coded as more democratic in 1914 than it was in 1840, and most states move a significant distance along the 20-point scale. Denmark, for example, moves from –9 to 10 between 1840 and 1915 (see Figure 2.1). There is significant democratization in Germany (see Figure 2.1) and to a lesser degree in Italy as well. Spain and Sweden appear equally democratic as of 1915, as do Greece and Norway (see Table 2.2).

Part of the reason that democratization appears to move stepwise is that Polity IV generally only records a small number of changes over a long period of time for each case.[31] For example, there is no change in either Belgium's or the Netherlands' score between 1848 and 1918. There are also only four changes in the UK between 1800 and 1918. Relatedly, some critical junctures that historians have identified do not appear in the data. The 1883 reform bill in Great Britain (The Third Great Reform), the 1893 universal manhood suffrage bill in Belgium, and the 1912 male suffrage bill in Italy all do not appear to influence the polyarchy score.[32] Most importantly, Polity IV does not include female suffrage in its measurement of democracy, hence Switzerland is coded as a (perfect) 10 since 1848.

The Varieties of Democracy dataset presents a very different impression of the first wave. Figure 2.2 shows movement along the scale is far more compressed for most states. Germany and Sweden barely budge

---

[31] Gleditsch and Ward. (1997). "On average, it takes between two and three decades before one observes a propensity for the authority characteristics to change."
[32] There are also problems with missing data, such as with Spain between 1860 and 1880.

## 2.2 Measuring the First Wave

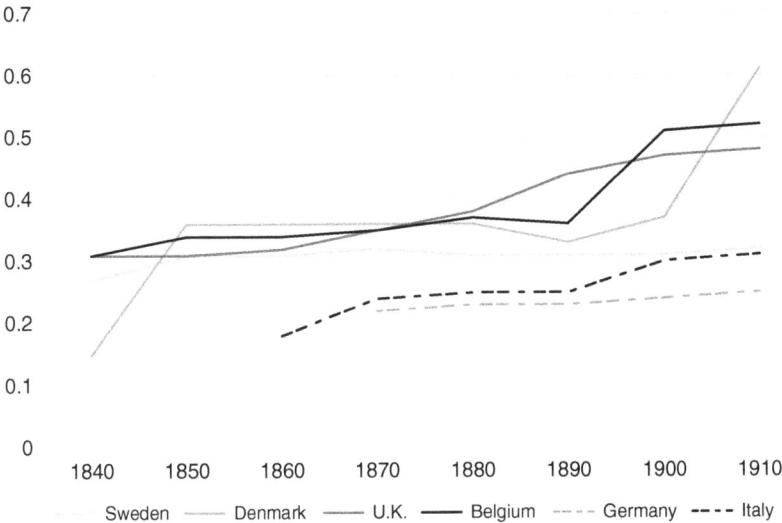

FIGURE 2.2 V-Dem electoral democracy scores 1840–1910 for select European states

from 1870 to 1910, and both Denmark and Belgium appear as stable oligarchies before rapid (not gradual) democratization. Portugal and Spain also do not democratize (or come close as in Polity IV) but remain under .25 for the entire first wave. Unlike with Polity IV, no state in Europe reaches a perfect score, and most are far away from the two most democratic states in the world as of 1915: New Zealand (.78) and Australia (.75).

The following list presents two of V-Dem's five measures of democracy – electoral democracy and liberal democracy – for a group of European countries as of 1914.[33] For comparison, the most democratic state in the world at the time was New Zealand, with an electoral democracy score of .80 and a liberal democracy score of .72. The V-Dem rankings confirm Norway's status as the most democratic state in Europe, followed by Denmark and Switzerland. They also better capture the historical consensus that Greece, Portugal, and Spain were far from democratic on the eve of World War I. Sweden and Germany are both clearly autocracies, and Italy is only a touch more democratic than Greece. The United Kingdom is in the middle of the pack. In sum, using V-Dem data

---

[33] The V-Dem project identifies five "high-level" principles of democracy: electoral, liberal, participatory, deliberative, and egalitarian. The first two principles are the ones most widely used in the empirical literature on democratization.

rather than Polity IV data leads to a very different typology of first-wave regime types. It also suggests an interpretation of authoritarian stability rather than stepwise democratization (compare Figures 2.1 and 2.2).

- **Polity (Polyarchy score)**
    - Denmark (10)
    - Greece (10)
    - Norway (10)
    - Switzerland (10)
    - France (8)
    - Sweden (8)
    - UK (8)
    - Portugal (7)
    - Belgium (6)
    - Spain (6)
    - Germany (2)
    - Italy (-1)
    - The Netherlands (-2)
- **V-Dem (Electoral democracy, Liberal democracy)**
    - Norway (.71, .64)
    - Denmark (.62, .56)
    - Switzerland (.60, .54)
    - France (.52, .47)
    - Belgium (.52, .45)
    - The Netherlands (.49, .43)
    - United Kingdom (.47, .41)
    - Italy (.40, .28)
    - Greece (.38, .26)
    - Sweden (.33, .35)
    - Germany (.25, .21)
    - Portugal (.24, .18)
    - Spain (.18, .17)

## 2.3 POLITICAL REGIMES DURING THE FIRST WAVE

Having now surveyed both master narratives of European democratization and empirical measurements of the first wave, the final section of this chapter offers a revised typology of European regimes on the eve of World War I that is more historically accurate, and hence more theoretically useful, than one based entirely on an authoritarian-democratic dichotomy.

## 2.3.1 Democracies and Male Democracies

What states combined a franchise of "one-person, one vote" with an executive authority that was responsible to a directly elected parliament? On the eve of World War I there were only four countries in the world that possessed both attributes: New Zealand, Australia, Denmark, and Norway. Two other states combined universal male suffrage with parliamentary responsibility, so one could classify France and Switzerland as male democracies as of 1914.

These states had arrived at democracy through very different paths. Norway was the most democratic state in Europe as of July 1914. The key events in Norwegian political development during the first wave all occurred in the context of nationalist agitation against Sweden. Despite having been granted autonomy in all but external affairs in 1814, in practice the Swedish throne controlled all aspects of Norwegian politics until 1884 when parliamentary sovereignty was introduced. Universal manhood suffrage followed in 1898 with female suffrage coming in 1913.

Denmark was the second most democratic state in Europe according to the V-Dem data, and this ranking is consistent with most analyses of Danish political development. However, and contrary to the Danish "Democracy Canon," there was nothing gradual about Danish democratization. The 1849 constitution had introduced universal male suffrage, but the franchise was then limited in 1866 following a military defeat by Prussia. Danish politics from 1870 to 1901 was marked by "bitter struggle over the constitution, where at times Denmark was on the brink of dictatorship."[34] Jacob Estrup, a conservative landowner and architect of the 1866 franchise rollback, was every bit the Danish equivalent of Bismarck. He served as prime minister from 1875 to 1894, and "from 1885 until 1894 Estrup essentially ruled by decree."[35] He dissolved the lower house of parliament ten times from 1876 to 1894.[36] A reform in 1901 forced the king to cede ministerial responsibility to parliament, yet on the eve of World War I the upper house of Parliament (*Landsting*) was still not based on universal suffrage and was dominated by conservative landowners who had blocked an effort to reform it in June 1914. It was also not until 1915 that Danish women gained the vote for national parliamentary elections.

---

[34] Stewart Oakley, *A Short History of Denmark* (New York: Praeger, 1972), 203.
[35] Goldstein, *Political Repression*, 266.
[36] Ibid., 25.

TABLE 2.2 *Year that parliamentary sovereignty/cabinet government/absence of veto players was achieved*

| Country | Year Dahl's Eighth requirement fulfilled |
| --- | --- |
| Belgium | 1830 |
| France | (1848), 1875 |
| Switzerland | 1848 |
| The Netherlands | 1868 |
| Italy | 1876 |
| Norway | 1898 |
| Denmark | 1901 |
| Portugal | 1910 |
| United Kingdom | 1911 |
| Sweden | 1917 |
| Germany | 1918 |
| Greece | 1974 |
| Spain | 1978 |

The 1901 reform is so significant that it is referred to as *systemskiftet*, or "change in system," in Danish. The act itself was very small, for all King Christian IX did was to invite a relatively minor liberal politician, Johan Deuntzer, to form a government. But since this was the first time the king had recognized a parliamentary majority rather than installing a conservative government, it marked the beginning of parliamentary sovereignty. Specifically, it met Dahl's eighth requirement that "institutions for making government policies depend on votes and other expressions of preference."[37] The requirement rules out a powerful monarch, an unrepresentative upper house, or a military with a political veto, and Table 2.2 presents the year when other European states met it.

France adopted universal male suffrage in 1848, rolled it back in 1849, and reinstituted it in 1851 under the Second Empire of Louis Napoleon Bonaparte. Four years after his competitive authoritarian regime collapsed as a result of a disastrous war with Prussia, France had arrived at a male democracy in 1875.[38] It took an additional seventy-one years and two World Wars for women to gain the vote in France. The conventional explanation for delayed female suffrage in France, as in Belgium (1948) and Italy (1946), is that Catholicism was more patriarchal than

---

[37] Dahl, *Polyarchy*, 3.
[38] For an analysis of democratization in the 3rd Republic, see Steven Hanson, *Post Imperial Democracies* (New York: Cambridge University Press, 2010).

Protestantism. However, it was not religious parties that opposed female suffrage in France but rather left-wing parties that calculated that women would vote with their priests.

Geoff Eley argues in his history of the European left that "theoretically, socialists were radical advocates of sexual equality."[39] The German Socialist August Bebel called for female suffrage in his 1879 essay "Women under Socialism," which was widely read in Germany before 1914 and translated into twenty languages. At the time, it was illegal for women to join and attend political activities in Germany, and female socialists who wanted to attend SPD meetings had to wear a disguise to evade the police who worked diligently to enforce this law.[40] Even as Socialist strength grew, the party did not push for female suffrage. Rather, "where working-class men had the vote, socialist parties failed to prioritize votes for women. Where struggles for manhood suffrage continued, they relegated female suffrage to the future."[41] One also cannot ignore that misogyny pervaded Socialist discourse. The German socialist newspaper *Sächsisches Volksblatt* wrote in 1900 that "women don't want to know about politics and organization ... they appreciate a May Day festival, with singing and speeches and dancing ... but they don't appreciate political and trade union meetings."[42] Edmund Fischer (SPD parliamentarian) said the "natural occupation" of women was "the care and upbringing of young children" and "the embellishment and stabilization of family life."[43] It was only after World War I that the SPD translated its theoretical demand for female suffrage into action, although the beneficiaries were not the Socialists but, ironically, the conservatives who had opposed giving the vote to women until the collapse of the empire.[44]

The Swiss case demonstrates that there is indeed no direct or inexorable path from universal male suffrage to female suffrage. Switzerland introduced universal suffrage and parliamentary sovereignty at the same time

---

[39] Geoff Eley, *Forging Democracy: The History of the Left in Europe, 1850–2000* (New York: Oxford University Press, 2002), 99.
[40] William Smaldone, *European Socialism* (New York: Rowman and Littlefield, 2014), 114.
[41] Eley, *Forging Democracy*, 103.
[42] Ibid., 100.
[43] Ibid.
[44] See Michael Bernard, *Institutions and the Fate of Democracy: Germany and Poland in the Twentieth Century* (Pittsburgh: University of Pittsburgh Press, 2005), 63. Hans Delbrück from the conservative DNVP argued during the writing of the Weimar constitution that women should be saved from the "dirt and despicableness" of politics and remain nonvoting citizens (quoted in Bernhard, 62).

in 1849, making it the oldest male democracy in the first wave. The Swiss Association for Women's Suffrage was founded in 1909, but it would take an additional half century before Swiss men voted on the question. When they did in 1959, they rejected female voting by a national score of 67 percent to 33 percent. During the 1960s some cantons introduced female suffrage, while others continued to deny it. In 1971, a second referendum passed that guaranteed the vote to women in federal elections. Some cantons still denied women the vote at the cantonal level, meaning that some of the first female members of parliament still could not vote on local matters. Only in 1990 did the federal Supreme Court guarantee women the vote in the last bastion of male democracy: the ultraconservative canton of *Appennzell Innenhoden*.

### 2.3.2 Competitive Oligarchies

The term competitive oligarchy comes from Dahl's mapping of regime types along two dimensions and represents cases in which participation is low but public contestation is high. Since Dahl did not define "competitive oligarchy" further, and since the term is virtually absent from the scholarly literature but central to the first wave in Europe, we need to specify what this arrangement looked like in practice. The most obvious check on participation was a restrictive franchise, but participation could also be skewed by plural voting and by arcane registration requirements. In cases where an upper house was unelected or elected through a restricted or unequal suffrage system, an oligarchy of old regime elites exerted veto power over a democratic lower house. Competitive oligarchies, in short, were defined by counter-majoritarian institutions. In most cases these were not the relics of feudalism but rather deliberate mechanisms of preserving political power. They were not only the creations of conservatives but also of liberals whose hostility to universal suffrage has been neglected in the democratization literature.

Great Britain was not a democracy in 1914; rather, it was a competitive oligarchy. An article in *Political Science Quarterly* from March 1911 titled "Barriers Against Democracy in the British Electoral System" reports that there were at least half a million plural voters.[45] A series of

---

[45] Edward Porritt, "Barriers against Democracy in the British Electoral System." *Political Science Quarterly* XXVI, 1 (March 1911), 1–31. The author notes other democratic deficits as well: "plural voting, university representation, non-payment of members of Parliament and the official expenses thrown upon candidates for the House of Commons are the four most obvious anomalies in the British electoral system (1)."

complicated registration requirements, combined with the checks on universal suffrage from the 1883 Reform Act, gave the United Kingdom one of the most limited franchises in Western Europe on the eve of World War I. The question of parliamentary sovereignty in the United Kingdom was also more unsettled in July 1914 than most accounts suggest. The period from 1906, the year the Liberals came to power, and 1911 was one of near-permanent constitutional crisis involving the power of the House of Lords. These unelected peers constituted as close to a physical embodiment of the "Old Regime" as one could imagine. The liberal press labeled this group the diehards or the ditchers (since they were willing to die in the last ditch), and so staunch was their defense of inherited privilege that they embraced these terms of abuse. The House of Lords lost its veto powers through the Parliament Act of 1911, but the battle against the legislation led to the coalescence of a radical right political faction that threatened violence to prevent Irish home rule. Several months before the outbreak of World War I, British military commanders began to draw up plans for disarming local military and police forces whose loyalty may be wavering, and German agents reported back that the United Kingdom was paralyzed by partisan conflict and could be drifting into civil war. Consider Churchill's account of July 1914:

> These shocking events caused an explosion of unparalleled fury in Parliament and shook the state to its foundations. We cannot read the debates that continued at intervals through April, May, and June [of 1914], without wondering that our Parliamentary institutions were strong enough to survive the passions by which they were convulsed. Was it astonishing that German agents reported and German statesmen believed that England was paralyzed by faction and drifting into civil war, and need not be taken into account as a factor in the European situation?[46]

In the Netherlands, the suffrage question had been the most divisive and enduring political issue since the 1870s. The Dutch had also not come terribly far since a suffrage reform of 1896 that expanded the suffrage from about 6 percent to 11 percent of the population. In the face of labor agitation, the liberal government of 1913 appointed an all-party commission to examine the issue of electoral reform. Its work was interrupted by the outbreak of hostilities and universal suffrage would not be achieved until 1919. Belgium was arguably more democratic than the Netherlands in 1914, but it is still better termed a competitive oligarchy than a democracy. On the one hand, labor agitation from the 1890s

---

[46] Winston Churchill. *The World Crisis: 1911–1914* (London: Thornton Butterworth, 1923), 181.

had succeeded in achieving close to universal manhood suffrage. Along with parliamentary sovereignty and civil liberties, this combination would have put Belgium squarely in the ranks of the most democratic states in Europe had it not been for plural voting. The electoral reform of 1893 – the reform that introduced near-universal male suffrage – had simultaneously safeguarded elite control by giving the wealthiest 30 percent of the population the majority of votes through plural voting. The labor movement, moreover, had spent two decades attempting to overturn Belgium's plural voting system, without success. As in both the Netherlands and Great Britain, a parliamentary committee was created by the Belgian government-in-exile during the war to examine the suffrage question. However, it was just that – a question – as of 1914, and a parliamentary commission hardly guaranteed a meaningful change.

Sweden was, along with Germany, the most authoritarian state in northern Europe as of July 1914. It combined a highly restrictive suffrage and plural voting with a lack of parliamentary sovereignty. The suffrage reform bill of 1907–1909 may have moved Sweden from autocratic to competitive oligarchic territory, but a real democratic transition only came at the end of the war.

Italy from 1860 to 1912 is the archetype of a competitive oligarchy. The adage was that the Italian government constituted political rule "over 30 million, by 3,000, for the benefit of 300,000."[47] This was an accurate description of a system in which only 2 percent of the adult population had the right to vote for over two decades. Suffrage reform only expanded to 7 percent under the new 1882 franchise reform. There were two major political parties, but they were nearly indistinguishable ideologically and governed in an oligarchic arrangement termed *trasformismo* throughout this period. Then, in 1912, Italy introduced universal manhood suffrage. This was a particularly dramatic extension of the restrictive 1882 law, and it came suddenly (not gradually). As late as 1906, Giovanni Giolitti (the dominant politician in Italian politics from the 1880s to the 1920s) had rejected universal suffrage on the grounds of Italy's high illiteracy rate. It was a classic liberal position, but he shifted course by 1911 and pushed an expansive franchise extension through a reluctant parliament. By 1912, Italy had both universal male suffrage and parliamentary sovereignty. At the same time, massive electoral corruption in the south of the country coupled with a secret electoral pact between Liberal and Catholic parties makes it difficult

---

[47] H. S. Hughes, *The United States and Italy* (New York: Norton, 1965), 53.

to claim that Italy was democratic before World War I. Rather, it had become a competitive authoritarian regime where elections were free but not fair.

### 2.3.3 Competitive Authoritarian Regimes

Other cases of competitive authoritarianism in first-wave Europe include the French Second Empire (1851–1870), Germany from 1871 to 1918, Italy after 1912, and Greece, Portugal, and Spain.[48] Elections under universal suffrage were held in all three states (although Portugal engineered a franchise rollback in 1911), but elites dominated the system. According to one historian, Spain "was not a parliamentary system with abuses; the abuses were the system."[49] The literature is scarcer on Greece and Portugal, but they appear to fall into the same category.

One benefit of V-Dem is that it includes some critical variables that Polity IV does not. One of these is free and fair elections, and the V-Dem "clean election" variable shows massive electoral corruption in Spain and Portugal, along with significant corruption in Italy and Germany. One of the core features of competitive authoritarianism – a tilted electoral playing field – thus appears to have been fulfilled in these cases. Interestingly, it also shows that some competitive oligarchies (the Netherlands and Sweden) ran mostly clean elections with a limited franchise, demonstrating again the asynchronous nature of democratization (Table 2.3).

TABLE 2.3 *V-Dem clean election scores*

|  | 1870 | 1880 | 1890 | 1900 | 1910 |
|---|---|---|---|---|---|
| The Netherlands | .84 | .84 | .84 | .85 | .78 |
| Sweden | .82 | .81 | .81 | .81 | .78 |
| Italy | .52 | .52 | .52 | .47 | .48 |
| Germany | .40 | .40 | .40 | .40 | .55 |
| UK | .34 | .46 | .61 | .70 | .72 |
| Portugal | .28 | .29 | .29 | .27 | .18 |
| Spain | .12 | .12 | .12 | .14 | .12 |

---

[48] It was a modified form of competitive authoritarianism in that it combined a powerful monarch with universal male suffrage, as per Bismarck's original design.

[49] Raymond Carr, R. *Spain, 1808–1939* (London: Oxford University Press, 1966), 367.

### 2.3.4 Authoritarian Regimes

One of the underappreciated features of the first wave is that even very undemocratic states felt pressure to hold elections of some sort. Spain held them, even though the newspapers reported the results before the votes were counted. There are relatively few cases of genuine autocracies in the Europe of July 1914, but they were important ones. Russia and the two empires of Austro-Hungary and the Ottomans were absolutist states. There was some internal differentiation in Austro-Hungary (see Chapter 6), but on the eve of World War I, the Austrian Reichsrat and all the provincial assemblies had been dissolved by Emperor Francis Joseph. The states that emerged from the two defeated empires had virtually no democratic experience, and none is generally considered to have been part of the first wave.

Box 2.1 summarizes my reconfiguration of West European regime types before World War I. As other scholars have pointed out, democratization

---

**Box 2.1 European Political Regimes before 1915**

- **Norway**
    - Universal and equal suffrage: Yes
    - Dahl's eighth requirement: Yes
    - Free and fair elections: Yes
    - Regime type: Democracy
- **Denmark**
    - Universal and equal suffrage: Yes
    - Dahl's eighth requirement: Yes
    - Free and fair elections: Yes
    - Regime type: Democracy
- **France**
    - Universal and equal suffrage: Male only
    - Dahl's eighth requirement: Yes
    - Free and fair elections: Yes
    - Regime type: Patriarchal Democracy
- **Switzerland**
    - Universal and equal suffrage: Male only
    - Dahl's eighth requirement: Yes
    - Free and fair elections: Yes
    - Regime type: Patriarchal Democracy

## 2.3 Political Regimes During the First Wave

- **Belgium**
  - Universal and equal suffrage: Plural/male
  - Dahl's eighth requirement: Yes
  - Free and fair elections: Yes
  - Regime type: Oligarchy

- **The Netherlands**
  - Universal and equal suffrage: Restricted male
  - Dahl's eighth requirement: Yes
  - Free and fair elections: Yes
  - Regime type: Oligarchy

- **United Kingdom**
  - Universal and equal suffrage: Plural/restricted
  - Dahl's eighth requirement: Yes
  - Free and fair elections: Yes
  - Regime type: Oligarchy

- **Sweden**
  - Universal and equal suffrage: Male/restricted
  - Dahl's eighth requirement: No
  - Free and fair elections: Yes
  - Regime type: Oligarchy

- **Portugal**
  - Universal and equal suffrage: Male only
  - Dahl's eighth requirement: Yes
  - Free and fair elections: No
  - Regime type: Competitive Authoritarian

- **Italy**
  - Universal and equal suffrage: Male only
  - Dahl's eighth requirement: Yes
  - Free and fair elections: No
  - Regime type: Competitive Authoritarian[a]

- **Germany**
  - Universal and equal suffrage: Male (federal)
  - Dahl's eighth requirement: No
  - Free and fair elections: Yes
  - Regime type: Competitive Authoritarian

[a] Before 1912, however, Italy was a competitive oligarchy, as was Portugal before 1911.

was often asynchronous during the first wave.[50] The Netherlands, for example, established parliamentary sovereignty nearly fifty years before universal male suffrage, and there was over a 100-year gap in full voting rights between Swiss males and Swiss females. By 1915, only two states in Europe met the three central criteria for democracy (universal and equal suffrage, Dahl's eighth requirement, and free and fair elections). Put another way, less than 3 percent of the population of Western Europe lived in a full democracy before the end of World War I.

## 2.4 CONCLUSION

The view that Western Europe – Germany aside – democratized significantly over the course of the first wave is over a century old and deeply rooted in comparative politics. So too is Polity IV data, which more or less endorses a gradualist (or Whiggish) view of European political development during the long nineteenth century. V-Dem provides a totally different picture, and future scholars would be well-advised to retest theories that were originally developed using Polity IV data. Both data sets are similar, however, in that they are based on individual opinions (either those of trained coders or international experts) about the historical record. The rest of this book engages deeply with the historiography and overall provides strong qualitative evidence for V-Dem's picture of either a muted first wave or of authoritarian resilience in an age of democratization.

---

[50] Capoccia and Ziblatt, "Historical Turn."

# 3

# Crafting Competitive Oligarchy in the United Kingdom

The "Age of Reform" refers to British political history in the first three quarters of the nineteenth century, punctuated by the two parliamentary reform acts of 1832 and 1867.[1] According to the Whig view, it was during this period that "the British genius for peaceful popular reform seemed to demonstrate a particular and significant ability on the part of the aristocracy, the middle classes and the people in harmonizing the institutions of the ancient kingdom with the advanced political ideals of the age."[2] This narrative appeared as early as 1848 with the publication of Thomas Macaulay's History of England and was very much a confirmation of Macaulay's and other Whig politicians' role in the reforms. Macaulay's became the textbook account of the period and the archetype for Dahl's first path to polyarchy. It is also the first – and in most cases probably the only – story that political scientists learn about British democratization. It is thus fair to say that the Whig view of the Age of Reform has had wide-ranging intellectual influence.

---

[1] The first regular scholarly use of the term "reform" was in the 1927 English translation of Elie Halévy's third volume in his six-volume history of England titled *The Triumph of Reform (1830–1841)*. A decade later, the term acquired additional intellectual cache with the publication of Llewelyn Woodward's *The Age of Reform: 1815–1870* for the Oxford History of England series. Scholars have since offered other adjectives for this period: Asa Briggs referred to it as the "Age of Improvement," while Miles Taylor casts it as an "Age of Uncertainty." Nevertheless, the "age of reform" has stuck to such a degree that there are volumes devoted to rethinking it. See, for example, Arthur Burns and Joanna Innes, eds., *Rethinking the Age of Reform: Britain 1790–1850* (Cambridge: Cambridge University Press, 2003).

[2] Francis Herrick, "The Second Reform Movement in Britain, 1850–1865." *Journal of the History of Ideas* 9, 2 (1948), 174.

At the same time, British democratization has also been framed as a triumph of societal pressures from below. Beginning in the late 1950s, a large literature has recast the working classes as the true agents of democratic change. Reviewing Llewellyn Woodward's Whiggish *The Age of Reform 1815–1870* in the Oxford History of England series in 1940, George Dangerfield questioned the title's premise. "In so far as the period covered here is an 'Age of Reform,'" Dangerfield wrote, "it is an age of negative reform, partly symbolic and partly humanitarian, and always subservient to the progress of unchecked capitalist enterprise."[3] Dangerfield then introduced a central rival hypothesis to the Whig interpretation of history: "it was the extra-parliamentary pressure of 'the mob' which affected the great Reform Act of 1832." In the 1950s and 1960s, E. P. Thompson and his disciples in social history began to reimagine "the age of reform" as seething with revolutionary potential. In their view, it was public agitation by the non-elite classes that forced suffrage expansion from an intransigent old regime.[4] Political economists formalized the "threat of revolution" (TOR) hypothesis four decades later and used both 1832 and 1867 as illustrative examples.

Both views of British democratization cannot be correct. The reforms of 1832 and 1867 cannot simultaneously be timely concessions by farsighted elites *and* last-ditch attempts to forestall an imminent revolution.[5] Fortunately, after decades of scholarship on the age of reform – much of which focused on the question of whether reform came from above or from below – it is possible to weigh the evidence in favor of each view, as this chapter proceeds to do. It finds that rather than conceding to extra-parliamentary pressure, the British elite met rising protest activity by strengthening the coercive forces of the state. The first modern police force was created in London in 1829 to deal with the types of social and political protests for which the traditional institutions or coercion – the army and the yeomanry – were ill suited. The Home Office proved adept at infiltrating groups that opposed the regime, and the information it provided to elite decision-makers usually pushed back on claims of imminent revolution.

The Whig view of the British age of reform cannot be sustained either, for three reasons. First, its traditional focus on two high points of reform – 1832 and 1867 – leaves out the two decades of repression that preceded

---

[3] George Dangerfield, "Review of Woodward." *Science and Society* 4, 1 (1940), 106.
[4] E. P. Thompson, *The Making of the English Working Class* (New York: Vintage, 1963).
[5] Some Whig accounts seek to reconcile these interpretations, making them even more difficult to potentially falsify. My view is that elites cannot logically be taking both preventative and emergency action simultaneously.

the First Great Reform, as well as the repression of the Chartists by reformers and conservatives alike thereafter. While revolutionaries won universal suffrage in Denmark, France, and Switzerland in 1848, the Chartist movement achieved none of its aims. Second, the architects of both reform acts were hardly nascent democrats. Rather, their starting point was the liberal proposition that "capacity" was a requirement for voting, with the implication that some individuals in a society will never possess it. Macaulay was one of many to argue against universal suffrage in Parliament: He warned that "universal suffrage would be fatal to all purposes for which government exists" and that it was "utterly incompatible with the very existence of civilization."[6] Remarkably, this view persisted throughout the entire "age of reform." Third, elites believed that they had succeeded in preserving the essential features of the old regime in the face of democratic challengers. In their minds, they had not constructed an inchoate democracy but a competitive oligarchy. This chapter argues that they succeeded.

## 3.1 HISTORIOGRAPHY AND DEMOCRATIZATION

In 1931, Herbert Butterfield lamented the dominance of a "Whig interpretation of history" among British historians that was political from its inception.[7] Macaulay's 1848 history of England, for example, asserted that "the history of our country during the last hundred and sixty years is essentially the history of physical, of moral, and of intellectual improvement."[8] As a historiographical school, Whig history engaged in a massive project of reading history backward rather than forward, and Butterfield summarizes the consequences of this method:[9]

---

[6] *Hansard*, 3rd series, Vol. LXIII, p. 46.
[7] Herbert Butterfield, *The Whig Interpretation of History* (New York: W. W. Norton, 1965). Other historians have agreed with Butterfield's characterization. According to Georg Iggers, Whig historians "were not writing the history of industrialization but history *for* the prevailing liberal/capitalist orthodoxy in the 19th century." Emphasis in original. George Iggers, *New Directions in European Historiography* (Hanover: University Press of New England, 1984), 156. Andrew Gamble writes that: "the leading practitioners of political science were convinced that change needed to be evolutionary and gradual and that there were strict limits to what could be achieved through political action. Study of the past revealed both the achievements of English political institutions and the difficulty of improving upon them without endangering their survival (Gamble 408–409)."
[8] Thomas Babington Macaulay, *The History of England from the Accession of James II* (1848). Vol. 1, p. 14.
[9] On the analytical problems, "reading history backward" creates for political science, see Amel Ahmed, "Reading History Forward: The Origins of Electoral Systems in European Democracies." *Comparative Political Studies* 43 (2010), 931–968.

The Whig historian can draw lines through certain events ... and if he is not careful, he begins to forget that this line is merely a mental trick of his; he comes to imagine that it represents something like a line of causation. The total result of this method is to impose a certain form upon the whole historical story, and to produce a scheme of general history which is bound to converge beautifully upon the present – all demonstrating throughout the ages the workings of an obvious principle of progress, of which the Protestants and Whigs have been the perennial allies while Catholics and Tories have perpetually formed obstruction.[10]

G. M. Trevelyan was an unabashed devotee of the Whig school and its most prolific historian. His works continues to be cited by political scientists, including by Acemoglu and Robinson, but among historians, his work began to fall out of favor by the 1950s, in large part because of its political slant. Trevelyan himself admitted that his works "reeked with bias" toward the end of his academic career.[11] Consider, for example, his analysis of British democratization from his 1926 *History of England* in which Trevelyan writes that "by a gradual transition toward democracy, seldom hastening and never turning back, political rights were extended to all without a catastrophe."[12] He continues: "this great maneuver was safely accomplished because all classes and parties showed, upon the whole, sound political sense and good humour."[13] Here, Trevelyan's view of democratization is not far from Dahl's point about elite learning. Two pages later, however, it becomes clear that British national character – personified through the acts of great men – is what mattered most to Trevelyan: "British methods of coping with the problems of the new era showed great practical inventiveness and were all in the line of a strong native tradition." It was not so much socialization of new classes, but the "good genius of English politics" that had "so often retrieved apparently hopeless situations," according to Trevelyan.[14]

Problematic as this line of reasoning is for contemporary political scientists – how can one ever hope to operationalize the "good sense" or "British genius" that underpinned the age of reform? – the Whig view of British political development has had a substantial influence on the field of

[10] Butterfield, *The Whig Interpretation of History*, 11.
[11] www.oxforddnb.com/display/10.1093/ref:odnb/9780198614128.001.0001/odnb-9780198614128-e-36554.
[12] G. M. Trevelyan, *History of England*, Vol. III, 3rd ed. (Garden City: Doubleday Anchor Books, 1945), 152.
[13] Ibid.
[14] Ibid., 154.

## 3.1 Historiography and Democratization

comparative politics. The European past – and particularly Britain's past as the first state to transition to modernity – became essential material for the construction of modernization theory.[15] Harry Eckstein's chapter on Britain in Samuel Beer and Adam Ulam's *Patterns of Government* is a case in point.[16] Eckstein wanted to explain the "political deference" of the British that was, in his view, central to its democratic stability. He argues that the "ultimate reason for 'political deference' in Britain is to be found in the gradual, predominantly peaceful development of British political institutions." He continues:

> The democratization of British politics in the nineteenth and twentieth centuries involved little more than still another restructuring of the balanced forces of the constitution and another grafting of new upon old and ancient principles. Revolutionary violence, aiming at a utopian reconstruction of society, was never required to accomplish it. Like the "absolutism" of the Tudors, and like the ascendancy of Parliament and the growth of the modern cabinet system in the eighteenth century, the expansion of the franchise was achieved more through acquiescence than intense struggles. The conservative forces sometimes yielded gracefully, sometimes indeed pushed the process along on their own initiative; and thereby, perhaps intentionally, they made it appear that democracy did not require any fundamental reconstitution of political life.[17]

It is difficult to tell where modernization theory ends, and Whig history begins, in such narratives of British democratization. Still, this basic view of English development was accepted as historical fact even by critics of the behavioral revolution. Barrington Moore, for example, seemed to reject any sanguine view of British history outright in his scorching critique of modernization theory. "It is not necessary to read English history very long," he notes, "to realize that there is an element of myth in common notions about the peculiar capacity to settle their political and economic differences through peaceable, fair, and democratic processes."[18] Violence, Moore reminds us, played a fundamental role in the transition from absolute monarchy to democracy in Britain. The English Civil War marked the emergence of a balance

---

[15] Nils Gilman, *Mandarins of the Future: Modernization Theory in Cold War America* (Baltimore: Johns Hopkins University Press, 2003).
[16] Though introduced as a textbook by its editors, *Patterns of Government* represents a good example of linking modernization theory and European history. Samuel Beer and Adam Ulam, eds., *Patterns of Government: The Major Political Systems of Europe* (New York: Random House, 1958).
[17] Harry Eckstein, "The Sources of Leadership and Democracy in Britain," in *Patterns of Government*, Samuel Beer and Adam Ulam, eds., 87.
[18] Barrington Moore, *Social Origins*, 3–4.

of power between the crown and the landed aristocracy that Moore claims to be a general prerequisite for democratic development. The Civil War itself was in turn the product of the enclosure movement, which Moore deems a form of "massive violence exercised by the upper classes against the lower." Yet, it was precisely the elimination of the peasant class that allowed for democratization centuries later. There was thus nothing peaceful about England's democratic transition when one takes the long view.

When the reader gets past the eighteenth century, however, Moore's view of English political development from 1848 to 1914 is not much different from the gradualist narrative. In fact, the title for the British case study in *Social Origins* is "England and the Contributions of Violence to Gradualism." Moore may date the formation of an "alliance between parliamentary democracy and capitalism" earlier than other scholars, but he agrees with the central claim of modernization theory that "men of commerce in both the countryside and the towns" were "the chief carriers of what was eventually to be a modern and secular society."[19] Four hundred pages later, Moore reaches his famous conclusion, "No Bourgeois, No Democracy." His summary of the English case is not as succinct, but it contains the causal mechanisms Moore found to be most important:

Governing in the context of rapidly growing industrial capitalism, the landed upper classes absorbed new elements into their ranks at the same time that they competed with them for popular support – or at the very least avoided serious defeat by well-timed concessions. This policy was necessary in the absence of any strong apparatus of repression. It was possible because the governing classes eroded slowly and in a way that allowed them to shift from one economic base to another with a minimum of difficulty.[20]

At the time Moore was writing *Social Origins*, social historians in Britain began to challenge pieces of the gradualist narrative. Once again, contemporary politics explains the development of a new historical school. Indeed, the links could not have been more explicit, as the academic network took the name the "Communist Party Historian's Group." As McWilliam summarizes, "Unashamedly partisan, the Group opened up the history of the working class and created a new approach that became known as 'history from below.'"[21] It included Eric Hobsbawm, George

---

[19] Ibid., 4.
[20] Ibid., 39.
[21] Rohan McWilliam, *Popular Politics in Nineteenth Century England* (London: Routledge, 1998), 19–20.

Rude, and E. P. Thompson, whose *Making of the English Working Class* was the first work to postulate a radical undercurrent among the masses. Thompson was upfront about his purpose: "I am seeking to rescue the poor stockinger, the Luddite cropper, the 'obsolete' hand-loom weaver, the 'utopian' artisan, and even the deluded follower of Joanna Southcott from the enormous condescension of posterity."[22] One of his central claims was that a coherent working-class movement was every bit as important in the agitation of 1830–1832 as the middle-class heroes of Whig accounts. A second was that Britain faced a series of revolutionary crises from the French Revolution through 1832. Thompson argues that "1819 was a rehearsal for 1832. In both years a revolution was possible (and in the second year it was very close)."[23] Royden Harrison, whose work will be discussed at length later in this chapter, pursued a similar line of argument in his analysis of suffrage expansion of 1867. Further studies in this vein continued to push the thesis that Britain was far closer to revolution than the gradualist narrative implies.[24]

There is a tight connection between such histories tracing the influence of "pressure from below" and the "TOR" hypothesis. According to Acemoglu and Robinson, democratization only "occurs because the disenfranchised citizens can threaten the elite and force it to make concessions. These threats can take the form of strikes, demonstrations, riots, and – in the limit – a revolution."[25] Unlike Moore, contemporary political economists argue that it is possible to have democracy without massive bloodshed and that the threat of mass violence was enough to convince reluctant elites to make concessions to democracy. Acemoglu and Robinson claim that "most transitions to democracy, both in nineteenth- and twentieth-century Europe and twentieth-century Latin

---

[22] Joanna Southcott was a prophetess who claimed to be the Woman of the Apocalypse mentioned in *The Book of Revelations* (12:1–6). Her movement numbered 100,00 followers in the first two decades of the nineteenth century. E. P. Thompson, *The Making of the English Working Class*, 12.

[23] Ibid., 671.

[24] Thompson's thesis provoked a powerful rebuttal from historians Malcolm Thomis and Peter Holt, who argued that the threat of revolution was inflated by government spies and panicky magistrates. See Malcolm Thomis and Peter Holt, *Threats of Revolution, 1789–1848* (London: Macmillan, 1977). A qualified defense of the threat of revolution thesis can be found in Edward Royle, *Revolutionary Britannia? Reflections on the Threat of Revolution in Britain, 1789–1848* (Manchester: Manchester University Press, 2000). Royle finds that revolutionary potential existed in Britain but that a revolution did not occur as a result of multiple factors, chief among them being the coercive capacity of the British state.

[25] Acemoglu and Robinson, *Economic Origins*, xii.

America, took place amid significant social turmoil and revolutionary threats."[26] Regarding the United Kingdom, they state simply that "the threat of social disorder was the driving force behind the creation of democracy in Britain."[27] The Great Reform Act of 1832 serves as a primary illustration in their original article and in their 2006 book. They also suggest in both works that the Second Great Reform was a product of revolutionary threat.

Such theoretical and empirical claims have provoked many compelling critiques over the last two decades.[28] They have also resulted in many extensions, such as Aidt and Jenson's hypothesis that revolutionary threats internationally trigger domestic liberalization, as the opposition becomes inspired by the liberalizing example of foreigners, and the old regime comes to feel more threatened by the existing domestic opposition when it sees foreign regimes collapse in revolution.[29] The rest of the chapter uses the British case to assess these and other claims.

But rather than beginning with the reform of 1832 – the conventional starting point for political scientists in particular – I begin two decades earlier with the Luddite disturbances and the state's reaction to them. I argue that the age of reform – at least in a political sense – had scarcely arrived before 1832 and that the British state had developed new coercive institutions to deal with political mobilization before the first major suffrage expansion.

## 3.2 DEFENDING THE OLD REGIME: 1811–1829

If there was indeed an age of reform in Britain, it was preceded by an age of repression. This was true not only of the decade of anti-Jacobin reaction that followed the French Revolution but indeed of the entire quarter century before the passing of the First Great Reform. The Tories ruled from 1806 to 1830 and blocked parliamentary reform throughout. They practiced a "policy of consistent repression, which showed scant sympathy for the impoverished circumstances and political aspirations of ordinary

---

[26] Ibid., 27.
[27] Ibid., 4.
[28] Notable criticisms include Ansell and Samuels, *Inequality and Democratization*; Capoccia and Ziblatt, "Historical Turn," 2010; Daniel Treisman, "Democracy by Mistake." *American Political Science Review* 114, 3 (August2020), 792–810.
[29] Toke Aidt and Peter Jensen, "Workers of the World Unite! Franchise Extensions and the Threat of Revolution in Europe, 1820–1938." *European Economic Review* 72, C (2014), 52–75.

people."³⁰ The repression of the Luddites, the Peterloo Massacre, and the growth of policing of everyday life in London and other major cities have been neglected in Whig narratives of the period but are as crucial to it as the democratic reforms that are identified with it.

The Luddite disturbances that began in Nottingham on March 11, 1811, demonstrated the potential of widespread social protest and exposed the shakiness of the institutions available to enforce public order. The Luddites lacked a political program and generally focused on destroying the textile machinery that they feared was replacing them.³¹ Nevertheless, scenes of Luddites drilling and practicing maneuvers on the edges of industrial towns created a perception of crisis. One journalist wrote menacingly that "the insurrectional state to which this country has been reduced for the last month has no parallel in history, since the troubled days of Charles the First."³² This was an exaggeration: Conservative estimates put casualties in the English Civil War at upwards of 100,000. Still, the Luddites could be violent. When a group of 150 of them attacked Rawfolds Mill on April 11, 1812, and then murdered mill owner William Horsfall several weeks later, the British state responded in draconian fashion: Three Luddites were hanged for the murder, and fourteen more were hanged for their attack on property. Machine breaking had only been made a capital offense in February, so the state was sending a clear message by executing fourteen British subjects. It was also responding to a generalized fear of revolution captured by the romantic poet Robert Southey (who began as a political radical but had since become a conservative) in 1812. "At this time," Southey wrote, "nothing but the Army preserves us from the most dreadful of all calamities, an insurrection of the poor against the rich, and how long the Army may dare be depended upon is a question which I scarcely dare ask myself."³³

The government deployed the largest force to suppress domestic disorder in English history, as one parliamentarian noted at the time in the House of Commons.³⁴ Somewhere around 12,000 men were required to crush the Luddites, and contemporary newspaper accounts warned that "the great

---

[30] David Cannadine, *Victorious Century: The United Kingdom, 1800–1906* (New York: Penguin, 2017), 134.
[31] The best study of the Luddites remains Frank Ongley Darvall, *Popular Disturbances and Public Order in Regency England* (London: Oxford University Press, 1934).
[32] *Leeds Mercury*, December 26, 1811.
[33] Quoted in Elie Halévy, *A History of the English People*, Vol. 1 (New York: Pelican Books, 1912), 292.
[34] *Parliamentary Debates*, xxi. II. 808.

bodies of troops, the continual coming and going of parties of cavalry, the frequent and ubiquitous military patrols, the garrisons of soldiers, large and small, in the different centres and factories gave the district a most warlike appearance."[35] For many observers, the solution was not to be found in the three existing coercive institutions: the army, the yeomanry, and the voluntary defense force. One wrote to the Home Office that "a permanent police establishment with regular police is the only solution."[36]

Discussion of a police force for the city of London, in fact, predated the French Revolution. The first of many failed police bills for London became the basis for the Dublin Police Act of 1786, which created a professional, uniformed, and armed police for the first time.[37] The Royal Irish Constabulary was a colonial occupation force from the outset, and it was not originally viewed as a potential model for London. And perhaps it never would have been, had it not been for Robert Peel, the future prime minister (1834–1835 and 1841–1846) and founder of modern British conservatism. Peel launched his political career at the age of twenty-one when he was given the "rotten borough" of Cashal in Tipperary – with its twenty-four total electors – by his father.[38] He served as Chief Secretary for Ireland from 1812 to 1818 and responded to the problem of chronic disorder by creating salaried positions of magistrates and constables. As Home Secretary from 1822 to 1827 and from 1828 to 1830, he embarked on major reforms of the courts and penal system. During those years, he worked on plans for reform of the British police.

Initially, Peel met little success. The basic practices of English policing had not changed for centuries. Volunteer forces composed of men of social standing were in charge of maintaining order in rural areas, while towns and cities sometimes paid constables for night watches. There was no standardization or centralization, and police operated within a patchwork of local customs and legal precedents. Elite opinion was also against putting more coercive power in state hands. A parliamentary committee on police reform in 1818 rejected Peel's first plan in no uncertain terms: "Such a system would of necessity be odious and repulsive ... It would be a plan which would make every servant of every house a spy on the actions of his master, and all classes of society spies on each other."[39]

[35] Darvall, *Popular Disturbances*, 263.
[36] Allsop to H.O., in H.O. 42. 153.
[37] Glasgow became the first city on the British Isles to create a similar force in 1800.
[38] A rotten borough was a constituency with a very small electorate that could be controlled by a patron.
[39] Parliamentary Papers 1818, viii, 32.

## 3.2 Defending the Old Regime: 1811–1829

The ruling class, ironically, believed that an organized police force would undermine, rather than solidify, their position.

Given such resistance to the very concept of policing, how was it that the first modern police force was created in London in 1829? Unsurprisingly, there is both a Whiggish and a Marxist answer to this question.[40] The traditional Whiggish account portrayed it as "something created by far-sighted men to solve very real problems of crime and disorder."[41] Social historians, by contrast, viewed police as the agents of the dominant class.[42] In this view: "police work was as much about keeping the 'dangerous classes' under surveillance and control as about fighting crime."[43] The social historians are on firmer ground in this debate, for it is very difficult to support the Whig position that policing arose as a progressive solution to a rise in crime. Policing was political from its inception in Great Britain, just as it was elsewhere. It resulted not from a functional imperative of social improvement, but rather from the failure of other forces of coercion to handle growing popular agitation.

Consider the position of the British state circa 1815. It had two primary ways of dealing with extra-parliamentary challenges to its authority. The first was spying, a broad range of practices from mail tapping to infiltrating opposition networks that had grown exponentially during the Napoleonic Era.[44] As Darval notes, "in the absence of any organized system of police, lacking the most rudimentary detective staff, the only way in which the authorities could discover what was going on in the country was by the employment of informers or by the confession of accomplices."[45] He describes this surveillance system as follows:

---

[40] For an introduction to the historiography of British policing, see Robert Reiner, *The Politics of the Police* (New York: Oxford University Press, 2010).

[41] Clive Emsley, *The English Police: A Political and Social History* (New York: Longman, 1996), 4; A key author in this tradition is Charles Reith. See Charles Reith, *The Police Idea: Its History and Evolution in England in the Eighteenth Century and After* (London: Oxford University Press, 1938); Charles Reith, *The Blind Eye of History: A Study of the Origins of the Present Police Era* (London: Faber and Faber, 1952); Charles Reith, *A New Study of Police History* (London: Oliver and Boyd, 1956).

[42] David Jones, *Crime, Protest, Community and Police in Nineteenth Century Britain* (Boston: Routledge and Kegan Paul, 1982); Robert Storch, "The Plague of the Blue Locusts." *International Review of Social History* 20, 1 (1975), 61–90.

[43] David Taylor, *The New Police in Nineteenth-Century England: Crime, Conflict and Control* (Manchester: Manchester University Press, 1997), 8.

[44] Bernard Porter, *Plots and Paranoia: A History of Political Espionage in Britain 1790–1988* (London: Unwin Hyman, 1989).

[45] Darval, *Popular Disturbances*, 277. This was not unique to early nineteenth-century Britain. Two of the most notorious secret police systems in world history – the Gestapo and the Stasi – also depended on voluntary informers. See Robert Gellately, *The Gestapo*

The Home Department itself was approached by volunteers, convicts, soldiers, labour leaders, and anonymous members of the public, who were anxious to be employed as spies. Magistrates and other authorities wrote frequently to Whitehall to ask either for Bow Street runners and other persons to procure information or for authority to incur expense in hiring their own informers. The Government itself sent down, either on its own initiative, or at the request of the appropriate authorities, its own agents and spies. Large sums of money were spent in this manner. When money was not spent directly in payment to secret agents it was offered in rewards to people who should give information. The procuring of secret information was almost the major activity of many of the authorities.[46]

Such surveillance worked, to a degree. Royle concludes that "most of the [revolutionary] plots from 1794 to 1848 were exposed by spies" and further notes that "as the schemes matured, the government knew as much about them as the plotters."[47] Darval similarly finds that "spies played an important role in Regency disturbances" and that "they were one of the most important, and not the least expensive, instruments of Government in its attempt to work a medieval system of local and internal government under modern conditions."[48] One of the central problems with relying so heavily on voluntary informers, however, was that their motives and methods in espionage were usually suspect. As General Maitland put it: "those who are willing to undertake mixing with the Disaffected are generally of a Character whose information must be received with extreme Caution."[49] Surveillance, moreover, was primarily for detecting and foiling the most serious threats to political order; they were of little help once major social protests began.

In such an event, the state had two options: the army and the yeomanry. The Luddite disturbances revealed how unwieldly, and unpopular, the army was as a solution to domestic conflict. An alternative to the army was the yeomanry cavalry, which was the mounted division of the British Volunteer Corps founded in the 1790s for national defense

---

*and German Society* (New York: Oxford University Press, 1990); Mary Fulbrook, *The People's State* (New York: Oxford University Press, 2005).

[46] Darvall, *Popular Disturbances*, 275–276. Darvall identifies the correspondence between Colonel Fletcher of Bolton-le-Moors and the Home Office as "the best single source of information with regard to the contemporary spy system." The "Bow Street Runners" was originally a derogatory name for the law enforcement officers of the Bow Street Magistrate's Court in Westminster.

[47] Edward Royle, *Revolutionary Britannia? Reflections on the Threat of Revolution in Britain, 1789–1848* (Manchester: Manchester University Press, 2000), 183.

[48] Ibid., 299.

[49] Maitland to Beckett, July 18, 1812, in H.O. 42.125.

against revolutionary France. Local authorities soon began to use them for "dispersing disorderly mobs" such as in the food riots of 1795 and against the Luddites.[50] The non-mounted component of the Volunteer Corps was disbanded following Napoleon's defeat in 1815, but the yeomanry was retained. Since the price of membership in the yeomanry was one's own mount, it was always a force drawn primarily from the ranks of the landed elite, though the newly rich also entered in large numbers for social prestige.

The Peterloo Massacre showed the problems with relying on such a force for handling social and political protest. Long marginalized in standard history texts in the UK, the massacre only received official commemoration in 2007 when the Manchester City Council voted to replace a blue plaque noting only a "dispersal by the military" with a red one that contained a more accurate description of the event.[51] The *Guardian Newspaper* – itself a direct outgrowth of the Peterloo Massacre – editorialized that "the uncomfortable truth about a defining moment in the history of democracy in Britain has finally been recorded – 188 years after the event – on a red plaque fixed to a wall in the centre of Manchester."[52]

Peterloo began as one of many mass meetings intended to pressure the government into democratic concessions following the end of the Napoleonic wars. A mass petition for universal manhood suffrage gained 750,000 signatures in 1817 but had been roundly rejected by the House of Commons. The Manchester Political Union organized the St. Peter's Field meeting and invited the well-known orator and radical Henry Hunt. The specific grievance was that Manchester had no representation in parliament while rotten boroughs proliferated, but there was a general call for political reform and a program that would later be adopted by the Chartists. The first meeting, scheduled for August 9, was cancelled because spies had learned of the event and the organizers wanted to stay within the law. Instead of demanding that Manchester receive parliamentary representation, the organizers claimed that they were merely meeting to "consider the propriety" of such a move, and the meeting was rescheduled for week later. The *Manchester Observer* reported that the purpose of the meeting was "to take into consideration the most speedy and effectual mode of obtaining Radical reform in the Common House of Parliament."

[50] Darvall, *Popular Disturbances*, 255.
[51] The original blue plaque erected in 1972 read only "The site of St. Peter's Field where on 16th August 1819 Henry Hunt radical orator addressed an assembly of about 60,000 people. Their subsequent dispersal by the military is remembered as Peterloo."
[52] www.theguardian.com/uk/2007/dec/27/past.politics.

Members of the crowd held banners with the following slogans: "universal suffrage," "annual parliaments," "no corn laws," and "vote by ballot."

The red plaque tells what happened next: "On 16 August 1819, a peaceful rally of 60,000 pro-democracy reformers, men, women and children, was attacked by armed cavalry resulting in 15 deaths and over 600 injuries." Far from a simple "dispersal" by the military, Peterloo was the single most deadly use of state power against English protestors in British history to that point. When local magistrates commanded the yeomanry to arrest Hunt and the other speakers, the inexperienced and numerically overwhelmed members of the Manchester and Salford Yeomanry got stuck in the crowd. At that point, it appeared to Lieutenant Colonel Guy L'Estrange of the 15th Hussars, a cavalry regiment of the British army that had been summoned by the magistrates, that the yeomanry was being attacked by the mob. The resulting cavalry charge by the British army caused most of the casualties, though the yeomanry were widely recognized to have been the instigators. Many members of yeomanry quit after Peterloo upon receiving threatening letters.[53] The tragedy was immediately dubbed "The Peterloo Massacre" by James Wroe, editor of the *Manchester Observer*, who compared the bloodshed at St. Peter's Field to Napoleon's defeat at Waterloo four years earlier. Wroe was subsequently arrested and charged with sedition, and a crackdown on his paper led to its closure in February 1820. The Manchester *Guardian*, founded in 1821 by John Edward Taylor who was present at the massacre, promised to continue Wroe's work.

Politically, the consequence of Peterloo was increased repression. The preamble to what would become known collectively as the "Six Acts" began with the statement that "every meeting for radical reform is an overt act of treasonable conspiracy against the King and his government." The goal was to prevent a repeat of Peterloo by severely curtailing the political liberties of the radical opposition. Two of the acts were concerned primarily with arms: the *Training Prevention Act* outlawed drilling and private military training, while the *Seizure of Arms Act* allowed for the search of private property for weapons. A further two acts concerned freedom of speech: the *Blasphemous and Seditious Libels Act* raised the penalties for distributing radical literature and the *Newspaper and Stamp Duties Act* increased taxes on political pamphlets and required newspaper editors to post bonds. Freedom of assembly was curtailed through the *Seditious Meetings Act*, which

---

[53] Ione Leigh, *Castlereagh* (London: 1951), p. 132.

limited the size of public meetings, and the right of due process was undercut by the *Misdemeanors Act* that sped up trials and restricted the use of bail. All told, the Six Acts represented one of the most striking curtailments of political rights in British history.

Opposition to the Six Acts generated the so-called Cato Street Conspiracy. Arthur Thistlewood, who had been imprisoned following the Spa Fields Riots in 1816 and had been released in the fall of 1819, was the leader of a spectacular, and entirely unworkable, plan that involved killing the entire Cabinet, along with Prime Minister Lord Liverpool, seizing government buildings, and creating a Jacobin-inspired "Committee for Public Safety." But Thistlewood's second in command was a police spy and agent provocateur. The plot was foiled, and one policeman was killed. Five conspirators (including Thistlewood) were executed, and five were sent to Australia.

While the Cato Street Conspiracy could be dismissed as outlandish, the British state could not ignore the fact that public agitation for reform, however vaguely defined or imperfectly understood by its champions, had become a permanent feature of the political landscape. Its tools for disarming this threat – from spies, to troops, to repressive legislation – were all widely recognized as unwieldy. The funeral of Queen Caroline in August 1821 provoked another mass mobilization against the government that required the movement of 9,000 troops and 5 military regiments.[54] Once again, there was a chorus for a new police force to regulate such disturbances and to control the "dangerous classes." A typical one read:

The most superficial observer of the external and visible appearance of this town, must soon be convinced, that there is a large mass of unproductive population living upon it, without occupation or ostensible means of subsistence; and, it is notorious that hundreds and thousands go forth from day to day trusting alone to charity or rapine; and differing little from the barbarous hordes which traverse an uncivilized land ... The principle of [their] action is the same; their life is predatory; it is equally a war against society, and the object is alike to gratify desire by stratagem or force.[55]

The Duke of Wellington, military hero of the Napoleonic wars and future Tory prime minister, laid out his concerns about relying on the army for public order in London (Box 3.1):

I feel the greatest anxiety respecting the state of the military in London ... Very recently strong symptoms of discontent appeared in one of the battalions of the guards ... Thus, in one of the most critical moments that ever occurred in this

---

[54] David Taylor, *The New Police*, 21.
[55] George Mainwaring, *Observations on the Present State of the Police of the Metropolis* (London, 1821), 4–5.

> **Box 3.1 Timeline of the Age of Repression in Nineteenth-century England[a]**
>
> - **1811 – March 11:** Luddite disturbances begin in Nottingham
> - **1812 – February:** Machine breaking is made a capital offense
> - **1812 – April 11:** 150 Luddites attack Rawfolds Mill
> - **1816 – November/December:** The Spa Field Riots
> - **1817 – Fall:** House of Commons rejects petition for universal suffrage
> - **1819 – August 16:** The Peterloo Massacre
> - **1819 – December:** The Six Acts passed
> - **1820 – February:** Cato Street Conspiracy
> - **1821 – August:** Funeral for Queen Caroline provokes agitation against the government
> - **1829 – April:** Catholic Emancipation Act passed
> - **1829 – June:** Metropolitan Police Act passed
> - **1829 – December:** Birmingham Political Union formed
> - **1830 – July:** French Revolution
> - **1830 – November:** Formation of Whig government
>
> [a] This timeline refers strictly to repression in England and not in the United Kingdom as a whole. There was severe repression in Ireland throughout this period.

country, we and the public have reason to doubt the fidelity of the troops, the only security we have, not only against revolution but for the lives and property of every individual in this country who has anything to lose.[56]

And yet the report of a second parliamentary committee on policing in 1822 was no more favorable to Peel's proposal than the one from 1818. It reasoned that:

It is difficult to reconcile an effective system of police with that perfect freedom of action and exemption from interference, which are the great privileges and blessings of society in this country; and your Committee think that the forfeiture or curtailment of such advantages would be too great a sacrifice for improvements in police, or facilities in detection of crime, however desirable in themselves if abstractly considered.[57]

---

[56] Quoted in Reith, *The Police Idea*, 213. Wellington is referring to Queen Caroline's funeral as "one of the most critical moments that ever occurred in this country."

[57] Report of the Select Committee on the Police of the Metropolis, *Parliamentary Papers* 1822 (440): iv, p.11.

## 3.2 Defending the Old Regime: 1811–1829

And then, after a decade of failure, Peel succeeded. The parliamentary committee drafted a plan for the Metropolitan police (for the City of London) with little parliamentary opposition in 1829. It is still not entirely clear what had shifted elite opinion enough to conquer the traditional British fear of a French style police force. Peel wielded statistics showing a rise in crime in London, though "it seems clear that Peel was primarily concerned with the threat posed by political radicalism."[58] Peel assuaged concerns about the police becoming a standing army by specifically designing the new uniforms to look different from military ones and only arming them with wooden truncheons rather than firearms. The police carried badges so that the public could easily identify them. Peel pledged his commitment to civil liberties: "God forbid that [I] should mean to countenance a system of espionage."[59] He also articulated a set of practices – later known as Peelite Principles – that came to define modern policing. The foundation of these principles was "to prevent crime and disorder, as an alternative to the repression of crime and disorder by military force." Although the purported other eleven Peelite principles look to have been "an invention of twentieth-century policing textbooks," the romantic view of the unarmed "bobbies" (named after Peel) persists.[60]

Robert Storch finds that ordinary citizens called the bobbies by other names, such as "Peel's bloody gang" and the "blue devils." From the moment they were founded, the new police were used as riot squads and were understood to be "hired mercenaries" and "unconstitutional bravoes."[61] Elements of the public considered then parasitic – "blue locusts" was yet another derogatory term for police that appeared to earn money for doing little other than bothering ordinary people. Most importantly for our purposes is that the police were viewed as agents of the political class. One working-class political weekly warned that the police were "a *political*, not a *protective* force" and that their "object is not so much to prevent thieving as to watch political feeling, and give reports to the Ministers of the political movements of the working class."[62] Storch finds

---

[58] David Taylor, *The New Police*, 21.
[59] Emsley, *The English Police*, 24.
[60] Peel in fact did not list his principles, leaving it to later police historians to summarize them. As a result, there are multiple variations of the supposed "Peelite principles" in the literature. Susan A. Lentz and Robert H. Chaires, "The Invention of Peel's Principles: A Study of Policing 'Textbook; History.'" *Journal of Criminal Justice* 35 (2007), 69–79.
[61] Storch, "Blue Locusts," 71.
[62] Poor Man's Guardian, November 2, 1833.

that the police did indeed have "an omnibus mandate to detect and prevent crime, to maintain a constant, unceasing surveillance upon all facets of life in working-class communities – to report on political opinions and movements, trade-union activities, public houses, and recreational life."[63] These practices were well captured by the axiom "you guard St. James by watching St. Giles."[64] The anti-police riots of the 1840s and 1850s speak to the societal resistance that the new police generated in the following decades.[65] But the critical point is that the British state responded to societal resistance by constructing a new coercive institution. The political agitation of the 1830s accelerated that trend.

### 3.3 THE FIRST GREAT REFORM

On March 2, 1831, Thomas Babington Macaulay (future author of the *History of England*) addressed the House of Commons and spoke in favor of the bill that would ultimately result in the Great Reform Act of 1832.

I support this plan, because I am sure that it is our best security against a revolution ... We say, and we say justly, that it is not by mere numbers, but by property and intelligence, that the nation ought to be governed. Yet, saying this, we exclude from all share in the government great masses of property and intelligence, great numbers of those who are most interested in preserving tranquility, and who know best how to preserve it. We do more. We drive over to the side of revolution those whom we shut out from power.[66]

Whig politicians like Macaulay had made a remarkable conversion to the cause of reform by 1830. Although some liberals like Lord Russell had long advocated electoral reform, it was hardly a mainstream position among the Whigs. Writing in the wake of the passing of the Six Acts, Lord Charles Grey noted in a letter to a friend and supporter of parliamentary reform that "the leaders of the popular party, or rather of the Mob" wanted "not Reform but Revolution." He further warned his friend that "if a convulsion follows their attempts to work upon the minds of the people, inflamed as they are by distress, for which your reform would afford a very inadequate remedy, I shall not precede you

---

[63] Storch, "Blue Locusts," 64.
[64] "The Police System of London," *Edinburgh Review* July 1852, p. 5. St. James was the wealthy section of London and St. Giles was a slum.
[65] Storch, "Blue Locusts," 72–76.
[66] *The Miscellaneous Writings and Speeches of Lord Macaulay* (London: Longmans, Green, Reader, and Dyer, 1871), 485.

many months on the scaffold."⁶⁷ Given that these views were prevalent among liberals – the most likely elite advocates of reform – it is not surprising that from "1822 to 1830 popular support for reform was virtually dormant."⁶⁸

Three historical events changed this situation. The first was the formation of the first Whig government after nearly a quarter-century of Tory dominance.⁶⁹ Many Whigs had long wanted to reform the system of rotten boroughs that produced dependable Tory majorities, and this was their first real opportunity to do so. Second, the death of King George IV on June 26, 1830, and the subsequent succession of William IV meant that a monarch opposed to any reform was replaced with one with Whig sympathies. The new king's actions would later be decisive in the passing of the Great Reform Bill, particularly his pledge to create new peers. Third, and probably most consequential, was the Catholic Relief Act of 1829 that allowed Catholics to enter parliament. According to Michael Brock, Catholic emancipation destroyed "the mystique of an unalterable, Protestant constitution."⁷⁰ The effect was not only psychological. Many Tory "Ultras" switched from being unshakeable defenders of the old system to supporters of expanding the franchise because they hoped the "anti-popery" of the public would constitute a check on the new Catholic influence.⁷¹ The first divisions thus emerged in the Tory oligarchy that had ruled Britain uninterruptedly since 1806, and several of the Ultras became unabashed enemies of Wellington.⁷²

Thus, as Geoffrey Finlayson and other historians explain, "by 1830, the general aim of parliamentary reform commanded wide acceptance."⁷³ And yet such acceptance did not lead automatically to reform. Duke Wellington (Tory) defended the old system in the House of Lords in November 1830 and refused to consider any changes to it.

---

⁶⁷ Quoted in J. R. M. Butler, *The Passing of the Great Reform Bill*, 33–34.
⁶⁸ Quinault, 378.
⁶⁹ Cannadine, *Victorious Century*, 166.
⁷⁰ Brock, 57.
⁷¹ Cannadine, *Victorious Century*, 154, explains their logic as follows: "They [the Ultras] rightly noted that Catholic Emancipation had been deeply unpopular among the people of predominantly Protestant Britain, which meant that a more representative House of Commons would never have passed such a measure. They accordingly embraced reform in the hope of preventing any such similar calamity in the future." In this sense, the Tory Ultras were harbingers of conservatives in Prussia and France who believed that suffrage expansion could serve reactionary interests (see Chapter 4).
⁷² Gash, 270.
⁷³ Geoffrey Finlayson, *Decade of Reform: England in the Eighteen Thirties* (New York: W. W. Norton and Co., 1970), 7.

In his view, the strength of the old system was its foundation in class inequalities – that it "contained a large body of the property of the country, and in which the landed interests had a preponderating influence" was its chief selling point. At the same time, Wellington also claimed the current arrangements were far more inclusive than those that had preceded it, in Britain and elsewhere. "Britain," according to Wellington, already "possessed a Legislature which answered all the good purposes of legislation, and this to a greater degree than any legislature ever had answered in any country whatsoever."[74] Regarding electoral reform, he stated during the same parliamentary debate that "as far as he was concerned, as long as he held any station in the government of the country, he should always feel it his duty to resist such measures."[75] His government fell on a confidence vote a week later, and Grey's Whig government came to office with the expectation that it would introduce parliamentary reform. Given that other reform bills had stalled over the previous decades, the successful passing of the Whigs reform bill was far from guaranteed.

The Whigs touted the conservative nature of their project. The instructions for the parliamentary committee preparing the bill were to craft "the outline of a measure … large enough to satisfy public opinion … yet still based on property."[76] According to Lord Russell: "the electors should … be intelligent, incorrupt and independent. In other words, they should have the capacity to make a choice, the wish to make a good choice, and the power to carry that wish into effect."[77] He sought to "bring into the constituency those who are best qualified to exercise the important privilege, from their education, from their general intelligence, and from the stake [i.e., property] which they have in the country."[78] This meant the middle class, which had, according to liberals, undergone a profound transformation in recent years:

The rapid and astonishing influx of wealth had absolutely changed the whole state of the middle classes of society. Those middle classes now consisted of persons well acquainted with every useful branch of art and science; they were fully capable of forming enlightened views and sound principles upon all political and moral questions, and upon all points connected with the State.[79]

[74] Cannadine, *Victorious Century*, 156.
[75] *Hansard*, November 2, 1830, 3rd series, Vol. I, c. 53.
[76] Brock, *The Great Reform Act*, 136.
[77] Russell, December 12, 1832, *Hansard*, p. 497.
[78] Russell, December 12, 1831, *Hansard*, p. 166.
[79] Lord Plunkett, March 28, 1831, *Hansard*, p. 1044.

These were mere assumptions, however. Cannadine reminds us that: "in reality there was little solid information about who these people were, what they did, where they lived, or how many of them there were."[80]

### 3.3.1 Threat of Revolution?

Did Macaulay and Grey view revolution as imminent in 1832? There are at least two problems with taking their words as face value. First, they were repeating a well-worn justification for franchise expansion that Whigs had been using for forty years.[81] They were enmeshed in a Victorian political culture in which the fear of revolution in general was salient.[82] Much of the talk of revolution was simply performative: Royle cautions that "the language of revolutionary oratory may have been empty rhetoric conditioned by the dramatic conventions of the day and understood for what it was by both speaker and audience."[83] Moreover, as Brock argues, the Tory's had used the "good fright" argument so many times that it had lost its effect: "It was by now very well known to the progressives. They had suffered much from its application over the years. Tory governments had cried wolf too often. Their opponents could easily represent these cries as false alarms, designed to whip the doubtful into line."[84]

Second, as Joseph Hamburger points out, it was far from clear that Grey was referring to an imminent revolution: "the Whigs ... were mainly concerned about the possibility of a revolution in the future – not in 1831 but in, say, 1851 – or as it turned out, in 1842 and 1848. They thought the present unrest was under control for the time being, and that it would subside with the passing of the Reform Bill."[85] The opposition Tories, for their part, also cried revolution, but for them it was the passing of the Reform Bill that would constitute the overthrow of the social order. According to Wellington, for example, "Beginning reform is beginning revolution."[86] While there was much talk of revolution in the parliamentary debate, there

---

[80] Cannadine, *Victorious Century*, 161.
[81] Bateman, *Disenfranchising Democracy*, 261.
[82] Walter Houghton, *The Victorian Frame of Mind, 1830–1870* (New Haven: Yale University Press, 1970), 54–58.
[83] Royle, *Revolutionary Britannia?*, 8.
[84] Brock, *Great Reform*, 127.
[85] Joseph Hamburger, *James Mill and the Art of Revolution* (New Haven: Yale University Press, 1963), 37.
[86] Roland Quinault, "The French Revolution of 1830 and Parliamentary Reform." *History* 79, 257 (1994), 385.

were few signs that the public was preparing for one. Two prominent reformers – O'Connell and Russell – lamented that "the country was in a state of perfect tranquility" in the Spring of 1830.[87]

What had changed between the spring of 1830 and the collapse of Wellington's government in November 1830? One possibility is that the French Revolution of 1830 intervened and, following Aidt and Jenson, shifted the calculations of both the British opposition and the British regime.[88] At first blush, the historiography of the period provides some support for this claim. In his review of the literature, Roland Quinault writes that "the stimulus which the French revolution of 1830 gave to the campaign for parliamentary reform was subsequently noted by a long line of historians, from the Trevelyans, to Halévy, Woodward and Thompson."[89] However, each of these historians only notes the 1830 revolution in passing and provides few details on how exactly it mattered. Halévy's strongest piece of evidence is Wellington's quote that he would have remained in power "had not the late revolution in France occurred at a critical period."[90] Norman Gash, however, claims that this was sour grapes on Wellington's part. The French Revolution of 1830, Gash argues, had little effect on the outcome of the elections, as most of them were already over by the time news of the revolution reached Britain in early August.[91] The political elite and the press also failed to see the relevance of it for their domestic politics. "United as Englishmen were in welcoming the revolution," Gash writes, "they were not necessarily conscious of any need to extract from the scenes evaluated in France a lesson for their own political behavior."[92] Roland Quinault tries to show that the 1830 revolution had a greater influence than this, and he demonstrates that it appeared in political discourse and the media. Elites drew the opposite conclusion from it that TOR theories would predict, and Quinault concludes that "the revolution convinced Wellington that parliamentary reform should be vigorously resisted."[93] In November 1830, Wellington still believed he could govern without committing to any electoral reform. There is little convincing evidence that the French

---

[87] Brock, *Great Reform*, 77.
[88] Aidt and Jensen, "Workers Unite."
[89] Quinault, "French Revolution," 379.
[90] Ibid., 392.
[91] Norman Gash, "English Reform and French Revolution in the General Election of 1830," in R. Pares and A. J. P. Taylor, eds., *Essays Presented to Sir Lewis Namier*, 260.
[92] Ibid., 266.
[93] Quinault, "French Revolution," 383.

Revolution mattered much in the reform of 1832, leading to the conclusion that their chronological proximity is coincidental, not causal.

What about the political unions that were founded in 1830 and agitated for electoral reform? Did they constitute a credible revolutionary threat? Some of their leaders certainly believed so, and their version of events has often been taken as evidence that revolution was imminent at two points in the passing of the Great Reform: November 1831 and May 1832.[94]

Middle-class reformers followed the Irish example and founded political unions to advocate for political change. The Birmingham Political Union (BPU) was founded in 1829 "to obtain by every just and legal means such a reform in the Commons House of Parliament as may ensure a real and effectual representation of the lower and middle classes of the people in that House."[95] The political unions (there were other significant ones in Leeds, Manchester, and Sheffield) were pro-government: "the political unions became the center of support for the Grey's government outside of Parliament – They were a source of strength."[96] Grey counseled the king that the political unions championing reform did not constitute a revolutionary threat: "The excitement which now exists is directed to what, I think, is a safe and legitimate object. In the event of a dissolution, it would act in support of the King and Government."[97]

The opposition Tories attacked the government for being too cozy with a seditious organization. Much like Whig predictions of revolution without reform, this was a standard rhetorical device. Neither of the two major studies that examine the political unions find them to be revolutionary.[98] Rather, leaders of the groups made every effort to distance themselves from revolutionary rhetoric and excluded potential troublemakers from membership. This was largely out of necessity, for as Flick reminds us, the "basic problem in organizing national political agitation was that in most respects it was illegal."[99] Before forming the

---

[94] They exaggerated influence from the beginning. Flick (29) finds no evidence for Attwood's claim that the BPU was responsible for Whigs taking over the government in 1830. See Carlos Flick, *The Birmingham Political Union and the Movements for Reform in Britain 1830–1839* (Hamden: Archon Books, 1978).
[95] Finlayson, *Decade of Reform*, 7.
[96] Ferguson, 264.
[97] Quoted in Briggs, 2000, *Chartism*, 215.
[98] In addition to Flick's monograph, the other standard reading on the BPU is Nancy LoPatin, *Political Unions, Popular Politics and the Great Reform Act* (London: Macmillan, 1999).
[99] Flick, *Birmingham Political Union*, 42.

BPU, Attwood consulted with both attorneys and experienced agitators to ensure that the *Rules and Regulations* of the union would not get him in legal trouble.[100]

The second reading of the Reform Bill passed the Commons by a vote of 302 to 301 on March 22, 1831. However, an attempt by the Tories to add an amendment led to a de facto no-confidence vote in the Whig government. Russell then asked the king to dissolve parliament and to call new elections.[101] This amounted to a public referendum on the Reform Bill and constituted the first "single issue" campaign in English politics. The elections demonstrated the overwhelming popularity of the reform and gave the Whigs a strong mandate. According to Brock, at this point "every MP with constituents knew that a vote against the Bill meant expense at the next election whenever it came, and perhaps a risk of being unseated."[102] Furthermore:

The election might have shown that it was unwise for MPs to defy the government. A peer was more happily placed for a display of independence. Alarm at Reform mobs had little effect except among those noblemen whose country seats lay near great towns. Many opposition and doubtful peers regarded the possibility of disorder if the Bill were rejected as a bogey raised by the government. Moreover, the fear of being thought afraid was even more powerful among the peers than in the Commons. Their principles forbade them to yield to threat, especially to threats in which they did not believe. The government's attempts to show that the king would allow a large creation were unconvincing; and no other threat counted.[103]

The barely modified Reform Bill passed the Commons with a vote of 345 to 236 and was sent to the House of Lords, which proceeded to reject it on October 8, 1831, by a vote of 199 to 158. The Lords were once again unmoved by the social unrest. The BPU had held a meeting on October 3, 1831, on Newhall Hill in what was "probably the largest political gathering held in Britain to that date."[104] The Lords' rejection then set off a series of disturbances, and it is from this point forward that

---

[100] According to a description from a contemporary (Parkes), Attwood "was a cautious, even timid, man; Parkes was later to declare that physical courage was one of the traits that the banker lacked to be a great agitator. He often expressed his fear of being seized and lodged in a dungeon or otherwise 'destroyed like the reformers of old.' Thus, he determined to follow a course of great discretion."
[101] Bateman, *Disenfranchising Democracy*, 259. The Tory amendment would have stripped Scotland and Ireland of their proposed redistribution of seats.
[102] Brock, *Great Reform*, 171.
[103] Ibid., 232–233.
[104] Flick, *Birmingham Political Union*, 63.

## 3.3 The First Great Reform

the proponents of the revolutionary threat theory marshal most of their evidence. According to this view, a series of riots in Derby, Nottingham, and, most significantly, Bristol allowed the reformers to argue that the country was in fact on the verge of revolution. The supposed participation of the political unions in these disturbances, coupled with signs that the largest of these unions (the BPU) was adopting a military structure and arming itself, meant that the revolutionary threat was not emanating from "ill-organised working-class groups" but rather from a "well-organised middle-class group."[105]

Upon closer inspection, however, the political unions were unlikely revolutionaries. Once again, they repeatedly professed their loyalty to the king and their support for the Whig government. After the Lords rejected the first reform bill, the BPU issued the following statement:

> Friends and Fellow Countrymen! The Bill of Reform is rejected by the House of Lords! Patience! Patience!! Patience!!! Our beloved King is firm – his patriot ministers are firm – the House of Commons is firm – the whole nation is firm. What then have the people to fear? Nothing! – unless their own violence should rashly lead to anarchy, and place difficulties in the way of the King and his Ministers. Therefore, there must be no violence. The people are too strong to require violence. By peace – by law – by order – everyone must rally round the throne of the King. The small majority of the Lords will soon come to a sense of the duty which they owe to their Country and to the King – or some other legal means will be devised of carrying the Bill of Reform into a law without delay. Fellow countrymen – be patient – be peaceful – be strictly obedient to the laws, and everything is yet safe. God bless the King![106]

Plans circulated to form a militia to protect private property and preserve order – but the goal was to control a potential mob and not to intimidate the government. At a meeting of the BPU council in November, there was discussion of creating an unarmed force "to render the physical powers of the Union available for the preservation of life and property." Flick recounts that "Parkes then went to Attwood and Scholefield and told them that the proposed plan was illegal; as usual he found the banker highly sensitive to any such possibility." Flick finds that the "Bristol riots [were] especially upsetting to Attwood, for he held that no disturbances would take place in towns that possessed active political unions."[107]

Critically, those most responsible for monitoring internal security did not consider the Unions dangerous. LoPatin's analysis of reports from

---

[105] Thomis and Holt, *Threats of Revolution*, 89.
[106] Flick, *Birmingham Political Union*, 65.
[107] Ibid., 67–69.

the Home Office reveals that the state was not overly concerned about either the Nottingham or Derby riots. Even the more tumultuous riots in Bristol also did not provoke undue alarm: "The government looked at the events in Bristol and saw that the Political Unions were responsible and level-headed, not revolutionary."[108] If anything, it was the enemies of reform (the Tories) that tried to use the disturbances to their advantage and warn that the reform push had ignited a revolutionary situation. Hamburger also analyzes Home Office reports and similarly concludes that "the government's confidence that it could control the disorder and its calm evaluation of its significance contrasts sharply with the frightened and alarmist statements made by some Tory politicians."[109] The combination of Home Office reports and assurances from Lord Grey alleviated concerns about Bristol.[110] The government took the precautionary step of issuing the Proclamation against Political Unions on November 21, 1831, but neither the government nor local officials did anything to implement it. By this point, the BPU had completely backed away from whatever paramilitary plans it had made and public agitation appeared to have subsided by December 1831.

In summary, the historical record does not provide much direct evidence of fear of social unrest dictating government policy in 1831. Nor does a recent quantitative analysis that compares roll call votes on the Reform bill on March 22, 1831, with those on December 17, 1831.[111] The authors consider the first vote to have occurred in a "low-tension" environment, while the second occurred in a "high-tension" one. As we have seen, this coding is broadly consistent with the historical record. Their econometric analysis finds that "the threat of revolution had an impact, if at all, only on reluctant Whig politicians." Put another way, some very conservative Whigs were probably moved by public opinion and popular unrest to drop their opposition to electoral reform. Yet, the authors also find that "social unrest hardened the anti-reform stance of the Tory MPs and of their patrons, many of whom stood to lose directly from the reform."[112] This finding is strikingly similar to Brock's answer to the same question.

---

[108] LoPatin, *Political Unions*, 100.
[109] Hamburger, *Art of Revolution*, 237.
[110] LoPatin, *Political Unions*, 101.
[111] Aidt and Jenson, "Workers Unite." The authors rightly note that the two bills were virtually identical.
[112] Ibid., 242.

- 1830 – June 26: Death of King George IV
- 1831 – March 2: Macaulay addresses the House of Commons in favor of what would become the Great Reform Act of 1832
- 1831 – March 22: The second reading of the Reform Bill passes the Commons by 302 to 301
- 1831 – April 22: The king dissolves Parliament and calls new elections
- 1831 – September: The Reform Bill passes the House of Commons by 324 to 236
- 1831 – October 3: The Birmingham Political Union (BPU) holds a meeting on Newhall Hill
- 1831 – October 8: The House of Lords rejects the Reform Bill by 199 to 158
- 1831 – November 21: The government issues the **Proclamation against Political Unions**
- 1832 – January: William IV decides not to object to the creation of peers in the House of Lords to ensure passage of the Reform Bill
- 1832 – April 13: The Reform Bill passes the House of Lords 184 to 175, with thirty-nine peers abstaining or reversing their votes
- 1832 – May 7: Diehard opponents of the Reform Bill effectively block it through postponement in the House of Lords by 151 to 116
- 1832 – May: The **May Crisis of 1832**—Grey's government resigns, and William IV calls on Lord Wellington to form a new government to carry through the Reform Bill
- 1832 – May 20: The king's secretary signals to diehard opponents that new peers would not be created if opposition is dropped
- 1832 – June 4: The Reform Bill is read again and passed by 106 to 22

In January 1832, William IV made a critical decision: He would not object to the creation of peers in the House of Lords to ensure the passage of the Reform Bill. The king's hesitancy in the past had signaled to peers that the threat was not credible, but on this occasion, his support for the measure to overcome the crisis spread quickly.[113] When the Bill was brought again to the House of Lords on April 13, 1832, thirty-nine peers either reversed their vote or abstained, allowing the Bill to pass by a vote of 184 to 175. The closeness of the vote suggests that the fear of revolution was not considerable enough to convince close to half of the

[113] Brock, *Great Reform*, 269.

peers of the necessity of reform. Moreover, a move by diehard opponents of the Bill to effectively block it through postponement succeeded in the House of Lords by a vote of 151 to 116 on May 7, 1832.

The May Crisis of 1832 marked a second round of public agitation. When Grey's government resigned, King William IV called on Lord Wellington of the Tories to form a government to carry through the Reform Bill. Wellington failed, and for several tense days, the constitutional crisis was accompanied by massive public protests, bank runs, and apparent preparations for armed resistance by Attwood's BPU and Francis Place's group in London. According to Thomis and Holt, "the plan was for revolution, however respectable its organisers, however determined they were that a revolutionary seizure of power should not precipitate social revolution in Great Britain."[114] Attwood believed his plan had worked: "Our declaration against the Duke ... has done the business."[115]

Attwood and Place, however, were really engaging in "legend-making."[116] Place himself did much to encourage the view that the TOR forced the Lords to back down: "much of the available information about the crisis comes from the archive to which Francis Place devoted his declining years. In it his own power and prescience receive the fullest recognition."[117] Royle cautions that "whereas Place was always ready to regard the revolutionary threats of others as foolish or empty, he did not see his own involvement in this light."[118] Place wrote of his plans for the insurrection in his diary: "Birmingham was the place in which to hoist the standard of revolt." London would then follow, and key members of Parliament would continue the rebellion in the House of Commons.

The problem, however, was that the supposedly key figures were never aware of the plan. There is no evidence that any member of parliament had heard of it. Brock writes that "there was a touch of comic opera about Attwood's army ... Its chances against regular troops would have been poor. It was not intended for fighting regulars, still less for defeating them. Its function was to put Wellington in the position where he must give the order to fire on the reformers or concede defeat."[119] And again, Attwood was too obsessed with the rule of law to be an effective

[114] Thomis and Holt, *Threat of Revolution*, 92–93.
[115] Quoted in Flick, *Birmingham Political Union*, 88.
[116] Ibid., 94.
[117] Brock, *Great Reform*, 296.
[118] Royle, *Revolutionary Britannia?*, 76.
[119] Brock, *Great Reform*, 309.

revolutionary: It took attorneys so long to review the BPU's "Solemn Declaration" for any traces of illegality that it was published too late to influence Wellington.[120]

In the end, the only measure that persuaded the Lords was the threat of mass peerage. On May 20, the king's secretary Sir Herbert Taylor sent a note to the diehard opponents of reform, indicating that the new peers would not be created if opposition were dropped.[121] When the Bill was read again on June 4, it passed by a vote of 106 for and only 22 against.

### 3.3.2 A Modest Reform

While the passing of the First Great Reform is now widely viewed as a critical juncture in British democratization, it was not viewed so at the time, particularly by the working class. Even before it had been passed, the National Union of the Working Classes – which demanded annual parliaments, universal manhood suffrage, vote by parliament, and no property qualifications for members of parliament – blasted the bill as "a mere trick to strengthen ... the tottering exclusiveness of our 'blessed constitution.'"[122] Radicals like G. J. Harney described the legislation as "mock reforms." This was not a surprising reaction given the modest changes that followed from the Great Reform. From the start, the Whigs were "convinced that their task was essentially conservative, a rescue operation on behalf of rank and property."[123] Practically, this meant abolishing the qualifications that had allowed some members of the working class to vote under the old system. Russell and other Whigs had long claimed that the Tories regularly "swindle[d] the poor and ignorant out of their votes by beer and bribery." Their transparent goal was to put "the franchise as much as possible in the hands of the middle classes."[124] As Lord Grey put it, the goal of the reform was to "satisfy all reasonable demands, and remove at once, and forever, all rational grounds of complaint from the minds of the intelligent and the independent portion of the community."

Grey reassured the king that "in truth, the right of voting, taken generally, will be found much less popular than the old one."[125] And if "popular" is taken to mean working class, then Grey's prediction was largely

---

[120] Flick, *Birmingham Political Union*, 86–88.
[121] Briggs, *Age of Improvement*, 223.
[122] Ibid., 286.
[123] Finlayson, *Decade of Reform*, 10.
[124] Quoted in Bateman, *Disenfranchising Democracy*, 255.
[125] Bateman, *Disenfranchising Democracy*, 256.

correct. The three lowest categories in the class structure of English borough constituencies – agriculturalist, semi/unskilled laborer, and craftsman – all saw their enfranchisements rates *decline* after 1832.[126] For Charles Wood, the Bill was "an efficient, substantial, anti-democratic, pro-property measure."[127] Grey called it "the most aristocratic measure that ever was proposed in parliament."[128] As one historian concludes, "there seems no escape from the conclusion that the 1832 Reform Act diminished the penetration of the electorate down the social scale."[129] Bateman considers it a case of democratic disenfranchisement in which a suffrage expansion is accompanied by new forms of electoral exclusion.

It was not the expansion of the electorate that was most important about the Reform Act, but rather its recomposition – the extension of voting rights to the middle classes, the disenfranchisement of the working classes of the boroughs, the increased size of the constituency electorate, and the redistribution of seats to the growing cities, centers of religious dissent, liberal economics, and reformist politics.[130]

Sheri Berman writes that:

while in retrospect the Great Reform Act may appear as the first step on Britain's long path to democracy, it is important to remember that its supporters viewed it in the opposite way: as a way of preventing democratization and preserving the reigning order by bringing into it those who could be trusted to support it and defer to the elites dominating it.[131]

Lord Russell, one of the architects of the reform, was unwilling to consider further expansion of the suffrage. Speaking against a measure to amend the bill in 1837, Russell warned that "the entering again into this question of the construction of representation so soon would destroy the stability of our institutions."[132] The speech earned him the nickname "Finality Jack," but it was actually Peel who had used those terms three years earlier in his Tamworth Manifesto, a foundational document of modern British conservatism written in the town of Tamworth. There

---

[126] Ibid., 267.
[127] Quoted in Brock, *Great Reform*, 170.
[128] Ibid., 152.
[129] T. J. Nossiter, *Influence, Opinion, and Political Idioms in Reformed England: Case Studies from the North-East, 1832–74* (Hassocks: Harvester Press, 1975), 166.
[130] Bateman, *Disenfranchising Democracy*, 272. The other cases that Bateman analyzes are the United States in the 1810s–1820s, when the white working class won the franchise in many states while free blacks lost it, and the founding of the French Third Republic, when a bill for disenfranchising the working class was only barely defeated.
[131] Sheri Berman, *Democracy and Dictatorship in Europe*, 196.
[132] Lord Russell, November 20, 1837. Hansard, 3/xxxix/68–71.

Peel had called the Reform act a "final and irrevocable settlement of a great constitutional question."[133] Indeed, the consensus among its designers was that the Bill was supposed to have solved the issue for "at least thirty or forty years." Their estimates proved to be accurate.

### 3.4 THE REPRESSION OF THE CHARTISTS

The Chartist movement was born directly from the disappointment of the First Great Reform. Robert Owen created the Grand National Consolidated Trades Union in 1834 as a "direct answer to the Reform Act of 1832 which had left five out of six working men without votes."[134] While Owen's movement collapsed within two years, the London Working Men's Association was founded in 1836 and revived the idea of a national petition from the BPU. One petition from the BPU in 1837 read as follows:

Your present petitioners feel compelled to declare that ... Reform ... has most grievously disappointed the hopes and expectations of the country. After five years of patient trial your petitioners have no reason to believe that the wants and interests of the industrious classes are better understood, or their rights and liberties better protected now, than they were in the unreformed Parliament; and your petitioners are convinced, that it is absolutely necessary to effect a further and much more extensive Reform of the Commons House of Parliament before the industrious classes can hope to enjoy any permanent relief and protection.[135]

The original petition included six points: (1) universal manhood suffrage, (2) vote by ballot, (3) equal electoral districts, (4) payment for M.P.s, (5) annual parliaments, and (6) abolition of the property qualification for a seat in the House of Commons.[136] These were not new political demands: "all had a radical pedigree stretching back into the eighteenth century and sometimes even earlier."[137] Over the next twelve years, the Chartists brought three petitions with millions of signatures to the House of Commons. The three crests of Chartist agitation (1839, 1842, and 1848) followed the overwhelming rejection of these democratic demands by Parliament.[138]

---

[133] www.historyhome.co.uk/peel/politics/tam2.htm.
[134] Woodward, *Age of Reform*, 129.
[135] Finlayson, *Decade of Reform*, 92.
[136] The third petition of 1848 dropped the ballot demand and thus contained only five points.
[137] Briggs, *Chartism*, 35.
[138] On July 12, 1839, commons refused to consider the Chartists' national petition by a vote of 235 to 46. On May 2, 1842, the vote was 287 to 49. In 1848, there was not even a vote to consider the petition on the basis that many signatures had been forged.

The Chartists barely figured into Whig histories of the age of reform, and they received little academic attention until Asa Briggs's edited volume *Chartist Studies* (1959). Historians of the labor movement, by contrast, tend to place the Chartists within E. B. Thompson's unbroken radical tradition and to consider them a revolutionary force.

When reports of workers arming themselves first reached Lord Russell in February 1839, the Home Secretary discounted the threat. Russell had recently signed a warrant ordering the Postmaster General to intercept, read, and then pass on the correspondence of Chartist leaders. And on this basis, he concluded that: "as far as I can perceive [the] exhortation to the people to arm is not likely to induce them to lay out their money on muskets or pistols. So long as mere violence of language is employed without effect, it is better, I believe, not to add to the importance of these mob leaders by prosecution."[139] Russell followed this up in a letter to the Duke of Newcastle in March 1839, noting that "it does not appear to me that those who have encouraged their followers to provide themselves with arms are ready to encounter so fearful a risk."[140] Resisting demands of magistrates to break up Chartist meetings, Russell ordered them to simply send in reports so that the Home Office could continue to monitor the situation, much as it had during the turbulence of 1832.

The government again acted quickly when reports of increased arming and drilling reached the Home Office in April and May 1839. A royal proclamation outlawed drilling, authorized local authorities to arm special constables, and gave magistrates the legal authority to arrest armed Chartists. In February, the army had appointed Sir Charles Napier to take over the command of the Northern District (where most of the Chartist agitation was coming from), an interesting choice given that Napier – a distinguished soldier with a radical streak – appeared sympathetic to the Chartist demands. Napier first sought to deter the Chartists by reminding them of the army's overwhelming power advantage:

> He invited a number of the Chartist leaders to a demonstration of artillery fire, and pointed out to them that they could not move, feed, or keep under control a large force. Napier explained that he could fall on them if they dispersed to collect food, "maul them with cannon and musquetry" if they tried to march, and, if they ventured upon an attack with pikes, scatter them before they reached him, or countercharge with his own cavalry.[141]

---

[139] Russell to Harewood, September 18, 1838, H.O. 52/38.
[140] Russell to Newcastle, March 16, 1839, H.O. 41/13.
[141] Woodward, *Age of Reform*, 138.

Like Russell, Napier saw little potential for revolution from the Chartists and looked at them with more pity than hostility. In a letter from December 1839, he wrote: "an anonymous letter come, with a Chartist plan. Poor creatures, their threats of attack are miserable. With half a cartridge, and half a pike, with no money, no discipline, no skillful leaders, they would attack men with leaders, money and discipline, well-armed, and having sixty rounds a man. Poor men![142]" At the same time, Napier urged the government to find another alternative to suppressing the Chartists with army units. In a letter to the Home Office dated July 20, 1839, Napier called for the "establishment of a strong police force" and warned that "if the police force be not quickly increased, we shall require troops from Ireland."[143]

In the proceeding decade, the model of the Metropolitan Police had been extended to other parts of the country. A Royal Commission set up in 1836 published their report in March 1839:

*Having specially examined the state of public security against breaches of the peace in the manufacturing districts, we find,*

1. that the free investment of capital and employment of laborers and the progress of manufacturing industry are impeded and endangered, and combinations carried on by violent and unlawful means; that murder has been resorted to; and that threats of murder, and arson, and personal violence are resorted to by such combiners as means to affect their objects;
2. that for the prevention of the disturbances peculiar to such districts, as well as for the prevention of the more ordinary breaches of the peace, amidst the new and increasing population, no other efficient force than a military force is provided;
3. that such force is inadequate for the purpose of the prevention of disorders, and that from the reluctance that is felt in having recourse to it for the purpose of repression, it is rarely used until considerable evil has been occasioned; and
4. that from the want of an efficient preventive force, the peace and manufacturing prosperity of the country are exposed to considerable danger.[144]

The result was the Rural Constabulary Act (also referred to as the Rural Police Act) of 1839. The name is misleading, as its passage had

---

[142] Journal, December 1, 1839, in *Napier*, Vol. 2, p. 98.
[143] Quoted in Taylor, *The New Police*, 28.
[144] www.historyhome.co.uk/peel/laworder/constab.htm.

major ramifications for policing in urban areas as well, including the cities of Manchester, Bolton, and especially Birmingham. The legislation took policing out of municipal control and essentially extended the Metropolitan police system to these cities. The bill enabled any county to raise taxes to establish its own police force. Birmingham was not a coincidental choice: It was the site of the National Chartist Convention in July 1839 after the organizers had moved it from London to escape repression by the Metropolitan police. The Home Office then sent sixty police to Birmingham in July to serve until a local force could be established.[145] Chartists railed about the "wanton, flagrant, and unjust outrage ... made upon the people of Birmingham by a bloodthirsty and unconstitutional force from London."[146] They attacked the Rural Constabulary Act as "one of the most barefaced assaults which ever had been attempted to be perpetrated against a nation's rights" and as "the first step toward despotism."[147] At the same time, the presence of the police helped the Chartists recruit. As Storch notes: "The radical and chartist leaders of the 1830s and 1840s articulated the resentment felt against the police on a day-to-day basis in working-class neighborhoods."[148] They printed pamphlets that read: "Would the people ... submit to 27,000 rural police being placed all over the Kingdom ... in effect, another standing army, to make the people submit to all the ... oppressions which Government contemplate forcing on them?"[149]

The Newport Rising on November 4, 1839, was the climax of the first Chartist agitation. A group of Chartists led by John Frost and armed with homemade weapons launched an ill-advised assault on the town of Newport, hoping to stimulate outbreaks elsewhere. A detachment from a garrison of soldiers met the Chartists at the Westgate hotel where twenty-four men were killed and at least fifty seriously injured. The Newport Rising thereby surpassed Peterloo and marked the deadliest clash between British forces and English civilians in the nineteenth and twentieth centuries.[150] Frost and two other leaders were sentenced to treason (later commuted), and a legal attack on Chartism began in earnest. Around 500 Chartists were jailed during the Winter of 1840.

---

[145] Royle, *Revolutionary Britannia?*, 101.
[146] *Northern Star*, July 13, 1839; Lovett and John Collins were imprisoned for a year.
[147] Quoted in Emsley, *The English Police*, 40.
[148] Storch, "Blue Locusts," 71.
[149] *Northern Star*, March 9, 1839.
[150] David Jones, *The Last Rising: The Newport Insurrection of 1839* (Oxford, Clarendon Press, 1985), 156. British forces killed exponentially more civilians in Ireland and India.

## 3.4 The Repression of The Chartists

The government refined its techniques during the second major wave of Chartist activity in 1842. A deep economic downturn in 1841 had led to work stoppages and other disturbances in the Midland coalfield, and Chartist organizers had organized and presented the second great National Petition to Parliament on May 4, 1842. Once again, it found little support and was rejected. Agitation spread to Scotland and to the textile districts of Lancashire and Yorkshire, and workers threatened to remain on strike until the Charter became law. Calculating that "force alone can subdue this rebellious spirit," the Home Secretary Sir James Graham directed large military forces to the site of the agitation and suspended the right of free assembly: "All meetings in large numbers in present circumstances have a manifest tendency to create terror and to endanger the public peace, that as such they are illegal, and upon notice given that they will not be allowed to be held, they ought to be dispersed."[151]

Although there was no equivalent to the Newport Rising in the second round of Chartist activity, the reaction of the government was more severe than it was in 1839. As Mather argues, the Tory government under Peel (in contrast to the Whig government in power during 1839) "was not satisfied with a simple restoration of order. It was determined to probe to the depths of what it regarded as a very dangerous conspiracy, and to discredit the instigators of the outbreak by exposing the enormity of their transactions."[152] Once again, the use of government informants was widespread and effective.[153] One observer described the trials that followed as a "Tory reign of terror," and in Staffordshire county alone, there were 274 trials that resulted in 154 sentences of imprisonment and 54 sentences of transportation.[154]

It was not enough that the hundreds of working men who had been rounded up by the authorities should be brought before the Special Commissions at Stafford, Chester and Liverpool on charges of riot, obstruction of labour and demolition of dwelling houses, and mercilessly sentenced to seven or ten or twenty-one years' transportation. The whole episode of the strikes must be presented to the nation, through the law courts, as a cold-blooded act of treason, in which Chartist leaders were deeply involved.[155]

---

[151] Quoted in Mather, "The Government and the Chartists," 388–389.
[152] Ibid., 390.
[153] According to Royle, "The real reason why the risings fizzled out was that in both south and west Yorkshire the authorities had eventually found local Chartists willing to inform on what was being planned." Royle, *Revolutionary Britannia?*, 110–111.
[154] Briggs, *Chartism*, 87.
[155] Mather, "The Government and the Chartists," 389–390.

The revolutions of 1848 led directly to a third, and final, Chartist campaign. On April 3, the Chartists announced plans to march their petition from Kennington Common in London to the House of Commons on April 10. The government deployed 100,000 special constables, drawn from the middle classes to London, and the Duke of Wellington commanded an additional 8,000 concealed army troops to meet the Chartists.[156] According to Briggs, this event did not itself "bring Chartism to an end, but it demonstrated clearly why from the start the movement had been doomed to failure." His description of the "fiasco at Kennington Common" draws upon newspaper reports and eyewitness accounts, an excerpt of which follows:

Before the mass demonstrations took place, the Home Secretary, the Duke of Wellington, and a large number of special constables (including Prince Louis Napoleon, soon to be Napoleon III), took formidable precautions to protect property and to preserve law and order in the metropolis. The Chartists' decision to go ahead with their plans even though the Home Secretary announced that a procession from the Commons to Westminster would be illegal was bravado in a sense: as Harney remarked later, "every hour the strength of our adversary, and our own weakness became more and more apparent." Yet there seemed to be little alternative. When the great day came, there was a smaller Chartist crowd on the Common than had been anticipated, and O'Connor immediately capitulated when Richard Mayne, the Superintendent of the Metropolitan Police, told him to abandon the idea of carrying the Petition *en masse* across the river to Westminster. Heavy rain brought the speeches to an end, and the crowd was dispersed. The Petition was subsequently shown to include large numbers of forged signatures – what petition of the period (and there were many) would not? – and Parliament was able to dismiss Chartism for a third time with no great difficulty. This time there was no vote.[157]

By the summer of 1848, the Chartist movement had been all but extinguished. It then vanished in the 1850s. Cobden, writing in 1861, lamented the passivity of the working class: "I wonder the working people are so quiet under the taunts and insults offered them. Have they no Spartacus among them to head a revolt...? I suppose it is the reaction from the follies of Chartism, which keeps the present generation so quiet."[158] Austen Henry Layard speculated similarly in 1866: "where is now the Charter with its six points of which we used to hear so much? We hear no more of it now."[159]

---

[156] Briggs, *Chartism*, 22,
[157] Briggs, *Age of Improvement*, 268–269.
[158] Quoted in J. L. Hammond and M. R. D. Foot, *Gladstone and Liberalism* (London: The English Universities Press, 1967), 76.
[159] Layard, April 16, 1866, *Hansard*, p. 1450.

## 3.4 The Repression of the Chartists

- **1836, October** – The London Working Men's Association is founded in place of the failed Grand National Consolidated Trades Union
- **1839, February** – Lord Russel first hears about workers arming themselves
- **1839, March** – A Royal Commission (established in 1836) publishes its report on the model of the Metropolitan Police Force for use outside of London
- **1839, July 20** – The Rural Constabulary Acts are passed
- **1839, July** – National Chartist Convention in Birmingham
- **1839, November 4** – The Newport Rising
- **1842, May 4** – Chartists present the second great National Petition to Parliament
- **1848, Winter–Spring** – Revolutions in Denmark, France, and Switzerland achieve universal suffrage
- **1848, April 3** – Chartists announce plans to march their petition from Kennington Common to the House of Commons
- **1848, April 10** – The Fiasco at Kennington Common
- **1856, September** – The police expand via the County and Rural Borough Police Act
- **1866, March** – Lord John Russell introduces the Reform Bill
- **1866, July 23** – Hyde Park Railing Affair
- **1867, May 6** – Hyde Park Riots
- **1867, June** – Reform Bill of 1867 passed

The repression of the Chartist movement does not fit easily into Whig accounts of the age of reform. Trevelyan devotes less than one page to the movement in his three-hundred-page *History of England* from the late eighteenth to early twentieth centuries. He notes that the Chartists' "political program of Universal Suffrage had no chance of success so long as it was demanded as a class measure, to be won not by the help of middle-class organization and leadership, but as an attack on employers." He argues further that "success crowned the movement in the 'sixties' when middle-class reformers joined the workers in demanding suffrage expansion."[160] This is a superficial reading of 1867, as I shall argue later. But social historians, following E. P. Thompson, have also erred by exaggerating long-run Chartist victories at the expense of what were clearly both short- and medium-term defeats.

---

[160] Trevelyan, *History of England*, 187.

In line with the argument of this chapter, the repression of the Chartists demonstrates two critical features about the age of reform. The first is just how profoundly unsuccessful was the effort to achieve universal suffrage in a supposed vanguard of democracy. The Chartists not only failed to achieve what similar movements elsewhere had – France and Switzerland in 1848 – but they never even succeeded in the short term (as in Prussia in 1848). A corollary to this is the endurance of the belief in capacity as a requirement to voting among many reformists themselves. The second feature is the growing power of the state to deal with mass political agitation. The expansion of police forces helps explain the successful repression of Chartism. And whereas the Chartists disappeared, the police expanded again following the 1856 County and Borough Police Act that completed the process of police nationalization. Once again, the fear of social disorder – this time it was ex-soldiers (so-called ticket-of-leave-men) roaming the streets after the Crimean War – accelerated the growth of the state's coercive power.

## 3.5 THE SECOND GREAT REFORM

The Second Reform Act of 1867 doubled the size of the electorate, from roughly 20 percent of adult males to 40 percent, and enfranchised the urban working class for the first time. Historians agree that the original bill did not intend such a wide suffrage expansion. When a Whig government came to power under Earl Russell in 1866, it introduced a reform bill in 1866 that would have set a seven-pound threshold in the towns and fourteen-pound one in the counties. This would have enfranchised about 400,000, but it was defeated by a group of breakaway Whigs that led to the formation of Benjamin Disraeli's conservative government. The passing of the Second Great Reform occurred alongside protest from the Reform League – founded in 1865 to agitate for universal male suffrage. It was this group that was instrumental in both the Hyde Park Railing Affair on July 23, 1866, and the Hyde Park Riots of May 6, 1867. As with 1832, the influence of social pressure on elite decision-making is the subject of some controversy, which will be discussed at length later in this chapter. The surprising outcome of the bill was that it was far more expansive than William Gladstone's, which the Tories had voted down. Disraeli – Gladstone's archrival – then pushed through a reform that set the threshold at five in the towns and twelve in the counties. The differences between the two bills may appear small, but changing the rates doubled the size of the newly enfranchised electorate. Contemporaries marveled at how parliament had turned a modest revision of 1832 into a "leap in the dark."

## 3.5 The Second Great Reform

According to the Whig view, the Second Reform Bill was the product of an enlightened and skillful elite and another milestone in the progressive march toward democracy. Trevelyan, for example, writes that: "the governing and conservative classes had grown accustomed to change as a normal condition of political life, instead of regarding it as the end of all things." Reading gradualism into the texture of British political culture, Trevelyan continues: "one might almost say that Darwin's then much contested doctrine of 'evolution' had already won its place in political consciousness."[161]

Gertrude Himmelfarb's spirited essay "The Politics of Democracy: The English Reform Act of 1867" contests this interpretation.[162] She decries the "rewriting of history to conform to the liberal image" in which "the Liberals are made out to be the rightful, legitimate parents of the act, and the Conservatives its nominal, foster parents."[163] Her thesis is that "the Reform Act was a Conservative measure, initiated and carried by a Conservative Government," but she does not replace the "good sense" of the Liberals with that of the Tories. Rather, she draws out the role of interparty factions, misperceptions, and miscalculations in the passing of the Second Reform Act.

To clear space for her argument, Himmelfarb dismantles Trevelyan's interpretation of 1867. Determined to make this Leap in the Dark conform to his view of history as an "orderly and gradual" accommodation to "social facts," Himmelfarb writes, led Trevelyan into "tautological arguments about the good sense of the elite."[164] Consider Trevelyan's claim, for example, that "the upshot of these ... confused Parliamentary operations of which not one of the statesmen concerned had quite foreseen the issue, was that the governing classes had recognized the needs of the new era with a wise alacrity."[165] The problem, according to Himmelfarb, was that the "needs of the new era" were neither defined nor articulated in the years prior to the Second Reform Act. Rather, "political commentators made much more of the public's political apathy than its zeal for reform."[166] Reform bills had been introduced in the House of Commons in 1852, 1854, 1859, and 1860, none of which came to anything. After pulling his reform bill of 1860, Lord Russel complained that "the apathy of the country is undeniable. Nor is it a transient humor; it seems rather like a

---

[161] Trevelyan, *History of England*, 204.
[162] Gertrude Himmelfarb, "The Politics of Democracy: The English Reform Act of 1867." *Journal of British Studies* 6 (1966), 97–138.
[163] Ibid., 118–119.
[164] Ibid., 97–98.
[165] G. M. Trevelyan, *British History in the Nineteenth Century* (London, 1922), 347.
[166] Himmelfarb, "Politics of Democracy," 98–99.

confirmed habit of mind."[167] The Second Great Reform thus began its life as one of many legislative proposals that were expected to fail. That it was introduced in a House of Commons that was viewed by contemporaries as "richer, and more aristocratic, than any which had preceded it,"[168] makes its transformation into a much broader bill all the more puzzling.

Himmelfarb thus asks: "How did an act so unanticipated and unsought, so uncongenial to public and Parliament alike, come to pass?"[169] If it was not through evolutionary processes, then what was the spark? As with the First Reform Bill, there is a Marxist interpretation of the Second Reform Act that Acemoglu and Robinson use to claim that "the threat of violence has been seen as a significant factor in forcing the pace (of the 1867 Reform Act); history was repeating itself."[170] The major proponent of this view is Royden Harrison, one of the founders of the Society for the Study of Labour History in 1960 and the successor to E. P. Thompson at the University of Warwick's Center for Social History (1971). In his study *Before the Socialists: Studies in Labour and Politics, 1861-1881*, Harrison claims that the immediate backdrop to the Second Great Reform was growing public protest following an economic depression and cholera outbreak. In his narrative of the bill's passage, the Hyde Park Riots of May 6, 1867, assume central importance.[171] "The historians, however distinguished and luminous their writings, who have omitted all mention of 6 May," Harrison claims, "have inevitably understated and misunderstood the part played by mass agitation in carrying the Second Reform Act."[172] It was on that day that 200,000 people disregarded government warnings and demonstrated in Hyde Park for suffrage reform. Harrison interprets May 6, 1867, as well as the "Hyde Park Railing Affair" of July 23, 1866, as a credible TOR that forced the government to concede to popular pressure.[173] His thesis is that "all the most influential men of

---

[167] Spencer Walpole, *The Life of Lord John Russell* (London: 1891) Vol. II, 342.
[168] Maurice Cowling, *1867 Disraeli, Gladstone and Revolution: The Passing of the Second Reform Bill* (New York: Cambridge University Press, 1967), 20
[169] Himmelfarb, "Politics of Democracy," 100.
[170] Acemoglu and Robinson, *Economic Origins*, 142.
[171] Royden Harrison, *Before the Socialists: Studies in Labour and Politics 1861–1881* (London: Routledge and Kegan Paul, 1965).
[172] Ibid., 100–101.
[173] The Hyde Park Railing Affair unfolded as follows: The Reform League, led by Edmond Beales, announced a mass meeting in Hyde Park for July 23 for universal suffrage. Sir Richard Mayne, Commissioner of the Metropolitan Police, informed Beales on July 18 that the meeting would not be permitted because the Home Secretary, Walpole, had banned it. The Reform League then challenged the legality of the ban on the grounds that the park belonged to the people and the monarchy, not the Home Secretary. When

property and power were persuaded that they must make a substantial concession in order to break up the agitation and remove the danger that prolonged intransigence, accompanied by police violence, would cause the popular forces to assume a truly menacing character."[174]

A second major critique of Harrison's thesis appeared two years later in the form of Malcolm Cowling's *1867: Disraeli, Gladstone and Revolution: The Passing of the Second Reform Bill*. Like Himmelfarb, Cowling stresses the weakness of the reform league and the "meagerness of their expectations" when it came to the possibility of reform.[175] "The commonplace to anyone who reads the letters of advanced advocates of electoral reform," Cowling notes, "is not the certainty of victory but the consciousness of weakness in face of working-class deference, middle-class complacency, [and] aristocratic monopoly." The archival material reflects "the manifest feeling of powerlessness which reformers outside the Parliament felt at the strength and obstinacy of [the] House of Commons."[176] Although May 6 may have demonstrated the reform league's organizational power, the mass meeting was little more than an assertion of the right to use Hyde Park.

Cowling does note that "the belief that there was a revolutionary situation in 1866/7, or that Disraeli's remedy was a revolutionary one, was shared by some public figures at the time. The Queen, Lowe, Beresford-Hope, Cranborne, Carnarvon and Earl Grey are some of those who agreed with Carlyle and Dr. Harrison." Yet Cowling questions why Harrison relied on these figures who "apart from the Queen ... were not in office when the crucial decisions were made, or, when active in Parliament, inhabited an intellectual world far different from that of most ministers

---

Beales and the rest of the executive committee arrived to find Hyde Park blocked by between 1,600 and 1,800 policemen on July 23, the Reform League chose not to confront the police but rather head to Trafalgar Square instead, where their right to public space was not in question. However, a large group of rank-and-file who were left behind ended up pushing over the railings around Hyde Park and trampling some flowerbeds. No one was injured, and it was treated as minor disaster in the press. The end result was a meeting between Walpole and Beales where the Reform League agreed to restore order on its members so long as the police and army troops withdrew. According to Harrison's view: "It is scarcely too much to say the fall of the park railings did for England in July 1866 what the fall of the Bastille did for France in July 1789." Himmelfarb is skeptical: "The violence of this affair has been as grossly exaggerated as its significance. In fact, its true significance may be precisely this exaggeration: the other demonstrations must have been pacific indeed for contemporaries and historians alike to have been so outraged by little more than broken railings and trampled flower beds (104)."

[174] Harrison, *Before the Socialists*, 108.
[175] Cowling, *1867*, 20.
[176] Ibid., 19.

and members of parliament."[177] He continues: "Whatever impression one gathers from studying Cranborne's or Lowe's writings and speeches, it is not the impression one gathers from those who were important in office or effective in Parliament."[178] They were hardly representative of the political class, and each had an axe to grind: "Cranborne, Carnarvon, Beresford-Hope, Lowe and Earl Grey were highly articulate political intellectuals with a doctrine to peddle, a review to produce, reputations to make or disappointments to make up for."[179]

Much like the "Revolutionary Britannia" view of 1832 draws uncritically on the papers of Francis Place and other protagonists with an interest in exaggerating their own role, Harrison's account of 1867 draws on selective evidence from a couple of sources that fit his narrative. He describes Frederic Harrison (no relation) as a "contemporary observer who furnished a shrewd and penetrating analysis" primarily because he "saw in 'the great Surrender' of 1867 the character of panic."[180] Similarly, he quotes a Tory backbencher, who noted during parliamentary debates on May 17, that "no one could watch what was passing in the country, or read the newspapers, without coming to the conclusion that, if that question of Reform were kept open for much longer, the hon. Member for Birmingham (John Bright) would be in the position of a Girondin."[181]

These were hardly representative of elite opinion, however. Much like in 1832, most conservatives were against making any concessions as a direct result of public agitation. According to Cowling:

Examination of the letters of politicians nearest to events shows that those who came closest to *fearing* the mob were not Conservatives, but Gladstone and the Whig/Liberal leaders ... Conservative backbenchers disliked mass demonstrations, objected to the government's failure to restrain them and demanded strong measures to preserve the peace and order of the capital. But the intensity of distaste which Conservatives felt for public displays of mob power prevented them from being "awed into submission" ... The Conservative attitude throughout the session of 1867 was that though *something* must be done, no countenance should be given to "the mere riots of a mob."[182]

Consider the Reform League, the group that Harrison claims influenced elite views. He writes: "The first and most certain consequence of 6

---

[177] Ibid., 20–21.
[178] Ibid., 24.
[179] Ibid., 21.
[180] Harrison, *Before the Socialists*, 103.
[181] Ibid., 112.
[182] Cowling, *1867*, 26.

May was the enormously enhanced prestige of the League and its increasing independence of its parliamentary and middle-class patrons."[183] Cowling argues that Harrison is once again writing his politics into his history: "Because the Reform League was politically active at moments of crisis, it is easy to attribute outstanding importance to its role. This is doubly easy when the historian has an interest in the working-class movement or the historical sociologist a belief that political maneouvre is incidental to the progress of popular social movements."[184] Much like the political unions during the passing of the First Great Reform, the reform leagues were hardly revolutionaries and operated in an "atmosphere of controlled legality."[185] Cowling is also skeptical of Harrison's argument that the agitation pushed conservatives toward reform, particularly the claim that it had softened Disraeli. "So far as it had an impact on him," Cowling writes of Disraeli, "it was in a reactionary direction, making Conservative backbenchers so hostile to the government's failure to resist the League's use of the Park that he could not concede as much as he wanted to."[186] Rebutting Harrison directly, Cowling concludes:

There was no "capitulation" to popular pressure. The Conservative party was not overborne by Beales and Bright. Disraeli did not revert to being a Radical. Derby did not suddenly discover Marx ... There was nothing inevitable about the course they followed. If a restrictive Act could have been passed on a conservative basis, they would have passed it. If party conditions had been suitable, they would have persisted in March 1867 with a restrictive proposal, and would have appealed to the existing electorate if defeated on it.[187]

Like the First Great Reform, the Second Great Reform was designed by liberals who still linked voting to capacity.[188] Gladstone announced that he was "a firm believer in the aristocratic principle – the rule of the best. I am an out-and-out inequalitarian."[189] Disraeli attacked Gladstone's bill

---

[183] Harrison, *Before the Socialists*, 98.
[184] Cowling, *1867*, 3.
[185] Ibid., 37.
[186] Ibid., 40.
[187] Ibid., 310.
[188] "Where democrats talked about universal rights (and conservatives talked about historical or hereditary rights) liberals talked about capacity: who possessed it, who might acquire it, and by what means ... The discourse of capacity enabled liberals to continue to pursue the progressive goals of the Enlightenment while avoiding the pitfalls of the Revolution and the dangerous language of 'rights.' Through a discourse of capacity, liberals could establish and legitimize a rational and progressive hierarchy strong enough to withstand the threats they faced, both old and new." Kahan, *Liberalism*, 6.
[189] John Morley, *Life of William Ewart Gladstone* (1906), Vol. II, 190.

on the grounds that the House of Commons should "not become a House of the People, a House of a mere indiscriminate multitude."[190] Gladstone then warned that Disraeli's more expansive bill was unwise: "you should not proceed so fast as to outrun the competence and disregard the condition of the people."[191] In the very speech in which he introduced the bill, Disraeli expressed his hope that it would "never be the fate of this country to live under a democracy."[192] He liked the Second Reform Bill precisely because it had, in his estimation, "really no spice of democracy."[193] Cowling summarizes the narrow parameters of the legislative architects:

> Wherever one looks in the parliamentary debates on the Reform Bill of 1867, one finds no general advocacy of a democratic franchise, electoral districts or equality between the worth of one vote and another. One finds, on the contrary, in both parties and all sections, an overwhelming anxiety to establish that nothing should be done to destroy the alliance between responsibility, respectability, wealth and status on one hand and the possible new electorate on the other.[194]

There was a cross-party consensus that a "hovel suffrage" – one that allowed illiterate lodgers to qualify for the vote – was a direct threat to the principle of fitness to vote. Writing in 1859, Sidney Herbert in 1859 explained the goals of political reform as follows:

> the first end is to bring the best men into this House; the second, the importance of which I do not undervalue, is, that the mass of population should have the sense of contributing to the common welfare. But we must not sacrifice the first principle to the second; we may reconcile both, and that is what I want the Government to do.[195]

According to Lord Stanley, a Whig in 1832 who had since become a conservative, "the real difficulty of the case ... is, how to admit the working class on any principle of selection to a share of the representation without admitting them indiscriminately as a body."[196] Lowe was more explicit in his class bias: "If you want venality, if you want ignorance, if you want drunkenness, and facility for being intimidated; or if, on the other hand, you want impulsive, unreflecting, violent people, where do

---

[190] Parliamentary debates, Vol. 183 c. 102–103.
[191] Gladstone, *Hansard*, April 12, 1867, p. 1694.
[192] Quoted in Donald Read, *The Age of Urban Democracy* (New York: Longman, 1994), 145.
[193] Buckle Letters, 407–408.
[194] Cowling, *1867*, 59–60.
[195] S. Herbert, March 22, 1859, *Hansard*, p. 593.
[196] Lord Stanley, March 21, 1859, *Hansard*, pp. 413–414.

you look for them in the constituencies? Do you go to the top or the bottom?"[197] And even an advocate of reform such as Bright noted:

> At this moment, in all, or nearly all our boroughs, as many of us know, sometimes to our sorrow, there is a small class which it would be much better for themselves if they we not enfranchised, because they have no independence whatsoever, and it would be much better for the constituents also that they should be excluded, and there is no class as much interested in having that small class excluded as the intelligent and honest working men. I call this class the residuum, which there is in almost every constituency, of almost hopeless poverty and dependence.[198]

Capacity, according to politicians on both side of the debate, could be measured in pounds sterling. "Gladstone himself candidly explained that he chose the 7-pound figure because it ensured that the working class would remain a minority of the electorate whereas under the 6-pound franchise it might become a majority."[199] Samuel Laing wanted the franchise for those with an "ability to act upon solid sense and reflection rather than from inconsiderate impulse," and he felt that the ten-pound franchise "drew that line in a general way very clearly and very distinctly" and that it was "a motive for good conduct and provident habits."[200] When Bright once intimated that there was little difference between an eight-pound and a seven-pound franchise, Lowe protested: "His one pound is no joke. The honorary Member for Birmingham's one pound means 100,000 men, and 100,000 men of whom he may know a great deal, but of whom we … know nothing."[201]

## 3.6 CONCLUSION

The most remarkable thing about the "age of reform" in Great Britain is how little democracy had progressed between 1832 and 1870. According to V-Dem, Great Britain scored a 0.30 on the electoral democracy index in 1830 and had only moved to 0.35 forty years later. The standard view of Britain as a democratic vanguard assumes that liberalism would eventually lead to democratization. In so doing, it underestimates the tenacity of liberals' hostility to universal suffrage and the degree to which they had defeated it from Peterloo onward. Social historians raised similar points in their critique of Whig history, but the narrative they have offered in its place is arguably even less consistent with the evidence. While it is true

---

[197] Lowe, Parliamentary Debates, Vol. 182, C.220.
[198] 3 Hansard 186: 636–637, March 26, 1867.
[199] Himmelfarb, "Politics of Democracy," 102.
[200] Gleig, "The Conditions of the Government," 534.
[201] 3 Hansard 182: 2093, April 26, 1866.

that popular agitation accompanied the passage of both reform acts, neither was the product of it, and it is difficult to draw any direct connections to elite behavior, other than stiffening the resolve of hardliners. One must also agree with Robbins' conclusion that "it is ... highly selective to appeal to only one instance in which popular pressure contributed to a reformist outcome."[202] The state crushed popular pressure multiple times between 1811 and 1867 and repressed rather than reformed.

This chapter has broadly agreed with Himmelfarb's claim "that so much of English government and society should have remained intact while so much else changed was a proper cause for gratification among Conservatives."[203] It also echoes Cowling's conclusion that:

> It is idle to ask: why did the Parliament of 1867 not resist democratic reform? The fact is that many of its members thought that they had resisted it, had taken the wind out of the democratic movement, had made plausible the claim that Parliament had moved with the opinion not of the mob (for that would matter little) but of the bulk of the class now actually voting and holding political power.[204]

Both historians reflect a basic sympathy with Polanyi's classic question about measuring change: "Why should the ultimate victory of a trend be taken as proof of the ineffectiveness of efforts to slow down its progress?" As Cowling puts it, British elites "felt they had delayed, for at least a generation on a matter in which delay was of first consequence, the democratizing of the British political system."[205] Walter Arnstein similarly posits that the seminal question about nineteenth-century Britain is not: "how did the middle class come to predominate?" but rather "how can we account for the remarkable survival in prestige and influence of landed aristocrats and squires in a society increasingly based on industrial wealth?"[206] Given that the goals of the Chartists were not realized until a half-century after the Second Great Reform, it is surprising how infrequently the question of authoritarian endurance in the United Kingdom has been posed. I have argued that the growth of domestic coercion coupled with liberal hostility to a wide suffrage were not only two central features of the "age of reform" but also two political pillars of competitive oligarchy.

---

[202] Bruce Morrison, "Channeling the 'Restless Spirit of Innovation': Elite Concessions and Institutional Change in the British Reform Act of 1832." *World Politics* 63, 4 (2011), 686.
[203] Himmelfarb, "Politics of Democracy," 137.
[204] Cowling, *1867*, 47.
[205] Ibid.
[206] Walter Arnstein, "The Myth of the Triumphant Victorian Middle Class." *The Historian* 37, 2 (1975), 207.

# 4

# The European Origins of Competitive Authoritarianism

The political rise of Louis Napoleon Bonaparte ranks as one of the most improbable in European history. Born in Paris in 1808, Louis Napoleon was seven when his uncle was defeated at Waterloo and spent his early adult years nourishing the cult of Napoleon, writing political tracts, and plotting a Bonapartist restoration. However, the pretender's two attempts to launch a coup against the regime of Louis Philippe (1830–1848) were notable only for their amateurishness. In 1836, Louis Napoleon tried to gain control of Napoleon's old artillery regiment garrisoned in Strasbourg and lead a march on Paris. He and his coconspirators, including his future Interior Minister Jean Gilbert Victor Fialin (who would later take the title the *Duc de Persigny*), were easily captured. Not wanting to make a martyr of a man they viewed as an inveterate, and likely harmless, schemer, the Orleanist regime handed Bonaparte money and banished him to America. Six months later, the pretender returned to Europe and resumed his plotting from Switzerland and London.

Bonaparte's chief asset was his resilience. In 1840, he and Persigny made a second attempt at power in which they chartered a pleasure boat in England and landed with sixty men across the Channel in Boulogne. When the townspeople failed to follow him on a march to Paris, and when the national guard began firing on the party, the future emperor beat a hasty retreat. His boat capsized in the kerfuffle, and Louis Napoleon was unceremoniously fished out of the Channel by the French authorities with a boat hook. He immediately became the subject of much ridicule in the press. This time, he was sentenced to life at a state prison in Ham. For six years, Napoleon read, wrote, and entertained numerous visitors in what he would later refer to as the "University of Ham," which proved to be a minimum-security facility. In May 1846, he disguised himself as a worker, walked out of the prison, and returned to London.

The regime blocking Bonaparte's dreams of a restoration – the "July Monarchy" – had been founded in July 1830 following the revolution against Charles X (1815–1830). It was more liberal than the monarchy it had replaced: it abolished hereditary peers in the upper chamber of parliament and doubled the size of the electorate for the lower house. Still, the suffrage was restricted to about 250,000 people (less than 3 percent of the French population), and the monarch still held absolute power.[1] A series of poor harvests in 1846 sparked protests and demands for expanded participation, but a bill to expand the franchise was rejected. Alexis de Tocqueville reminded his fellow members of the Chamber of Deputies on January 29, 1848, that "they were sleeping on a volcano" and asked them "do you not feel ... that the earth is quaking once again in Europe." He continued: "Can you not perceive that their passions, instead of political, have become social? ... that they are gradually forming opinions and ideas destined to upset not merely this or that law, or ministry, or form of government, but society itself?"[2]

Tocqueville's warnings about revolution went unheeded. Five weeks later, Louis Philippe abdicated and fled to England after his government's banning of banquets led to popular mobilization that the army showed no intention of repressing. When the Second Republic was proclaimed on February 24, its first move was to grant universal male suffrage. France had been transformed from a monarchy to a democracy within a matter of days.

When news of the February revolution reached him in London, Louis Napoleon told his cousin Marie that "I'm going to Paris, the Republic has been proclaimed. I must be its master." Marie responded that "you are dreaming, as usual."[3] Undeterred, Napoleon went to Paris on February 28th and was immediately expelled. This did not stop him from running for office, and he was elected twice within the space of three months.[4] He did not appear to be a political threat. When he took his seat in parliament on September 26th, the deputies present felt it "was hardly worth insisting on the ban which might still exclude him

---

[1] Berman, *Democracy and Dictatorship in Europe*, 86.
[2] de Tocqueville, speech to Chamber of Deputies, January 29, 1848.
[3] Louis-Dominique Girard, *Napoléon III* (Paris: Fayard, 1986), 83.
[4] Louis Napoleon was initially elected to the National Assembly on June 4, 1848, but resigned his seat after ten days because he was still considered a fugitive. He did, however, take the seat he won in the elections of the following September.

from the House."[5] The liberal politician Adolphe Thiers admitted later that the ban was abrogated "partly from pity" for the Bonapartist pretender who had, apparently, become a Republican.[6]

Louis Napoleon then ran for the presidency as a heavy underdog against General Cavaignac, whose brutal suppression of an urban insurrection in Paris from June 23 to June 26, 1848 (the 'June Days') had turned him into the savior of the Republic. Against all expectations, Bonaparte crushed his opponent in the presidential elections of December 10, 1848. The British ambassador Lord Normanby noted at the time that "history affords no parallel to this spectacle of all the eminent men of all former political parties uniting in support of a man whom not one of them would personally have selected. They, in fact, follow whilst they assume to direct, a popular impulse which they could not resist."[7] Three years later, Louis Napoleon orchestrated a successful coup d'etat and, following the results of a plebiscite, proclaimed himself emperor.

Bonaparte had baffled most contemporary political observers, but the most astute among them soon began to analyze the collapse of the Second Republic. Marx asked famously how "it was possible for a grotesque mediocrity [Bonaparte] to play a hero's part"? His answer was that Bonapartism had little to do with the political skills of Louis Napoleon – rather, the emperor himself was a reflection of the class alliances possible during that particular stage of capitalism.[8] The eminent liberal Charles de Rémusat noted that "he lacks so many of the qualities of an ordinary man of merit, judgement, education, conversation, experience, all these are subject to so many gaps that one is easily tempted to class him as utterly mediocre."[9] Thiers too initially viewed Louis-Napoleon as a promiscuous incompetent: "we will give him women and we will lead him."[10]

This turned out to be a profound miscalculation, as most subsequent historical accounts have stressed. While this chapter begins with

---

[5] J. M. Thompson, *Louis Napoleon and the Second Empire* (New York: W. W. Norton & Company, 1955), 92.
[6] Nassau William Senior, *Conversations with M. Thiers, M. Guizot, and Other Distinguished Persons during the Second Empire* (London: Hurst and Blackett, 1878), Vol. I, 31.
[7] Lord Normanby, 1851, Vol. II, 361.
[8] Karl Marx, "The Eighteenth Brumaire of Louis Bonaparte." *Die Revolution* (1852).
[9] Louis Girard, *Napoleon III*, 104.
[10] Adrien Dansette, *Louis Napoléon à la conquête du pouvoir* (Paris: Hachette, 1961), 243.

the short-lived Second Republic, the focus is the Second Empire that survived for twenty years and may very well have lasted much longer had it not been for a disastrous foreign policy blunder that precipitated the Franco–Prussian War. Bonaparte's second most significant political achievement – the construction of the original competitive authoritarian regime – has not received the same attention as his dismantling of France's first democracy.[11] Yet the political system that came to be referred to as Bonapartism is now associated less with Napoleon the conqueror than with Napoleon III.

This chapter develops three arguments about the Second Empire. The first is that Bonapartism and competitive authoritarianism (CA) overlap to a high degree. Political scientists have largely ignored Bonapartism as a distinct regime type, but I argue that it fits the criteria outlined by Levitsky and Way. The second is that the Second Empire was a consolidated regime that was toppled by loss in war rather than through the rise of domestic opposition. On the basis of post-Cold War cases, scholars have taken two mutually exclusive positions on the stability of CA. The first is that CA regimes are inherently unstable, for once voters begin to express their preferences through elections and practice democracy, they create dynamics that lead either to an authoritarian crackdown or a democratic transition. The second is that elections – and other democratic looking institutions – help keep CA regimes in power. In this view, CA is a stable political equilibrium. The preponderance of evidence from the Second Empire supports the second view of CA. There is a strand in the historiography of the Second Republic that views it as a liberalizing regime that was showing increasing signs of democratization in the late 1860s, but I show below that this interpretation is misleading and ignores the degree to which opposition forces had become co-opted into the system.

The third argument of this chapter is that Bonapartism was the model for the second competitive authoritarian state in Europe: Imperial Germany (1871–1918). There are many studies of democratic diffusion, some studies of authoritarian diffusion, but no studies to date of the

---

[11] There are some exceptions. These include Brison Gooch, *The Reign of Napoleon III* (Chicago: Rand McNally and Company, 1969); Alain Plessis, *The Rise of Fall of the Second Empire, 1852–1871* (New York: Cambridge University Press, 1979); Roger Price, *Napoleon III and the Second Empire* (New York: Routledge, 1997); Roger Price, *The French Second Empire: An Anatomy of Political Power* (New York: Cambridge University Press, 2001); Theodore Zeldin, *The Political System of Napoleon III* (New York: W. W. Norton, 1971).

diffusion of CA.[12] I review the evidence that Bismarck learned directly from Bonapartism and find that there is a compelling case that his analysis of the Second Empire contributed to his advocacy of universal suffrage within an otherwise absolutist framework.

## 4.1 SECOND REPUBLIC TO SECOND EMPIRE

In February 1848, the same year as the failure of the third Chartist petition, France became the first European state to enfranchise its entire male population.[13] In terms of participation and contestation, France was far more democratic than the United Kingdom, and indeed any other state in Europe, following the revolutionary crest of 1848. The Second Republic possessed all the other Dahlian checkmarks – freedom of association and the press, parliamentary sovereignty, and so on – that qualify it as the first democracy of the nineteenth century. The democratic experiment was short-lived: The Republic began to collapse months after its proclamation, in a stepwise progression characteristic of most democratic breakdowns.[14] Merriman's classic study demonstrates that: "The coup d'etat was not one single event, but the culmination of a long series of blows."[15] The Second Republic was thus an original case of democratic breakdown, which is interesting in its own right but also critical for understanding the origins of the Second Empire.

There were two primary democratizing forces in the Second Republic. The first were the Montagnards (also referred to as demo-socs or simply socialists). They fused universal suffrage and the social question, and when in power they immediately introduced legislation on the right to work that created national workshops. The second were the Republicans, many of whom favored a suffrage expansion while opposing universal suffrage. Republicans were caught off guard by the rapid dissolution of the July Monarchy, and agreed to universal suffrage largely because the Parisian workers who had actually toppled the regime were demanding

---

[12] On democratic diffusion, see Kurt Weyland, *Making Waves: Democratic Contention in Europe and Latin America since the Revolutions of 1848* (New York: Cambridge University Press, 2014); on authoritarian diffusion, see Agnes Cornell, Jørgen Møller, and Sven-Erik Skaaning, *Democratic Stability in an Age of Crisis: Reassessing the Interwar Period* (New York: Oxford University Press, 2020).

[13] Switzerland and Denmark also did so later in 1848.

[14] Steven Levitsky and Daniel Ziblatt, *How Democracies Die* (New York: Crown, 2018).

[15] John Merriman, *The Agony of the Republic: The Repression of the Left in Revolutionary France 1848–1851* (New Haven: Yale University Press, 1978), xxi.

it. It was a concession made in the moment, along with the appointment of four socialists to cabinet positions.[16]

Ten million French men cast a ballot in the elections of April 1848, making it one of the most dramatic cases of moving from extremely limited to universal male suffrage. It was the original "leap in the dark," far more significant than the British Second Reform Act, and there was genuine uncertainty about the outcome. However, this was a period in which conservative forces were far better organized than either the Republicans or the Montagnards. According to Magraw: "The April elections gave the conservatives the opportunity to restore their class rule through the manipulation of universal suffrage in a still rural France. They hoped to scare peasant proprietors with talk of Jacobin *commissaires* and urban *partageux*, to infuriate them with images of idle Parisian socialists living on the dole."[17]

The elections indeed produced a constituent assembly that was far less radical than the Republicans and Montagnards who had brought the Second Republic into existence. Two-thirds of the deputies elected on April 23 were conservatives, and de Tocqueville claimed it was even more conservative than the Orleanist parliament.[18] This is partly explained by a major tactical mistake by an inchoate working-class party engaging in mass elections for the first time. Sperber argues that the socialists' decision to put forth candidates that would represent all major trades led to their electoral underperformance. While this practice was consistent within guild organization, it was "completely inappropriate for manhood suffrage" and "resulted in a slate of totally obscure figures, each one known only to the workmen in his particular craft."[19]

The conservative majority also had much to do with the conservatism of peasants; Marx referred to December 10, 1848, as the "the day of the peasant insurrection."[20] Universal suffrage had been suddenly introduced into a largely agricultural society, with a huge peasant class that was controlled by landowners and local notables. This was hardly limited to France. In Chapter 3 we saw that the Great Reform of 1832 did

---

[16] Roger Magraw, *France 1815–1914: The Bourgeois Century* (New York: Oxford University Press, 1983), 120–121.
[17] Ibid., 123–124.
[18] Ibid., 124.
[19] Jonathan Sperber, *The European Revolutions, 1848–1851* (New York: Cambridge University Press, 1994), 154.
[20] Karl Marx, "Class Struggles in France," *Selected Works*, 173.

not profoundly alter the social or political composition of the House of Commons. In the rest of Europe, Sperber argues that "elections held under a broad, sometimes universal male suffrage favored most those political forces that were the most skeptical about both elections and democracy." He continues that "everywhere, a majority of the candidates elected represented conservative or at best very moderately liberal viewpoints." The irony was that the "Radicals, that is, the supporters of democracy, people who had pressed for the broadest possible franchise, were the big losers in elections held under the franchise they advocated."[21]

The first lesson of elections under universal suffrage was that they could produce conservative majorities. The second lesson – that mass elections were not predictable – unsettled liberals. Informed observers had not expected Bonaparte to win seats, and it was only after the results were known that they recognized the degree to which the popularity of Bonaparte derived simply from name recognition.[22] Liberals were similarly unprepared for the demo-soc's electoral recovery in the elections of May 1849. Roger Magraw notes that the socialists' "sweeping success in rural areas of central and southern France shook the conservatives' naïve trust in the peasantry as a solid anti-socialist bastion."[23] Liberal politician Adolph Thiers expressed these fears in the assembly: "Neither my friends nor I have ever hidden from ourselves the dangers of universal suffrage, such as it is organized today in France; but do you know what these two elections have done? They have given so much proof of danger that this proof has become an opportunity."[24] The procureur general in Limoges lamented: "What more terrible threat than this revolt of the lower classes, armed with universal suffrage, against the necessary condition, against the eternal laws of human society."[25] The procureur general in Rouen put the matter even more strongly:

---

[21] Jonathan Sperber, *European Revolutions*, 152–153.
[22] Price writes that

> Louis-Napoleon was the beneficiary of a sentimental cult of Napoleon kept alive by an outpouring of books, pamphlets, plays, songs, the lithographs which decorated so many poor homes, and, perhaps most potently, the stories told by old soldiers keeping alive the myth of a more prosperous, happy, and glorious epoch in sharp contrast to the misery and strife which appeared to accompany the Republic.

Price, *Second Empire*, 16.
[23] Roger Magraw, *France*, 137.
[24] Thiers, May 24, 1850, *Compte Rendu des Seances de l'Assemblee Nationale Legislative*, vol. 8, May 16–June 26, 1850 (Paris: 1850), pp. 149–152.
[25] AN BB 18, 1468, April 8, 1850; Merriman, *Agony of the Republic*, 135.

## 4 The European Origins of Competitive Authoritarianism

When it consented to the periodic renewal of political power by election, society committed a type of suicide, in that it thus placed a weapon that could be used against it in the hands of enemies. By offering the communists the possibility of becoming kings one day by a "*coup de scrutin*" [electoral coup] we have offered the most irresistible encouragement for the propagation of their doctrines ... the repression becomes insufficient protection for the country as, however energetic we can never neutralize ... the hope of conquering the leadership of society and all its advantages ... legally and without much waiting. As long as the government lacks the force and toughness necessary, as long as we are without powerful barriers against the invasion of communism, the country will continue to be in the hopeless and ruinous grasp of the social evil delivered to us by 1848.[26]

Thiers designed a new electoral law that required three years of continuous legal residence. Since the constitution of 1848 that introduced universal suffrage had a six-month residency requirement, French liberals could claim they were simply altering the residency requirement to reflect the minimum time period required to become an active member of the community.[27] In practice – and undoubtedly by design – the 1850 law disenfranchised about 30 percent of the adult male population. The numbers were much higher in Paris (56%) and in the working-class bastions of Lille (70%), Roubaix (80%), Nîmes (59%), and Creuset (52%).[28]

Liberals realized almost immediately that their new suffrage law had been a strategic blunder. The republican and socialist left called on their supporters to abstain from elections, thereby handing conservative forces even more representation. It also gave Louis Napoleon Bonaparte an additional source of legitimacy and another weapon against the parliamentary majority: he came out as a proponent of a return to universal suffrage on November 4, 1851. Liberals failed to abrogate the electoral law and reintroduce the six-month residency requirement on November 13.[29] Less than one month later, Napoleon engineered a coup d'état on December 10th and proclaimed universal suffrage by decree.[30]

Napoleon had been preparing for a coup as the president of the Second Republic. With his term set to run out in 1852 (the 1848 constitution allowed for no second term), he behaved very much like contemporary autocrats by seeking to modify the constitution in July 1851. Although he did not receive the 75 percent majority in the National Assembly required to do so, the dismantling of the republic had clearly begun from

---

[26] AN BB18 1468, Extract of PG Rouen, June 13, 1850; Merriman, *Agony*, 135.
[27] See, for example, Faucher, May 18, 1850, *Compte Rendu*, pp. 48–51.
[28] Kahan, *Liberalism in Nineteenth-century Europe*, 83.
[29] Merriman, *Agony*, xxxvi.
[30] Kahan, *Liberalism*, 103–106.

within. As Baguely summarizes, "the recourse to legal means, the degree of support of a hostile Assembly, and the outcome of the vote seemed to provide in a perverse way a legal mandate and a license to act."[31]

Napoleon chose the date of December 2, 1851, for his coup d'état for its dual Napoleonic symbolism: It marked both the day of Napoleon's founding of the First Empire in 1804 and the date of his military victory in the battle of Austerlitz in 1805. Troops seized key buildings in Paris during the night, police arrested seventy potential organizers of resistance, and supporters distributed public notices of the coup that read as follows:

> Frenchmen! The present situation cannot continue. Every day that passes aggravates the danger of the country. The Assembly, which ought to be the firmest support of order, has become a center of conspiracy ... Instead of passing laws in the public interest, it is forging weapons for civil war: it is attacking the power that I hold directly from the people; it is encouraging all kinds of evil passions; it is ruining the repose of France. I have dissolved it, and I call on the whole people to judge between it and me.[32]

Bonaparte then asked the French electorate to sanction his seizure of power in the plebiscite of December 20, 1851. There was little protest from liberals or conservatives. One conservative noted a consensus among his ranks that Louis-Napoleon was "the man around whom we need to rally, until things are sufficiently stable to move to a definitive form of government, which will most certainly not be his."[33] The Legitimist Paul Benoist d'Azy wrote to his father:

> We are caught between the regime of the sabre which has violated the constitution as it was sworn to uphold and the hideous socialists. There is really no choice, and just as we supported the Republic we will accept the existing government ... if it can persuade us to forget its origins by means of energetic action against the socialists and vigorous encouragement of business.[34]

Napoleon made a similar case to the country at large. Presenting himself as the only option to either a socialist revolution or the restoration of the old monarchic regime, he received a resounding 7,5000,000 'yes' votes against a mere 640,000 'no' votes (with 1,5000,000 abstentions).

---

[31] David Baguley, *Napoleon III and his Regime: An Extravaganza* (Baton Rouge: Louisiana State University Press, 2000), 12.
[32] J. M. Thompson, *Louis Napoleon*, 118.
[33] Undated letter in AN 271 AP 4.
[34] R. R. Locke and R. E. Cubberly, "A New Memoire on the French coup d'etat of December 1851." *French Historical Studies* 12, 4 (Autumn 1982), 584.

A second plebiscite on November 21–22, 1852, confirmed the destruction of the French Second Republic and its replacement by a hereditary empire.

- 1848, February 23–24 – Revolution and founding of the Second Republic
- 1848, June 23–26 – Popular insurrection in Paris crushed by General Cavaignac ("June Days")
- 1848, December 10 – Bonaparte elected President of the Republic
- 1851, December 2 – Coup d'état
- 1852, January 14 – Promulgation of new constitution
- 1852, November 21 – Plebiscite on reestablishment of the hereditary empire
- 1852, December 2 – Founding of the Second Empire
- 1857, March 5 – Five Republicans elected to Parliament
- 1858, January 14 – Plot to assassinate Napoleon fails (Orsini affair)
- 1860, November 24 – Publication of decree on political reform
- 1861, March 14 – Ollivier announces he will support liberalization
- 1863, May 31 – General election begins
- 1867, January 19 – Publication of plans for further reforms
- 1869, May 3 – General election begins
- 1869, May 8–10 – Serious disorders in Paris
- 1869, July 12 – Napoleon announces further reforms
- 1869, December 27 – Napoleon asks Ollivier to form a ministry
- 1870, March 21 – Napoleon proposes a "Liberal Empire"
- 1870, May 8 – Plebiscite on constitutional reform
- 1870, July 19 – France declares war on Prussia
- 1870, September 1–2 – France defeated at Sedan
- 1870, September 4 – Republican deputies proclaim the return of the Republic

## 4.2 BONAPARTISM AS COMPETITIVE AUTHORITARIANISM

What type of polity had Napoleon conjured into being? Roger Magraw writes that "the regime's political system was *sui* generis, without contemporary European parallel."[35] Engels noted in 1865 that "Bonapartism is the necessary form of government in a country in which the working classes have reached an advanced stage of development in the cities but

---

[35] Roger Magraw, *France*, 164.

## 4.2 Bonapartism as Competitive Authoritarianism

are outnumbered by the small peasantry and have been defeated by the capitalist class, the petty bourgeoisie and the army in a great revolutionary battle."[36] This became the working definition for socialist and communist theorists, producing a large literature that is mostly self-referential and did not really improve upon Marx's initial assessment.[37]

One of the most perceptive non-Marxist contemporaries was Walter Bagehot, who considered Bonaparte a "democratic despot" who wanted to establish "an absolute government with a popular mandate."[38] In other words, Bonaparte was a pioneer of CA. Levitsky and Way define competitive authoritarian regimes as "civilian regimes in which formal democratic institutions exist and are widely viewed as the primary means of gaining power, but in which incumbents' abuse of the state place them at a significant advantage vis-à-vis their opponents."[39] The contemporary proliferation of competitive authoritarian regimes – the authors count thirty-five cases between 1990 and 2008 – is in large part a result of the end of the Cold War, according to Levitsky and Way, as the United States (and to a lesser extent the European Union) was no longer willing to blindly support anti-communist authoritarian allies when the Soviet threat suddenly disappeared. Regimes that had previously repressed any and all forms of opposition now had to at least appear to accept the democratic rules of the game in exchange for support from the democratic west.

Levitsky and Way insist that CA is a post-Cold War phenomenon. Yet, as Dan Slater argues, "if this is true, [then] *Competitive Authoritarianism* risks not being able to travel outside the regime type's particular epoch, much like a book on fascist regimes become a book about the interwar period, and a book about communist regimes becomes a book about the Cold War era."[40] Levitsky and Way are forced to accept this point because their *explanation* for regime outcomes includes a temporally bounded set of international factors (specifically, the end of the Cold War and the nature of links to the West).

---

[36] Friedrich Engels, "Die preussische Militarfrage und die deutsche Arbeiterpartei," Marx-Engels Werke, Vol. 16, 71.

[37] Jost Dueffler, "Bonapartism, Fascism and National Socialism." *Journal of Contemporary History* 11 (1976), 109–128.

[38] Thomas Corley, *Democratic Despot: The Life of Napoleon III* (Westport: Greenwood Press, 1961), 354.

[39] Levitsky and Way, *Competitive Authoritarianism*, 5.

[40] Dan Slater, "Review of Competitive Authoritarianism." *Perspectives on Politics* 9, 2 (June 2011), 386.

There is nothing in the *concept* of CA, however, that prevents it from traveling across time.[41] According to Levitsky and Way, a key difference between CA and (full) authoritarianism is the presence of "constitutional channels ... through which opposition groups compete in a meaningful way for executive power." The Second Empire was the only European regime at the time other than Switzerland and Denmark with universal manhood suffrage and where opposition candidates seriously contested each election for the National Assembly, in addition to mounting their own campaigns against Louis Napoleon's most important plebiscites. Repression, as discussed in more detail further, was a critical feature of the Second Empire (during both its authoritarian and "liberal" stages), but this did not mean that opposition forces viewed elections as futile exercises; at several important junctures (most notably in 1852 and 1870) opposition forces actually expected to triumph at the polls and were bitterly disappointed by their defeats. Importantly, these defeats were rarely attributed solely to massive voter fraud. Historians note that "even Napoleon III's most bitter opponents never charged that official results and counts were fraudulent."[42] The democratic components of the Second Empire were robust enough that opposition forces viewed them as a means to power, irrespective of whether their ultimate goal was to erect a democratic republic or to restore a monarchy. Competition was meaningful in that outcomes were uncertain.

At the same time, the regime of Louis Napoleon did not win every single election because of advantages that often redound to the incumbent in truly democratic systems. Rather, it systematically violated some attributes that Levitsky and Way, following Dahl, identify as defining characteristics of democracy. First, while elections were free in that they were not marred by extensive corruption or intimidation, they were not fair because the opposition did not have anything approaching equal access to resources. The practice of selecting and marketing "official candidates" had been part of the French electoral experience for decades, but Louis Napoleon supercharged it. The Ministry of Interior set the pattern in 1852 by asking prefects to recommend candidates according to the "sincerity and energy of the support they would offer to the Prince-President."[43]

---

[41] Michael Bernhard also makes this point in "The Leadership Secrets of Bismarck: Imperial Germany and Competitive Authoritarianism." *Foreign Affairs* 6, 4 (November/December 2011), 150–154.

[42] Stuart Campbell, *The Second Empire Revisited* (New Brunswick: Rutgers University Press, 1976), 15.

[43] Price, *Second Empire*, 99.

## 4.2 Bonapartism as Competitive Authoritarianism

The prefect's job was to look for local notables that would support the Bonapartist program and whose preexisting standing in the community gave them a high likelihood of winning. In addition to identifying themselves with the popular emperor, the official candidates also received free advertising and all the help the prefecture could provide in their responsibility for "making elections." The system was not foolproof: sometimes the prefect chose a poor candidate that the opposition could then defeat, and sometimes the official candidate strayed too far from the Bonapartist program (though the vagueness of Bonapartist ideology rarely rendered this a major problem). Moreover, by the late 1860s the regime's margin of electoral victory began to decline and forced a recalibration of the practice. Still, the system worked to a remarkable degree, as the next section demonstrates.

### 4.2.1 Managing Elections

While the practice of nominating official candidates for office did not begin with the Second Empire, it took on additional dimensions under the new system. "What was really novel in the official candidature system of the fifties," writes Payne, "was the unabashed frankness of its sponsors, the attempt for the first time to fuse the system with universal suffrage, and the thoroughness with which administrators at all electoral levels supported the approved candidates."[44] The system was directed from the Interior Ministry. In a draft letter to prefects before elections in 1852, Interior Minister Persigny warned that while they may not be able to prevent a few "notorious enemies" from entering parliament,

> what matters is that there should be no canton where the hand of the government has not at least sapped the foundations on which the old influences rested ... Overthrow the hold of the old influences on the minds of the people ... Do not fear to fight against the old parties ... our business above all is to create a party.[45]

The prefect was thus instructed to find candidates who could both win in their local districts and were willing to take an oath of loyalty to the Empire. Persigny did not demand that official nominees make a standard pledge, but that "the candidates should in their circulars express themselves clearly in favour of the new order of things." One example, written in 1852, read as follows: "I am firmly convinced that to desert the cause

---

[44] Howard Payne, *The Police State of Louis Napoleon Bonaparte* (Seattle: University of Washington Press, 1966), 163.
[45] Zeldin, *Political System*, 17.

of Louis Napoleon in the present or in the future would be to desert the cause of France and of civilisation. In a word I make profession of devotion, of loyalty, of respect and of sympathy, absolutely and without mental reservations, for the prince and for his government." The aim here was "not to make such men puppets but to compel them to burn their boats and to ostracize themselves from their former party. They would thus be forced to stay on Napoleon's side since they were traitors to their old friends."[46] Persigny was happy with the results of the first election: "We have openly supported and chosen our candidates, but from the highest ranks of society, from the great landowners, wealthy mayors and so on."[47]

The French prefect was the most important local electoral manager. The prefectorial system was established in 1800, and under it career local administrators could rise to the level of prefects and subprefects. Former prefects, in turn, came to occupy key positions in state administration. The prefecture was thus an important career stepping-stone, and it came with major responsibilities.[48] One of these responsibilities was to complete reports monitoring the "moral and political situation" in their domains. According to a circular sent to prefects in 1853, this required gathering information on the following topics:

> *Public opinion:* its principal concerns and manifestations related to governmental policies. Attitude toward military commanders.
> *Political parties:* their importance and activities.
> *Secret societies:* evidence revealing or justifying suspicion of their existence.
> *Behavior of persons condemned for political offenses.*
> *Political offenses:* the circumstances, culprits, and prosecutions involved.

---

[46] Ibid., 39.
[47] G. Goyau, *Un Roman d'amitié* (Letters of Persigny and Falloux, 1928).
[48] According to Price:

> The nineteenth century prefect was the depository and the direct representative of the executive power in the *department*. The prefect, armed with the entire administrative power, wielded an authority that in varying degrees penetrated all the ministerial bureaucracies. He was the sub-ministerial agent most responsible for initiating and supervising measures of public order. He indirectly controlled municipal police. Responsibility for the general security made him chief of general police, into whatever administrative domain this duty might lead him. As a result, the prefect directed political police activities, open and secret, everywhere in the *department*. For the safety of the state, administrative doctrine prescribed that "all must converge into the one center, the prefecture. The prefect must know everything."

> Price, *Second Empire*, 15.

## 4.2 Bonapartism as Competitive Authoritarianism   105

*False news:* information on persons circulating it.

*Newspaper press:* its tendencies, influence, and number of subscribers to political newspapers.

*The book press and bookselling:* activities, violations, and prosecutions.

*Elections:* their political characteristics; results of by-elections.

*Clergy and religious organizations:* their influence, activities; public complaints against them.

*Civil functionaries generally:* their attitudes, conflicts, and relations with the public and other authorities.

*Functionaries in detail:* personal conduct, performance of duties, influence, attitudes, relations with the public, complaints against them.

*Teachers:* appointments, dismissals, and the reasons therefor.

*Gendarmerie:* conduct, etc.

*Public health:* epidemics, mortality.

*Important events:* fires, crimes, noteworthy trials.

*Miscellaneous:* drinking, establishments; direct and indirect taxes; mendacity; societies of mutual assistance; savings banks.

This was indeed a long list of activities. But according to Payne, "no routine" political duty of Louis Napoleon's prefects was more important than to "make" elections at the national, departmental, and communal levels by ensuring the victory of government-sponsored "official candidates."[49] Price concurs: "To a substantial degree, prefects were assessed by their superiors according to their success in managing elections."[50] Prefects warned mayors in their official correspondence (circulars) that supporting opposition candidates was "incompatible with their duties as officials and that, if they persisted, the most basic demands of honor would require them to offer their resignations."[51] Responding to the results of the 1857 election, with which he was generally very satisfied, Napoleon asked Minister of Interior Adolphe Billault to "point out to me as well as to your colleagues the officials who did not do their duty."[52] The prefects, in turn, closely monitored individual mayor's ability to deliver votes for the government according to the principle that "a mayor who has not enough influence over the people he administers to

---

[49] Payne, Police State, 162.
[50] Price, *Napoleon III*, 29.
[51] Price, *Second Empire*, 109.
[52] Zeldin, *Political System*, 75.

make them vote for the official candidate of the government ... ought not to hold his post."[53]

The mayors had the local organization to assist the official candidates.

In each commune, the official candidate has the services of ten civil servants, ten free and disciplined agents who put up his posters and distribute his ballot papers and his circulars daily; one mayor, one deputy mayor, one schoolmaster, one constable, one road-man, one bill-sticker, one tax-collector, one postman, one licensed innkeeper, one tobacconist, appointed, approved and authorised by the prefect.[54]

Price reconstructs this process:

As polling day approached every local official, from the mayor to the roadsman, would be expected to put up the posters and deliver the brochures and ballot papers printed on the white paper that was the exclusive right of the government candidate. They were to praise the official candidate and criticise his opponents. Typically the prefect of Ille-et-Vilaine instructed his mayors that "No electoral poster, other than that of the official candidate, can be put up in the commune without the authorization of the mayor, who is always free to refuse." The posters and ballot papers of opposition candidates "must be on coloured paper." In practice gendarmes and other zealous government officials frequently tore down opposition posters. Voting took place in the *chef-lieu* of each commune. On polling day, particularly in the small communities, voters could be expected to be harangued by the mayor, often in the intimidating presence of a gendarme. For those who regarded local officials and gendarmes with a mixture of fear and respect the simple fact of being presented simultaneously with a voting card and a ballot paper for the official candidate often must have appeared to be an instruction.[55]

Zeldin summarizes the next steps:

The voter was not presented with a list of candidates and asked to place a cross against one of them. Instead, he was required to put in the box a ballot paper which he had to produce himself, bearing the name of his favourite. These ballot papers were generally supplied by the candidates, and the practice was for them to print about three times as many ballot papers as there were electors and to distribute them widely. The government would send the ballot paper of its candidate, together with a card which entitled a man to vote, to all electors. Every elector thus inevitably received a government ballot paper. The ignorant among them, therefore, frequently came to vote with their electoral card and their government ballot paper, which they would put in the box as though it was the only ballot paper available.[56]

---

[53] Ibid., 81.
[54] Ibid., 85.
[55] Price, *Second Empire*, 112.
[56] Zeldin, *Political System*, 83–84.

## 4.2 Bonapartism as Competitive Authoritarianism

In the event a peasant came with an opposition ballot, the mayor could intervene along the following lines:

"Ah! Haven't you got any other ballot paper apart from that one?"
"Why, yes, M. le Maire."
"Show me."
The elector shows several. The mayor takes the official candidate's and says, "Here, my good man, this is the *good one*, put the others down----" Then the mayor puts it into the box. Or he would say, "Put the ballot paper you've got into your pocket and take this one; this is the *good one*.[57]

Prefects and mayors directed a third type of electoral manager: the police.

Political police engaged in constant surveillance of and opportune action upon public opinion, the press in all its forms, and associations of all kinds. Its business included police operations ranging from the suppression of rebellions to arrests for political conspiracy or other activities legally defined as subversive or considered to be so by the authorities entrusted with the protection of the sûreté générale. Political police maintained surveillance of the national frontiers, and of persons or groups abroad, for reasons considered politically relevant to the state's security. Sometimes the political police operated secretly through specialists in undercover work or part-time informers. But its essence was inseparable from the routine performance of certain functionaries whose general police powers formed only part of their broader administrative assignments.[58]

The prefect of Bas-Rhin's instructions to his police commissaire read as follows:

You should pay constant attention to the false news, the alarming rumors spread by the malicious through the countryside and avidly listened to by the rural population ... Visit each commune at least once a month, speak to the mayors on all matters concerning rural policing, and avoid adopting a severe or superior attitude towards them in order to win their confidence. Inform yourself about the political sympathies of the population, about their needs, listen with care to their complaints. You should also pay attention ... to the intrigues which are often hatched against the municipal authorities, try to discover the cause, identify the authors, and especially find out who is in the wrong.[59]

All sorts of local notables became involved with the business of managing elections. One schoolmaster boasted about "the influence which I have the good fortune to exercise over my friends and peaceful inhabitants of Bellecombe, who never go to vote without dropping in on me to

---

[57] National Archives Paris C. 1367, Rouxin's protest (Zeldin, 84).
[58] Payne, *Police State*, 7.
[59] Circular of February 17, 1853.

collect their ballot papers."[60] One judge of the peace of Seilhac reported his outlook for the election of 1863:

> The commune of Beaumont will be unanimous. This commune has just voted for the levying of an extraordinary rate to raise 500 francs to mend its church; the cost of the work is 800 francs. It awaits the subsidy of the remaining 300 francs from you ... The commune of Pirrefitte will also be unanimous. Like the former it has voted an extraordinary rate of 4000 francs for a parsonage. The cost will be 600 francs. It is asking you for a subsidy of 2000 francs ... It is important, M. le Prefet, that the grant of these subsidies should be announced before the date of the election ... Before yesterday I visited the whole of the commune of Chamboulive and despite all that has been done, it will vote unanimously and with enthusiasm. The change in the direction of the [proposed] road has produced its effect.[61]

The government totals in the communes came in close to unanimity: Beaumont 133 to 2 for the government and 130 to 1 in Pirrefitte. The totals were closer in Chamboulive (528 to 71), so perhaps the change to the road was left until too late to return the unanimous consent that the judge had promised his prefect.

Patronage was at the heart of the system of official candidature, as Persigny recognized:

> The patronage powers of the government are immense. By the eighty thousand remunerated positions of which it disposes, by all the funds of all types it can distribute as assistance to communes, to different establishments, to churches, to presbyteries, to schools; by the favors of all kinds that its decisions can procure, by its honorific and other rewards, by the very manner – more or less gracious, more or less favorable, more or less prompt – in which it decides the matters with which it is referred, it is possessed of enormous means of influence, and no government in history ever disposed of such powers.[62]

After the elections of 1863, Persigny was dismissed as Interior Minister because he did not manage elections well enough. In an extraordinarily frank letter, the emperor wrote to his original loyalist:

> Your maintenance in office will cause the agitation to continue, it will excite opinion and make the verification of the elections disastrous for the government. What do you want people to say in support, for example, of the candidatures of MM. Seneca and Boitelle, discredited men who were elected only as the result of the most culpable pressure of the administration! Well, I say it with regret, your temporary withdrawal can alone re-establish calm in public opinion. I recognize

---

[60] Zeldin, *Political System*, 85.
[61] Ibid., 83.
[62] *Memoires (acc) du duc de Persigny* (Paris: Plon, 1896), 313.

the great devotion you have shown me and I am far from bearing you any grudge for not having succeeded everywhere. But it must also be acknowledged, your superior and lucid mind is worthless for administration where all must be prepared long before by perpetual regular conduct. How could you succeed, for example, where the candidature of M. Delessert was improvised ten days before the election?[63]

The system of official candidature was showing signs of strain by the late 1860s, but that in no way diminishes the fact that, within only a couple of years, the regime had succeeded in building a Bonapartist party that won every election and plebiscite in the Second Empire. Some contemporaries, including the emperor himself, worried that Bonapartism was a paper tiger: Napoleon once allegedly quipped that "The empress is legitimist, my cousin is republican, Morny is Orleanist, I am a socialist; the only Bonapartist is Persigny and he is mad."[64] And still the Bonapartist party survived not only the firing of Persigny but also the collapse of the Second Empire and the transition to democracy. The elections of 1877 in the French Third Republic returned 104 Bonapartist deputies to the National Assembly.[65]

### 4.2.2 Policy of the Balanced Press

Louis Napoleon was terrified by the role that the press had played in fomenting the revolution of 1848, and he began a crackdown on opposition newspapers while still president of the Second Republic. He increased the level of control significantly as emperor. Many opposition papers, particularly those with republican or socialist leanings, were forced to close. The new government taxed others so heavily that they were pushed out of business. The regime was more lenient toward the Orléanist and *Legitimist* papers that continued to favor the restoration of the monarchy, but even some of these were subjected to the same treatment. Most of those newspapers that did not become semiofficial outlets for Bonapartism engaged in a high degree of self-censorship to ensure their continued existence. While the Second Empire permitted a degree of press freedom, the playing field for the opposition – particularly during elections – was hardly fair to the opposition.

Immediately following the coup, Persigny argued that controls were necessary until "a new political generation – young, vigorous, and

---

[63] Napoleon to Persigny, November 6, 1863, Persigny papers.
[64] Zeldin, *Political System*, 46.
[65] Price, *Napoleon III*, 64.

independent – arises to replace minds distorted and enervated by our revolutions."⁶⁶ The Interior Ministry gave prefects wide discretion to ban papers based on whether their publication "would tend to diminish or to weaken governmental authority."⁶⁷ In a December 1851 confidential circular to prefects, Morny suggested that this policy would become permanent:

> You should tolerate only those newspapers which conform to the prescriptions I have already outlined ... If some of them seem disposed to assist the liberating action of the government ... treat them with just favor. As for those journals that solicit permission to reappear, approval must not be readily given. Although a formerly hostile and dangerous paper might be restrained through fear and become more circumspect, it would still cater to its old confederates ... whom it would regroup into a kind of alliance and over whom it would retain an influence that we would be wiser to eliminate.⁶⁸

The press laws of February 1852 expanded the state's capacity to discipline the media. They set the amount of "caution money" required to publish newspapers at a rate that only individuals of great means (and thereby presumably of conservative opinions) could afford. Stamp taxes were increased (and applied selectively) to cut down on circulation rates of newspapers, making them both less influential and less profitable.

In addition to these disincentives, the 1852 press law also gave the prefects three new mechanisms of directly influencing the content of newspapers. The first was the power to insert communiqués in the form of official rebuttals of previously published editorials. The regime thereby reserved the right to respond in unmediated form to any argument with which it took issue. The second was the right to insert official corrections to any "false news" on the front page of the offending newspaper. The regime thus appeared as the ultimate arbiter of the truth. Third, prefects could issue *avertissements* (official warnings) that the government described as "invitations[s] given a newspaper to take a more moderate course."⁶⁹ Given that these warnings were published on the front page of the wayward newspaper, and that two of them resulted in suspension or suppression of the offending press, the *avertissement* was clearly much more than an "invitation." And if any of these disciplinary mechanisms failed, the state could always withdraw the authorization to publish by claiming that a newspaper represented a threat to the *sûreté générale*,

---

⁶⁶ Payne, *Police State*, 182.
⁶⁷ Ibid., 50.
⁶⁸ Ibid.
⁶⁹ Ibid., 184.

## 4.2 Bonapartism as Competitive Authoritarianism

meaning to the security of the state itself. Maupas' circular of March 30, 1852, reassured prefects that they possessed wide latitude in interpreting when a newspaper had crossed the line into endangering public order:

> Repressive measures by pure administrative decision derive from the ... right of authorization. As soon as a newspaper ceases to observe the conditions of authorization ... or persists in polemics that make it an instrument of disorder to the point of endangering public security, the government ... has the right to withdraw its authorization. You will use this right with impartial severity against those journals whose editorial policies, without specifically becoming liable to judicial action, are nonetheless dangerous for public order, morality, and religion.[70]

The goal was to maximize self-censorship and put the costs on the newspapers themselves. To a large degree it worked:

> Censored by himself, his copy pored over and corrected meticulously by the editor-in-chief, given a last check by the printer (who was responsible to the courts for every line that came off his press), deprived of scope and movement, drawing the thunderbolts while chained to the lightning rod, compelled by his job to strike sparks while seated on a powder keg, the journalist of 1860 was indeed the tortured victim of the imperial regime.[71]

Still, it was not enough to stamp out the most threatening opposition newspapers and harass opposition journalists. The government needed to construct its own media outlets in haste. According to Payne, "lacking a widespread Bonapartist press, the prefects sought to gain control over newspapers of diverse opinions, thus at once creating a tolerable medium for official propaganda while preserving the appearance of a press 'balanced' by moderately critical opposition."[72] In a circular of December 22, 1852, Persigny urged "an energetic intervention on the part of the administration in favour of good social principles. This intervention can best be accomplished by means of publications and pamphlets encouraged, and if need be, financed by the administration."[73]

The press law of 1852 gave prefects the right to distribute the *announces judiciaries* to whichever newspapers they wanted. Payne argues that: "The grant or refusal of this indirect subsidy could make or break many small papers whose meager advertising revenue made them depend upon printing business to augment the income from a few hundred subscribers. Disgruntled publishers who lost the annonces repeatedly challenged the

---

[70] Ibid.
[71] Ibid., 186.
[72] Ibid., 54.
[73] Price, *Second Empire*, 173.

prefects' new power. They were as many times rebuffed by the Council of State." Prefects met yearly to discuss the distribution of the annonces "according to their sense of political strategy." One prefect boasted of his prowess in targeting the annonces to his favored paper, "killing the small local sheets, and ending with only one political organ, influential and easy to manage."[74]

The policy of the balanced press also required the co-optation of the two largest opposition newspapers. Siècle had the largest circulation in France with close to 44,000 as of 1866. *L'Opinion nationale*, founded only in 1859, enjoyed exponential growth in its first several years. Persigny made the editors-in-chief of *both* newspapers members of Parliament with governmental support.[75] As of 1852, the regime could count on the support of about 3/4 of the provincial press: of an estimated 258 newspapers, only 60 were aligned with the Orléanist (13), Legitimist (34), or Republican (13) oppositions.[76] Zeldin finds that in 1862 the distribution of the provincial press was virtually the same as ten years earlier. The situation remained essentially unchanged as of 1867, when only 50 of the 272 provincial newspapers supported the opposition.[77] Circulation figures across time are difficult to find, but in both 1862 and 1867, government papers outpaced opposition ones in the provinces by about two and a half to one.[78] Throughout the entirety of the Second Empire, about half of the departments of France never had an opposition paper at all.

## 4.3 THE STABILITY OF BONAPARTISM

Does partial democratization – the proverbial halfway house between two regime types – inevitably lead to either full democratization or to an authoritarian crackdown? The history of the French Second Empire bears directly on this question. Indeed, the meaning of the Second Empire has been bitterly contested by historians – particularly French historians – since the battle of Sedan.[79] These intellectual battles were as much about contemporary politics as they were about the French past. For example,

---

[74] Payne, *Police State*, 194–196.
[75] Zeldin, *Political System*, 112; Campbell, *Second Empire Revisited*, 74.
[76] Price, *Second Empire*, 173.
[77] Zeldin, *Political System*, 85.
[78] Price, *Second Empire*, 176.
[79] On the historiography of the Second Empire, see Campbell, *The Second Empire Revisited*.

## 4.3 The Stability of Bonapartism

during the early years of the French Third Republic, those historians who defended Republican values cast the Second Empire as an authoritarian interlude with few redeeming features. Later, as the Republic appeared sclerotic and ultimately fell, once again, to the Germans in 1940, historians began to reframe the Second Empire as an experiment in state-led development that had some positive impacts on France's economic modernization.

More recently, a revisionist historiography has sought to connect developments during the liberal period of the Second Empire to the consolidation of the Third Republic in the 1870s. The general argument that Louis Napoleon's political system unintentionally contributed to a successful democratic transition takes several different forms. For Philip Nord, the liberalization of the Empire in the 1860s led to a "resurrection of civil society" in which a rising political elite was trained to think and behave like democrats, even though the system remained authoritarian.[80] "What makes possible a democratic transition," Nord writes, "is the prior elaboration, while dictatorship is still in place, of a counter-elite anchored in autonomous institutions and buoyed by an alternative political culture."[81] Nord's study builds on that by Katherine Auspitz, who argued that "the character of French politics in the first decade of the Third Republic was determined, not uniquely but necessarily, by the ascendancy of men whose political positions had been strengthened and, sometimes, established in the secularist voluntary associations of the 1860s."[82] Sudhir Hazareesingh takes a slightly different view by focusing on the ideological battles over the issues of citizenship and decentralization in the 1860s, but shares Nord's conclusion that "the Second Empire represented an important stage in the emergence of modern democratic norms and values in France."[83]

---

[80] Philip Nord, *The Republican Moment: Struggles for Democracy in Nineteenth Century France* (Cambridge: Harvard University Press, 1995). According to Nord (252):

> The republican awakening of midcentury France coincided with a general stirring of civic activism, which republicans both fed upon and incited. The authoritarian and statist political conjectures simplified the politicization of civic discontents, and with considerable political skill republicans capitalized on the moment. The result – a resurrection of civil society under republican auspices – swept aside the dynastic parties of old, which never again occupied center-stage in French political life.

[81] Ibid., 9.
[82] Katherine Auspitz, *The Radical Bourgeoisie: The Ligue de l'Enseignement and the Origins of the Third Republic, 1866–1885* (New York: Cambridge University Press, 1982), 7.
[83] Sudhir Hazareesingh, *From Subject to Citizen: The Second Empire and the Emergence of Modern French Democracy* (Princeton: Princeton University Press, 1998), 306.

If the Second Empire did indeed set the stage for the "republican moment" of the 1870s, this would suggest that Europe's first competitive authoritarian regime was democratizing to some degree. There is some evidence, to be sure, for this interpretation. One indicator is the declining performance of official candidates. According to the state prosecutor in Angers: "in 1852, and even in 1857, voters almost everywhere relied on the authorities' chosen candidates. Nomination as an official candidate was sufficient to ensure election. In 1863, the prestige derived from this designation had, already, substantially diminished; in 1869 it had almost completely disappeared."[84] While the Legitimist and Orleanist blocks remained essentially stagnant, the steady decline in the Bonapartists' huge electoral margins redounded to the Republican opposition. The increasing pace of liberal reforms over the course of the 1860s also appeared to suggest that the regime was responding to growing domestic demands for democracy. And naturally the growing use of the designation "liberal empire" implied that the empire had shed its most authoritarian characteristics and was heading in the direction of a parliamentary regime with full civil liberties.

We will see in Chapter 5 that historians of Imperial Germany have made similar claims about the self-reinforcing nature of quasi-democratic institutions. The balance of evidence – both for the Second Empire and for the Second Reich – suggests that such liberalization was directed by the old regime, was often of a token nature, and was never a serious challenge to autocratic power.

Louis Napoleon introduced political concessions from a position of strength, and in retrospect one can see that he controlled the pace and degree of liberalization. He followed the recommendation of Prince Napoleon that he "put himself at the head of the liberal movement, vigorously impose a sense of direction on it, and achieve dominance over it."[85] After a decade of reactionary authoritarianism, Napoleon announced on November 15, 1860, "nonchalantly" and without any warning, that he would allow the publication of parliamentary debates and would henceforth appoint ministers to explain government policy.[86] Some in his cabinet recoiled in horror at these tiny gestures toward parliamentary government, and several noted that the emperor had made concessions when they did not appear necessary, given the lack of political demand

---

[84] Quoted in Price, *Second Empire*, 127.
[85] Ibid., 74.
[86] Corley, *Democratic Despot*, 236.

## 4.3 The Stability of Bonapartism

for them. As Buffet wrote, "for nine years ... one has seen liberal ideas discussed and ridiculed by the immense majority of this country; one has seen ... public opinion crumble up more and more and become little by little stranger to the most simple notions of liberty."[87]

Napoleon's announcement also caught the opposition off-guard and presented it with the difficult choice of embracing the reforms or rejecting them outright. Many were naturally dubious of the emperor's motives but were caught in a bind. Thiers noted their dilemma: "It is impossible for the liberal monarchical party which has always demanded liberty to refuse any grant of it when it is offered. What matters is not the sincerity of the offer, but the sincerity of its acceptance."[88] He advised patience:

> If the government resists, when it sees that liberty will challenge a part of its omnipotence, a revolution will follow and it is disagreeable for those who have been in three revolutions to take part in a fourth. If the government yields with prudence, we are quite simply its prisoners and in good faith, we must agree, not to become its ministers, but to be its applauders.[89]

It is important to stress the timidity of these initial "liberal reforms." They amounted to the following: merely permission to the Chamber to hold a "debate on the Address", in the course of which the government might be interpellated on its policy, and be obliged to explain its projects of law – any member of the Council of Ministers might be called before the House: and a detailed daily report of the Chamber's proceedings to be issued to the press.[90]

In other words, the government granted a degree of transparency. The emperor made a seemingly more substantive concession when the Corps législatif was given power to discuss and vote on the budget, line by line. Yet "in practice this right was emptied of meaning by a subsequent decree which enabled the Government to 'rectify' the budget; and the old system returned in a new guise."[91]

Napoleon introduced further reforms in 1867 as his New Year's gift to the people. Chief among these were the right of deputies to ask parliamentary questions of the government and a law on public meetings that permitted gatherings of scientific and literary societies. The emperor assured his ministers that these would not develop into revolutionary clubs as in 1848, and that "if the attempt [to allow for more freedom of

---

[87] Zeldin, *Political System*, 107.
[88] Ibid., 109.
[89] Ibid., 110.
[90] Thompson, *Louis Napoleon*, 250.
[91] Ibid., 251.

association] is unsuccessful, the law will simply be repealed."[92] Napoleon was already noting regrets in October 1869 about liberalization. In a letter to his wife, he lamented that "the country is unfortunately incapable of coping with liberty ... incitement by the democratic newspapers and public meetings is bound to lead, sooner or later, to a riot, which will have the effect of a storm in purifying the atmosphere."[93]

"There is a myth," writes Zeldin, "that the liberal empire represented the abdication of Napoleon III, giving up his prerogatives in order to keep his throne; that it was forced on him by the strength of the opposition, who thus succeeded to his power."[94] In a letter to Metternich, the emperor stressed that he had no intention of conceding his core powers: "you understand ... that there are limits, both foreign and domestic policy, which I will not see overstepped."[95] He had worked on the text of the new constitution himself for nearly a year. Article 13 stated that: "The Emperor is responsible to the French people to whom he retains the right of appeal." This preserved the emperor's power of plebiscite and right to dissolve parliament. The constitution also "placed the question of dynasty outside the powers of parliament and made it a matter between the people and the sovereign."[96] And perhaps most critically, there was no solution to a possible deadlock between the monarch and the legislature. To call the new regime "liberal" stretched the meaning of the term to such an extent that one needs to compare across centuries to find a plausible case. As Zeldin concludes:

> The point was that it did not intend to establish parliamentary government and that the correct analogy for comparison is not the English constitution of the nineteenth century, but that of the late seventeenth ... Since so many people believed that France was not ripe for the institutions of nineteenth century England, it was perhaps not as silly as it might appear to start with those of seventeenth-century England.[97]

The emperor was masterful at presenting dilemmas for the opposition, beginning with the system of official candidates. One prefect explained the logic as follows: "The most certain method of dissolving the old parties in this department," he suggested, "is to borrow their leaders whenever they frankly accept the new order of things, and the

[92] Corley, *Democratic Despot*, 300.
[93] Price, *Second Empire*, 185.
[94] Zeldin, *Political System*, 120.
[95] Corley, *Democratic Despot*, 316.
[96] Zeldin, *Political System*, 153.
[97] Ibid., 151–152.

## 4.3 The Stability of Bonapartism

number as well as the opportunity of these borrowings must be determined, it seems to me, by the real strength of the local influences which we wish to win over."[98] By forcing these candidates to represent the government's positions, Persigny argued that campaigns would turn official candidates into convinced Bonapartists: "Napoleon's supporters, who were still an incoherent body formed of diverse elements, would be forced to cut their ties with these old parties and would be made into a solid party by the attack they would experience from all sides."[99] In the elections of 1863, "almost exactly half of the *opposition* or independent candidates entered parliament with, as it were, the co-operation of the government."[100]

The next step was to incorporate the Republicans. In the early 1850s, "suffering repression, humiliation, and disrepute, the republican party temporarily disappeared as an active political force."[101] When a mere five Republicans were elected to parliament in 1857, there was a tremendous uproar. According to Darimon's account, they were treated as pariahs in the National Assembly:

They found that seats had already been chosen for them all alone on the highest benches of the left. In the lobbies and public rooms of the house they were similarly kept at a distance. Old school friends turned their backs and refused to speak to them. They were regarded with fear and dislike, as dangerous intruders from the mob.[102]

"How was it, then," Zeldin asks, "that the leader of the ostracized group became the prime minister of the liberal empire?"[103] The answer is that the emperor succeeded in coopting moderate Republicans just as he had Legitimists and Orleanists. The Republican Émile Ollivier [one of the five elected in 1857] noted in a journal entry of November 25, 1860, in response to the initial reforms: "I do not think that these measures will undermine the Empire; they will *consolidate it. And yet I rejoice that this is a beginning ... I rejoice all the more, even* if this is only an expedient, because we have gained another means of attack."[104] The first public break in Ollivier's principled opposition to the new regime appeared in 1861 when a fiery speech by a clericalist politician prompted him to give

---

[98] Ibid., 37–38.
[99] Ibid., 114.
[100] Ibid., 139. Emphasis added.
[101] Campbell, *Second Empire Revisited*, 36.
[102] Zeldin, *Political System*, 120.
[103] Ibid.
[104] Price, 76.

the emperor his conditional support.[105] Ollivier's journal entry of March 13, 1861, suggests a change of course: "I fearfully think of the counterrevolution invading the world if this man [Napoleon III] was overthrown, and for the first time I understand and excuse Beranger and the liberals of the Restoration."[106] The Republican Carnot accused Ollivier of treason in 1861, after Ollivier had promised to support the emperor so long as Bonaparte was committed to political reform.[107] Still, Ollivier retained his identity as part of the republican opposition until 1865, when he accepted the role of parliamentary rapporteur for legislation legalizing strikes.[108] The emperor, for his part, believed that Ollivier "has two precious qualities which make me forget his failings. He believes in me and is the eloquent interpreter of my ideas, especially when I let him think they are his own."[109]

"Liberalization" exposed and magnified a basic cleavage in the republican forces between those who rejected any cooperation with the regime and those like Ollivier who were willing to work with it. Bitter invective was hurled at Ollivier – he was called the "man of lies and hypocrisy," and mention of his name caused uproars at republican meetings. Responding to his critics, Ollivier claimed a moral high ground:

to accept the institutions of his country, even whilst wishing they were better, then to use every legal means of improving, modifying, transforming them, that is the duty of a true patriot to strengthen itself, democracy must expand and not close in on itself ... It must prefer ideas to phrases, a realistic limited improvement to the vague hope of total reform, pursue liberty and not upheaval, progress and not revolution.[110]

Ollivier's government, formed on December 31, 1869, "included four ministers of the authoritarian empire and the continuity between the new and the old was thus preserved."[111] Ollivier deployed troops against demonstrators on January 12, 1870.[112] On April 30, 1870, he directed state prosecutors to "no longer hesitate to prosecute newspapers ... which contain a call for civil war and insult the Emperor. We cannot simply sit back ... and watch the revolutionary flood. Respect liberty; but

---

[105] Plessis, 159.
[106] Ollivier, *Journal*, II, 12.
[107] Price, *Second Empire*, 367.
[108] Price, 367.
[109] G. P. Gooch, "The Second Empire." *Contemporary Review* (July–Dec 1958), 130.
[110] Price, *Second Empire*, 368.
[111] Zeldin, *Political System*, 144.
[112] Price, *Second Empire*, 316.

provocations to murder and civil are the opposite of liberty."[113] Ollivier had become a Bonapartist in all but name, demonstrating the capacity of CA to transform even the most principled democrats into defenders of the system.

In May of 1870, Napoleon called a plebiscite on "the liberal reforms introduced into the constitutions since 1860." The Republican opposition was caught flat-footed once again and warned its members that a "yes" was tantamount to a vote of confidence in the regime. An editorial in Le Temps reminded its readers of the regime's subterfuge and urged a no vote: "in appearance it [the liberal constitution] represents a call for the definitive approval of our liberal conquests but in practice the victory would be that of the personal power."[114] The moderate Republican Ernest Picard wrote in his newspaper L'Electeur libre that "the sovereignty of the nation has no more dangerous enemy than the plebiscite. The plebiscite invokes national sovereignty the better to confiscate it. Through the plebiscite, the executive power retains for itself ... the formidable personal appeal to the people which results in the surprise votes which precede or follow a coup d'etat."[115] Jules Grevy urged his constituents in Jura to vote no because "France remains bowed down under the hand of a man, and in the future, the coup d'etat will remain suspended like a sword above its head ... The Empire is despotism behind the mask of democracy."[116] Eugene Spuller wrote a brief history of the Second Empire as part of the campaign to vote "no" in the 1870 plebiscite, and described the nature of the regime in similar terms: a "hybrid mixture of democracy and caesarism – which suffocates liberty while appearing to serve it – a bastard and corrupt system of government, which has no other restraint than the personal will of the Prince who operates under the cover of popular consent."[117]

The "no" campaign was trounced by a score of 7,300,000 to 1,600,000. Republican leaders were stunned by the result. Although it is difficult to compare the results of the 1870 plebiscite with that of the 1869 elections, it clearly represented a crushing defeat. Compared with the plebiscite of 1852, "support for the regime had grown in the west, remained at least stable in the north and north-east, stagnated in the

---

[113] Ibid., 186.
[114] Price, Second Empire, 316.
[115] Ibid., 75.
[116] Quoted in P. Jeanbrun, Jules Grevy (Paris: Tallandier, 1991), 125.
[117] Eugene Spuller, Histoire parlementaire de la seconde République suivie d'une petite histoire du second Empire. 2nd ed. (Paris: Alcan, 1893), 341.

south and much of the centre and south-west, and declined only in Paris and the east." And in addition: "the Parisian vote – 184,000 *non* and 138,000 *oui* – was much less hostile to the regime than the 1869 election results, as middle-class voters, disturbed by the extremism of the public meetings and by disorder in the streets, opted for the liberal regime."[118]

The Republican opposition acknowledged its defeat. Leon Gambetta, who proclaimed the French Third Republic on September 4, 1870, had lamented only several months earlier that "the Empire is stronger than ever," while Jules Favre depressingly admitted that there "was nothing more to do in politics."[119] The emperor, by contrast, was jubilant. "I'm back to my old score," he boasted, and the magnitude of his victory in 1870 did indeed approach those of 1851 and 1852.[120] Historians have largely agreed with Georges Weill's assessment that "the divisions among republicans had never been as strong as at the end of the Empire."[121] The author of the most comprehensive analysis of the Second Empire concludes that "as late as the early summer of 1870 there thus appeared to be no real threat to the survival of the regime" and that "it would be defeat in war, and not political opposition, which would destroy the Second Empire."[122]

What are the most compelling explanations for this persistence? The evidence is most consistent with an institutionalization of elections thesis, even though the Bonapartist party was hegemonic in the first decade of the regime and merely dominant in the second. The party may have lost votes, but it also integrated opposition figures into the governing party, and Louis Napoleon won his final plebiscite in convincing fashion after allowing a significant degree of liberalization. The fact that the Bonapartists never lost also means that we cannot imagine what it would have done had the opposition claimed victory, though Louis Napoleon's remarks to Metternich suggest that there were limits. He was, after all, a three-time coup plotter who helped destroy the Second Republic and proclaimed himself emperor.

There are several alternative explanations to consider. The first is that the economic performance of the regime bought a high degree of social peace. According to Alain Plessis, it was "the first regime to have given such distinct priority to economic objectives."[123] Louis Napoleon

---

[118] Price, *Second Empire*, 389.
[119] Ibid., 393.
[120] Plessis, *Rise and Fall of Second Empire*, 166.
[121] Georges Weill, *Histoire du parti republican 1814–1870* (1928).
[122] Price, *Second Empire*, 401.
[123] Plessis, *Rise and Fall of Second Empire*, 62.

believed that the state could play a positive role in economic development and his regime concentrated on the construction of rail networks and urban renewal. Whether his policies created economic growth is unclear, however. Price concludes that "the rate of growth does not appear to have been any more rapid than during the July Monarchy, which might suggest that market forces rather than state policy were the decisive element shaping long-term economic change."[124] Louis Napoleon, moreover, promoted almost exactly the sorts of policies that could have been predicted to foment opposition. Rather than favor the more powerful protectionist interest groups, the emperor was an advocate of free trade. His statist policies were also often bitterly resented by organized economic interest groups.

A second group of explanations for authoritarian persistence focuses on the weakness of the political opposition.[125] According to this logic, autocracies endure not primarily because they have captured or bought the allegiance of important social and economic groups – indeed, these groups may be either apolitical or even hostile to the regime – but because their opponents cannot muster the resources to topple them. Whether this failure stems from preexisting divisions among opposition forces, strategic miscalculations by opposition leaders, or a high degree of wealth inequality within society that provides would-be opposition forces with few tools in their political arsenal, the key insight here is that a stronger opposition – all other variables being equal – would have toppled the regime.

This is not an implausible counterfactual for the Second Empire. Indeed, in perhaps no other European state was the opposition so divided in terms of ideology and strategy. The monarchist forces were split between two rival camps: the Legitimists who favored the restoration of the Bourbon Monarchy and the Orleanists (some of whom favored the restoration of a powerful monarchy, and some of whom favored the installation of a parliamentary regime alongside a monarch as in Great Britain). These movements were so hostile to one another that – when given an actual opportunity to reinstall the monarchy before the consolidation of the Third Republic – they split over the issue of the design of a flag. Divided, the monarchists were then defeated by the Republican opposition.

---

[124] Price, *Second Empire*, 211.
[125] Ellen Lust-Okar, *Structuring Conflict in the Arab World* (New York: Cambridge University Press, 2005); Marc Howard and Philip Roessler, "Liberalizing Electoral Outcomes in Competitive Authoritarian Regimes." *American Journal of Political Science* 50, 2 (March 2006), 365–381.

Political reformers were also split. The historical divisions of French Socialists have been well chronicled, and it is worth emphasizing that such divisions were present from the founding of the French labor movement. Republicans were internally divided over their relationship to the Socialists. Republicans and Liberals disagreed fundamentally over the magnitude of democratic reforms that were necessary, as well as over a host of other issues like decentralization, free trade, and foreign policy. The conflict between religious and anticlerical forces added yet another important cleavage that enervated the opposition to Bonapartism.

Still, the weakness of the opposition in the Second Empire had more to do with the behavior of the regime than with the structure and competence of the forces that were challenging it. As Beatriz Magaloni's analysis of the endurance of CA in Mexico reveals, hegemonic parties go to the trouble of running up massive electoral margins, as opposed to taking the easier route of simply making sure it wins a legislative majority, because such a strategy creates enormous problems for the opposition. Potential opposition candidates, as well as potential defectors from the hegemonic party, are intimidated by displays of electoral omnipotence. Voters, in turn, come to believe that a vote for the opposition is wasted. In short, massive shows of strength can be self-reinforcing in competitive authoritarian settings.[126] As this chapter has argued, the evidence in favor of co-optation is strong.

There is a final explanation worth considering. Since the Second Empire ultimately fell because of international war, could it be that the war was diversionary, meaning it was conducted precisely to distract from, and ultimately bring into line, an increasingly powerful opposition? Historians of Wilhelmine Germany have claimed that World War One was, in part, a diversionary war to outflank the SPD. But this is not the case with the Franco–Prussian War. According to Ollivier, in the months before the collapse of the Second Empire, "there was never a time at which peace in Europe seemed to me more assured."[127]

The origins of the Franco–Prussian War are complicated, but the central facts are as follows. The spark for the conflict was the candidacy of Leopold of Hohenzollern-Sigmaringen for the Spanish throne. Bismarck had encouraged this prince from the Hohenzollern family to become king of Spain, knowing full well the provocation it would be to France. As with so many other matters, Bismarck calculated correctly, and a "war

---

[126] Beatriz Magaloni, *Voting for Autocracy: Hegemonic Party Survival and Its Demise in Mexico* (New York: Cambridge University Press, 2008).
[127] Thompson, *Louis Napoleon*, 293.

party" within the press and Bonapartist circles began to press a reluctant emperor to demand that Leopold not only retract his candidacy but also that the King of Prussia personally guarantee that there would be no further Prussian interference in Spanish affairs. The second demand – which was designed to inflict reputational damage on Prussia – was unnecessary, and the Prussian King politely refused this unreasonable request during a meeting at the Spa town of Ems. The matter might very well have ended there, had not Bismarck doctored a telegraphic account of the meeting and released a new "Ems Telegram" on July 14, 1870, that made it appear as if the Prussian King had been insulted and humiliated by the French Foreign Minister. Bismarck had set his second trap, and Napoleon fell headlong into it when he declared war on July 19. He would surrender at Sedan a mere six weeks later.

## 4.4 CONCLUSION: THE DIFFUSION OF BONAPARTISM

The young Bismarck, A. J. P. Taylor remarks, "had no vision that he would unify Germany on the basis of universal suffrage."[128] Born in Prussia in 1806, Bismarck embraced the values of the Junker class of landowning elites – monarchism, militarism, and anti-liberalism. After a short and unproductive career in the civil service, Bismarck returned to his estate in 1847. By his own account, "no one would have ever heard of me, in my rural retreat, if I had not become a member of the united diet by chance."[129] Perhaps, though most historians have tended to discount this confession of a political animal and assumed that Bismarck – much like Bonaparte – would have found another entry way into politics. In any event, by 1847 Bismarck "had made a name for himself in a narrow reactionary circle."[130] His reputation grew in 1848, when he tried to entangle first the Prussian army and then the Prussian monarch in his counter-revolutionary plots. The King of Prussia quipped that Bismarck was so reactionary that he was "only to be used when the bayonet rules." Indeed, Bismarck's most famous quote was his prediction in 1864 that "the great questions of the time will not be resolved by speeches and majority decisions – that was the great mistake of 1848 and 1849 – but by iron and blood."

Bismarck's path from a diehard opponent of suffrage expansion in 1848 to one of its foremost advocates within Prussia led through the

---

[128] A. J. P. Taylor, *Bismarck* (New York: Vintage, 1955), 13.
[129] Ibid., 23.
[130] Ibid., 24.

French Second Empire. According to Peter Steinbach, Bismarck saw in Bonapartism "how easily a monarchical government can exploit liberal-national ideas and parliamentary institutions to enhance its power." And for this reason, Steinbach continues, Bismarck "increasingly regarded the universal franchise as an expedient that strengthened authority and the monarchical principle by means of the plebiscite."[131] Bismarck was also one of the first politicians to turn toward what was emerging as a new center of power and to seek to make personal contact with Napoleon III.[132] In an 1851 letter to his conservative patron Ludwig von Gerlach, Bismarck notes a connection between the emerging Bonapartist system and Prussian tradition. He writes that "I would venture to say that, here in Prussia, Bonapartism is older than Bonaparte, only in milder German form."[133] His first documented visit with Napoleon III occurred in 1855, though the substance of their conversation is unknown. But in subsequent letters to Gerlach in 1857, which Bismarck decided to place in the chapter of his memoirs titled "Visit to Paris" that had taken place two years earlier, we find his most detailed comments on the nature of Bonapartism.

"News from Berlin apprises me that they regard me at Court as a Bonapartist," Bismarck begins. Whereas Gerlach considered Bonaparte's regime revolutionary and hence illegitimate, Bismarck disagreed. "By aiding the spread of revolutionary institutions among his neighbours, the French Emperor would be creating danger for himself, he will rather, in the interests of the maintenance of his rule and dynasty and with his conviction of the faultiness of present French institutions, seek to gain for himself firmer foundations than those of the Revolution." Bismarck viewed Bonapartism as a restoration, not a revolution, and did not consider it to be transitory. He continues:

the present form of government in France is not arbitrary, a thing that Louis Napoleon can correct or alter. It was something that he found as a given and is probably the only method according to which it will be possible to govern France for a long time to come. For everything else the basis is missing either in national character or has been shattered and lost.[134]

---

[131] Peter Steinbach, "Reichstag Elections in the Kaiserreich," in Larry Jones and James Retallack, eds., *Elections, Mass Politics and Social Change in Modern Germany* (New York: Cambridge University Press, 1992), 133.
[132] Lothar Gall, *Bismarck: The White Revolutionary* (London: Unwin Hyman, 1986), 132.
[133] Ibid., 134.
[134] "Visit to Paris," *Bismarck, The Memoirs. Vol I* (New York: Howard Fertig, 1966), 198.

## 4.4 Conclusion: The Diffusion of Bonapartism

Bismarck held two ambassadorial posts from 1858 to 1862 while he awaited political events to play out in Prussia. His first posting, in St. Petersburg, allowed him to observe unreconstructed monarchic absolutism in practice. When he was recalled from St. Petersburg to Berlin in July 1861, he advocated, to the horror of the monarch, the creation of a "German parliament, elected by universal suffrage, to sweep away all the little princes."[135] He was then posted to Paris because he refused to take a ministry without portfolio in the Prussian government. There is little in the historical record of note regarding his short stint in Paris other than his terrible boredom. "There is absolutely no reason why I should be either here," he wrote, "swallowing the hot dust of Paris, yawning in cafes or theatres, or camping in Berlin at the Hotel Royal as a political dilettante. I could spend my time better at the baths."

He did not have to suffer Paris for long. He was appointed Prime Minister and Foreign Minister of Prussia in 1862. In 1863, he sprang "the idea of universal suffrage on a startled German public."[136] Bismarck then introduced universal male suffrage in Prussia in 1866. It was a shock to former conservatives and former friends like Gerlach:

> In the midst of the clanging of weapons Prussia introduces at the Bund a demand for universal suffrage. Universal suffrage means political bankruptcy – in place of living relations of law and political thought, instead of concrete personalities, we get numbers and exercises in addition.[137] (243)

> [Memorandum against Bismarck's design for the north German confederation:]
> How is it remotely conceivable, all old Prussian institutions, all elements of its power, are to be surrendered through this one declaration in the Speech from the Throne and that through it – its finances, its army, its House of Lords, the Monarchy, Prussia itself – is to be given over to the temporary majority of a second chamber which will emerge from its new provisions? It will in the short or long run hopelessly go under in an unfathomable whirlpool. Prussia without the spirit which made it is as good as dead ... without an independent Monarchy.[138]

Bismarck, however, viewed elections as a means of solidifying monarchy and conservative rule. He argues:

> At the moment of decision, the masses will stand on the side of kingship, regardless of whether the latter happens to follow a liberal or a conservative tendency ... [T]he artificial system of indirect and class elections is much more dangerous than that of direct and general suffrage, because it prevents contact between the

---

[135] Taylor, *Bismarck*, 49.
[136] Jonathan Steinberg, *Bismarck: A Life* (New York: Oxford University Press, 2013), 8.
[137] Ibid., 243.
[138] Ibid., 260.

highest authority and the healthy elements that constitute the core and the mass of the people. In a country with monarchical traditions and loyal sentiments the general suffrage, by eliminating the influences of the liberal bourgeois classes, will also lead to monarchical elections.[139]

Louis Napoleon Bonaparte had discovered this formula twenty years earlier in what was the first attempt to harness universal suffrage to support an authoritarian regime. As we have seen, elections did not undermine the French Second Empire but rather helped to consolidate it. Had Bonaparte not made the disastrous mistake of declaring war on Prussia, there is every reason to believe that Bonapartism would have endured. This case study of the Second Empire cannot answer the question of whether elections support competitive authoritarian regimes in general, but as the original case of CA, is it relevant to that debate.[140] So too is the case of Imperial Germany, where the evidence once again points to the stability of CA.

---

[139] Otto von Bismarck, *Die gesammelten Werke*, vol. 429, 457.

[140] Daniela Donno, "Elections and Democratization in Authoritarian Regimes." *American Journal of Political Science* 57, 3 (July 2013), 703–716. Michael Miller, "Elections, Information, and Policy Responsiveness in Authoritarian Regimes." *Comparative Political Studies* 48, 6 (November 2014), 691–727. Miller concludes that "elections serve as tools of autocratic control and resilience." Michael Bernhard, Amanda Edgell and Staffan Lindberg, "Institutionalizing Electoral Uncertainty and Authoritarian Regime Survival." *European Journal of Political Research* 59, 2 (2020), 465–487, find that it takes about three electoral cycles for institutionalization. See also: Lee Morgenbesser and Thomas Pepinsky, "Elections as Causes of Democratization: Southeast Asia in Comparative Perspective." *Comparative Political Studies* 52, 1 (January 2019), 33–35.

# 5

# Wilhelmine Germany and Edwardian England

On July 30, 1914, the Austrian Foreign Minister Leopold von Berchtold received a pair of contradictory telegrams from the German government. The first, from Chancellor Bethmann Hollweg, urged the Austro-Hungarians to accept mediation with the Serbs and avert a war over the assassination of Franz Ferdinand. The second, from army chief of staff Moltke, demanded an immediate escalation of the conflict. A bewildered Berchtold reportedly asked, "Who rules in Berlin, Moltke or Bethmann?"

Berchtold was hardly the only one to wonder where power lay in Imperial Germany (1871–1918). The political system that Bismarck had designed to preserve autocracy appeared, without him in command of it, to lurch from one crisis to another under an assertive monarch and an insecure Junker class. The basic problem was that the old regime appeared incapable of stemming the electoral rise of the Social Democratic Party (SPD). In this view, Imperial Germany entered WWI as a combustible political system in which mass democracy pushed against authoritarian institutions. Many historians even see the roots of WWI in the turbulence, or the "primacy," of German domestic politics, whereby international conflict seemed to offer a respite for an embattled and unstable regime.[1]

By contrast, the standard view of the United Kingdom is that its domestic political arrangements were largely settled before WWI. The Third Great Reform of 1884, in this reading, had pushed the UK over

---

[1] See, for example, Wolfgang Mommsen, "Domestic Factors in German Foreign Policy before 1914," in J. J. Sheehan, ed., *Imperial Germany* (New York: New Viewpoints, 1976).

the democratic threshold, and with the Parliament Act of 1911, the landed elite had finally lost their veto power in the House of Lords. The liberal victory of 1906 brought a "people's budget" and two electoral campaigns where the party profited from pitting the "peers against the people." Mass democracy had triumphed over competitive oligarchy, and Great Britain entered WWI as a stable democracy at war against an unstable dictatorship.

This chapter contests this conventional framing. The Third Great Reform, in fact, left the United Kingdom far short of democracy, and different elements of the Edwardian crises were all rooted in its restrictions on political participation. Britain had one of the lowest suffrage rates among Western European states on the eve of WWI. The Parliament Act was not necessarily the final victory of representative democracy over the principle of heredity, and upon closer inspection it is not so clear the Lords' power had been eviscerated. And most alarmingly, elements within the landed elite looked prepared to fight against Irish Home Rule to the end, and – critically – had their views magnified by the leader of the conservative opposition – Andrew Bonar Law. Here I agree with Ian Lustick's thesis that the Tories and the Ulster rebels constituted a "regime threatening alliance" that "produced a constitutional crisis more serious than any to befall a British government since the seventeenth century."[2]

The question of Home Rule for Ireland brought Great Britain perilously close to both civil war and constitutional deadlock by the summer of 1914. On the very day, July 24, that the cabinet received the government's report on the failure of the Buckingham Palace Conference on Ireland, it also received news of the Austrian ultimatum to Serbia from Foreign Secretary Sir Edward Grey. The outbreak of WWI then pushed domestic politics aside in Great Britain, as it did in the other belligerent states. Although it is impossible to speculate on the course of British democracy absent WWI, this chapter argues that – at the very least – both the seriousness of the Edwardian crisis and the persistence of competitive oligarchy until the end of WWI cast doubt on the gradualist (or settled) narratives of British political development.

The political regime of Imperial Germany, by contrast, appeared immutable to most contemporary observers. This chapter begins by examining the evolution of the Sonderweg thesis in Germany (see Chapter 2 as well) and its connection to debates about democratization. It concludes

---

[2] Ian Lustick, *Unsettled States, Disputed Lands: Britain and Ireland, France and Algeria, Israel and the West Bank-Gaza* (Ithaca: Cornell University Press, 1995), 194.

that the most convincing interpretation of Wilhelmine Germany was that it was a case of stable competitive authoritarianism, and much like Bonapartist France, it would have endured had it not been for international war.

## 5.1 HISTORIOGRAPHY OF THE SECOND REICH

The first histories of Imperial Germany were unmistakably political. This was hardly surprising given the longstanding links between German academics – historians and political scientists in particular – and the state.[3] Historians like Werner Sombart and Wilhelm Riehl celebrated Germany's political differences with other European states, particularly France and Great Britain. Their project was to demonstrate that "German political order was in no way inferior to that of the west but that Germany's semi-constitutional system ... was immeasurably superior to that of western democracies."[4] The first iteration of the "Sonderweg" thesis was thus a robust defense of Germany's rejection of parliamentary democracy in favor of "constitutionalism." This view was not seriously challenged during the Weimar era, as Germany's conservative historical establishment continued to venerate the old regime.[5] German historians also overturned the view that Germany was overwhelmingly responsible for the outbreak of WWI.[6]

After World War II, however, scholars reintepreted Germany's "Sonderweg" as a case of pathological political development that produced Nazism. The new "German question" was twofold: how did things go so wrong in Germany, and what did other states do right? To recall, Dahrendorf's answer (see Chapter 2) was that "industrialization in Germany failed to produce a self-confident bourgeoisie with its own political aspirations." Since the German bourgeoisie was small and "unsure of itself and dependent in its social and political standards," Dahrendorf argues, "German society lacked the stratum that in England

---

[3] Georg Iggers, *The German Conception of History: The National Tradition of Historical Thought from Herder to the Present* (Hanover: University Press of New England, 1967).
[4] Wolfgang Mommsen, *Imperial Germany 1867–1918: Politics, Culture, and Society in an Authoritarian State* (London: Bloomsbury Academic, 2009), ix.
[5] On the German historical profession during this period, see Fritz K. Ringer, *The Decline of the German Mandarins: The German Academic Community, 1890–1933* (Hanover: Wesleyan University Press, 1969).
[6] Holger Herwig, "Clio Deceived: Patriotic Self-Censorship in Germany after the Great War." *International Security* 12, 2 (Fall 1987), 5–44.

and America, and to a lesser extent even in France, had been the force of a development in the direction of greater modernity and liberalism."[7]

This new Sonderweg thesis produced a massive literature. Since three of its proponents – Hans-Ulrich Wehler, Jürgen Kocka, and Hans-Jürgen Puhle – taught at the University of Bielefeld, this Sonderweg view became synonymous with the Bielefeld school, or simply the "Bielefelders."[8] The Bielefelders revisited the work of Eckhart Kehr and Hans Rosenberg, two historians whose critical views of Imperial Germany were iconoclastic in the 1930s. Wehler's *The German Empire* synthesized the Bielefeld school in the guise of a standard textbook on German history from 1871 to 1918. His basic proposition was deliberately provocative. "The thread which is running through this book," Wehler writes, "is the basic assumption that we cannot adequately grasp the history of the Third Reich without recourse to the history of the German Empire."[9] Wehler dismissed conservative historians like Gerhard Ritter, who argued that the German Empire was a constitutional regime. "Pseudo-constitutional semi-absolutism" was a more appropriate term, according to Wehler, for a regime where "the socio-political power structure ... with its supporting ideologies remain[ed] strong enough to impose its restrictive conditions on Germany society up to the autumn of 1918."[10] Wehler further locates a "flexible readiness on the part of the ruling elites to move with the times while all the more ruthlessly defending their traditional positions behind its façade."[11]

No sooner had this new historiography of Imperial Germany coalesced in the 1970s than two British historians, David Blackbourn and Geoff Eley, identified it as the "New Orthodoxy." What Wehler and the other Bielefelders had in common, according to Blackbourn and Eley, was that "they view 1933 as the final outcome of a particular historical continuity; they see that continuity as the product of German peculiarity; and they see a crucial element of that peculiarity in the aberrant behavior of the German bourgeoisie."[12] Blackbourn and Eley mounted two central objections to this view of German history, and the history of Imperial

---

[7] Ralf Dahrendorf, *Society and Democracy in Germany*, 52.
[8] R. Fletcher, "Recent Developments in West German Historiography: The Bielefeld School and Its Critics." *German Studies Review* 3 (1984), 451–480.
[9] Hans-Ulrich Wehler, *The German Empire 1871–1918* (Providence: Berg Publishers, 1985), 7.
[10] Ibid., 239.
[11] Ibid., 244.
[12] David Blackbourn and Geoff Eley, *The Peculiarities of German History* (New York: Oxford University Press, 1984), 287.

Germany in particular. The first was that, by reading history backward from the rise of Nazism, the Bielefelders set up the entire inquiry as the search for pathological deviations from an idealized Western (usually British, though sometimes French), norm. Blackbourn and Eley rejected the Whiggish view of British political development that representatives of the Sonderweg school, like modernization theorists before them, implicitly accepted. Drawing on historians like Tom Nairn, Blackbourn and Eley countered that "the British bourgeoisie was as spineless as the German. It failed to transform society in its own image. It failed to control the state. It failed to generate its own distinctive, combative, unifying view of the world."[13]

The second critique is embedded in the chapter titles "The Discreet Charm of the Bourgeoisie" and "A Silent Bourgeois Revolution." Blackbourn and Eley dispute the claim that the German middle class had been "refeudalized" a la Dahrendorf and Wehler. Major political and cultural changes – the growth of associational life in particular – were spearheaded by the German bourgeoisie. By looking at German history from this angle and by dropping the Whiggish view of British history as a point of comparison, Blackbourn and Eley concluded that there was in fact no "Sonderweg." Rather, Germany was typical of many modernizing societies where incomplete political rights coexist alongside a vibrant political society and rapidly growing economy.

### 5.1.1 Democratization in Imperial Germany?

Although Bismarck designed universal male suffrage for Prussia, he was clearly never a principled democrat and thought about revoking suffrage at several points, including, as we shall see later, in 1890. Given Bismarck's multiple assaults on basic democratic rights (the anti-socialist legislation, the *Kulturkampf*, the anti-Polish politics, the anti-Semitism, to name just a few), there was no prospect of meaningful democracy under his rule, and there is no serious historical dispute on that question. The controversy begins with the fall of Bismarck in 1890 and the extent to which universal suffrage and parliamentary practices were indeed creating a participatory political culture that – absent WWI – would have led to genuine democracy. As Michael Bernhard puts it: "The crux of the debate is whether competitive authoritarianism can serve as a useful

---

[13] Ibid., 136; Tom Nairn, "The English Working Class." *New Left Review* 24 (1964), 45–47; Tom Nairn, "The British Political Elite." *New Left Review* 23 (1964), 19–25.

halfway house toward a better political future – whether institutions that offer some form of open contestation, even if seriously flawed, inculcate good habits that eventually facilitate the emergence of liberal democracy, or whether they constitute a detour away from it."[14]

Sheri Berman argues that the answer is dependent on historiography.[15] Using the Blackbourn and Eley frame, she recodes Imperial Germany a "partial success" of democratization through economic development rather than a glaring exception to modernization theory. Berman stresses the high levels of political participation and vibrancy of civil society in the Second Reich. Turnout in Reichstag elections rose from barely over 50% in 1871 to 85% by 1912, and Berman interprets this as a rising sense of political efficacy. "If elections had truly been seen as meaningless," she writes, "then German citizens would not have bothered to participate in such droves."[16] As German voters became less deferential over time, and as vote totals for the two main challengers to Bismarck's conservative political coalitions – the SPD and the Zentrum – increased from election to election, the entire system appeared headed toward crisis. "A soft authoritarian political system designed to safeguard the power of traditional elites," Berman claims, "simply could no longer be reconciled with the increasing middle-and working-class political participation and the demands generated by economic development."[17]

This portrait of a democratizing Imperial Germany has both institutional and cultural components. Marcus Kreuzer analyzes the former and concludes that a significant degree of parliamentarization had occurred by the eve of WWI.[18] Building on a different historiography than the Bielefelders, Kreuzer draws on Werner Frauendienst, who claimed that the Reichstag had become increasingly willing to censure the chancellor and the minister in the late Wilhelmine period.[19] Specifically, Frauendienst noted that

Even in a constitutional system heavily dominated by the emperor, no minister had any prospects of working successfully, let alone in the long run remain in

---

[14] Bernhard, "Leadership Secrets of Bismarck," *Foreign Affairs*.
[15] Sheri Berman, "Modernization in Historical Perspective: The Case of Imperial Germany." *World Politics* 53, 3 (April 2001), 431–462.
[16] Ibid., 444.
[17] Ibid., 454.
[18] Marcus Kreuzer, "Parliamentarization and the Question of German Exceptionalism." *Central European History* 36, 3 (2003), 327–357.
[19] Werner Frauendienst, "Demokratisierung des deutschen Konstitutionalismus in der Zeit Wilhelms II." *Zeitschrift für die gesamte Staatswissenschaft* 113 (1957).

## 5.1 Historiography of The Second Reich

office, if he did not enjoy a reliable parliamentary majority. A hostile parliament could not necessarily topple him but it could become obstructionist enough ... so that the chancellor's and the emperor's decision to keep him were considerably complicated.[20]

Kreuzer also borrows from Manfred Rauh's *Federalism and Parliamentarization in Germany*, which argued that a "silent parliamentarization" had occurred in late Wilhelmine Germany as the Reichstag gained power over the Bundesrat, and Reichstag deputies began behaving like their counterparts in true parliamentary systems.[21] This occurred despite open resistance to and lukewarm support for the principle of parliamentarism itself among deputies. Kreuzer concludes that, contrary to the Wehlerite view, the Reichstag had in fact amassed a "wide range of prerogatives that significantly limited the government's ability to act unilaterally."[22] Chief among these, Kreuzer argues, was the norm of ministerial resignation following the loss of the Reichstag's confidence and the growing importance of parliamentary committees to design and review legislation. Like Berman, Kreuzer rejects the Sonderweg thesis and argues that the powers of the Imperial Reichstag compare favorably with a range of postwar democratic governing institutions in Europe.

Margaret Anderson's *Practicing Democracy: Elections and Political Culture in Imperial Germany* represents the most significant effort to reinterpret the period as one of incipient, yet meaningful, democratization.[23] It follows on the important works of Stanley Suval, Brett Fairborn, and Jonathan Sperber, each of whom argued that imperial elections were much more than a symbolic form of political participation.[24] Like Berman, Anderson characterizes Imperial Germany as a "macro political success story" in which "after fifty years of going to the polls, Germans assumed that democracy was both desirable and inevitable."[25] Her core claim is

---

[20] Ibid., 738.
[21] Manfred Rauh, *Föderalismus und Parlamentarismus im Wilhelminischen Reich* (Düsseldorf: Droste, 1973). Kreuzer notes that there has been no refutation of Rauh (344, fn. 47) and finds it curious that Frauendienst and Rauh have not received the same attention as Wehler.
[22] Kreuzer, "Parliamentarization," 343.
[23] Margaret Anderson, *Practicing Democracy* (Princeton: Princeton University Press, 2000).
[24] Stanley Suval, *Electoral Politics in Wilhelmine Germany* (Chapel Hill: University of North Carolina Press, 1985); Jonathan Sperber, *The Kaiser's Voters: Electors and Elections in Imperial Germany* (New York: Cambridge University Press, 1997); Brett Fairbairn, *Democracy in the Undemocratic State: The Reichstag Elections of 1898 and 1903* (Toronto: University of Toronto Press, 1997).
[25] Anderson, *Practicing Democracy*, 241; Ibid., 399.

that even imperfect democratic institutions that were designed explicitly to preserve authoritarianism can create a democratic political culture over the long run. Voting, in short, becomes a self-reinforcing habit that leads to demands for more democracy. Whereas Wehler and others had downplayed the significance of universal suffrage within an authoritarian state, Anderson views elections as "genuine democratic contests for the hearts and minds of the German people – even in places where the balloting itself was not yet free."[26] Such a growing normative commitment to democracy among the German electorate explains the creation of a standing parliamentary Election Commission (*Wahlprüfungskommission*) to handle the volume of complaints of electoral misconduct. Had elections been viewed as an empty exercise, Anderson argues, ordinary Germans would not have petitioned the government to investigate purported irregularities, and the state itself would not have responded by forming a robust institution charged with retrospective electoral monitoring. Nor would Germans have gained the secret ballot in 1903, an event that Anderson describes as "perhaps the most significant contribution of Germany's elected deputies to their country's democratic development."[27] Her argument is built on critical junctures like this, but also on the cumulative effects of regular democratic practice. She writes that "each plebiscitary campaign ... encouraged the very mobilization that was drawing wider and wider sections of the population into the orbit of the parties and destroying the consensual political culture for which many older Germans so longed – and on which the monarch's authority ultimately depended."[28]

To be clear, none of these scholars claim that Imperial Germany was anywhere close to a real democracy by the outbreak of WWI. What their work does do, however, is challenge the view that elections were empty political rituals and that the Reichstag was simultaneously a debating society and a rubber stamp. If they are correct, this rereading of Imperial Germany would have important implications for subsequent work on European political development and democratization more generally.

### 5.1.2 The Endurance of Competitive Authoritarianism

The strength of Anderson's book is its empirical base, and no work rivals its meticulous reconstruction of the practice of elections in Imperial Germany. Yet the first half of the book (well over 200 pages of text)

---

[26] Ibid., 305.
[27] Ibid., 242.
[28] Ibid., 411.

actually describes an entrenched system of electoral intimidation and corruption that is not far from Wehler's depiction. To be sure, documenting how social forces (landowners, the clergy, and industrialists), in addition to state power (such as Bismarck's anti-socialist legislation), is an important contribution. However, it is one in tension with the book's central thesis about the democratizing effects of universal suffrage in an authoritarian system. For if Anderson's detailed accounts of electoral coercion are merely stage-setting for the eventual emergence of democratic practices, the reader wonders why she has given it such asymmetric attention. Her conclusion, for example, that "in no other country – at least among the 'civilized lands' to which Germans liked to compare themselves – was the practice of electoral intimidation by bread lords felt to be so universal, so unvarnished, and so enduring" is arresting only in light of arguments to come.[29] Anderson anticipates this objection in her conclusion, noting that "much of our discussion in these pages has concerned itself with barriers to exercising a free vote."[30] This is an understatement, for it is difficult not to agree with Volker Berghan's comment that

> the book contains, page after page, descriptions of how elite groups in the rural and the urban parts of Germany put innumerable obstacles in the way of making a free, secret, and equal vote a reality for at least the male part of the population, never mind the other half that remained completely disenfranchised until the fall of the monarchy in 1918.[31]

Anderson makes much of the adoption of the secret ballot for elections to the Reichstag in 1903. "Neither the parties nor the government knew for certain what the consequences of the reform might be," she writes. "For all of them, it was a decision to subject their interests to uncertainty," she continues before asserting that "it is precisely the continuing uncertainty a reform like this builds into the system that constitutes, for institutionalists like Dankwart Rustow and Adam Przeworski, the decisive milestone in the transition to democracy."[32] This is true with respect to Reichstag elections, which was the most democratic aspect of the entire system. We will turn to the question of how much power the Reichstag had really amassed later, but it is first important to note how most *state* elections – including, but not limited

---

[29] Ibid., 226.
[30] Ibid., 415.
[31] Volker Berghahn, "The German Empire, 1871–1914: Reflections on the Direction of Recent Research." *Central European History* 35, 1 (2002), 78.
[32] Anderson, *Practicing Democracy*, 242.

to, Prussia's infamous three-class electoral system – were not direct and equal. Moreover, the trend was toward restrictive rather than expansive suffrages in the two decades before WWI.

### 5.1.2.1 *State Elections in Imperial Germany*

In 1868, Saxony introduced direct, secret, and equal voting. Conservatives dominated state elections until 1887, when the SPD won five seats in the Landtag of the rapidly industrializing "Red Kingdom." Following the elections of 1896, when the SPD won fifteen seats, the conservative government switched to a three-class suffrage system modeled on the Prussian variant. This reactionary measure – dubbed "Mehnert's law" as it was the design of conservative leader Dr. Paul Mehnert – included only minor attempts "to diminish the [Prussian three-class system's] reactionary reputation and plutocratic effects."[33] Mehnert's law appeared to be working too well, so "that by 1899 the Saxon Interior Minister hoped that the SPD would retain 'a few seats' in the Landtag, so that the new franchise would not appear too reactionary."[34] To no avail: by 1901 the SPD had lost all representation in the Landtag, which was startling given that the SPD was clearly the largest party in the state. In the Reichstag elections of 1903, for example, the SPD won nearly every constituency in Saxony. Even conservatives found Mehnert's law draconian, but their central pitch to the Saxon monarch was that the system had the unintended effect of shifting the locus of Saxon domestic affairs from the Landtag to the Reichstag. Saxon Foreign Minister Georg von Metzsch-Reichenbach recalled his discussion with the monarch as follows:

After [I] told him that statistics gathered under the present franchise indicated that 80 percent of voters have no influence on the choice of deputies and are therefore unrepresented in the Landtag – which contravenes principles of fairness – also that among this 80 percent are found not only social democrats but also many clergy, teachers, lower and middle-ranking officials, etc., who are embittered because of this disadvantage; and finally, that as a result of these circumstances, the Reichstag has been made into a forum for discussing the domestic political affairs of Saxony, which properly belong only in the Landtag – the king agreed that the government should proceed with electoral reform.[35]

---

[33] James Retallack, "What is to Be Done?" The Red Specter, Franchise Questions, and the Crisis of Conservative Hegemony in Saxony, 1896–1909." *Central European History* 23, 4 (December 1990), 277.
[34] Ibid., 278.
[35] Quoted in Ibid., 286.

The Saxon government announced its openness to franchise reform in 1903, but it took six years of party negotiations (primarily between different factions of the conservatives and the National Liberals) and major suffrage demonstrations organized by the SPD to finally arrive at the new electoral law of 1909.[36] Saxony replaced the three-class system with a relatively simple plural voting scheme whereby individuals cast between one and four ballots, meaning that Saxony introduced secret, direct, but unequal suffrage. The SPD was able to recapture twenty-five seats at the next election, partially confirming conservative and liberal fears that even plural voting would not be enough to stem the "red tide." The system was only tested once (in 1909), and the other Saxon parties did not coordinate versus the SPD in those elections; they may very well have done so in the next.

Hamburg was like Saxony in that the SPD did well in Reichstag elections but not in local ones. The SPD had won all three Reichstag seats in Hamburg since 1890, but elections to the Hamburg City Council (*Bürgerschaft*) were based on a property qualification, and half of all seats were reserved for "notables." Even under such a restrictive system, the SPD still managed to win twelve seats in the elections of 1904. Finding this development "alarming in the extreme," the Hamburg City Senate – whose members were elected for life – pushed for a constitutional revision in 1906 to sharply increase the property qualification.[37] The 1906 Hamburg "franchise robbery" (as the SPD deemed it) introduced plural voting whereby the wealthiest third of voters elected around twice as many deputies as the rest of the electorate. Elsewhere in Germany, Lübeck and Brunswick tightened their election laws during this period and one-third of adult males were excluded in Bavaria because they did not meet income requirements. Baden (known as the *Musterlaendle* or "Model State") and Württemberg were the only states that liberalized during this period.

The Prussian electoral system, of course, was unreformed from 1848 to 1918. According to one estimate, by 1903 the 3% of voters who belonged to the "first class" as a result of their tax contributions possessed equal electoral influence as the entire "third class" that included

---

[36] On the Dresden suffrage demonstrations, see Christoph Nonn, "Putting Radicalism to the Test: German Social Democracy and the 1905 Suffrage Demonstrations in Dresden." *International Review of Social History* 41 (1996), 183–208.

[37] Richard Evans, "Red Wednesday in Hamburg: Social Democrats, Police and Lumpenproletariat in the Suffrage Disturbances of 17 January 1906." *Social History* 4, 1 (January 1979), 3.

85% of all voters.³⁸ Everyone recognized the regressive nature of the system that, as Max Weber famously noted, "poisoned the political system as a whole." Future Chancellor Bethmann Hollweg complained in 1906 that "Our Prussian franchise is impossible to preserve in the long run ... Its Conservative majority is so banal in spirit and so complacent in its feelings of inviolable power that it must be humiliating to any progressively minded man; we *must* find a new basis."³⁹ Yet Bethmann's attempt to reform the Prussian electoral system, just like sixteen previous efforts before it, failed.⁴⁰ When he proposed a new election law for the Prussian diet in 1910 that would have eliminated the three-class system but introduced plural voting for certain groups, the chancellor was forced to table the bill after the Prussian conservatives came out against it and it became clear to him that they "would have let only a farcical bill pass."⁴¹

After the elections of 1912 made the Social Democrats the largest party in the Reichstag, Bethmann tried to reform the Prussian electoral system again. And once again he was met with a conservative opposition that viewed the three-class system as "the last bulwark against the red flood."⁴² Conservative Party leader Ernst von Heydebrand laid out the stakes in a parliamentary debate in May 1912:

Rule by the undifferentiated masses – which is the core ideal of universal equal suffrage – is an attack against the basic laws of nature, according to which the capable, the best and the worthiest [should] contribute to a country's fate; and this contribution of the ablest and the best has been the foundation of every civilization. In fact, it is impossible to conceive of a civilization that makes no such distinctions.⁴³

It is thus not surprising that "the burning issue for political parties was not parliamentary government at all, but rather the reform of the three-class franchise used for Prussian state elections." In this specific historical context, Jeffries continues, "the clamor for further democratization made parliamentarization seem a rather esoteric issue, of interest only to constitutional lawyers, historians, and newspaper columnists" on the eve of WWI.⁴⁴ This,

---

³⁸ Thomas Kühne, *Dreiklassenwahlrecht und Wahlkultur* (1994), 423.
³⁹ James Retallack, *Notables of the Right: The Conservative Party and Political Mobilization in Germany, 1876–1918* (Boston: Unwin Hyman, 1988), 163.
⁴⁰ Ziblatt, *Conservative Parties*, 215.
⁴¹ Hajo Holborn, *A History of Modern Germany, 1840–1945* (New York: Alfred A. Knopf, 1969), 365.
⁴² Quoted in Ibid., 365.
⁴³ Stenographische Berichte, Haus der Abgeordneten, May 20, 1912.
⁴⁴ Jeffries, *Contesting the German Empire*, 107.

however, was not always the case. During the 1890s there had been a serious push to create a cabinet government that could reign in an all-powerful chancellor like Bismarck.

### 5.1.2.2 The Nondevelopment of Cabinet Government

Bismarck's fall begins in the year 1888, known to historians of Germany as the "year of the three Kaisers." On March 9, 1888, William I, German Emperor and King of Prussia, died at the age of 91. Bismarck may very well have continued his role under the new Kaiser, but on June 15, 1888, Frederick III died and Wilhelm II assumed the throne at age 29. Bismarck was 73, and the generational difference was one of a host of factors that brought the new monarch into conflict with the "Iron Chancellor." A second was the presence of a camarilla that sought to dislodge Bismarck and reassert monarchic power. Three members were particularly important. The first, Prince Philip Eulenburg, was "an ultra-reactionary troublemaker" who had become Wilhelm II's best friend following a hunting trip on April 19, 1886.[45] Although he held no official position, the ubiquitous Eulenburg probably had the most influence over Kaiser Wilhelm during the 1890s. The second was General Alfred von Waldersee, who shared Eulenburg's anti-Semitic, reactionary, and occultist views. He wrote in his diary in 1886 that "we are probably facing major catastrophes" as "everywhere the masses are on the move, everywhere there is rebellion against authority, the negation of all religion, the generation of hatred and envy against those with wealth."[46] The third member of the camarilla was Friedrich von Holstein, a career civil servant in the Foreign Office, whose nondescript appearance and manner concealed his brutal and effective scheming: Waldersee once described Holstein as "one of the worst agents" and as "so clever as never to show himself in the world."[47]

These and other members of the camarilla had initially hoped that an aging Bismarck could be convinced to scrap universal suffrage. Eulenburg wrote in his diary:

> How about a demand by all the Federal Princes for a revision of the electoral law under the Chancellor's leadership? I admit that this would amount to a coup d'etat and that shooting could hardly be avoided. But I almost think that the

---

[45] Wolfgang Mommsen, *Imperial Germany 1867–1918: Politics, Culture, and Society in an Authoritarian State* (New York: Arnold, 1995), 153.
[46] Quoted in John Röhl, *The Kaiser and His Court: Wilhelm II and the Government of Germany* (New York: Cambridge University Press, 1994), 200.
[47] Steinberg, *Bismarck: A Life*, 428.

Prince [Bismarck] could be persuaded to accept such a course, for at bottom he is dissatisfied with his electoral law ... But enough, these are only fantasies after a few glasses of 'Braunschweiger Mumme.'[48]

It was not, in fact, fantasy. Gordon Craig writes that: "throughout the 1880s, as his parliamentary troubles increased, the Chancellor's mind had turned more and more frequently to the idea of cutting the Gordian knot by means of a radical revision of the constitution."[49] Bismarck told General Hans von Schweinitz in 1886 that: "It can very well happen ... that I will have to destroy what I made. People forget that the same thing can happen to the existing federation that happened to the Frankfurt Bundestag in 1866; the princes can withdraw from it and form a new one without the Reichstag."[50] Bismarck confided to the Prussian diplomat Prince Heinrich Reuss in December 1889 that:

With the eventuality of a hostile majority we must always reckon. You can dissolve three or four times, but in the end you have to smash the crockery. These questions – like that of Social Democracy and that of the relationship between Parliament and the separate states – will not be solved without a bloodbath, just as the question of German unity was not.[51]

Relations between Wilhelm and Bismarck deteriorated rapidly. When Alexander III asked Bismarck on October 12, 1889, if he was certain of his position with the Kaiser, Bismarck answered, "I am certain of the confidence of Kaiser William II and do not believe that he would ever dismiss me against my own will." Alexander III replied that "it would give me great pleasure if your optimism were to be fully confirmed."[52] The elections of March 1890 were a defeat for the Cartel parties (and thus for Bismarck) while the Social Democrats became the largest party with 19.7 percent of votes cast. Having failed to make his anti-socialist legislation permanent five weeks earlier, Bismarck sought to introduce even harsher anti-socialist legislation into the Reichstag, expecting that it would fail and provoke a crisis. He once again signaled that he might abolish universal suffrage.[53] Reviving an old idea, he suggested that "the

---

[48] John Röhl, "Staatsstreichplan oder Staatsstreichbereitschaft? Bismarck's Politik in der Entlassungskrise." *Historische Zeitschrift* 203, III (1966), 613.
[49] Craig, *Germany*, 174. Here Bismarck is referring to the German Confederation (which had its seat in Frankfurt) that existed from 1815 to 1848 and from 1851 to 1866 before being dissolved following the Austro–Prussian War of 1866.
[50] Schweinitz, *Denkwürdigkeiten*, ii. 317.
[51] Zechlin, *Staatsstreichpläne*, 26.
[52] Steinberg, *Bismarck*, 441.
[53] Hajo Holborn, *History of Modern Germany* (New York: Alfred. A. Knopf, 1969), 300.

princes ... could decide, if need be, to withdraw from the joint treaty. In this way it would be possible to free oneself from the Reichstag if the results of the elections continued to be bad."[54]

Bismarck's enemies recognized that this was a cunning plan: one member of the camarilla called it "the most masterful move in the whole game of chess: it means checkmate for the king."[55] Bismarck could claim that the new monarch was the underlying cause of the crisis and at the same time strike again at social democracy. This time it was not to be. When on March 16 Bismarck invoked an arcane cabinet order of 1852 that prevented ministers from speaking to the emperor without the chancellor being present, Wilhelm demanded that he rescind it. This was a de facto request for Bismarck's resignation, which he duly submitted on March 20, 1890. Bismarck wrote a long memorandum in defense of the cabinet order, which he described as "decisive for the position of the Minister-President and alone gave him the authority which made it possible to exercise that level of responsibility for the collective policies of the cabinet."[56] He composed this defense even as his successor – General Leo von Caprivi – had taken over and was working in the next room. Ultimately, Bismarck was replaced by the only force that could: the king. As Theodor Fontane noted at the time: "Bismarck is the greatest scorner of principle who has ever existed and a 'principle' finally brought him down, the same principle that he carried written on his banner all his life and in accordance with which he *never* acted. The power of the Hohenzollern monarchy ... was stronger than his genius and his falsehoods."[57]

Wilhelm II had certainly grabbed power away from Bismarck, yet it took a while for the "personal regime" of Wilhelm II to emerge. Röhl writes that "when Bismarck was dismissed in 1890, it was widely believed that the system could not continue without him. Some observers expected that Germany would revert to the loose federation which had existed until 1866, others that she would become a parliamentary republic, and others again that Bismarck would return to establish a kind of dictatorship."[58] The decade of the 1890s opened with all sorts

---

[54] Steinberg, *Bismarck*, 444.
[55] Ibid., 445. The camarilla member was Paul Kayser, head of the Colonial Department in the Foreign Office.
[56] Ibid., 449.
[57] Fontane, *Briefe* ii, 324.
[58] John Röhl, *Germany without Bismarck: The Crisis of Government in the Second Reich* (New York: Cambridge University Press, 1967), 9.

of political possibilities, but by the turn of the century none of them had come to pass.

General Leo von Caprivi, chief of the admiralty from 1883 to 1887, succeeded Bismarck as chancellor and prime minister of Prussia in 1890. He was not an obvious candidate: "Politics had no attraction for him, and he agreed to serve as chancellor most reluctantly."[59] Caprivi sought to make the position of chancellor less powerful, raising conservative suspicions that he was "bent upon constitutional experiments that would subvert the political and social foundations of the Prussian state."[60] Their perceptions were at odds with Caprivi's modest aspirations, for upon closer inspection: "Caprivi's aim would seem to have been to give up much of his power to the Prussian Ministers and Reich Secretaries. He wanted the Chancellor, the Prussian Ministers and State Secretaries to take decisions jointly, in the manner of a modern Cabinet."[61] Caprivi wrote later that he had "tried to encourage the Ministry of State to act like a corporate body, first so as to create a better substitute for the *personal* authority of Bismarck, second so as to be in a better position to offer resistance to the Kaiser's tendency to make sudden decisions."[62]

Bismarck had treated his ministers as his own agents. He noted that: "it is a fact that in Prussia the King commands and the Ministers obey so long as they feel they can accept the responsibility." If not, they resigned and "the King, if what he wants is not totally eccentric, will always ... find new Ministers easily enough."[63] Holstein appreciated Bismarck's handiwork in crafting the Prussian Ministry of State even while plotting to remove him in 1890. The ministers were civil servants rather than aspiring politicians, making it "more comfortable for the monarch and more efficient technically than a parliamentary Cabinet." Holstein admitted: "It is one of the Chancellor's greatest achievements to have isolated the Cabinet from parliamentary majorities and made it independent of them."[64]

Caprivi was not alone in his desire to strip power from the position of Chancellor. According to Röhl: "Bismarck's unwillingness to relinquish control over the central departments convinced many observers that the all-powerful office of Chancellor would have to be cut down to size or

---

[59] Holborn, *History of Modern Germany*, 303.
[60] Craig, *Germany*, 253.
[61] Röhl, *Germany Without Bismarck*, 67.
[62] Ibid., 65.
[63] Bismarck, *Gesammelte Werke*, XII, 324ff.
[64] Memorandum of 10 February 1890 by Holstein, Marschall, Kayser and Fischer, BA Koblenz, EP, 8, 122ff.

even abolished."⁶⁵ Caprivi gave up the Minister-Presidency of Prussia to a political rival – Count Botho Eulenburg (cousin of Philip) – in 1892 in a sincere effort to create a separation of power.⁶⁶ From the moment "Caprivi announced that he was giving the Prussian ministers the freedom that Bismarck had denied them, he lost control over them, and some of them began to intrigue against him."⁶⁷ The camarilla worked to convince Wilhelm that Caprivi was not an authentic Prussian. By the summer of 1894 there were "many voices close to the Emperor's ear that were insisting that the time was ripe for action against the forces of revolution, but that Caprivi was not the man to lead the assault."⁶⁸ Outmaneuvered, Caprivi submitted his resignation in October 1894 and was replaced by Chlodwig, Prince of Hohenlohe-Schillingfuest, whose early career successes first in the Prussian diplomatic service and then as the Minister-President of Bavaria had been replaced by indolence. His nickname was the "leafless branch." Hohenlohe had refused to become chancellor in 1890, and listed his reasons in a note dated October 1894:

1. Age, poor memory, illness.
2. Poor public speaker.
3. Unfamiliarity with Prussian laws and politics.
4. Not a soldier.
5. Insufficient means. I could probably manage without the *Statthalter's* salary, but not in Berlin. I shall be ruined. (Roehl 121)

And yet now he not only accepted the chancellorship but also took back the post of Prussian Minister-President, reversing Caprivi's decoupling of these positions from 1892 to 1894. He remained financially dependent on the Kaiser throughout his time as chancellor, and indeed his financial need was a chief reason Eulenburg had favored him for the position.⁶⁹ Hohenlohe's weak leadership was perfect for camarilla operations: Craig concludes that "under Hohenlohe the palace intrigues and the internecine warfare between the agencies that had characterized Caprivi's last years continued and, indeed became so intense as to defeat sound policy initiatives."⁷⁰ Walter Bronsart von Schellendorff (Prussian

---

⁶⁵ Röhl, *Germany without Bismarck*, 37.
⁶⁶ Bismarck had of course held the positions of Chancellor of Germany and Chancellor of Prussia simultaneously.
⁶⁷ Craig, *Germany*, 255.
⁶⁸ Ibid., 260.
⁶⁹ Röhl, *Germany without Bismarck*, 176.
⁷⁰ Craig, *Germany*, 262.

Minister of War 1893–1896) once complained that "the position of the Ministers is becoming utterly impossible. One wears oneself out in parliament trying to achieve something, and then anonymous advisors come along and ruin everything."[71]

Although Hohenlohe had not shown any of Caprivi's tendencies toward parliamentarism, he too was becoming frustrated with Wilhelm's style of rule: "The departmental heads work out questions of domestic policy without my participation because they know H.M. does not listen to my advice. I am held responsible in the press and must answer in the Reichstag for policies about which I know nothing. All personnel decisions are decided without my advice and even without my knowledge."[72] After four years of service to the king, Hohenlohe was replaced by Bernhard von Bülow, who had been Eulenburg's choice all along. Dubbed "the eel" for his unctuous behavior, Bülow lacked any principles other than his own advancement within the diplomatic corps. "It is no exaggeration to say," writes Craig, "that [Bülow] worked harder at keeping himself in the Emperor's good graces, upon which he knew that his position was absolutely dependent, than he did at any other aspect of his office, and he did not hesitate to employ the most byzantine forms of flattery to achieve his purpose."[73] He had clear anti-parliamentarian views.[74] Before his promotion, for example, Bülow promised that he:

> would be a different kind of Chancellor from my predecessors. Bismarck was a power in his own right, a Pepin, a Richelieu. Caprivi and Hohenlohe regarded or regard themselves as the representatives of the 'Government' and to a certain extent of the Parliament against His Majesty. I would regard myself as the executive tool of His Majesty, so to speak his political Chief of Staff. With me, personal rule – in the good sense – would really begin.[75]

Eulenburg seemed satisfied: "I feel that after nine years of frightening storms I have finally succeeded in steering the ship of the Kaiser's *Government* –the governmental machine – into a tolerably safe

---

[71] Röhl, *Germany without Bismarck*, 136.
[72] Hohenlohe, III, 582.
[73] Craig, *Germany*, 273.
[74] In Bülow's own words:

> I do not wish ... to advocate the parliamentary system as it is understood in the west of Europe. The worth of a constitution does not depend on the way it reacts on the party system. Constitutions do not exist for parties, but for the state. Considering the peculiarities of our government, the parliamentary system would not be a suitable form of constitution for us.

Hewitson, "Kaiserreich in Question," 766.
[75] Röhl, *Germany without Bismarck*, 194.

## 5.1 Historiography of The Second Reich

harbour ... The matter is now in the able hands of Bülow, whom the Kaiser thinks of as 'his Bismarck.'"[76] Opponents of the regime recognized its strength as well. The liberal Friedrich Naumann lamented in *Demokratie und Kaisertum*, published in 1900, that:

> There is no stronger force than the Kaiser. The very complaints of the anti-Kaiser democrats about the growth of personal absolutism are the best proof of this fact, for these complaints are not pure invention but are based on the repeated observation that all policy, foreign and internal, stems from the will and word of the Kaiser. No monarch of absolutist times ever had so much real power as the Kaiser has today. He does not achieve everything he wants, but it is still more than anybody would have believed possible in the middle of the last century. That century, whose middle years echoed with the dreams of a German republic, ended with more power in the Kaiser's hands than even Barbarossa possessed.[77]

The *Daily Telegraph* affair of November 1908 exposed just how little parliamentarization – the growth of cabinet government and parliamentary sovereignty – had progressed eight years later. It began when the Kaiser allowed the publication of a year-old interview in the British newspaper *Daily Telegraph* in which he accused the British of being "mad, mad, mad as March hares." This would have constituted a clear violation of the norm that the king confer with the chancellor before releasing statements on foreign policy. Yet Wilhelm had uncharacteristically followed proper procedure and given a copy to Bülow before publication. The problem was that Bülow never read the document, though he was loath to admit that to the Reichstag as it would, in the words of the Austrian ambassador, highlight the *"cascade de negligences"* that sparked the crisis.[78]

There was much debate about the affair in the Reichstag, but when the critical moment arrived, the National Liberals stopped short of pushing for a vote of no-confidence in the chancellor. This would have touched the monarchy, and "the National Liberals were not yet ready to question the powers or the wisdom of the monarchy."[79] For Craig, the *Daily Telegraph* affair represents another of the "lost opportunities that marked the course of Germany's constitutional history" when political parties, "momentarily united in a demand for a diminution of the royal prerogative, a greater degree of responsibility of the Chancellor to the

---

[76] Eulenburg's Notes on the Year 1898, BA Koblenz, EP, 50, 1a ff.
[77] Friedrich Naumann, *Demokratie und Kaisertum*, 167f.
[78] Craig, *Germany*, 284.
[79] Beverly Heckart, *From Bassermann to Bebel: The Grand Bloc's Quest for Reform in the Kaiserreich, 1900–1914* (New Haven: Yale University Press, 1974), 76.

Reichstag, and the granting to that body of the right of interpellation, did not remain so."[80] The proposed changes from the *Daily Telegraph* affair were subsequently buried in committee.[81] Bülow did manage to coax a promise from the Kaiser that he would respect constitutional procedure in the future, and Wilhelm retreated from public view for a while. The real political casualty, however, was Bülow: the Kaiser waited until enough time had passed, then replaced him with Theobald von Bethmann Hollweg.

Two other lost opportunities, according to Beverly Heckart, were two short-lived experiments in opposition party coordination. Friedrich Naumann had promoted the idea of a "Grand Bloc" from "Bebel to Bassermann" (the leaders of the Social Democrats and National Liberals, respectively) to unite the forces in favor of parliamentary government in his book *Demokratie und Kaisertum*, first published in 1900. Heckart argues this aspiration was temporarily realized in Baden from 1910 to 1914 and nationally from 1912 to 1913. She also suggests that the experiment might have been repeated had the war not intervened.[82] Published when the "New Orthodoxy" of the Bielefelders was at its height, Heckart's book received mixed reviews among historians. Ekkehard-Teja Wilke noted that "Heckart's optimistic assessment for the possibility of Wilhelmian Germany evolving into a parliamentary democracy is unsubstantiated."[83] She also gives "temporary, improvised cooperation an appearance of consistency it lacked (Hunt)."[84] Geoff Eley claims that her argument about "tentative parliamentary overtures" are built on "superficial generalities."[85] And Wilke again: "Naumann's slogan 'from Bassermann to Bebel' actually seems to have been more the wishful thinking of a few politicians and a convenient façade for parties lacking the courage of their clichés than a serious guide to political action."

---

[80] Craig, *Germany*, 284.
[81] Heckart, *Bassermann to Bebel*, 207.
[82] Ibid., 278. Specifically, she writes: "If the war and its effect had not occurred, however, the failure of 1910 [the collapse of the Grand Bloc] could not be viewed as the final act in the peacetime drama of reform. The problem would have continued to exist, and the Grand Bloc would have been the only group capable of achieving its solution."
[83] Ekkehard-Teja Wilke, *American Historical Review* 81, 2 (April 1976), 409.
[84] Hunt points out that Heckart "tends to employ the term 'Grand Bloc' to denote any cooperation among the non-conservative parties. See Hunt, "The Bourgeois Middle in German Politics." *Central European History* 11, 1 (1978), 94.
[85] Geoff Eley, "Review of From Bassermann to Bebel." *The Historical Journal* 19, 1 (March 1976), 301.

## 5.1 Historiography of The Second Reich

These all seem to be unfair readings of her argument, which is more about why the Grand Bloc was unlikely to succeed at the national level, and why even in the liberal bastion of Baden its existence was short-lived. Indeed, "many passages in the book document that such a process was unrealistic."[86] For example, she writes that "in the spring of 1914, the schemes of *Demokratie und Kaisertum*, so promising a short time before, seemed no closer to achievement than when Naumann had first proposed them."[87] She also argues at length why such efforts were doomed to fail: "The nationalism of the National Liberals during the decisive crisis of the monarchy explains why a permanent Grand Bloc, and hence an evolution toward parliamentary democracy, was almost impossible in peace or war."[88] Only one reviewer seems to have registered these points, finding that the book "makes a genuine contribution to our empirical understanding of the *failure* [not the qualified success] of parliamentary government in Germany."[89]

The collapse of the Grand Bloc was in fact part of a more general failure of the opposition in Wilhelmine Germany to fully support parliamentary government. Even among liberals, support for it was weak.[90]

Although most left liberals in Prussia shared Rathenau's support for electoral reform, responsible government, and the rule of law, they were also, like him, 'visibly patriotic and not *insistent* on full parliamentary rule.' When these men added up the numbers, they saw no need 'to trouble their heads' about the imminent introduction of a system whereby shifting parliamentary majorities could force a change of government. As Friedrich von Payer declared in December 1908: 'We can leave this question to future generations; for we lack the unavoidable prerequisite for it, namely a closed, capable, enduring majority, as in England.'[91]

Only the SPD was serious about parliamentary government and universal male and female suffrage, but there were splits within it as well. Orthodox Marxists like Rosa Luxembourg had come to see

---

[86] Wilke, 409.
[87] Heckart, *Bassermann to Bebel*, 268.
[88] Ibid., 283.
[89] Thomas Knapp, "Review of Bassermann to Bebel." *History: Review of New Books* 3, 7 (1975), 182.
[90] On the liberals and the question of parliamentary government, see Alastair Thompson, *Left Liberals, the State, and Popular Politics in Wilhelmine Germany* (New York: Oxford University Press, 2000).
[91] James Retallack, *The German Right, 1860–1920: Political Limits of the Authoritarian Imagination* (Toronto: University of Toronto Press, 2006), 122.

parliamentarism as an adversary before the "great schism" that divided the German left. Even revisionists viewed parliamentarism as a means to an end. The SPD's view of the parliamentary system as the "characteristic institution of the capitalist order" helps explains its "tenuous support for a parliamentary system of government."[92]

In sum, it seems difficult to defend Kreuzer's claim that "ministerial responsibility gradually expanded from 1890 onward (338)." Rauh's thesis of "silent parliamentarization" has, according to James Retallack, been "rightly discarded" by subsequent historians.[93] Contrary to Rauh's claim that the Empire was "on the threshold of a parliamentary system" at the outbreak of WWI, Christopher Schönberger argues that in fact "the Empire was further from parliamentarization at its end than it had been in its early years."[94]

An article from the *American Political Science Review* from 1911 by W. J. Shepard makes similar points.[95] The author notes three "signs of change" in Imperial Germany, but then proceeds to argue that each is illusory. The first was rising discontent at the personal regime of Kaiser Wilhelm. "There is no doubt," Shepard reports, "that the feeling of dissatisfaction and protest at the personal regime is almost universal."[96] But "this protest and discontent at arbitrary personal government does not, however, imply a desire for parliamentary responsibility." Rather, Shepard speculates, "it may mean, and among large sectors of the people does mean, nothing more than a demand for a return to Bismarckian traditions – a restoration to the Chancellor of the functions of a Grand Vizier." Moreover, expressions of outrage, as during the *Daily Telegraph* affair, had, at best, only a short-term restraining influence on the Kaiser's behavior.

---

[92] Mark Hewitson, "The *Kaiserreich* in Question: Constitutional Crisis in Germany before the First World War." *The Journal of Modern History* 73, 4 (December 2001), 761, 757.

[93] Retallack, *German Right*, 116: Two critiques of Kreuzer raise similar objections. See Jonathan Sperber, "Comments on Marcus Kreuzer's article." *Central European History* 36, 3 (2003), 359–366; Kenneth Ledford, "Comparing Comparisons: Disciplines and the Sonderweg." *Central European History* 36, 3 (2003): See also the extended critique of the "parliamentarization" thesis in Volker Berghahn, *Imperial Germany 1871–1918: Economics, Society, Culture and Politics* (New York: Berghahn Books, 2005), 177–203.

[94] Christopher Schönberger, "Die überholte Parlamentarisierung. Einflussgewinn und fehlende Herrschaftsfähigkeit des Reichstag im sich demokratisierenden Kaiserreich." *Historische Zeitschrift* 272 (2001), 655.

[95] W. J. Shepard, "Tendencies toward Ministerial Responsibility in Germany." *American Political Science Review* 5, 1 (February 1911), 57–69.

[96] Ibid., 59.

"Thus far it is evident," he writes, "that the national revolt against the personal regime has produced no perceptible effect upon the mind of the Emperor."[97]

The second trend was increased ministerial responsibility, which Shepard argues "has been greatly exaggerated." He acknowledges that "there has grown up ... the practice of interpellating the Chancellor" but stresses that it "is entirely an extra-legal development."[98] He is pessimistic about any further movements along those lines, as for him, "it is clear that the obstacles to an effective enforcement of a responsibility by the Reichstag upon the Chancellor are well-nigh insuperable." The key issue was the power of the purse: "The Reichstag's control over the budget, the power over supply, which has been in England the most important instrument for establishing parliamentary domination, cannot be used as a sanction for enforcing ministerial responsibility."[99] And unlike in the United Kingdom, the monarch still acted like a chief executive: "[Wilhelm's] chancellors have been mere personal secretaries with very little power of initiative. To do the Kaiser's bidding has been almost their sole function."[100]

Democratization was the third trend. Whereas Kreuzer considers Shepard an "optimist" in this respect, I read his argument quite differently.[101] After acknowledging some suffrage expansions in other states of the Reich – particularly Baden – Shepard turns to the critical case of Prussia. Here he is dubious that any reform is possible given the power of the Junker elite: "The three-class system is the citadel of their powers; its abandonment would give the enemy possession of the entire fortress."[102] They would never surrender power willingly, and "even with the entire Left united it is difficult to see how the forces of reaction can be dislodged without a resort to force."[103] The outlook for peaceful democratic change in Imperial Germany was thus quite poor: "a voluntary abnegation of the advantages which *Junkertum* and *Beaurokratie* now enjoy is scarcely to be looked for. The application of some form of compulsion will probably be necessary."[104]

---

[97] Ibid., 60.
[98] Ibid., 61.
[99] Ibid., 63.
[100] Ibid., 59
[101] Kreuzer, "Parliamentarization," 332.
[102] Shepard, "Tendencies," 66.
[103] Ibid., 67.
[104] Ibid., 66.

### 5.1.2.3 The "State within the State"

This was a prescient reading, for it was only after total military capitulation that democratization occurred in Germany. It is difficult to exaggerate the role of the military in defending the authoritarian order. Although it never attempted a coup, it served as an enormous constraint on political action. As Berghahn explains:

> The workings of the Reich Constitution ... can only be fully understood if we take into account that, in principle, the Kaiser had at his disposal the use of military force and could set in motion a violent solution to any domestic political conflict. Even if this instrument was never used, the threat of it was a powerful political tool to wield.[105]

The Reichstag was dissolved four times – three times because of military expenditure.[106] We have seen how Bismarck contemplated a coup d'etat in 1890 and how multiple critical actors in the Imperial government considered it seriously throughout the 1890s. Historians of the period are united on this point. "From Bismarck's fall until the acceptance of the Navy Bill in 1898, the threat of a coup d'etat overshadowed Berlin politics."[107]

The Prussian army was an antidemocratic institution. Indeed, an officer could not be both a soldier and a democrat, as a training manual explained:

> the officer in reserve status must never, while an officer, belong to a party which places itself in opposition to the government of our Emperor or of the *Landesherr*. If he feels conscientiously restricted by this, then he must request his dismissal. As an officer, he is his imperial master's 'man' in the old German sense of the word. Under no circumstances must he place himself in opposition to him. On the other hand, however, he is fully justified in making use of his political rights and intervening in the political struggle on behalf of the objectives which the *Landerherr* and the Emperor pursue.[108]

This conformed fully to William II's view of the military. According to Prince Eulenburg: "Emperor William II (who, unlike his highly educated progenitors, 'finished' his education as an officer in the First Regiment of the Guards) sucked in like an infant at the breast the tradition that every Prussian officer is not only the quintessence of honour, but of all good

---

[105] Berghahn, *Imperial Germany*, 179.
[106] Jeffries, *Contesting the German Empire*, 98.
[107] Röhl, *Germany without Bismarck*, 277.
[108] Gordon Craig, *The Politics of the Prussian Army* (New York: Oxford University Press, 1955), 236.

## 5.1 Historiography of The Second Reich

breeding, all culture, and all intellectual endowment."[109] Wilhelm promised he would never "seek popularity with the street mob at the expense of my army."[110] He imitated the military's disdain for the Reichstag, once referring to it as "a troop of monkeys and a collection of blockheads and sleepwalkers."[111] In a letter to the Tsar, he called Reichstag deputies "scoundrels without a fatherland" that were behaving "more and more like pigs."[112]

It is therefore not shocking that Wilhelm II appeared open to a Staatsreich from the beginning of his rule. The Kaiser told Eulenburg during a North Sea Cruise during the summer of 1891 that he "did not dream of avoiding a conflict" with the Reichstag and that he was only prepared to postpone a coup d'etat for three years. The Kaiser realized that there would be opposition at first, but that "things will be different later, when the Reichstag has absorbed a new generation."[113] Another serious attempt followed in 1894 when Botho Eulenburg (cousin of Philip) introduced a bill against 'revolutionary tendencies' into the Reichstag. It was clear that a bill of this kind would be defeated: Eulenburg's motive was undoubtedly to begin a coup d'etat policy with a view to overthrowing the chancellor.

Although a Staatsreich did not occur, Eulenburg's chilling memorandum of August 1, 1896, makes clear that it was really a permanent plan. In it, Eulenburg lays out a number of scenarios and their ramifications. He drew a crucial distinction between a "First Combination, in case His Majesty does not want a policy of violence" and a "Second Combination, in case His Majesty does not wish to avoid a Policy of Violent Clarification, or is forced to accept one." The latter course, Eulenburg imagined, might unfold as follows:

> In this case Bülow would have to be spared, since lots of new men would be required when the violent struggles are over. It is not impossible that even Bronsart could survive without a constitutional conflict, but the prospects are slight. The appointment of a battle-hungry Minister of War to the Chancellorship implies ipso facto that the Government has thrown in the gauntlet and is turning sharply to so-called Reaction, and this would lead to the strongest opposition throughout the whole Reich, even to the dissolution of the Reichstag and certainly to a tremendous increase in the difficulties with the Bavarians, Württembergers and Saxons.[114]

[109] Ibid., 241.
[110] Kaiser to Eulenburg, May 4, 1896.
[111] Craig, *Germany*, 292.
[112] W. Goetz (ed.), *Briefe Wilhelms II. an der Zaren*, 290.
[113] Quoted in Röhl, *Germany without Bismarck*, 72.
[114] Eulenburg memorandum, August 1, 1896, BA Koblenz, EP, 43, 547ff.

Waldersee's January 1897 memorandum to the Kaiser was more optimistic about the chances of immediate success than Eulenburg's:

> In view of the tremendous growth of the Social Democratic organization, it seems ... certain that the time is approaching when the power of the State will have to do battle with that of the working masses ... But if the battle is inevitable ... the State has nothing to gain by waiting ... It is in the State's interest not to allow the Social Democratic leaders to choose when to begin the great reckoning: rather it should do everything possible to force an early decision. The State is certainly still strong enough to suppress any rising at present.[115]

The Kaiser told General Waldersee in response: "I know you will do the job well if shooting becomes necessary."[116] Around the same time, Hohenlohe also was informed of a plan to end universal suffrage and fill the Reichstag with representatives from state diets. He reported that Wilhelm answered "all objections with the remark that nothing could be achieved without a struggle, that it was his duty to safeguard Germany's military strength, and that he was prepared and determined to fight a life or death struggle."[117] According to Craig: "By the middle of 1897 a complete breakdown of the constitutional system seemed at hand, and rumours of an imminent coup d'etat were more widespread than at any other time since the beginning of the reign."[118]

These constant threats of coup d'etats had direct – and profoundly negative – effects on the morale of the Reichstag. Centre party leaders noted in 1897 that "never before have we been threatened so openly with a coup d'etat."[119] Those deputies who were still reluctant to accept the Government's new policies were persuaded to do so by their fear of a coup d'etat. Looking back in June 1898, Karl Bachem justified his party's support for the Government by pointing to Miquel's plans for replacing two-thirds of the Reichstag with representatives from the State parliaments. The only way of stopping him from taking this step, Bachem claimed, was for the Centre to cooperate. "On two previous occasions – 1887 and 1893 – we had fallen into the trap of a Reichstag dissolution. *We* were returned, but the bills went through all the same. Should we have made that hopeless attempt yet again? There was now a real danger of a violent alteration of the electoral law."[120]

---

[115] Quoted in Röhl, *Germany without Bismarck*, 218.
[116] Ibid.
[117] Ibid., 220.
[118] Craig, *Politics of the Prussian Army*, 250.
[119] Quoted in Röhl, *Germany without Bismarck*, 215.
[120] Ibid., 250.

The status of the army as "a state within the state" was reaffirmed during the Zabern (Saverne) affair in the borderland of Alsace-Lorraine.[121] During a lecture to recruits on the nature of Alsatian civilians in late October 1913, a twenty-year-old lieutenant named von Forstner nearly single-handedly sparked a civil–military conflict. Specifically, von Forstner turned to a soldier who had previously been disciplined for knifing a civilian and said: "if you knife an Alsatian 'wackes' you won't get 2 months for each dirty 'wackes' you bring me – you'll get 10 marks."[122] Wackes was an ethnic slur for Alsatian and was offensive enough that its use was banned in the German military. Thus, the publication of von Forstner's remarks in the local newspaper (the *Zabern Anzeiger*) on November 6, 1913, sparked a series of public disorders. Civilians heckled von Forstner in the streets, and von Forstner responded with more obscenities that were once again reported in the local press. Von Forstner was disciplined with six days of house arrest, but the public disorder continued and the garrison commander, Colonel von Reuter, declared martial law on November 28. Specifically, Reuter invoked an 1820 royal order that authorized the military to seize control from local civilian authorities should the latter be unable to quell disturbances. Dozens of Alsatians were arrested for the charge of laughing at military officers, and when von Reuter's actions came under national scrutiny three weeks later, he became defensive and vowed to escalate if necessary: "Look here, the people are standing there again. If the Schlossplatz and the Hauptstrasse are not kept free, if people hang around and laugh, then I shall take action. There will be shooting."[123]

Kitchen notes in his account of the Zabern affair that "although this incident seems trivial, and many much more serious cases of this type had happened previously, relations between the army and the civilian population had become so bad that a wave of indignation spread throughout the country."[124] Wilhelm II interfered immediately and directly by hastily approving the military's report that blamed the entire incident on the media and Alsatian activists. "The affair grew into a national scandal when it became clear that the Kaiser, as commander-in-chief, was not prepared to accept even the slightest criticism of 'his' military."[125] When another (unarmed) civilian mocked Forstner on the street on December 2, the young lieutenant slashed him with his sword, causing severe injuries and escalating the crisis.

---

[121] The phrase is from Craig, *Politics of the Prussian Army*.
[122] Martin Kitchen, *The German Officers Corps, 1890–1914* (Oxford: Clarendon Press, 1968), 197.
[123] Quoted in Ibid., 199.
[124] Ibid.
[125] Berghahn, *Imperial Germany*, 252.

154   5 Wilhelmine Germany and Edwardian England

The Reichstag discussed the Zabern affair during parliamentary sessions on December 3–4, 1913. The heart of the debate was whether the army stood above the law. The problem was not just the pugilistic Forstner, but also the draconian Reuter, who had no basis, it was argued, for declaring martial law. The Social Democrats spoke of a military dictatorship and demanded the resignation of Chancellor Bethmann Hollweg. The chancellor believed that the army was at fault but could only say that excesses had been committed and that "the king's uniform must be respected under any circumstance."[126] Politicians across the party spectrum found the army in the wrong, and a (nonbinding) vote of no-confidence against Bethmann Hollweg passed by 293 to 54.

As with many of the other potential turning points in Imperial Germany, there are alternative readings of the Zabern affair. David Schoenbaum tried to argue that Zabern brought Wilhelmine Germany closer to, rather than further from, parliamentary democracy.[127] He concludes that: "Zabern showed imperial Germany to be neither significantly more nor less repressive than other Western societies ... There was reason to note and deplore the easy brutality of a Prussian lieutenant. There were also grounds to admire the spontaneous dismay of a Germany outraged by the relative inconvenience caused a remote handful of provincials by their overnight arrest."[128] The outcry in parliament, the censure of Bethmann Hollweg, and the abrogation of the 1820 royal decree were all signs of the growing power of the Reichstag.

Peter Paret's review of Schoenbaum's study argues that this is the minority view. The supposed achievements of the Zabern affair, Paret writes, "seem feeble vindications, similar to the so-called moral victories that had followed on the earlier scandals, such as the *Daily Telegraph* affair, which never touched, let alone altered, the structure of power."[129] We should also recall that "the Kaiser remarked with glee that he could simply ignore the vote of no-confidence."[130] Moreover, "The subsequent debate showed that in the face of such a radical demand parties other than the Social Democrats were unwilling to continue to attack

---

[126] Reichstag Debate, December 3, 1913.
[127] David Schoenbaum, *Zabern 1913: Consensus Politics in Imperial Germany* (London: George Allen and Unwin, 1982).
[128] Ibid., 184.
[129] Peter Paret, review of Zabern Affair. *Journal of Modern History* 56, 3 (September 1983), 577–579.
[130] Berghahn, *Imperial Germany*, 253.

the government and thereby force through a major constitutional change."[131] Heckart writes that "it was a measure of their monarchism that none of the German parties suggested a constitutional change during the Zabern Affair" and continues that "no one wanted to exploit the Zabern Affair to increase the powers of the Reichstag."[132] Craig offers a similarly damning verdict:

> Not used to authority, they were no more inclined than they had been at the time of the *Daily Telegraph* affair to make experiments in exercising it; the idea of using the boycott to force changes in the government frightened them ... The middle class parties, which were composed of people who admired the military and imitated its values, could not be moved to more than momentary irritation over its faults, and a Reichstag that had voted the biggest peacetime military budget in history in October 1913 was not a body that was capable of disciplining the army three months later.[133]

Thus far I have argued that the Wehlerite view of Imperial Germany as a deeply authoritarian state remains far more convincing than alternative interpretations. Many scholars cede this point while still suggesting that the combination of universal suffrage, monarchism, and militarism was highly combustible. An entire strain of historiography has explored how the "primacy of domestic politics," particularly the need to stop the march of Social Democracy, led to foreign policy adventurism and, ultimately, the catastrophe of WWI. Critics of the Sonderweg, as we have seen, also rejected Wehler's static view of Imperial Germany. If their case for "silent parliamentarization" or "practicing democracy" makes too much of particular episodes of political liberalization, perhaps they are still correct in their view that there were long-run democratic trends that would have eventually led to either democratization or an authoritarian crackdown.

Mark Hewitson casts doubt on this proposition by demonstrating that the political system rested on firm ideational foundations.[134] Hewitson finds that political elites – including vocal opponents of the regime – "had accepted the institutional structure of the *Kaiserreich* as the invisible framework of their thought" during the Second Reich's first three

---

[131] Martin Kitchen, *The German Officers Corp 1890–1914* (Oxford: Clarendon Press, 1968), 210–211.
[132] Heckart, *Bassermann to Bebel*, 253–254.
[133] Craig, *Germany*, 300.
[134] Mark Hewitson, "The *Kaiserreich* in Question: Constitutional Crisis in Germany before the First World War." *The Journal of Modern History* 73, 4 (December 2001), 725–780.

and a half decades. Then, according to Hewitson, there was a period of debate running from roughly the *Daily Telegraph* to the Zabern affairs. Rather than undermining the legitimacy of the system, however, these debates consolidated ideological support for the regime. He concludes: "When, during critical junctures between 1908 and 1914, German politicians were faced with the prospect of crossing the threshold between a constitutional and a parliamentary system of government, all except those of the SPD refused to do so."[135]

German politicians and academics considered two basic regime types – parliamentary and constitutional – to be the only possible ones for their state. Russian despotism, Swiss direct democracy, and American representative democracy were viewed as impossible developmental paths. That left France and Britain as points of comparison. The first was rejected and derided.[136] The second was deemed both a "swamp of corruption" and a product of British exceptionalism. Delbrück argued that both cases demonstrated how parliamentarism led "self-perpetuating oligarchies" and that for him: "Germany constitutes the real, archetypal obverse of the parliamentary states."[137] He was echoing themes from Treitschke's speech marking the 25th anniversary of Wilhelm's I regime in 1886 when he said:

We do not consider that we have found the only true form of constitutional system; but the only possible form for Germany, which the history of this century teaches on every page, is a free popular representation, which seeks to reach agreement with a free crown and does not claim the right to subordinate the monarchy to its own will.[138]

Hewitson concludes that: "most Germans had acknowledged during the early twentieth century that Germany's constitutional regime was a discrete, functioning system of government, separate from western European parliamentarism."[139] Rather than moving toward parliamentarism, "most deputies, including Naumann, were content to consolidate Germany's constitutional regime rather than raise the prospect of a parliamentary alternative."[140] Max Weber's view on

---

[135] Ibid., 767.
[136] Mark Hewitson, *National Identity and Political Thought in Germany: Wilhelmine Depictions of the French Third Republic, 1890–1914* (Oxford: Oxford University Press, 2000).
[137] Hans Delbrück, *Regierung und Volkswille* (Berlin: Georg Stilke, 1914), 126.
[138] Hewitson, "*Kaiserreich* in Question," 730.
[139] Ibid., 780.
[140] Ibid., 772.

parliamentarism was that "its solution would perhaps be consigned to the distant future."[141]

In sum, of the two books written in 1973 – Wehler's *The German Empire* and Rauh's *Federalism and Parliamentarianism in Wilhelmine Germany* – the arguments of the former remain persuasive while those of the latter do not. This is not to say that Sonderweg debate has not been productive, or that it is even over.[142] It is time, however, to reject the view that Wilhelmine Germany was a rapidly democratizing society. The balance of evidence supports Holborn's conclusion that "fundamentally the structure of state and society that Bismarck had built remained unchanged to the end of the Empire in 1918."[143] Retallack points out the inherent difficulty in accepting this view for (many) historians:

> As historians, we are inclined to think that right-wing diehards deserved the dismal fate that awaited them at the polls. We don't like their politics, and so we tend to see the tide of world history arrayed against them. But as German scholars have pointed out with increasing vehemence in the last half-decade, this emphasis on failure does not take full account of the persistent power of those institutions of authority in Imperial Germany on whose survival or demise the fortunes of the German Right hinged.[144]

Political scientists have learned much from historians about Imperial Germany. It is less clear what, if anything, historians of the period have learned from political scientists. The intellectual exchange has been mostly in one direction. In part this occurred because the Sonderweg debate occurred at a time when comparative politics as a field classified regimes as *either* democratic or authoritarian.

Much of the dissonance in the historiography arises from a juxtaposition of the "antidemocratic, anti-parliamentary, and anti-liberal encumbrances from the Bismarckian age with an image of Wilhelmine society and culture as extraordinarily pluralistic, reformist, and modern."[145] Competitive authoritarianism allows for all these trends to exist simultaneously, and classifying Imperial Germany as such can help resolve some intractable debates. The Reichstag need not be understood as either toothless or rapidly aggrandizing if we accept that quasi-democratic institutions in CA regimes are usually neither rubber stamps nor democratic

---

[141] Ibid., 754.
[142] Jürgen Kocka, "Looking Back on the Sonderweg." *Central European History* 51, 1 (March 2018), 137–142.
[143] Holborn, *Modern Germany*, 296.
[144] Retallack, *German Right*, 13.
[145] Ibid., 23.

incubators. We can reject the proposition that Imperial Germany would have either democratized or suffered a coup d'etat in the absence of WWI if we consider the growing evidence that competitive authoritarian regimes can be durable rather than transitory. According to Holborn: "The pseudo-constitutional system that Bismarck created even worked in the hands of his inferior successors. Only two eventualities could have broken its hold." The first was a coalition between the Social Democrats and the bourgeoisie, and that coalition repeatedly failed to form before the war. The second eventuality was "a decisive defeat of the army that would jeopardize the whole nation."[146] As in Bonapartist France, it was loss in war that led to the collapse of competitive authoritarianism in Imperial Germany.

## 5.2 THE EDWARDIAN CRISIS IN BRITAIN

The Edwardian period does not figure prominently in most studies of British democratization.[147] Collier, drawing on Pugh, claims "by 1884 Britain could be said to have become a mass democracy with the working-class constituency a majority of voters."[148] This view, I argue later, seriously overestimates the degree of democracy in Britain until the Parliament Act of 1911. In one of the most trenchant and enduring analyses of the period, George Dangerfield posited that the crises of the Edwardian period amounted to the "strange death of liberal England."[149] Had it not been for the outbreak of WWI, Dangerfield argues, Britain may very well have experienced the collapse of parliamentary democracy and civil war. Although not all elements of Dangerfield's thesis remain persuasive today (the threats to political order from both labor and suffragette movements appear overblown), there is a historical consensus that there was a significant danger that Ulster would go to war to prevent Irish Home Rule. Compared to previous cases of domestic unrest, the old regime appeared genuinely unable to manage it. As scholars put it: "It used to be an old staple university exam question: *When did Britain*

---

[146] Holborn, *Modern Germany*, 297.
[147] Ziblatt (*Conservative Parties*) is an important exception. He views Edwardian England as a "settled democracy" that flirted with democratic breakdown. My interpretation of the Edwardian period is similar, though I contend that the chances of democratic backsliding or a democratic breakdown were higher than he suggests.
[148] Collier, *Paths toward Democracy*, 96.
[149] George Dangerfield, *The Strange Death of Liberal England 1910–1914* (London: Penguin, 1961).

*come nearest to revolution: 1832, 1866, 1912, 1919, 1926...?* The correct answer is none of these, but spring and summer 1914."[150]

### 5.2.1 Democratic Deficits after the Third Reform 1884

The electoral reform of 1884 has not received nearly the scholarly attention of either 1832 or 1867.[151] Once again, the Whig claim that "the Franchise Act of 1884 went almost all the way to universal male suffrage" needs to be seriously revised. As Neal Blewitt notes in his study of the franchise from 1885 to 1918, "historians have tended to over-emphasize the achievement of the reforms of the mid-1880s and to overlook the anomalies remaining. They have magnified the triumph of principles, minimized the reality of the practice."[152] Given that only 59 percent of adult males possessed the vote in 1911, we need to consider why the Third Great Reform failed to mark the advent of universal male suffrage.

Part of the answer is that universal suffrage was never its intention. Gladstone supported "the broad principle that the enfranchisement of capable citizens, be they few or be they many – and if they be many so much the better – gives an addition of strength to the state."[153] The key word here is "capable": Gladstone was still offering the same argument as liberals did in 1832 about fitness for the franchise (see Chapter 3). Suffrage remained based on qualifications, even if those qualifications had multiplied to now include the majority of the adult male population. Ascertaining who did and did not meet the various parameters was complicated. J. A. Pease, who was preparing the Franchise and Registration Bill of 1912, lamented that "the intricacy of our franchise laws is without parallel in the history of the civilized world."[154] To his chagrin, he found that there were eleven distinct ways of qualifying for the franchise, with a total of nineteen different variations.[155] Many adult males still fell outside of them altogether. Domestic servants, adult sons living with their parents, and recipients of poor relief were some of the largest

---

[150] Iain McLean and Alistair McMillan, *State of the Union* (Oxford: Oxford University Press, 2005), 126.
[151] Ziblatt is an exception and considers 1884 to be a critical juncture. Cannadine concurs that 1884 was profound.
[152] Neal Blewett, "The Franchise in the United Kingdom, 1885–1918." *Past and Present* 32 (1965), 27.
[153] Gladstone, *Hansard*, February 28, 1184, p. 108.
[154] Quoted in Blewett, "Franchise," 30.
[155] Goldstein, *Political Repression*, 10.

disenfranchised groups. Concerns about vote tampering and corruption also meant the exclusion of certain categories of state and election officials. Blewitt estimates that the franchise provisions excluded at least 12 percent of the total adult male population, although the true figure is certainly higher, as the author was unable to calculate the number of sons living under their parents' roofs.

It was, above all, the system of registration – inefficient, arcane, and burdensome to the would-be franchise holder – that "explains the gap between the franchise principles of 1884 and their implementation in the ensuing three decades."[156] Politicians at the time recognized it as anachronistic. According to one writing in 1892, "The existing registration law in this country is utterly bad. It belongs to a time when a vote was a privilege and not a right, and when it had the effect of keeping people off the register."[157] Another noted that the system was "so replete with technicalities, complications, and anomalies, that every obstacle is put in the way of getting on, and every facility exists for getting struck off, the register."[158] For example, since several of the franchise categories (occupation, household, lodger, and service) required that the registrant possess the qualification for a year, and since there was a six-month delay before the registration became effective, many voters had to wait one and a half years before being able to vote. If they changed qualifications, they needed to wait up to an additional two and a half years. Since most property holders did not face similar delays in getting on the role, this aspect of the registration system tilted the democratic playing field further toward the landed elite. For, as one contemporary observed: "it is when you come to the working classes, who have to follow the tide of industry from one place to another, that the hardship of twelve months occupation most harshly operates."[159]

A comparison of the total percentage of the population enfranchised (lower chamber) in the UK with other European states as of 1915 reveals it to be a laggard, as opposed to the vanguard it is often assumed to have been (see Table 5.1).

Plural voting – one of the counterweights to the suffrage expansion of 1884 – also persisted. Blewett recounts how "every election witnessed the spectacle of the pluralist hastening around the countryside to record his parcel of votes, a sight arousing Conservative praise and inciting Radical

---

[156] Blewett, "Franchise," 28.
[157] Ibid., 34.
[158] Ibid., 28.
[159] Ibid., 36.

TABLE 5.1 *Suffrage rates in 1915 in Europe*

| Country | Percentage of total population enfranchised for lower house in 1915 (Vdem) |
|---|---|
| Norway | 100 |
| Finland | 100 |
| France | 50 |
| Italy | 50 |
| Switzerland | 50 |
| Belgium | 50 |
| Denmark | 45 |
| Sweden | 40 |
| **United Kingdom** | **35** |
| The Netherlands | 35 |

wrath."[160] One speaker in favor of the Plural Voting (Abolition) Bill of 1892 made the following observations:

> I have myself five votes for five different constituencies – not that I have sought the votes by purchasing property for that purpose; but they have come to me accidentally on account of holding property in different places. Two are occupation votes, two freehold votes, and one is for a University. But I know many who have a great many more votes than five. I think it was Sir Robert Fowler, a late Member of this House, who used to boast that he had no fewer than thirteen votes in different constituencies, and that he was able at one General Election to record them all. Then there is the well-known case of the Oxford tutor – a man who had eighteen different qualifications, and, at the Election of 1874, voted in respect of these different qualifications eighteen times. But this case pales before one I heard of recently. A clergyman of the Church of England, who has a hobby for acquiring qualifications in different constituencies, has been able to obtain fifty votes in different places, and I was informed that at a certain General Election he contrived to vote in no fewer than forty different places.[161]

The best available estimate is that around 7 percent of the electorate – which we have seen was already limited – were plural voters.[162] A contemporary explained the logic: "Is the man who is too illiterate to read his ballot paper, who is too imprudent to support his children, to be placed on the same footing as the man who by industry and capacity has acquired a substantial interest in more than one constituency?"[163] The

---

[160] Blewett, "Franchise," 44.
[161] Mr. Shaw Lefevre, Plural Voting (Abolition) Bill (No. 42), Wednesday May 18, 1892.
[162] Blewett, "Franchise," 46.
[163] Ibid., 45.

clear answer for liberals was no, and in this sense plural voting was a pure institutional expression of competitive oligarchy. It was also very effective, and the democratic deficit created through plural voting was considerable. Donald Read estimates that "the middle classes retained about twice the electoral weight which they would have carried within a 'one man one vote' system."[164] There was no reform of plural voting before WWI, though this was not for a lack of trying. The House of Lords vetoed efforts to abolish it in 1892 and 1906. It remained unreformed on the eve of WWI: one conservative backbencher defended the practice in 1913 as "a very good thing [that] has only one fault – there is not enough of it."[165]

The House of Lords was the most powerful of Britain's oligarchic institutions. It is easy to downplay the political significance of Britain's unelected upper chamber, and Bagehot's recommendation to those who venerated the Lords to "just look at it" was one of the gentler barbs directed at it. "Absenteeism is the first great recognized blot of the Upper Chamber," admitted one of the defenders of the House of Lords in 1888.[166] Lords sittings were both short and poorly attended, and for most peers "the Lords was primarily a social club, not a legislative chamber."[167] As one peer put it: "The first principle of debate in the House of Lords is that, except under direct pressure, discussion shall be concluded in time to dress for dinner."[168] Lord Willoughby de Broke believed that "such work as a back-bench peer wanted to do need not interfere with hunting; questions could always be asked on non-hunting days; committees could be attended to in the summertime."[169]

One should not be fooled by such professions of amateurism. The House of Lords – as we have seen in 1832 – constituted a major barrier to democratization. Defenders of the unelected upper chamber of parliament had long argued along the lines of the Earl of Meath, who worried that "a single omnipotent assembly ... might by a bare majority take an irretrievable step ... entailing wide-spread misery, or even shaking, if not destroying, the foundations of the social fabric."[170] Conservative leaders

---

[164] Donald Read, *The Age of Urban Democracy: England 1868–1914* (New York: Longman, 1979), 303.
[165] Blewett, "Franchise," 44.
[166] Andrew Adonis, *Making Aristocracy Work: The Peerage and the Political System in Britain 1884–1914* (Oxford: Clarendon Press, 1993), 52.
[167] Ibid., 54.
[168] Ibid., 57.
[169] Ibid., 58.
[170] G. D. Phillips, *The Diehards: Aristocratic Society and Politics in Edwardian England* (Cambridge: Mass, 1979), 137.

offered a solution to this problem in the form of the "referendal theory," according to which the Lords was "an instrument for reserving on all great and vital questions a voice for the electors and for the people."[171] Lord Salisbury put it as follows:

> The second chamber ... exists ... for the purpose of insisting on delay, and on an appeal to the people whenever an accidental, temporary and unreal advantage is to be used for the purpose of permanently modifying the constitution ... We quite acknowledge that the House of Lords must submit to the will of the nation, but we must have the will of the nation clearly ascertained.[172]

Similarly, for Lord Balfour, prime minister from 1902 to 1905 and leader of the Unionist party from 1905 to 1911, the purpose of the Lords was "not to prevent the people of this country having the laws they wish to have" but rather to prevent the "hasty and ill-considered offspring" of "one passionate election."[173] Lord Selbourne too viewed the House of Lords as a necessity: "I say that there is no depth of malignant lunacy to which such a majority, if constitutionally uncontrolled, would not sink."[174]

These arguments were at once "dubious, disingenuous, and dangerous."[175] Rather than enhancing democracy, the House of Lords diminished it in two distinct ways. First, and most obviously, the very existence of an unelected upper house with veto power over legislation stemming from the House of Commons undercut the principle of parliamentary sovereignty. Even if the Lords did not behave exactly like the Prussian Bundestag, and even if the scope of the Lords' authority was limited by norms and practices, it was nevertheless in the institutional position to do so. Secondly, the dominance of the Tories in the House of Lords gave one of the political parties a built-in advantage over the other. As Ensor observed: "In the accident of its permanent control over a second

---

[171] David Cannadine, *The Decline and Fall of the British Aristocracy* (New York: Random House, 1990), 44; For a recent study of the development of the "mandate" or "referendal" theory, see Ben Sayle, "'Populist Constitutionalism' and the Unionist Party during the House of Lords' Crisis of 1911." *Parliamentary History* 40, 3 (2021), 521–542.
[172] Ibid., 46.
[173] Ibid., 47.
[174] Phillips, *Diehards*, 137.
[175] Cannadine, *Decline and Fall*, 44. Specifically, the theory implied that the hereditary and unrepresentative peers could challenge the lower house in the name of the nation as a whole, and that the Lords possessed the right to force a dissolution on the Commons – both conventions quite unknown to the British constitution. Moreover, it soon emerged that the only measures the Tory-dominated upper house felt bounds to refer to the people were the radical proposals of successive Liberal governments, which showed up their claim of non-partisan concern for the national will as ridiculous humbug.

chamber having such large powers of rejection in the abstract, the conservative party held a one-sided advantage, which could not be theoretically justified to a democracy."[176]

### 5.2.2 People's Budget to Parliament Act

The Liberals came to power in 1906 with a huge majority in the House of Commons and with plans of implementing major social legislation. Over the next several years, however, the House of Lords blocked major elements of their program. Whereas the Liberals had won 400 seats to the Unionists 157 in the House of Commons, they constituted only 15 percent (88 of 602 peers) in the House of Lords.[177] The Education Bill of 1906, the cornerstone of the Liberals' legislative agenda, was so amended by the Lords that the final version proved a humiliation for the government of Prime Minister Campbell-Bannerman. A bill to end plural voting was defeated in the upper house in the same year. In 1907, Campbell-Bannerman won a Commons majority for restricting the House of Lords' absolute veto to a suspensory veto, but this was never implemented. "The lords' destruction of liberal bills had seemed thus far to be wearing the government down. They were in the position of a blockaded city, whose supplies must steadily run out, so long as it remains powerless to shake off the blockader. Only a direct counter-offensive could save it."[178]

David Lloyd-George, liberal leader and future prime minister (1916–1922), served as Chancellor of the Exchequer from 1908 to 1915 in the government of Prime Minister H. H. Asquith (1908–1916). Loyd-George used the 1909 budget to escape a political siege. According to B. K. Murray, "from the moment Lloyd George began the active preparation of his Budget in October 1908, he was determined that its yields should be as much political as financial."[179] This did not necessarily mean that Lloyd George was deliberately provoking a constitutional crisis by introducing his "People's Budget" on the assumption that the Lords would reject it. In fact, there was only muted opposition from conservatives when the budget was introduced in the House of Commons. And at this point, Lloyd-George had yet to adopt an openly confrontational stance with the House of Lords.[180] What he had tried

---

[176] R. C. K. Ensor, *England 1870–1914* (1936), 431.
[177] Norton, 446–447.
[178] Ibid., 413.
[179] B. K. Murray, *People's Budget*, 117.
[180] Powell, 46–47.

## 5.2 The Edwardian Crisis in Britain

to do in the budget was smuggle in measures that Lords had previously rejected, such as licensing and education and land reform, and put them either in the difficult position of rejecting the budget outright or acceding to these reforms. It was not, in short, designed to provoke the constitutional crisis that resulted.

After analyzing the budget in depth, conservative leader Lord Balfour decided that it was an assault on the landed elite and rallied the conservative party against it. The *Times* called it "a vindictive budget, which strikes heavily and repeatedly at the classes which do not favor the party in power."[181] Political strategists warned of social revolution:

> The methods of this budget would be quite as audaciously applied in 1911 as now, and the possibility of a campaign of promises with respect to old age pensions, insurance against unemployment, Poor Law reform, and the rest are simply limitless. Larger pensions at an earlier date will be offered. Men like Lloyd George and Winston Churchill will do anything to win. Upon the lines of the budget they will keep on winning, if we submit now ... with direct taxation heaped upon home capital and enterprise, [England] would be a Socialist republic in all but name.[182]

This theme was repeated in the debate in the Lords, which was uncharacteristically well attended. One claimed the budget represented "the thin end of the wedge of State proprietorship," while another suggested that it was "purposely formed so as to lead to the nationalisation of land ... so as to lead to the nationalisation of all sources of production."[183] Summing up was Lord Milner: "If we wish to maintain the principle of private ownership, if we believe the country is not prepared for the threatened gigantic change, we cannot shirk from the conflict that is now forced upon us."[184] Willoughby de Broke, a member of the landed elite whom Dangerfield referred to as living "no more than two hundred years behind his time," warned that if the budget passed, "we shall have both Houses of Parliament definitely committed to a policy of socialism and nothing else but socialism."[185] De Broke offered his own robust defense of the hereditary principle: "I have been brought up in the midst of stock-breeding of all kinds all my life, and I am prepared to defend the hereditary principle ... whether the principle is applied to Peers or ... to foxhounds."[186]

---

[181] Adonis, *Making Aristocracy Work*, 147.
[182] Ibid., 150.
[183] Ibid., 156.
[184] Ibid.
[185] Ibid., 155.
[186] Phillips, *The Diehards*, 128–129.

Politicians did not varnish their words during the "Peers versus the People" crisis, as Lloyd George had succeeded in framing it. In October of 1909, he referred to the House of Lords as "500 men chosen accidentally from the ranks of the unemployed." He continued his attack on the hereditary principle, barking in January 1910 that the peers "need not be sound, either in body or in mind. They only require a certificate of birth, just to prove they are the first of the litter. You would not choose a spaniel on those principles."[187] Lloyd George also likened the House of Lords to "broken bottles stuck on a park wall to keep off the radical poachers from lordly preserves."[188]

When the House of Lords rejected the budget by a vote of 350 to 75 on November 30, 1909, Landsdowne invoked the "referendal theory" in his motion: "That this House is not justified in giving its consent to the Bill until it has been submitted to the judgement of the country."[189] Asquith won a motion in Commons two days later that the Lords' action was "a breach of the constitution and a usurpation of the rights of the Commons."[190] Given that the Lords' rejection of a "money bill" went against all precedent, Asquith had no choice but to resign. When the king permitted the dissolution of the lower house, he forced an election in January 1910. Neither party could claim a major victory, as the Liberals were returned to power with a reduced majority and the Unionists improved somewhat upon their terrible results of 1906.

The unexpected death of King Edward and the accession of King George V in May of 1911 injected more uncertainty into the unfolding constitutional crisis. Neither party seemed capable of negotiating out of the impasse on its own, so Asquith called on leaders from both parties to work out a solution, and a constitutional conference met twenty-two times between June 17 and November 10, 1911. Conservatives pushed for a codification of the referendal theory, but this was anathema to the Liberals. The convention ended in failure, as even the intense participation by political heavyweights – Lloyd George and Asquith represented the Liberals, while Balfour, Lansdowne, and Chamberlain negotiated for the Unionists – could not produce a breakthrough. Thus, a second election in 1910 was called for December and once again returned a Liberal government while leaving the parliamentary math unchanged. Having fought two elections, more or less successfully, on the issue of the House of

---

[187] Quoted in Goldstein, *Political Repression in Europe*, 261.
[188] Cannadine, *Decline and Fall*, 50.
[189] Ibid.
[190] David Powell, *The Edwardian Crisis: Britain 1901–1914* (London: Palgrave, 1996), 48.

Lords, the Liberals moved quickly to reintroduce their Parliament Bill on February 22, 1911. The bill sought to constrain the Lords in two fundamental ways; first, by taking away their ability to amend or reject money bills, and second, by stripping the chamber of its veto power altogether.

In a stunning parallel with the passing of the First Reform Act, the royal threat to create new peers – around 300 in this case – was what ultimately convinced enough of them to vote for the Parliament Bill on its third reading in the House of Lords in July of 1911. Put another way, eighty years after the First Reform Act, the monarch still played a critical role in settling basic constitutional questions. The Unionist leadership in the Lords ultimately recommended that their party members "hedge" their position on the constitutional question, wagering that there were enough safeguards in the Parliament Bill to preserve the Lords' power and making the compelling point that even a diminished House of Lords was better than one mangled through mass peerage.

The vote passed by a single vote, and many peers defended the principle of a hereditary upper chamber to the end. These so-called diehards – or ditchers, as they were "prepared to stand in the last ditch" to protect the House of Lords – mounted a furious campaign against the Parliament Bill in the summer of 1911.[191] Of the 112 diehard peers, 100 were members of the landed elite. Willoughby de Broke captured their philosophy: "our only hope ... is to fight like blazes against enemies within and without."[192] Their politics was reactionary: during debate on the Parliament Bill, the earl of Meath criticized the Lords for allowing the reform of 1832 to pass in the first place.[193]

It is tempting to view the passing of the Parliament Act as a democratizing moment that created another massive and permanent check on the power of hereditary legislators, the embodiment of the Old Regime. Lloyd-George viewed it that way: in a letter regarding the passing of the act, he wrote: "I can hardly believe it ... The dream of Liberalism for generations realised at last."[194] Bonar Law replaced Balfour as leader of the Unionist party after the act passed, a reflection of the conservatives' massive political defeat.

---

[191] The term "ditchers" originates from conservative politician Lord Curzon's advice to die in the last ditch resisting the Parliament Act, which is ironic as Curzon ended up being a "hedger" rather than a "ditcher." Norton, "Resisting the Inevitable?" 453.
[192] Cannadine, *Decline and Fall*, 523.
[193] Ben Sayle, "'Populist Constitutionalism' and the Unionist Party during the House of Lords' Crisis of 1911." *Parliamentary History* 40, 3 (2021), 534.
[194] Quoted in Norton, "Parliament Act," 453.

Yet, while the Lords lost the power of absolute veto to avoid mass peerage, they preserved some blocking powers. The centerpiece of the Lords' reassembled institutional arsenal was the two-year suspensory veto, an idea that had been discussed for decades and that was reintroduced in 1907 by Campbell-Bannerman. In place of an absolute veto over the House of Commons, the Parliament Bill provided the Lords the power to delay a bill for up to two years. Specifically:

> If any Public Bill ... is passed by the House of Commons in three successive sessions ... and is rejected by the House of Lords in each of those sessions, that Bill shall, on its rejection for the third time by the House of Lords ... become an Act of Parliament ... Provided that this provision shall not take effect unless two years have elapsed between the date of the second reading in the first of those sessions of the Bill in the House of Commons and the date on which it passed the House of Commons in the third of those sessions.[195]

These two years were critical, as the term of the House of Commons was cut from seven to five years. This meant that the Lords could use their delaying power of two and a half years to block any major initiatives of a government halfway into its term. In this sense, the Lords' power of referendum was preserved to some degree. Second, a little noticed provision of the act required that the two public bills be identical. "The bulk of the moderate men," wrote one contemporary observer, "see that the [Parliament] bill offers such ample opportunities for effective delay and revision that they are satisfied anything like dangerous or precipitate legislation is impossible."[196] According to Powell: "The Parliament Act did as much to conserve as to curtail aristocratic power – something of which some Liberals were only too well aware, and which provided a platform for continuing aristocratic revolt against the Liberal government between 1911 and 1914."[197]

The landed elite had by no means conceded permanent defeat on the issue either.[198] De Broke wrote to Selbourne that: "We have now got all the men on our side both in and out of Parliament that are worth having. We must keep them going."[199] While de Broke briefly considered forming a new political party, Selbourne persuaded him that a strategy of party capture would be more effective. On October 11, 1911, a prominent

---

[195] www.legislation.gov.uk/ukpga/Geo5/1-2/13/data.pdf.
[196] Ibid., 158.
[197] Powell, *Edwardian Crisis*, 64.
[198] Sayle finds evidence that the ditchers were intent on restoring the Lords' veto and considered the Parliament Act illegitimate. Sayle, "Populist Constitutionalism," 540.
[199] Phillips, *Diehards*, 143.

group of diehards founded the Halsbury Club, a radical right faction that Lord Middleton viewed as a legitimate threat to the Tories. "Unless something is done" Middleton warned, "three-quarters of the [Unionist] party will drift into the Halsbury club."[200] Much like the Dreyfus Affair led to the construction of the proto-fascist *Action Française*, Smith claims that "six years of radical legislation, dramatically heightened by the passage of the 1909 budget and the Parliament Act of 1911, had encouraged a militant right wing in the party, disillusioned with, if not actually against, representative government."[201] A more recent article reaches similar conclusions, such as "the ditchers embodied years of frustration among the radical right with Unionist and national politics" and that "the ditchers were the first groupings in which the 'radical right' gathered as part of a single body."[202]

De Broke told Halsbury in July 1911 that "we have used every weapon save personal violence. I should not be adverse to using even that."[203] He looked toward the impending crisis over Ireland with glee: "The real value of the Home Rule struggle will be to stiffen the sinews; warm up the blood and show all the enemies of England at home and abroad that they still have to reckon with the old spirit."[204] Even more ominously, de Broke insisted that "no one who seriously considers the state of the nation will assert that the present situation can be dealt with by a process of party politics, as we know them. On the contrary, it is the very system of party politics that has wrought so much havoc."[205]

### 5.2.3 Home Rule and Constitutional Crisis

In 1870, the Irish lawyer and Member of Parliament Isaac Butt founded the Irish Home Government Association, which quickly became a grassroots machine for electing Irish Nationalist MPs. Fifty-nine Nationalists gained seats in the elections of 1874, and when Charles Stewart Parnell took over from Butt in 1879, he increased this total to sixty-five in the elections of 1880. Following the Third Great Reform – which had quadrupled the electorate in Ireland – Nationalist representation rose to

---

[200] Ibid., 145.
[201] Smith 1993, 163.
[202] Sayle, "Populist Constitutionalism," 522–523.
[203] Cannadine, *Decline and Fall*, 526.
[204] Alan Sykes, "The Radical Right and the Crisis of Conservatism before the First World War." *The Historical Journal* 26, 3 (1983), 671.
[205] Ibid., 673.

eighty-six in the elections of 1885 and pushed Gladstone to introduce a Home Rule Bill in June of 1886. The bill was defeated, Gladstone's government fell, and the Unionists (the Tories and the Ulster Loyalists) won the elections of 1886 and ruled for the next twenty years. During this period politics was organized along a Liberal-Nationalist/Tory-Loyalist (Unionist) axis.

According to Lustick, "the regime-challenging character of Ulster 'loyalists' opposition had been evident as early as 1886."[206] Lord Randolph Churchill (leader of Unionist Party) noted in that year that "Ulster ... at the proper moment will resort to the supreme arbitration of force." Seven years later, Lord Balfour in 1893 similarly warned that "Ulster can at all events fight. The last refuge of brave men struggling for their freedom cannot be denied them."[207] This incendiary rhetoric served to strengthen the political connections between Ulster and the Tories, but so long as Tories controlled government, Irish Home Rule was effectively blocked and the violence purely theoretical. That changed in 1906, but conservative dominance in the House of Lords remained a last line of defense against Home Rule.

The passing of the Parliament Act in 1911 added to the urgency of the Irish question, for everyone understood the connection between the end of the Lords' veto and the arrival of Home Rule. During the King's Speech in February 1912, Asquith's government announced it would indeed introduce a Home Rule Bill, while Unionists began plotting to prevent it. In an open letter in *The Times* (July 26, 1911), conservative leader Andrew Bonar Law speculated: "It might or might not be wise to use this power, but if I am right in thinking that the House of Lords would have the means of compelling an election before Home Rule became law, that surely is a power which ought not to be lightly abandoned."[208] Recall that the Parliament Act had "condemned the Liberals to piloting the Bill unchanged through three successive session of parliament before it could become law."[209]

It was during this period that, Dangerfield claims, the conservatives "set out to wreck the Constitution" and "very nearly succeeded."[210] The central player here – Andrew Bonar Law – was an unlikely candidate for the role of political arsonist. Robert Blake pointed out the irony of a "Presbyterian

[206] Lustick, *Unsettled States*, 190.
[207] Ibid.
[208] Norton, 456.
[209] Powell, *Edwardian Crisis*, 144.
[210] Dangerfield, *Strange Death*, 96.

of Canadian origin, who had spent most of his life in business in Glasgow," taking over "the Party of Old England, the Party of the Anglican Church and the country squire, the party of broad acres and hereditary titles." Yet "Bonar Law's expertise was to cloak the intricate arguments of Balfour with blood-curdling rhetoric and yet remain within, if rather stretched, constitutional limits."[211] Speaking to a crowd of 100,000 Ulster unionists at Balmoral (outside of Belfast) on Easter Tuesday 1912, Bonar Law praised them for helping to "save the Empire." In his infamous Blenheim Speech of July 29, 1912, he called the Liberal government "a revolutionary committee which has seized by fraud upon despotic power" and referred ominously to "things stronger than parliamentary majorities" that were required in such desperate times. Specifically, Law proclaimed that "we shall not be restrained by the bonds which would influence us in ordinary political struggle. We shall use any means to deprive them of the power which they have usurped and compel them to face the people they have deceived."[212]

The most arresting and famous phrase from Law's Blenheim Palace speech, however, was his ambiguous quip that he knew "no length of resistance to which Ulster can go in which I would not be prepared to support them." This was neither an aberrant nor poorly phrased remark, but part and parcel of a strategy of "Bluff, Bluster, and Brinkmanship."[213] Bonar Law's central goal was to precipitate a general election on the question of Home Rule, wagering that the Unionists would win and that his new government could manage the Irish question better than Asquith's. It was a risky strategy because it depended on the credible threat of violent resistance to force such a referendum on Home Rule. Bonar Law recognized the risks himself when he asked, rhetorically: "What if the North men do fight, and fight over a bill not worth the bones of a Pomeranian puppy? What an implication we may be preparing for ourselves?"[214] Still, he persisted in his pressure campaign against the Liberal government. He put the following question to the Commons in debate in April of 1912: "Do Hon Members believe that any Prime Minister could give orders to shoot down men whose only crime is that they refuse to be driven out of our community and deprived of the privilege of British citizenship?"[215] He put

---

[211] Jeremy Smith, "'Paralysing the Arm': The Unionists and the Army Annual Act, 1911–1914." *Parliamentary History* 15, 2 (1996), 206.
[212] *The Times*, July 30, 1912.
[213] Jeremy Smith, "Bluff, Bluster and Brinkmanship: Andrew Bonar Law and the Third Home Rule Bill." *The Historical Journal* 36, 1 (1993), 161–178.
[214] Ibid., 170.
[215] Ibid., 195.

the choice as follows: "The prospect before us is either that the government go on with, as I fully believe, the certainty of disorder approaching at least civil war; or, that we compel an election." *The Economist* noted in August 1912 that its readers "cannot escape from the one outstanding and extraordinary fact – that the leader of the Conservative party had definitely and repeatedly encouraged the outbreak of civil war."[216]

Opponents of Home Rule, like Law, had previously sought to use the Annual Army Act to sabotage it. This idea was raised again during debate on the Parliament Act of 1911, the logic being that without the "recognized cornerstone of the English Parliamentary system" in place, governing would be impossible and the Lords' veto would be restored.[217] Bonar Law saw the potential for more targeted maneuvers. After he had calculated that the diehards would be unable to block the Parliament Bill, he wrote a portentous letter in the *Times* on July 26, 1911, in which he warned the conservatives could delay "the Army Annual bill [to] make the continuance of the Government impossible and compel an election."[218] Using the army for such nakedly political objectives would have constituted a major breakdown in civil–military relations, but up until the winter of 1914, such plans were just talk.

The Curragh incident of March 1914 changed that. At the very least, the incident was a poorly devised way of preventing a possible mutiny among Irish officers who would have been tasked with implementing Home Rule in Ulster.[219] Specifically, the commander-in-chief in Ireland, Major-General Sir Arthur Paget, ordered his generals to spread the word that any officer with a residence in Ulster would be allowed to "disappear" without the usual consequences of desertion. Additionally, any officer who was not prepared to undertake actions in Ulster was given the chance to submit his resignation. Paget then notified the war office that fifty-seven out of the seventy officers of the 3rd Cavalry Brigade (stationed in the Curragh Camp in County Kildare) "prefer to accept dismissal if ordered north." Paget did not have the authority, but rather than ordering him to enforce discipline, the government reached a bargain with the mutineers, signaling to one contemporary that "I do not believe that wild horses will drag the army into Ulster now."[220]

---

[216] *The Economist*, "Doctrine of Disorder," August 17, 1912.
[217] Smith, "Paralysing the Arm," 192.
[218] Ibid.
[219] The incident is sometimes referred to as a "mutiny."
[220] Smith, "Army Annual Act," 199.

## 5.2 The Edwardian Crisis in Britain

During the parliamentary debate on the Curragh incident, one member of the governing party warned that "for the first time in modern English history a military cabal seeks to dictate to government the bills it should carry or not carry into law." He continued that "we are confronted with a desperate rally of reactionaries to defeat the democratic movement and repeal the Parliament Act. This move by a few aristocratic officers is the last throw in the game."[221] Unionist leaders like Lord Balfour claimed instead that the Parliament Act had merely "suspended" the British Constitution and put in place an "interim constitution" that would not stand in the way of armed rebellion.[222] On the other side of the political aisle, Lloyd George warned that nothing less than democracy was at stake in the Home Rule controversy: "We are confronted with the greatest issue raised in this country since the days of the Stuarts ... We are not fighting about Ulster. We are not fighting about Home Rule. We are fighting for all that is essential to civil liberty in this land."[223]

Many diehards committed themselves to resisting the authority of Parliament should Home Rule come to pass. Sometimes the threat of violent disobedience was clouded in euphemisms. One swore in January 1913 that "we shall use to our utmost the time that is at our disposal in preparing for eventualities which might occur should they attempt to force the bill on us."[224] Similarly, de Broke claimed in a speech to the House of Lords in July 1913 that while "decent men" would sooner see the Irish question "fought to a finish at a General Election," he warned "if that means of settlement is denied to us, then we must fall back on the only other means at our disposal."[225] He reminded his colleagues that "we do not propose to allow our most vulnerable flank a separate existence to a nation whose very leaders have constantly declared war upon their country."[226] He continued by noting that the new organizations office was located "curiously enough, next door to a gunmaker's shop."[227] These were not empty threats: the private correspondence of leading diehards reveals that they "were prepared to spill blood to achieve their goals."[228] An all-party conference at Buckingham Palace

---

[221] Ziblatt, *Conservative Parties*, 155.
[222] Lustick, *Unsettled States*, 204.
[223] Ziblatt, *Conservative Parties*, 155.
[224] Phillips, *Diehards*, 151.
[225] Ibid., 152.
[226] Cannadine, *Decline and Fall*, 523.
[227] Ibid., 527.
[228] Phillips, *Diehards*, 155.

on Ireland broke up in July of 1914 without any sign of resolution or softening of positions. Lustick suggests that this stalemate was tactical as "each side wanted to use parliamentary debates during the final circuit of the Home Rule Bill to force the other into appearing responsible for the outbreak of violence."[229]

In July, the Irish nationalists landed a cache of weapons by daylight near Dublin. The harbormaster immediately alerted the local authorities, and both a unit from the Dublin Metropolitan Police and a detachment of the King's Own Scottish Borderers were deployed. The volunteers and the soldiers clashed after many police officers refused orders to disarm their co-ethnics. Although there were no casualties during this foray, a crowd had gathered to jeer and heckle the soldiers on Bachelor's Walk, thereby provoking an officer into ordering his army to face the crowd. In the tension a shot was fired, followed by a volley, followed by the death of three people instantly, a fourth later, and injuries to thirty-eight unarmed civilians. That was July 26, 1914. Two days later the *Times* warned that "there can no longer be any doubt that the country is now confronted with one of the greatest crises in the history of the British race."[230] Churchill recalled the mood similarly:

I remember on the eve of the Great War … for a long time … after the failure of the Buckingham Palace Conference, we discussed the boundaries of Fermanagh and Tyrone. Both of the great political parties were at each other's throats. The air was full of talk of civil war … The differences had been narrowed down … to parishes and groups inside the areas of Fermanagh and Tyrone, and yet, even when the differences had been so narrowed down, the problem appeared to be as insuperable as ever, and neither side would agree to reach any conclusion. Then came the Great War.[231]

## 5.3 CONCLUSION

Barrington Moore wrote that: "the theme of diehard opposition to the march of democracy is a rare and minor current among the landed aristocracy of England in the nineteenth century."[232] Chapter 3 challenged this view, and this chapter has documented just how far down the extra-parliamentary road some defenders of the old regime had travelled on the eve of WWI. Although scholars regularly ponder what would have

---

[229] Lustick, *Unsettled States*, 213.
[230] Quoted in Read, *Urban Democracy*, 497.
[231] Quoted in Mclean and McMillan, *State of the Union*, 128.
[232] Moore, *Social Origins*, 35.

happened in Germany had WWI not broken out, the Edwardian period is not usually the subject of such counterfactuals. Some major ingredients for democratic backsliding were present; these included a radical right wing that ranked stability of democracy below other objectives, an internal conflict (Ireland) that brought the UK close to constitutional deadlock several times, and a leader of the conservative party who showed "semi-loyalty" to democracy. On this third point, I agree with Ziblatt's analysis that: "[the Unionist Party] took on behavioral and rhetorical traits that arguably matched what Juan Linz identifies as precursors to democratic breakdown: opposition 'semiloyalty' and 'disloyalty' to basic democratic or constitutional procedures."[233] During debate on the Parliament Bill in 1911, Churchill excoriated the Conservatives for "their claim to govern the country whether in office or in opposition and to resort to disorder because they cannot have their way." In 1914, Churchill claimed that the "veto of violence has replaced the veto of privilege."[234] Ziblatt agrees: "As long as the conservatives won, democracy was settled; as soon as they lost, a constitutional crisis appeared to shake the state."[235] The Capitol Insurrection of January 6, 2021, in the United States laid bare the importance of accepting defeat for democratic stability not just in transitional regimes but also in longstanding democracies. Would Bonar Law have been able to control the centripetal forces he had unleashed?[236] We shall never know, but the fact is that England entered WWI in a deep domestic political crisis with some major elements of competitive oligarchy intact.

---

[233] Ziblatt, *Conservative Parties*, 144.
[234] Read, *Urban Democracy*, 495.
[235] Ziblatt, *Conservative Parties*, 110.
[236] Although some scholars claim that Law was ultimately bluffing, others disagree. Lustick, for example, writes that "according to his biographer, Bonar Law's violent public declarations were not belied by his public remarks" and that "he saw little hope of arresting civil war." Lustick, *Unsettled States*, 202.

# 6

# Authoritarian Resilience in Northern Europe

Northern Europe is currently home to some of the highest-quality democracies in the world, and most scholarly and official narratives of democratization in these states assume they have been democratic vanguards since the late nineteenth century. There is wide consensus in the academic literature that Belgium, Denmark, the Netherlands, and Sweden followed a gradualist path similar to the United Kingdom. For Dahl, they are all cases of "stable high-consensus polyarchies" that developed through "peaceful evolution within an already independent nation state."[1] For Ziblatt, the five states represent examples of "settled democratization" in which democracy was "gradually constructed via a relatively direct path, absent high-profile moments of backsliding, authoritarian detours, or disruptive coups."[2] Gradualism was thus not unique to the United Kingdom, and the same forces at work in British democratization – elite competition, middle-class activism, and elite political restraint – were common to the first wave in Northern Europe as a whole. Like in the United Kingdom, political elites in Northern Europe also built upon medieval institutions of local self-government – the "tings" in Denmark and Sweden and the urban centers of the Low Countries – during their transitions to mass politics. These narratives of progress, with national variations, have become part of the historical memory of contemporary Northern European states.

---

[1] Dahl, *Polyarchy*, 41–42; Dahl was hesitant to place Denmark squarely in this category, given that it had apparently taken a successful "shortcut" to democratization through the 1848 introduction of universal male suffrage and because "the Danish political experience has been subjected to so little extensive analysis." (footnote #5, 39–40).

[2] Ziblatt, *Conservative Parties*, 10.

As with the British case, there is also a challenger to this Whiggish view of political development, one in which the working class is the key democratizing force at crucial moments. Scholars have used suffrage expansions in both Belgium and Sweden, for example, as illustrative examples of the "threat of revolution" hypothesis. The Belgian Socialists pioneered the use of the general strike for political ends, and the 1893 suffrage expansion showed socialists across Europe its enormous potential. In Sweden, labor agitation before 1909 – and then again in 1918 – preceded major democratic reforms. The dynamics in these cases were, in this view, similar to those of 1832 in Britain. A second line of argument focuses less on the revolutionary potential of the working class and more on its success in gaining political representation.[3] Political pressure from below was channeled into socialist parties as well as into mass strikes and extra-parliamentary pressure campaigns. This perspective on democratization also has found its way into the official narrative in Northern Europe, particularly in Sweden – where the socialists helped craft "Nordic Democracy's" origin story in the 1930 – and in Belgium, where heavy industrialization had indeed produced a working-class party that could indeed claim some notable victories for democracy.

This chapter argues that both views – the Whiggish and the revolutionary – are misleading because each overstates the degree of democratization in what were competitive oligarchies (Belgium, the Netherlands, and Sweden) on the eve of World War I. Denmark was the most democratic of the four, but it had only been so for about thirteen years and had only become so after thirty-five years of conservative rule through emergency decrees and monarchic power. It also experienced one of the greatest suffrage rollbacks in European history following its defeat in war in 1864. The Netherlands still possessed one of the most restricted suffrages of any state in Europe on the eve of World War I, and plural voting still preserved the power of the old regime in Belgium following the introduction of universal manhood suffrage in 1893. The gradual view not only overestimates the degree of democracy in Northern Europe before World War I but also underestimates the ability of elites to construct new roadblocks as old ones were removed in the transition to mass politics. The "democracy from below" perspective, for its part, overstates the success rate of social

---

[3] Ruth Collier, *Paths Toward Democracy* (New York: Cambridge University Press, 1997); Dietrich Rueschemeyer, Evelyne Huber Stephens and John D. Stephens, *Capitalist Development and Democracy* (Chicago: University of Chicago Press, 1992).

protest in forcing elite concessions: In most cases the regime responded by ignoring or repressing popular demands for universal suffrage.

## 6.1 BELGIUM

When Belgium gained its independence from the Netherlands in 1830, it adopted a constitution that was widely hailed as among the most liberal in the world.[4] Along with wide protection of civil liberties and the press, the constitution created a very narrow suffrage that led to the Liberal domination of government until the early 1880s, when Catholics (who benefited from the method of means testing in rural areas) began to alternate in power with the Liberals. Carstairs finds that "the means-tested suffrage was so restrictive that everywhere it was the fairly affluent bourgeois class who had the vote."[5] Only 4 percent of the population could vote during the first sixty-three years following Belgian independence.[6] The introduction of universal male suffrage in 1893 occurred in the context of rapid industrialization and rising socialist power, but only after six decades of competitive oligarchy.

The two primary narratives of Belgian political development focus on the path toward democracy and have little to say about the reversals.[7] The Liberal story posits that Belgium's medieval urban centers were democratic bastions. Addressing parliament two months after the liberation of his country in 1944, the Speaker of the Belgian House asserted that: "This country has been, by age-old tradition, a country of liberty and self-conscious democracy. Its cities belong to the most ancient cradles of the rights of a free, self-governing citizenship, and however many occupations and dominations it may have undergone, it has never given up its attachment to this moral heritage."[8] Such ideas date back to at least the 1850s, when the Belgian journalist Louis Labarre wrote in 1856: "if there is one country in Europe where the democratic sentiments of equality and liberty have taken deep roots in the soil, that country is

---

[4] Belgium and the Netherlands had been joined into the United Netherlands at the Congress of Vienna in 1815.
[5] Andrew Carstairs, *A Short History of Electoral Systems in Western Europe* (Boston: George Allen and Unwin, 1980), 50.
[6] V-Dem.
[7] Marnix Beyen identifies two other narratives – the Flemish and the Catholic. See Marnix Beyen, "Multiple Democracies in One Country: Belgian Narratives of Democracy, 1830–1850." *Journal of Modern European History* 17, 2 (2019), 171–183.
[8] Parliamentary Proceedings, Extraordinary Session of the Combined Chambers, November 9, 1944, 9.

ours" continuing that "Belgian history is the history of the struggle of the proud citizens dictating to the sovereigns charters in which one can see the right of insurrection inscribed for centuries."[9] The socialist narrative, by contrast, begins with the industrial revolution and valorizes the working class in democratic development. As Beyen notes, this perspective is more prominent in official narratives in Belgium than the Whig (Liberal) view: "In the more or less official historiography created by the Belgian political and intellectual elites, collective actors of lower and middle strata much rather than monarchs and aristocrats were presented as the forerunners of the Belgian nation."[10] Common to both narratives – and to most academic analyses – is the misleading claim that Belgium democratized before World War I.

Belgium was one of the most industrialized states in the world in the 1880s and 1890s. Marx once referred to it as the "hell of the proletariat," a fitting description given that the economy was built on coal mining. Yet the misery of working conditions, coupled with the relative ease of organizing workers in a compact geographical space, also made it a center of working-class political activism. Belgian coal workers had begun striking with the explicit aim of winning universal suffrage in 1887. Massive demonstrations followed in 1890 before the Belgian Socialist Party decided to call its first general strike in 1893 to force parliament to grant universal manhood suffrage. The party's leader Emile Vandervelde proclaimed in front of a crowd outside of parliament that if the chamber "decrees political equality, it will be the army of labour that joyfully re-enters their factories. If they refuse us, we will become the army of the Revolution."[11] The Belgian parliament rewarded the protestors with a massive step toward universal male suffrage.

Socialists across Europe, including Friedrich Engels, Karl Kautsky, and Rosa Luxembourg, all praised Vandervelde on his political victory. Scholars have, quite reasonably, identified it as a case of democratization from below. One view is that it constitutes a clear case of political liberalization delivered through a credible revolutionary threat.[12] Another is that it represents a turning point in the political power of organized labor, the first concession of many by the old regime before the final transition to democracy. Collier, to take one example of this viewpoint,

[9] Quoted in Beyen, "Multiple Democracies," 177.
[10] Ibid., 171.
[11] Janet Polasky, "A Revolution for Socialist Reforms: The Belgian General Strike for Universal Suffrage." *Journal of Contemporary History* 27, 3 (July 1992), 453.
[12] Przeworski, "Conquered or Granted?"; Therborn, "Rule of Capital."

writes "the course of democratic reform in Belgium was characterized by a strong working-class role, one that was apparent through many phases as the process unfolded."[13]

The history of Belgian democratization needs to be revised in three respects. First, the reform of 1893 not only widened the franchise but also introduced plural voting.[14] While scholars have certainly noticed the counter-majoritarian elements of the 1893 reform, they have tended to downplay the degree to which plural voting dulled the impact of near-universal male suffrage. But what is one to make of a system where the wealthy and well-educated received enough additional votes so that about 30 percent of the electorate cast a majority of the total?[15] Was 1893 a step toward liberal democracy or the consolidation of competitive oligarchy? The Belgian Socialists came to the latter view quickly, particularly after an 1895 law extended plural suffrage to municipal elections and added a fourth possible vote based on residency requirements that favored landowners over laborers.[16] Members of the party referred to the 1895 law as the *loi des quatres infamies* ('law of the four disgraces,' a reference to the maximum four votes). Many of the Socialist party rank-and-file felt betrayed by the leadership's acceptance of plural voting, particularly since the party had pledged to never do so at its most recent party congress.[17] The elimination of plural voting was the central political goal of the Belgian Workers' Party for the next several decades. On the eve of World War I, it had still not achieved it.

Second, the qualified success of the 1893 reform needs to be weighed against the repeated failures of working-class mobilization both before and after it. As Goldstein notes, "huge strikes and demonstrations, attracting scores of thousands demanding suffrage reform, rocked Belgium every year between 1886 and 1892."[18] None of them, however, resulted in democratic concessions and instead revealed the willingness

---

[13] Collier, *Paths Toward Democracy*, 89.
[14] All males over the age of twenty-five received one vote. Those with a university education and an administrative position received an additional two votes. Additionally, males could receive an additional vote if they owned their property or paid a rent of five francs, or if they were at least thirty-five and married. No individual could cast more than three votes in parliamentary elections. See Frederick Dhondt, "Justice and Equality for All?" British Legal History Conference, 2019, 31.
[15] Goldstein, *Political Repression*, 263.
[16] Frederick Dhondt, "Justice and Equality for All?" 37.
[17] Janet Polasky, *The Democratic Socialism of Emile Vandervelde, Between Reform and Revolution* (Oxford: Berg Press, 1995), 29.
[18] Goldstein, *Political Repression*, 263.

of the Belgian state to repress. In March 1886, worker riots in Liege and Borinage took on political content as 260,000 copies of a pamphlet calling for universal suffrage were sold.[19] The Belgian authorities declared martial law and killed a dozen workers. The Belgian political class also tried to diffuse protests by promising to "take up the issue" in parliament, where most proposals either died in committee or were voted down. For example, a 75,000-person demonstration for universal suffrage in Brussels on August 10, 1890, forced the parliament to agree to initiate debate over suffrage reform.[20] These discussions stalled, and it was only the pressure of a miner's strike in Charleroi in 1891, and continual working-class mobilization in 1892, that forced a vote on universal suffrage in parliament. Even after seven years of continued labor pressure, the Belgian parliament rejected a constitutional revision for universal suffrage. It was this rejection that led to the general strike of 1893 (which was far from peaceful as eleven were killed and hundreds wounded) and the subsequent suffrage expansion that, as we have seen, can only be considered a partial success.

Even more telling is the failure of labor agitation after 1893. When workers struck in 1895 to protest the *loi des quatres infamies* that established plural voting, Vandervelde urged restraint and spoke out against another general strike: "It would be certain defeat, the loss of workers' reforms." Perhaps his seat in parliament led him to jettison the revolutionary talk of two years earlier, for in place of direct action he asked workers to "remain calm ... that will assure us victory in the future." When the Socialists again began to mount protest against the electoral system in 1899, it was primarily in reaction to the government's proposal to introduce proportional representation selectively, and to the benefit of Catholics. Vandervelde then momentarily ditched his revisionism and called "to arms, comrades, to arms, rally round the red flag."[21] Over the course of the next decade, the Belgian Socialist Party would be torn between a revolutionary and parliamentary strategy. The failure of two general strikes, the first in 1902 and the second in 1913, owed much to these divisions.

The general strike of 1902 – the second in Belgian history – was significantly larger than the first in 1893: 300,000 people demonstrated throughout the country for suffrage reform. The state responded

---

[19] Ibid., 262.
[20] Polasky, "Revolution for Socialist Reforms," 451.
[21] Ibid., 455.

by mobilizing 60,000 troops. When the Belgian parliament rejected Vandervelde's proposal for universal and equal male suffrage after two days of debate on April 18, the party leadership vowed to continue the general strike. But that evening, the civil guard in Louvain mowed down a peaceful procession of demonstrators, killing six and wounding fourteen. Vandervelde retreated immediately: "I recognize that it is no longer possible to win democracy by force .... It would be foolhardly to allow our admirable proletariat to be massacred."[22]

Vandervelde and Luxembourg debated the lessons of 1902 in the socialist press. Vandervelde claimed that the "real enemies of the strike were not the Liberals, but the 60,000 bayonets of the army."[23] Rosa Luxembourg revoked her previous endorsement of the Belgian Socialists and attacked their passivity and willingness to compromise with bourgeois forces. "If social democracy opposes the historically necessary revolution ... then the only result will be to transform social democracy from the avant-garde to the rearguard."[24] But Luxembourg's position – acceptance of violence and orthodox Marxism – was not widely represented within the Belgian Socialist Party, which was one of the least radical socialist parties in Europe.[25]

The third major revision to the official narrative of Belgian democratization before World War I is that it did not include women. The Socialists specifically stopped short of demanding universal adult suffrage. The prospect of female voting was raised in internal party discussions in the 1890s, and there was a full debate on the issue at the 1902 party congress.[26] Female suffrage was consciously left out of the party program. Patriarchal attitudes no doubt contributed to this omission, but electoral concerns – specifically the fear that women would overwhelmingly vote religiously – played a major role as well. Like France, Belgium only introduced female suffrage after World War II, decades after most states in Europe had done so.

The elections of June 1912 brought Belgium no closer to universal suffrage. "The Catholic domination of Parliament seemed fated to continue," Polansky writes, and "electoral reform through Parliament remained as distant a possibility as ever."[27] When workers demanded

[22] Ibid., 36.
[23] Polansky, 1992, 458.
[24] Ibid.
[25] Gary Marks, Heather Mbaye and Hyung Min Kim. "Radicalism or Reformism? Socialist Parties before World War I." *American Sociological Review* 74, 4 (2009), 615–635.
[26] Polasky, *Emile Vandervelde*, 44.
[27] Ibid., 46.

another general strike in 1912 for universal suffrage, Vandervelde tried to prevent it and negotiated with politicians and business leaders to find a peaceful resolution. He later wrote: "the principal leaders of the party very clearly opposed the strike and made every effort to forestall it. The resolution of the masses forced the leaders to play their part."[28] When Parliament defeated a proposal for universal suffrage on February 8, 1913, the Socialists announced their support for a general strike. This time, the state responded not with force but with an apparent concession as the parliament agreed to set up a parliamentary commission on electoral reform. Vandervelde counseled the demonstrators to be happy with their "half-victory," while many of the rank-and-file wanted to use the opportunity to finally enact universal and equal suffrage without qualifications.[29] When the general strike was called off, Luxembourg described it as "an even greater defeat than that of 1902."[30]

Collier summarizes the conventional academic view that "working-class pressure and particularly the use of the political strike were constant features of the process of Belgian democratization from the 1880s on."[31] There is some truth to this view, but it downplays the multiple crushing defeats of the movement for universal suffrage and suggests that Belgium had mostly democratized prior to World War I. It had not. Female suffrage was not on the table and the Socialists had failed, after two decades of effort, to change the *loi de quatres infamies* that had introduced plural voting. Would the parliamentary commission established in 1913 have successfully crafted and passed a bill for universal and equal suffrage had Belgium not been invaded in August 1914? Perhaps it would have succeeded where previous efforts had failed. It may also have found another path around democracy that preserved, through institutional design, a high degree of oligarchic rule. Had Germany won the war, one can only begin to speculate about what type of domestic political arrangements it would have allowed in Belgium, but democracy would hardly have been one of them.

## 6.2 THE NETHERLANDS

In *The Politics of Accommodation*, Arend Lijphart categorizes Dutch democratization as a "case of peaceful change." He notes that "all major

---

[28] Polasky, "Revolution for Socialist Reforms," 460.
[29] Ibid., 463.
[30] Polasky, *Emile Vandervelde*, 51.
[31] Collier, *Paths Toward Democracy*, 89.

political problems facing the Dutch during the past century have been resolved peacefully and constitutionally. The only big blot on their record is their failure to withdraw from the colonial empire without bloodshed and severe damage to their national interest."[32] Lijphart, to be fair, was more concerned with using the Dutch case to revise pluralist theory and outline a theory of consociational democracy than he was with the specifics of Dutch history. Still, his work offers a direct example of a modernization theorist – at least one with deep training by modernization theorists – applying a version of Whig history elsewhere. As one scholar wrote recently: "there is a strong tendency to present Dutch history from the perspective of continuity and conciliation, instead of breaks and conflicts. Even the introduction of mass politics at the end of the nineteenth century has been interpreted from a Whig perspective as a rather peaceful process of segmented emancipation, known as 'pillarisation.'"[33] The website of the national parliament (*Tweedekammer*) offered a similar take on the 100-year anniversary of the achievement of universal suffrage (male and female) in the Netherlands in 2019. Although the text accompanying the timeline "The Road Towards Universal Suffrage in the Netherlands" does include the proviso that it was "preceded by a long fight," it mostly focuses on how "slowly but surely, the right to vote was extended."[34]

In fact, the Netherlands from 1815 to 1886 was more oligarchic than even Great Britain. Table 6.1 shows male suffrage was extremely limited before a major reform of 1887.[35] Unlike the short-lived revolutionary constitution of 1798, the constitution of 1815 made no mention of popular sovereignty. The end of the Napoleonic wars brought a restoration that "re-installed the old ways of quiet negotiating in the inner circle of councils of the state and the provinces, and this time even without the pressure of the (lower) middle classes on the local government that had been quite normal

---

[32] Arendt Lijphart, *The Politics of Accommodation* (Berkeley: University of California Press, 1968), 77.
[33] Robert van der Laarse, "Bearing the Stamp of History: The Elitist Path to Democracy in the Netherlands," 50.
[34] www.houseofrepresentatives.nl/dossiers/hundred-years-universal-suffrage-celebration. The timeline also notes the extreme limitations of the franchise in the nineteenth and early twentieth centuries; Lijphart similarly refers to the period of conflict over the suffrage in the late nineteenth century (104–110) and clearly does not consider the Netherlands to have achieved democracy before 1918 (72).
[35] Table adapted from Jan Verhoef, "The Rise of National Political Parties in the Netherlands, 1888–1913." *International Journal of Politics* 4, ½ (Spring-Summer 1974), 207–221.

TABLE 6.1 *Male suffrage rates in the Netherlands, 1853–1917*

| Year | Registered voters as percentage of total male population |
|---|---|
| 1853 | 11.0 |
| 1870 | 11.3 |
| 1880 | 12.3 |
| 1887 | 14.0 |
| 1888 | 27.0 |
| 1890 | 26.8 |
| 1896 | 25.0 |
| 1897 | 52.2 |
| 1907 | 60.9 |
| 1917 | 70.8 |

during the Republic."[36] Although the United Netherlands (Belgium and the Netherlands were joined at the Congress of Vienna) was technically a constitutional rather than an absolute monarchy, the 1815 constitution gave the king the power to appoint ministers, declare war and peace, and raise revenue without consulting parliament. "I can reign without ministers," King William boasted: "It is I alone who govern and am responsible."[37]

The 1830 July Revolution in France sparked anti-Dutch rioting in Belgium to such a degree that middle- and upper-class Belgians formed civic guards to control the mass protest. When the Dutch army was forced to withdraw – 10,000 troops could not pacify the rioting cities – the Belgian civic guards declared independence and elected a constituent assembly. Unlike in newly independent Belgium, there was no significant domestic liberalization in the Netherlands as William kept the country on a war footing throughout the 1830s. William abdicated in 1840, but his son William II (1840–1849) refused to consider even modest changes to what had become an absolutist state. The Revolutions of 1848 produced a more liberal constitution in the Netherlands, but there was nothing like the mass enfranchisement in Denmark and France. In the first direct elections for the second chamber in 1850, property qualifications kept the suffrage rate to about 2.5 percent of the total population.[38] Goldstein

---

[36] Henk te Velde, "The Emergence of the Netherlands as a 'Democratic' Country." *Journal of Modern European History* 17, 2 (2019), 164–165.
[37] Golstein, *Political Repression*, 103.
[38] Carstairs, *Electoral Systems*, 61.

notes that "the totally unrepresentative character of parliamentary life in the Low Countries is clearly indicated by the fact that in 1850, 70 percent of the Dutch parliament held law degrees, at a time when less than 0.1 per cent of the Dutch population attended a university."[39]

Conflict between King William III – who had effectively controlled the government and ignored parliament despite the *recognition* of parliamentary sovereignty in the constitution of 1848 – and the two major Dutch political parties (Liberal and Conservative) led to the *implementation* of parliamentary sovereignty in 1868. It came with no major demands for suffrage reform, and it was not until the Eel Revolts of 1886 – along with an additional twenty years of socialist organization – that the political elite were forced to react. What began as a crackdown on the brutal sport of eel-pulling took on political dimensions as the riots showed "the extent of popular hatred for a police that for years had been brutally chasing socialists and putting down demonstrations."[40] Twenty-five people were killed and 100 were wounded in the state repression that followed. As demands for universal suffrage grew, the regime responded with a modest concession. The 1887 reform contained the "Caoutchouc Article" that stated that "signs of fitness and social well-being" were required to vote but did not specify those qualities further. When the liberal Minister for Home Affairs (1891–1894) Tak van Poortvliet tried to interpret "fitness" broadly to include all literate males not on public relief, the Chamber added amendments that would have limited Tak's franchise extension. His proposal split the Liberal Union and forced new elections in 1894 in which the "Takkite" liberals were defeated by the newly formed Free Liberals who opposed universal suffrage.

The new government passed a more limited reform in 1896 that doubled the electorate but left the Netherlands behind most states in Western Europe in terms of suffrage rates. The Liberals split again over the suffrage issue in 1901 when the base of the Liberal Union refused to endorse the party leadership's proposal that the party call for an immediate constitutional reform to introduce universal suffrage. The party executive then formed the Liberal Democratic Union, and in the elections of 1901, three different Dutch liberal parties won seats in the 100-member Lower House: Liberal Union (18), Free Liberals (8), and Liberal Democratic Union (9). With a comparatively weak socialist party and the liberals divided, suffrage

---

[39] Goldstein, *Political Repression*, 211.
[40] E. H. Kossmann, *The Low Countries 1780–1840* (Oxford: Oxford University Press, 1978), 316.

expansion was one of the three frozen conflicts (church/state relations and collective bargaining were the others) in Dutch politics that showed no signs of resolution. Like Sweden, the Netherlands appeared to be resisting the general democratic trend. "At the end of the 19th century, French or Belgian politicians would routinely assume that popular sovereignty and democracy were good things and democracy was increasingly praised in Britain," notes te Velde. "In the Netherlands," he continues, "politicians who advocated these things were still considered dangerous radicals."[41]

The mass protests that followed those of the 1880s and 1890s did not produce any further reforms. The 1903 general strike organized by the socialists was widely viewed as a "debacle" and no major protests for universal suffrage occurred again until the "Red Tuesdays" (the first Tuesday when the House convened) of 1910–1912. Lijphart writes that "around 1910 ... the political situation looked quite serious. The three major issues had reached a peak of tension, and the lines between rivals were sharply drawn. Especially the issues of the schools and the right to vote remained fundamentally unresolved with all of the contending groups hardening in their intention not to yield."[42] Whereas Collier views the Red Tuesdays as helping "to precipitate the introduction of universal suffrage for men in 1917," the only immediate reaction to them was the formation of a parliamentary committee.[43] In 1912, the Liberal government appointed two commissions to recommend solutions to the education and suffrage questions. Given that these conflicts had persisted for over three decades, there was no guarantee that another parliamentary committee would have solved them.

## 6.3 SWEDEN

Like the Netherlands, Sweden has somehow managed to elude its deeply authoritarian past in the literature on democratization.[44] Most scholars consider it an example of evolutionary democratic development or settled

---

[41] Henk te Velde, "The Emergence of the Netherlands as a 'Democratic' Country." *Journal of Modern European History* 17, 2 (2019), 166–167. Te Velde, 166: "Until the end of the 19th century, the Dutch parliament did not even debate democracy. The first real advocate of democracy only entered parliament in the late 1880s. Until the 1890s, even the *word* democracy was only used about a hundred times in the Dutch lower house and then another hundred times until the end of the century." Italics in original.
[42] Lijphart, *Politics of Accommodation*, 109.
[43] Collier, *Paths Toward Democracy*, 96.
[44] Dahl claims that Sweden followed the gradualist path like Britain, and Ziblatt considers Sweden a case of settled democratization.

democratization. This reading is derived both from political scientists with regional expertise in Scandinavia and from historians of Sweden. Stein Rokkan – one of the most influential European political scientists of the twentieth century – summed up the divergent paths of Sweden and Denmark as follows: "Sweden was able to keep up its estate representation through most of the era of absolutism and moved very gradually, step by step, toward mass democracy; Denmark, by contrast, was an absolute monarchy from 1660 to 1839 and moved quite suddenly to near-manhood suffrage already in 1849."[45] Another common reference to the gradualism of Swedish democratization is a 1974 article by Timothy Tilton in *The American Political Science Review*. His claim that "Swedish democracy does not owe its origins to a revolution, but to a series of reform acts in 1866, 1909, and 1918 extending the franchise in a way reminiscent of the English Reform Acts" has appeared verbatim in multiple studies.[46] Perhaps this is part of the reason that "researchers simply seem to reproduce the idea that Sweden's democratization, unlike Denmark's but like the United Kingdom's, was a slow, gradual process, although available quantitative comparative data and historical evidence tell the opposite story."[47] Indeed, Table 6.2 reveals that Sweden had the most restrictive franchise in Western Europe on the eve of the First World War.[48]

Nevertheless, the notion of "Nordic Democracy" is integral to these democratic narratives. In them, the "tings" of the Viking era assume the same liberalizing role as town councils in the Low Countries. According to one scholar of parliamentary history in Scandinavia, "the idea that there was a long democratic tradition in Sweden and in the other Nordic countries was … elevated to a national character and interpreted as an effective bulwark against totalitarianism."[49] Swedish elites crafted this story in the 1930s, and part of its goal was undoubtedly to make Swedish

---

[45] Stein Rokkan, "Dimensions of State Formation and Nation-Building: A Possible Paradigm for Research on Variations within Europe," in Charles Tilly, ed., *The Formation of National States in Western Europe* (Princeton: Princeton University Press, 1975), 588.
[46] Timothy Tilton, "The Social Origins of Liberal Democracy: The Swedish Case." *American Political Science Review* 68, 2 (June 1974), 561–571.
[47] Johan Schaffer, *The Forgotten Revolution: Challenging Conventional Wisdom on Sweden's Transition to Democracy* (Oslo: University of Oslo, 2010), 11.
[48] Table 6.2 is derived from T. S. Aidt, Jayasri Dutta, and Elena Loukoianova, "Democracy comes to Europe: Franchse Extensions and Fiscal Outcomes 1830–1938." *European Economic Review* 50, 2 (2006), 249–283.
[49] Jussi Kurunmäki, "The Making of 'Swedish Democracy': Anti-aristocratic, Royalist, Reformist and Exemplary." *Journal of Modern European History* 17, 2 (2019), 148.

TABLE 6.2 *Average total franchise (electorate as percentage of population over 20)*

| Country | 1830–1880 | 1881–1914 |
|---|---|---|
| Austria | n.a. | 38 |
| Belgium | 3 | 24 |
| Denmark | 26 | 29 |
| Finland | n.a. | 66 |
| France | 19 | 42 |
| Germany | 36 | 38 |
| Italy | 4 | 35 |
| The Netherlands | 5 | 18 |
| Norway | 9 | 55 |
| United Kingdom | 9 | 26 |
| **Sweden** | 10 | 15 |
| Switzerland | n.a. | 38 |

democracy appear older than it was. To mark the 500-year anniversary of the Riksdag, the Swedish Prime Minister pronounced in 1935 that "the ancient self-government of the Swedish people had been maintained" to allow them to "further develop our democratic order."[50] Even though they were the victims of a repressive political order for decades, the Social Democrats emphasized gradualism. According to one study of the SAP's historical memory, "by drawing a straight line from the self-owning peasant to the SAP, the party transmits the message of being an integrated part of a thousand years of Swedish history."[51]

Academics contributed to this democratic mythmaking: Nils Herlitz, professor of public law and the editor of *Nordisk Tidskrift* (Nordic Journal), claimed that Swedes were egalitarian "in their blood."[52] His book *Sweden: A Modern Democracy on Ancient Foundations* (1939) begins with the observation that "people have come to regard Sweden as a well-organized and happy democracy and to take interest in its social, economic, and political conditions."[53] He continued:

The country has retained throughout the centuries, from primitive times, some elements of popular government and political freedom. What the European peoples learnt in the 19th century from the American and French revolutions, and

---

[50] Ibid., 158.
[51] Schaffer, "Forgotten Revolution," 458.
[52] Kurunmäki, "Making of Swedish Democracy," 158.
[53] Nils Herlitz, *Sweden: A Modern Democracy on Ancient Foundations* (Minneapolis: University of Minnesota Press, 1939), ix.

from constitutional government in England, was not altogether new to Sweden, which affords the rare spectacle of a modern democracy with direct roots in the Middle Ages. Its constitutional history is comparable to that of England, but other countries offer no clear parallels.[54]

These views have found their way into Swedish democracy promotion efforts. A government publication uses Swedish history to conclude that, "the transition to democracy is often a gradual process. The first election can take years to prepare. It takes decades to build democratic institutions; it takes generation to develop a democratic culture. All democratic forces must have reasonable expectations and show patience."[55]

However, rather than a case of gradualism, Sweden's transition to democracy was rapid by any metric. Dankwart Rustow, whose work is paradoxically cited by some of the same scholars who adopt the gradualist view, pointed this out fifty years ago: "as recently as the beginning of this century, Sweden had one of the most restricted suffrage systems of any state with a representative constitution. It was a stable oligarchy. Yet by 1921 the right to vote had been extended to all adult men and women, and the accountability of the cabinet to the democratically elected legislature was beginning to be accepted. The transition to democracy, then, was late and rapid."[56] Second, Sweden's political regime resembled Wilhelmine Germany's far more than it did those of other northern European states. Monarchs in Germany and Sweden were looking for opportunities to enhance, not diminish, their own power. In both states, the upper house of parliament defended countermajoritarian institutions and principles. Despite challenges to competitive oligarchy, on the eve of World War I the Old Regime in Sweden remained intact: "Sweden was still governed by the King and the conservative elites that rallied behind him, including money and landed wealth, the nobility, and the officer corps. Old Sweden had triumphed for the time being."[57]

This portrait of prewar Sweden as an authoritarian state seems difficult to square with its contemporary status as a high-functioning democracy that aspires to egalitarianism, but it is entirely consistent with its political development to that point. For nowhere else in Western Europe had an essentially medieval system of representation remained intact

---

[54] Ibid., x.
[55] Cited in Schaffer, "Forgotten Revolution," 11.
[56] Dankwart Rustow, "Sweden's Transition to Democracy: Some Notes toward a Genetic Theory." *Scandinavian Political Studies* 6, A6 (1971), 12.
[57] Byron Nordstrom, *The History of Sweden* (Greenwood: Westport CT., 2002), 71.

for so long. Although the *Riksdag's* four-estate system (farmers, nobles, clergy, and burghers) was progressive in 1435, Sweden was still using the same system in the 1860s! The first electoral reform in modern Swedish history dates from 1866 and extended the vote to about 5 percent of the population. It was largely the creation of Louis De Geer, a conservative politician and member of the Swedish nobility. Writing in his memoirs, De Geer claimed that "In the passing of the Parliament Act [1866] the aim had chiefly been to abolish the Estates and prepare the entry of categories standing outside of the estates, though they could be considered of similar rank, but any need to extend the franchise was not yet recognized."[58] Members of the upper chamber were elected using a system of plural voting whereby a wealthy elector could cast thousands of votes, while the electorate of the lower chamber was limited by a high property qualification.[59] One senator referred to the new system approvingly as "a new chamber of nobles."[60] And in Rustow's own view: "De Geer's conservative reform brought oligarchy up to date by substituting property for status. It laid the foundations for an alliance between bureaucracy, landed wealth, and industry .... De Geer's reform may be compared in its effects to Bismarck's conservative unification of Germany."[61] Carstairs agrees with this analysis: "In effect, the reform of 1866 substituted control of parliament by a plutocracy for control by the nobility, and this was achieved by means of the property qualification for the electors of both houses."[62]

As in Belgium – and really throughout the rest of Europe – the demand for universal male suffrage in Sweden came primarily from the Socialists around the turn of the century. The repression of the Socialists in Sweden during the 1880s was on par with that in Germany – with the important difference that the Swedish Socialists had no political representation given the restricted suffrage. There was a softening in both states regarding the repression of the working class around 1889, but whereas the German Socialists used the 1890s for organizational development and ideological debate, the Swedish Socialists were singularly focused on the suffrage question. The party organized its first "People's Parliament" in 1893 to present the state with demands for political reform by a legislative body

---

[58] Douglas Verney, *Parliamentary Reform in Sweden, 1866–1921* (London: Oxford University Press, 1957), 92.
[59] Cairstens, *Electoral Systems*, 99.
[60] Rustow, "Sweden's Transition," 23.
[61] Ibid., 25.
[62] Carstairs, *Electoral Systems*, 99.

elected by universal male suffrage. If these demands were not met, they threatened a general strike followed by the convening of another people's parliament that would be "so all-inclusive and imposing that there can be no thought of further resistance on the part of the 'loyalists.'"[63]

While perhaps an organizational and symbolic success, the first people's parliament met the same fate as the English Chartists: representatives of the state listened politely to their demands and rejected all of them. No general strike followed, and while a second People's Parliament did indeed convene in 1896, it failed to live up to its revolutionary promise and "came as something of an anti-climax."[64] Once again, the state rejected all demands and there was no general strike. Adopting a different tactic, the party organized a petition calling for universal suffrage that gained 364,000 signatures and was presented to the king in 1899. In May 1902, 120,000 workers struck for suffrage reform. This time a bill did reach Parliament, but it was defeated in 1902, as were similar reform bills in 1904, 1906, and 1906.

Given this pattern of repression and political intransigence, what explains the franchise extension of 1909? One possibility is that it constitutes a moment where elites conceded in the face of a genuine revolutionary threat. Acemoglu and Robinson (2000), for example, rely on Tilton's claim that "the reform of 1909 had been preceded by strikes and demonstrations" to place it in the same category as 1832 in Britain.[65] However, the strike of 1909 that Tilton, and by extension Acemoglu and Robinson, cite was not about the right to vote but was rather sparked by a lockout by the Employers Association.[66] As in Belgium, the Swedish Socialists had become wary of calling general strikes and decided against doing so in both 1902 and 1907. Perhaps the 1909 reform can still be viewed as the upshot of decades of labor pressure. Collier, for example, argues that "popular pressure and labor agitation ... played an important role in the passage of this legislation."[67] No further evidence is provided, making it difficult to tell whether protest merely accompanied, rather than led to, political reform.

A more convincing interpretation is that the 1909 reform was, like the Second Great Reform in the UK, an attempt to adapt oligarchy to

---

[63] Rustow, "Sweden's Transition," 54.
[64] Ibid., 56.
[65] Tilton, "Swedish Case," 567; Acemoglu and Robinson, "Why Extend Franchise," 1185.
[66] Francis Sejersted, *The Age of Social Democracy: Norway and Sweden in the Twentieth Century* (Princeton: Princeton University Press, 2011), 139.
[67] Collier, *Paths Toward Democracy*, 83–84.

the industrial age. The conservative Prime Minister Arvid Lindman saw that an increasing number of workers were passing the existing property qualification to vote. Lewin summarizes Lindman's arguments to his fellow conservatives:

> What was necessary, Lindman argued, was to find some aspect of the suffrage issues that would split the growing Left. It could not be assumed that demands for universal manhood suffrage would continue to be defeated in Parliament. There were now too many people who supported such a reform. Sweden would soon be the only country in Europe that did not allow all adult men to vote. No, the introduction of universal manhood suffrage was certainly unavoidable. But could this process take place in a way less harmful to the Conservatives than by embracing the suffrage ideas of the Left? If such a solution could be found, it was better to act now, while the Conservatives were in government and could direct the political game. If this opportunity were squandered, the Left would soon get the chance to implement *its* suffrage program.[68]

Rustow concurs that elites were looking for ways to soften the blow: "If we wish to get universal suffrage with guarantees, we must get it now – if we tarry, make no mistake about it, we shall assuredly get it without guarantees."[69] Lindman's solution – one that had been suggested by conservatives as early as the 1890s – was to change the electoral system from majority elections to proportional representation while simultaneously introducing universal manhood suffrage. The 1909 reform thus included what Rustow termed the "Tory guarantee" of proportional representation for the lower house. Much like the Belgium reform of 1893, what appeared to be an unambiguous victory for democracy was tempered by – and perhaps even overwhelmed by – counter-majoritarian elements.

Although the 1909 reform was viewed as a success by conservatives, it constituted a franchise extension nonetheless with all its attendant effects on patterns of representation in the two chambers. On the one hand, it virtually ensured conflicts between the two houses, given that they represented different sectors of society. The increase in power of the legislature also raised demands for genuine parliamentary government in a state where it had never existed. For "although they might pay some attention to the outcome of elections, until 1917 Sweden's kings appointed the Government as they chose."[70]

---

[68] Leif Lewin, *Ideology and Strategy: A Century of Swedish Politics* (New York: Cambridge University Press, 1988), 70.
[69] Rustow, "Sweden's Transition," 22.
[70] Nordstrom, *History of Sweden*, 70.

The three years before the outbreak of World War I were marked by conflicts between the crown and the advocates of parliamentary government. During these years, "Sweden was thrown into a constitutional crisis whose high points were marked by the Farmer's March, the Palace Courtyard crisis, the resignation of the Staff government, and the formation of a 'royal government' the same year before World War One broke out."[71] These crises, recounted later, were all part of a deliberate strategy to "prevent parliamentarist (sic) concepts from being put into practice."[72] Indeed, there is a historical consensus that "the march and the Kings words were all carefully planned to force a crisis."[73]

The parliamentary elections of 1911 (the first held since the reform) returned a liberal and socialist majority to the lower house. King Gustav initially tried to form a government without the participation of the liberal leader Karl Albert Staaff before deciding to fight the new government on the terrain of national defense. When Staaff cancelled plans to build a light battleship (the F-boat *Sverige*) months after becoming prime minister, Gustav and his conservative allies mounted an intense pressure campaign in the press. Such a public break with his government was an ominous sign. A private campaign to raise funds from the population for the F-boat so surpassed all expectations that three light battleships were eventually built and the old regime was emboldened to continue the confrontation. When 30,000 farmers – along with leaders of conservative parties and organizations – marched to Stockholm on February 6, 1914, to express their support for increasing defense spending, the king took the opportunity to address his subjects from the yard of the Royal Palace. This so-called "Palace Yard Speech," the work of the famous explorer and monarchist Sven Hedin, rebuked the liberal government for its softness on defense and fanned the crowd's monarchism. It contained stirring lines like, "From ages so distant that they are hidden in the obscurity of sagas, the building of this realm has rested on a foundation of solid and unshakeable trust between King and people .... I will not retreat from the battle readiness and the war preparedness that the experts in my army regard as indispensable."[74]

The speech provoked the political crisis that it had intended. Former Prime Minister Lindman, who read the proposed speech on January 29, "told the King that it would cause the Government's resignation, and

---

[71] Lewin, *Ideology and Strategy*, 87–88.
[72] Ibid., 106.
[73] Nordstrom, *History of Sweden*, 71.
[74] Lewin, *Ideology and Strategy*, 110.

that he should let Hellner and De Geer II also read it in order to be sure that an alternative moderate-Liberal Ministry was feasible."[75] Lindman recognized the plot for what it was and lamented that "The King ... seems determined not to alter the speech. It is clear that there are advisors behind the King, and I think I know who they are."[76] According to Lewin: "sources say that at first the King was skeptical toward the idea of a farmer's march, but as the preparations proceeded and he heard more and more expressions of sympathy from Sweden's rural population, he snapped out of the lethargy into which the conflict with Staaff had led him, buoyed up by the thought of being able to demonstrate to the prime minister the strong ties between king and people."[77] Indeed, there were no alterations and the Palace Yard Speech was not an impromptu address from a monarch to his subjects but rather a carefully managed counterattack on proponents of parliamentary government.

After the address – of which Staaff was apparently oblivious beforehand – the prime minister demanded that the king, in the future, provide the government with advanced notice of his political statements. To which Gustav replied: "this request I cannot grant, for I will not deprive myself of the right to speak freely with the Swedish people."[78] Given that this was not an isolated quip but rather the culmination of a three-year-long fight between the king and the government, Staaff had no choice but to resign four days after the Palace Yard Speech. He was replaced by the "royal government" of Hjalmar Hammarskoeld. On the eve of World War I, Sweden remained the most authoritarian state in Northern Europe.

## 6.4 DENMARK

Denmark was the most democratic of the four cases discussed thus far in this chapter on the eve of World War I: It had universal, equal, and direct manhood suffrage along with parliamentary sovereignty. It was also a democratic vanguard in 1848 when it adopted universal manhood suffrage. Between 1864 and 1901, however, Danish politics was far from democratic. The 1901 system change that effectively established parliamentary sovereignty,

---

[75] Rustow, 188.
[76] Ibid., 189.
[77] Lewin, *Ideology and Strategy*, 110.
[78] Rustow, 187.

was preceded by 30 years of bitter struggle over the constitution, where at times Denmark was on the brink of becoming a dictatorship, and at times the difference between political confrontation and open revolt was hanging by a thread. At no point in the recent history of the country was Denmark closer to revolution and widespread civil disobedience than in the last quarter of the nineteenth century.[79]

As of 1814, the Danish realm consisted of the Kingdom of Denmark and the Duchies of Schleswig and Holstein. Both duchies – but particularly Holstein – had a significant and vocal German-speaking minority that, by the 1830s, had become enough of a separatist threat to force the Danish monarch into calling provincial assemblies in 1842. Although these bodies were only consultative, they became focal points for liberal demands and resulted in some protections for press freedom and civil liberties in the mid 1840s. In the revolutionary fervor of 1848, Danish liberal leaders organized a series of mass meetings that culminated in a march to the square of Christiansborg Palace to demand the removal of ministers. The marchers were shocked to learn that the king had already acceded to their demands, and the 1849 Constitution created a two-chamber parliament with both the upper house (Landsting) and lower house (Folketing) by direct, equal, and universal suffrage to males over thirty. The monarch remained but renounced absolute power and accepted the principle of ministerial responsibility.[80]

The advent of universal suffrage in Denmark seems a good fit for the "threat of revolution" theory, but upon closer inspection is only a partial one. The new king had already assented to the drafting of a new constitution in 1847, so at best the popular pressure accelerated his plans. In January 1848 (a month before the French revolution that set off the cascade), the king had proposed a new constitution that "was far too moderate to satisfy the democrats and conceded too much to German nationalism."[81] More importantly, it was less the revolutionary demonstration affects from France that were concerning the Danish crown than nationalist agitation in the provincial assemblies. In March 1848, the assemblies of both Schleswig and Holstein voted for a common constitution and sought membership in the German confederation. It was the war with Prussia over Schleswig that tipped the Danish Rigsdag from

---

[79] Knud Jespersen, *A History of Denmark* (New York: Palgrave, 2004), 76.
[80] Carstairs, *Electoral Systems*, 76.
[81] B. J. Hovde, *The Scandinavian Countries, 1720–1865: The Rise of the Middle Classes* (Boston: Chapman and Grimes, 1943), 549.

opposition to universal suffrage to support for it.[82] International war and nationalist mobilization were more important in the Danish franchise extension of 1848 than class-based revolution.

The fledgling democracy was nevertheless born with its own origin story of "Nordic democracy" in which Danes had been democratic since the Viking age. Scholarly and popular writings in the 1840s presented "the imagined historical legend tradition of the Folketing" and contained detailed description of the constitutional system of the Viking Age society. Like the "invented traditions" of nationalist awakenings elsewhere in Europe, elites deployed an idealized and largely fictional history to legitimate new institutions. The two bodies of the Danish parliament, for example, were originally referred to simply as "chambers" in the original two drafts of the June Constitution but were changed to Folketing and Landsting following a proposal from liberal leader Orla Lehmann to highlight a supposed historical continuity.[83] Like Whig history in Great Britain (recall that MacCauley published his history of modern Britain in 1848), the progressive narrative of historical progress came simultaneously with the expansion of the franchise.

The Danish narrative of Nordic democracy glosses over the half century of competitive oligarchy that followed its loss to Germany in the war of 1864, whereby Denmark lost both Schleswig and Holstein to Prussia. It was a devastating defeat: One-third of the land and population of the Danish Monarchy was lost. Rather than expanding the franchise as a result of international war, the Danish constitution of 1866 put control of the country into the hands of 1,000 wealthy landowners and the richest 20 percent of the urban population.[84] Like the Swedish electoral reform of 1866, it was a remarkable piece of oligarchic institutional engineering.[85]

---

[82] Ferejohn and Rosenbluth, *Forged Through Fire*, 245.
[83] Uffe Jakobsen and Jussi Kurunmäki, "The Formation of Parliamentarism in the Nordic Countries from the Napoleonic Wars to the First World War," in Pasi Ihalainen, Cornelia Ilie, and Kari Palonen, eds., *Parliament and Parliamentarism: A Comparative History of a European Concept* (New York: Berghahn, 2016), 100.
[84] Goldstein, *Political Repression*, 231.
[85] Carstairs's (77) painstaking explanation of the 1866 reform reminds us how the devil truly is in the details: "For the Landsting, the suffrage was now limited to electors who satisfied high property qualifications. Twelve of the sixty-six members of the Landsting were appointed by the Crown, one by the Faroese assembly and the remaining fifty-three by indirect election. Only half of the college of electors was now to be elected (by the relative majority system) by those electors who were enfranchised for the Folketing elections. For the other half of the college of electors, only those in Copenhagen were to be elected, and for these elections the franchise was restricted to persons eligible under a high property qualification. The rural members of the college of electors were to

Not only was the power of monarchy increased from 1849, but the old regime itself received increased representation through enfranchising civil servants, who, as in Prussia, could be counted on to vote conservative. In another departure from 1849, the ministers were not responsible to the Folketing, but to the king. They were also chosen from the Landsting rather than the Folketing. The new constitution also "ensured that the make-up of the two chambers would drastically differ" while making no regular provision "for resolving disputes between the two bodies."[86] In such a case, the king could invoke Paragraph 25 of the 1866 reform that gave the monarch special power to issue emergency legislation. All told, the 1866 constitution was a major rollback from the June 1849 constitution in terms of both suffrage rates and degree of parliamentary sovereignty. The Venstre (the liberal party of the left) and later the Social Democrats would demand a return to the "June Constitution" for the next four decades.

The most important politician during this period was undoubtedly J. B. S. Estrup. Born into a wealthy family, Estrup was elected to the Landsting as a member of the National Landowners Party in 1864 before becoming Minister of the Interior in 1865. One of the architects of the 1866 constitution, he once referred to universal suffrage as "the greatest folly in this otherwise so abundantly foolish age" as it would lead to the "collapse of everything we have learned to respect and to love."[87] He became leader of Højre (the conservatives) and prime minister in 1875. When the Folketing rejected his motion on defense appropriations, Estrup allowed the king to declare a provisional budget, as per Paragraph 25 of the constitution. The Venstre considered this unconstitutional, but Estrup used this mechanism repeatedly from 1875 to 1894 in what turned out to be the longest-serving government in Danish history. Following an assassination attempt in 1885, Estrup increased police action against the socialist press and trade unions and "began to rule in complete defiance of the Folketing."[88] He was so adept at this practice that a proponent of parliamentary democracy in Denmark lamented in

---

consist of persons with high property qualifications, who had the right of membership of the college without election. The system of election was to be Andrae's version of the single transferable vote, which had been used for the now defunct Rigsråd, but the element of fairness or 'proportional representation' which that system contained was in marked contrast with the highly restricted nature of the franchise – it was virtually on the wealthy and the conservative who were 'proportionally' represented."

[86] Oakley, *History of Denmark*, 91.
[87] Goldstein, *Political Repression*, 3.
[88] Caleb Woodhouse, "The Defense Question and Danish Politics, 1864–1914," 206.

1887 that "We can all agree that parliamentarianism is shot to hell, but nobody is willing to admit it."[89]

It is difficult to resist comparing Estrup with Bismarck. Both were reactionary landowners whose domineering position ultimately rested on monarchic power and not on democratic institutions. Their long periods in power overlapped to a remarkable degree, and it is difficult to imagine that they did not take notice of the other. One critical difference, however, was that Estrup – unlike Bismarck – was willing to retire. Whereas Bismarck tried desperately to hold onto power, Estrup was looking for a successor by the early 1890s. At the same time, he "was determined as ever not to let his withdrawal be an integral part of the settlement."[90] The first of two changes to the Danish system – the settlement of 1894 that followed Estrup's departure from government – produced a reconciliation between left and right, though it still left the king free to choose his ministers and to ignore a majority in parliament when forming a government. The second settlement was more dramatic: the so-called "system change" of 1901 that established parliamentarism in Denmark.

Still, on the eve of World War I, a return to the June Constitution had not been achieved. The March 1914 electoral reform would have introduced universal suffrage for both houses and was passed 102 to 2 in the lower chamber. But the conservative upper chamber blocked it and Estrup, who had voluntarily left as prime minister but remained politically active, warned against a return to the June Constitution.[91] The Landsting was dissolved and conservatives lost control of it. As in other states, it is possible that Denmark would have democratized fully before World War I. Collier, for example, claims that it was likely to have passed given the openness of the Venstre to it.[92] The fact remains, however, that the constitutional amendment of June 5, 1915 that abolished property qualifications for Landsting elections and introduced universal male and female suffrage (in 1918 women voted for the first time) only occurred after the outbreak of World War I. The major outlines of Danish political development from 1848 to 1914 was a massive suffrage expansion, a major suffrage rollback following defeat in war, and nearly half a century of trying to – but never ultimately achieving – a return to the June Constitution of 1849.

---

[89] Ibid., 212.
[90] Ibid.
[91] Ibid., 223.
[92] Collier, *Paths Toward Democracy*, 82.

## 6.5 NATIONALISM AND SUFFRAGE EXPANSION

Redistributive theorists of democracy (Acemoglu and Robinson, Boix, Przeworski, and Therborn) have looked toward franchise extensions in Austria, Finland, and Norway for evidence of mass class-based protest leading to democratization. The final section of this chapter argues that this view is misleading: It was independence movements within the Hapsburg Empire and national independence movements within Finland and Norway that really mattered.

### 6.5.1 Austria

The Austrian electoral reform of 1907 that created universal manhood suffrage throughout the Hapsburg empire is cited by Przeworski, as well as by Therborn, as an example of a case in which massive strikes preceded franchise extension.[93] The evidence supporting this claim comes from Jenks' (1974) study of the reform.[94] Yet while Jenks does argue that socialist agitation was an important factor in convincing the emperor in particular of the need for electoral reform, the backdrop for the reform was the complex politics of the national question in the empire. Indeed, Jenks frames his study as a "description of one of the last efforts made to reconcile nationalism and democracy with Hapsburg tradition in the period preceding the final collapse of the empire."[95] He stresses that support for franchise extension came from most national groups in the empire, with the notable exception of the Poles, whose elite were well entrenched in the Hapsburg political system and had no desire to diminish their influence. Czech pressure in the 1890s forced German leaders to concede that electoral reform was a possibility.[96] The Austrian Socialists joined in the nationalist demands, but the large demonstrations they organized for universal suffrage in 1893 and 1894 had little effect on the government.[97] As Jenks notes, "the factor which compelled Austrian politicians to pay attention to the issue [of universal suffrage] was not to be found in Austrian affairs."[98]

---

[93] Göran Therborn, "The Rule of Capital and the Rise of Democracy." *New Left Review* 103, 3–31.
[94] William Jenks, *The Austrian Electoral Reform of 1907* (New York: Columbia University Press, 1974).
[95] Ibid., 5.
[96] Ibid., 6.
[97] Ibid., 22–23.
[98] Ibid., 27.

## 6.5 Nationalism and Suffrage Expansion

Rather, it was the constitutional crisis in Hungary that was decisive. The development of the crisis is too complex to present here, but the key ingredient was the rising power of an ultra-nationalist Hungarian party of the Hungarian elite that threatened to overturn the compromise (*Ausgleich*) of 1867 that had established the dual monarchy. When the Hungarian Lower House refused to back the minority government of Baron Geza Fejervary, the Minister of the Interior Kristoffy proposed to introduce universal manhood suffrage to break the power of the Hungarian magnates. While this threat succeeded in taming the Hungarian opposition, it sparked a renewed push for universal suffrage within Austria. According to Jenks:

> Rumors and surmises of a possible Hungarian reform filled the columns of Austrian newspapers during the summer of 1905, and the possibilities of a similar reform in Austria were explored and exploited rather completely. Party leaders sensed a new issue which might blot out the sorry record of parliamentary turmoil and obstruction; they seemed ready to take full advantage of the opportunity of "serving the people" when parliament reassembled in September, 1905.[99]

This is similar to A. J. P. Taylor's interpretation in his classic study of the Hapsburg Monarchy:

> The Hungarian crisis had unexpected repercussions in Austria. The dynasty could not advocate universal suffrage for one parliament and oppose it in the other ... In Hungary universal suffrage was opposed by the united "Magyar nation;" in Austria, there was no unity in the Reichsrat, even among the parties who would be ruined by universal suffrage. The only organized opposition came from the Poles, who demanded – and secured – excessive representation at the expense of the Little Russians ... In Hungary, universal suffrage had never been more than a tactical threat; in Austria, it seemed a way of escape from the nationalist conflicts of the middle-class politicians.[100]

What all this meant is that, according to Jenks, there was an air of inevitability about the move to universal manhood suffrage that had much more to do with nationalist politics than it did with the threat of revolution by the working class. The nationalist parties in the empire supported universal suffrage (the Poles excepted), but so too did two other nonsocialist forces within Austria: the liberals, who may not have really welcomed universal suffrage but were committed to it in theory, and the Christian Socials, who accurately perceived that they would be big winners when conservative Catholics gained the right to vote.

---

[99] Ibid., 30.
[100] A. J. P. Taylor, *The Habsburg Monarchy, 1809–1918* (Chicago: University of Chicago Press, 1948), 212.

What role then did socialism and the Socialists play? The revolutionary disturbances in Russia "undoubtedly gave the Germans in Austria much to think about," but Jenks notes that the possibility of a pan-Slavic uprising in the empire "was seldom mentioned in the great debates on reform."[101] As noted, Przeworski is correct that Jenks does view the massive strikes organized by Austrian Socialists as the decisive factor that convinced the Emperor to decide for universal suffrage.[102] However, Jenks also recognizes that the Socialists' long-term crusade for universal suffrage had been unsuccessful before the Hungarian crisis, and that their threats had been dismissed in the past. A safe conclusion is that socialist agitation was important in the context of long-running nationalist problems and the spark of the Hungarian crisis but would have been unlikely to produce reform on its own.

### 6.5.2 Finland

Przeworski codes Finland as another case in which massive strikes preceded suffrage extension.[103] Yet the granting of universal suffrage in 1906 cannot be separated from the actual – and not the threat – of revolution in Russia, of which Finland was a part until 1917. Facing more serious problems elsewhere in the Empire, the Tsar conceded to Finnish demands for constitutional reform. The fact that these demands were pushed by the Socialists did not worry the Tsar unduly as "the Russians were much more alarmed by small bourgeois groups thought to be advocating separatism than by the Social Democrats."[104]

The political strikes of 1905 were also the culmination of national resistance rather than class-based agitation.[105] The most important political cleavage in Finnish politics leading up to the reform was not based on class but on the national question that pitted the Constitutionalists (a coalition of the Young Finnish Party, an upper-class nationalist movement, and the Swedish Liberals) against the Compliers (those groups that benefited from Russian rule). Since universal suffrage was championed by Finnish nationalists, Swedish liberals, and socialists, it meant that it

---

[101] Jenks, *Austrian Electoral Reform*, 31.
[102] Ibid., 41–45; 208–209.
[103] Przeworski, "Conquered or Granted?"
[104] Risto Alapuro, *State and Revolution in Finland* (Berkeley: University of California Press, 1988), 127.
[105] Klaus Tornudd, *The Electoral System of Finland* (London: Hugh Evelyn Limited, 1968), 28.

had close to universal consensus within the nationalist movement and helps explain why Finland adopted the most liberal constitution for its time in 1906. The fact that the Tsar stopped short of granting Finland independence and would proceed to trample on the new constitution until 1917 also helps explain such apparent magnanimity. The threat of class-based revolution had little direct role in the Finnish case.

### 6.5.3 Norway

Norway mirrors Finland in that franchise extensions were inextricably linked with the independence movement (in this case from Sweden). The main protagonists in this struggle were liberal nationalists that founded the Left party (Venstre) in 1884 after the supremacy of parliament was established. Although Collier's claim that this reform – which expanded the franchise – was a "result of a fierce struggle that almost erupted in civil war" would appear to fit the Acemoglu and Robinson narrative, this is an exaggeration.[106] The volunteer rifle clubs that would have compromised the armed resistance movement were peacefully disarmed when the Norwegian army authorities "went no further than to remove the bolts from stored rifles, put cartridge stocks out of harm's way, and load some of the cannons of the Oslo fortress."[107] The major battles for reform were fought not outside of parliament but within it between the early 1870s and 1884.

Therborn claims that the Left party "came out in opposition to universal suffrage" after 1884 and that it was only the labor movement's agitation that persuaded the liberals to overcome the resistance from rural interests.[108] Yet it is difficult to see how he arrived at this conclusion. Norway industrialized late, and the tiny Labor Party would not even gain parliamentary representation until 1905. The year before the extension of universal suffrage in 1898, it had won less than 1 percent in elections. Moreover, Collier, drawing on Luebbert and Derby, is correct in noting that the Liberals championed universal suffrage after a party split in 1884 in order to align themselves squarely with the nationalist movement for independence, which was achieved in 1905.[109] As in Finland, the overall picture that emerges in Norway is a fusion of the drives for independence and democracy with broad consensus for universal suffrage.

[106] Collier, *Paths Toward Democracy*, 67.
[107] Thomas Derry, *A History of Modern Norway* (Oxford: Clarendon Press, 1973), 58.
[108] Therborn, "Rule of Capital," 15.
[109] Collier, *Paths Toward Democracy*, 68; Luebbert, *Liberalism, Fascism, and Social Democracy*, 121; Derry, *Modern Norway*, 155.

## 6.6 CONCLUSION

Despite their revolutionary ideology, most working-class parties had in practice abandoned direct, extra-parliamentary confrontations with the state before most franchise extensions. In 1895, Engels himself had advised that socialist parties no longer adopt revolutionary tactics because technological change and growing state capacity made it too easy for capitalist forces to crush any uprising. It was not only the "policemen's truncheon" that the bourgeoisie now found soothing; it was also their machine guns. And yet repression was not really the central means by which the competitive oligarchies of Northern Europe retained their power. Counter-majoritarian institutions in the form of suffrage restrictions, plural voting, and unelected upper chambers with veto power were so effective that the threat of force – other than in Belgium – was rarely needed to defend the system. Neither was the systematic election rigging that, as Chapter 7 argues, was the old regime's solution to mass politics in Southern Europe.

# 7

# From Competitive Oligarchy to Competitive Authoritarianism in Italy

The Italian elections of 1913 were the first held under nearly universal manhood suffrage and produced yet another governing majority for Prime Minister Giovanni Giolitti. Hailing from a family of Piedmontese civil servants, Giolitti was the first Italian prime minister with no ties to the Italian wars of Unification of 1860 (the *Risorgimento*). His first ministry, which had ended abruptly in 1893 following a banking scandal and revolt in Sicily, gave no indication of future success. His comeback began amidst democratic backsliding in the late 1890s, when he stood with fellow liberals and socialists against an increasingly authoritarian government, and he was almost sixty when he became interior minister in 1901. But from 1903 to 1914, there were only 219 days when Giolitti did not control the Italian government, either directly or by handing power temporarily to a close ally, and this period in Italian history is rightfully known as "the Giolittian Age."[1] For some contemporary observers and historians, Giolitti had appeared to have successfully integrated the two major "subversive" political forces – Socialism and Catholicism – into a genuinely democratic system. In his *History of Italy, 1871–1915*, the liberal historian Benedetto Croce wrote that Italy had "one of the most democratic governments in Europe" on the eve of WWI.[2]

However, another contemporary, Orazio Raimondo, a socialist deputy from Sanremo (near Genoa), reached the opposite conclusion. During a

---

[1] Christopher Seton-Watson, *Italy from Liberalism to Fascism, 1870–1925* (London: Methuen, 1967), 225.

[2] Benedetto Croce, *A History of Italy, 1871–1915* (Oxford: Oxford University Press, 1929), 193.

speech in the Chamber of Deputies on December 6, 1913, Raimondo lamented as follows:

> The truth is, honorable colleagues, that under a democratic banner we have imperceptibly arrived at a dictatorial regime. The Honorable Giolitti has four times conducted the elections: in 1892, in 1904, in 1909, and in 1913. In his long parliamentary career he has, moreover, nominated practically all the senators (*Laughter*), all the prefects, and all the other high officials in the administrative, judiciary, political, and military hierarchy of our country (*Comments*). With this formidable power of his – let us all recite our *mea culpas* – he has done the work of drawing parties together by means of reforms and of drawing individuals together by means of personal attention (*Comments*). Now, Honorable Giolitti, when parties forget their programs, when those who come here leave at the doors the rags of their political convictions, it means a majority must be achieved by other means, as all personal powers are forced to do: with trickery and corruption (*Approval on the Extreme Left*). In this way, parliamentary institutions are annulled, party lines annihilated, and transformism, which has no justification whatsoever, is achieved.[3]

As with every speech in any parliament, we should consider the motives of the speaker as well as their words. Perhaps Raimondo was simply venting the Italian Socialist Party's (PSI) frustration with his party's electoral performance? The franchise extension had only raised the socialist vote by around 3 percent (from 19 percent in 1909 to 22.8 percent in 1913), and although the number of PSI deputies rose from 41 to 79, there were few signs of breakthroughs outside the party's traditional strongholds. Or perhaps Raimondo's comments were typical of an Italian parliamentary culture of hyperbole. Indeed, Gaetano Salvemini wrote that "Italian political literature from 1862 to 1922 is drenched with a flood of bitter criticism about everything and everybody."[4] The legacies of unification and the endurance of local loyalties created a deeply fractured political unit. One observer noted that, "The Catholics hated the liberal democratic unified secular kingdom, men from other regions hated the domination of the Piedmontese, Milan hated Rome, the Tuscans hated everybody else, the south hated the north, the republicans hated the monarchists, [and] the middle classes feared revolution."[5]

The Catholics, however, were not complaining in late 1913, for their electoral pact with Giolitti's liberal block (the Gentolini Pact) had

---

[3] *Atti Parlamentari.* "Discussioni della Camera dei Deputati. Tornata del 6 dicembre 1913," I, 184.
[4] Gaetano Salvemini, "Introduction," in Salamone, *Italian Democracy in Transition*, vii.
[5] Luigi Barzini, "Romance and the Risorgimento." *The New York Review of Books*, October 5, 1972.

## 7 From Competitive Oligarchy to Authoritarianism in Italy 207

produced major gains and brought them into the government. Monsignor Nicola Giannattasio communicated to the Bishop of Lecce that "the Gentolini program seems to me to have been worked out with Giolitti," adding that "I believe that we can be content."[6] Although the Gentolini pact had been secret, it was not undemocratic and constituted a partial settlement to the "Roman Question" that had poisoned Italian politics since unification. Even more importantly, it confirmed the Catholics as system-supporting rather than "subversive." Giolitti had also reached out to the Socialists repeatedly since becoming the prime minister in 1901, and although the "transformism" that Raimondo denounced had not worked as well as with the Catholics, the reformist wing of the party had become defenders of parliamentary democracy. The Socialists could not deny that Giolitti was the first Italian prime minister to regard trade unions as lawful associations and to maintain that the state must remain neutral in disputes between labor and capital. Even Giolitti's many critics acknowledged their freedom to engage in such polemics without retaliation.

Given the democratic features of Liberal Italy, it is understandable why political scientists have often considered Italy to be a case – albeit a late one – of first wave democratization. It meets the criteria in dichotomous coding schemes of Przeworski and Boix. According to Collier's more Dahlian approach, Italy passed the democratic threshold in 1913 with the first elections held under near universal male suffrage.[7] But this chapter argues that such coding was initially based on histories of the regimes written by liberals (like Croce) who emphasized the democratic achievements of the new Italian state and downplayed its oligarchic features. As with Imperial Germany, the evidence for authoritarian resilience outweighs that for genuine democratization in Liberal Italy (1860–1914). Put another way, Raimondo's diagnosis of the Giolittian system was basically right, as most of the rest of this chapter will argue. The comparison between Italy and Germany is tempting, particularly given the reproduction of a historical debate using the same basic terms.

---

[6] Alexander De Grand, *The Hunchback's Tailor: Giovanni Giolitti and Liberal Italy from the Challenge of Mass Politics to the Rise of Fascism, 1882–1922* (Westport: Praeger, 2001), 181.

[7] At the same time, Collier adds that "because of the ongoing informal practice of intervention in the electoral process, some analysts have dated the move to a democratic regime with the 1919 reforms, which, in addition to eliminating the remaining restrictions on the suffrage for males between twenty-one and thirty, introduced proportional representation, thereby substantially curbing those practices by giving an advantage to well-organized parties." Ruth Collier, *Paths Toward Democracy*, 72.

TABLE 7.1 *GDP per Capita by Decade in Select European Countries (Maddison Project)*

|  | 1830 | 1840 | 1850 | 1860 | 1870 | 1880 | 1890 | 1900 | 1910 | 1920 |
|---|---|---|---|---|---|---|---|---|---|---|
| Austria | 2,230 | 2,415 | 2,630 | 2,834 | 2,970 | 3,314 | 3,894 | 4,594 | 5,244 | 3,845 |
| Belgium | – | – | 2,944 | 3,655 | 4,291 | 4,886 | 5,464 | 5,947 | 6,478 | 6,315 |
| Denmark | 2,120 | 2,276 | 2,817 | 2,775 | 3,193 | 3,476 | 4,022 | 4,809 | 5,906 | 6,363 |
| France | 1,898 | 2,276 | 2,546 | 3,016 | 2,990 | 3,376 | 3,787 | 4,584 | 4,726 | 5,144 |
| Germany | – | – | – | – | 2,931 | 3,174 | 3,870 | 4,758 | 5,337 | 4,457 |
| Italy | 2,657 | 2,711 | 2,611 | 2,573 | 2,926 | 2,796 | 2,974 | 3,264 | 3,829 | 3,789 |
| Netherlands | 3,038 | 3,623 | 3,779 | 3,840 | 4,422 | 4,666 | 5,078 | 5,306 | 6,030 | 6,727 |
| Norway | 1,441 | 1,607 | 1,623 | 1,887 | 2,177 | 2,503 | 2,769 | 3,249 | 3,826 | 4,739 |
| Portugal | 1,721 | 1,503 | 1,470 | – | 1,554 | 1,510 | 1,798 | 2,075 | 1,957 | 1,959 |
| Spain | – | – | 1,706 | 1,930 | 1,809 | 2,520 | 2,463 | 2,676 | 2,823 | 3,244 |
| Sweden | 1,468 | 1,568 | 1,715 | 1,941 | 2,144 | 2,359 | 2,606 | 3,320 | 4,053 | 4,788 |
| Switzerland | – | – | – | 2,934 | 2,954 | 3,869 | 5,309 | 6,612 | 8,048 | 7,364 |
| United Kingdom | 3,550 | 4,018 | 4,332 | 5,086 | 5,829 | 5,997 | 6,845 | 7,594 | 7,718 | 7,017 |

Yet in many ways the more fruitful comparison is with other Mediterranean and Balkan states "where advanced constitutions proclaiming liberty, fraternity, and equality were proclaimed in the midst of poverty, slavery, and economic backwardness."[8] Data from the Maddison Project reproduced in Table 7.1 reveal that Italy, Portugal and Spain lagged most other Western European states at the end of the war.[9] Portugal's political development over the first wave reveals many parallels with Italy's. The system of Rotativismo was the Portuguese equivalent of *trasformismo* and similarly aided elite collusion. The franchise was limited and rolled back on several occasions. Elections were managed in similar ways. Indeed, electoral corruption in both Portugal and Italy was not product of the system, but rather its foundations. Spain, Romania, and potentially other cases in Central and Eastern Europe functioned similarly before WWI.

## 7.1 HISTORIOGRAPHY OF "LIBERAL" ITALY

How is it possible to study Italian history and arrive at diametrically opposed views of Giolitti's achievements? According to Martin Clark, the debate on Giolitti is in part a reflection of general trends in the Italian

---

[8] Tom Gallagher, *Portugal: A Twentieth Century Interpretation* (Manchester: Manchester University Press, 1983), 13–14.
[9] https://ourworldindata.org/grapher/gdp-per-capita-maddison-project-database

historical profession: "Italian historians are rarely shy, retiring scholars ... they are far more likely to be busy professional politicians ... the history they write has often been 'committed history' designed to cheer on their own." This "ensured that much Italian history-writing was hagiographical, or denunciatory, or 'Whig,' and that unwelcome facts would be ignored."[10] Indeed, some of these "busy professional politicians" include Benedetto Croce, Gaetano Mosca, and Gaetano Salvemini, each of whom contributed substantially to the historiography of Liberal Italy.

Croce is synonymous with the liberal view, which is based on the claim that "despite facing great obstacles and challenges, and despite some minor character flaws and failings, the liberal state was generally a success."[11] Croce took a similar attitude toward history as George Trevelyan (see Chapter 3) and believed that "what was important to stress in public was the good, the positive, the heroic, the liberal, for only thus would history be rightly educational."[12] According to Mack-Smith, this meant that "Croce sometimes relied on imagination rather than scholarly research, inventing and exaggerating facts to reinforce his eulogy of liberal patriotism."[13] Nevertheless, he was the most influential historian of his generation and "most post-war historians and their readers were reared on Croce's *History of Italy, 1871–1915*, a commemorative hymn to Liberal Italy."[14]

William Salamone's *Italian Democracy in the Making*, published in 1943, was the first rigorous study of Giolittian Italy to achieve a modicum of political neutrality. Although the book's title reflects a sympathy with liberals, it was very different in tone from Croce's work and did not whitewash electoral corruption.[15] Indeed, Salvemini – the greatest critic of the Giolittian system – wrote the introductory essay and used it to repeat many of the arguments he had made as Giolitti's political adversary. A major theme of *Italian Democracy in the Making* is the gradualism of the democratic transition, and though Salamone falls short of proclaiming liberal Italy a democracy on the eve of WWI, he does

---

[10] Martin Clark, *Modern Italy, 1871 to the Present*, 3rd ed. (New York: Pearson Longman, 2008), 5.
[11] Nick Carter, "Rethinking the Italian Liberal State." *Bulletin of Italian Politics* 3, 2 (2011), 227. See also Nick Carter, *Modern Italy in Historical Perspective* (London: Bloomsbury Academic, 2010).
[12] Mack Smith, "Benedetto Croce: History and Politics." *Journal of Contemporary History* 8, 1 (1973), 56.
[13] Ibid., 55.
[14] Clark, *Modern Italy*, 6.
[15] Mack Smith refers to Croce's *History of Italy, 1871–1915* as a "splendid apology for liberalism."

rule positively on the Giolittian age, referring to it as "a true nationalist resurgence."[16] Frank Coppa's 1971 study was even more laudatory, comparing Giolitti positively with Franklin Delano Roosevelt as the democratic founders of the modern welfare state and concluding that "modern industrial and progressive Italy stands as the greatest monument to the work of Giovanni Giolitti."[17] In a series of essays that were later published as a book, Raffaele Romanelli argued that liberal intentions were genuine, but that they lacked the capacity to enforce liberalism.[18] Other Italian social and economic historians challenged the empirical underpinnings of the "Sonderweg" thesis in the 1980s and 1990s, much like the "Peculiarities of German History" school had done in the 1970s.[19] American historians of Italy picked up these themes and reached conclusions similar to Coppa and Croce. One argued that,

> The liberals dealt with significant challenges to their principles and to their power before the war, and they met them in large part successfully. They kept Italy united; they upheld rights, although not always and not for everyone equally; they stretched the state to promote economic growth and to provide a modicum of protection to workers. In the process, they admitted the weight of circumstances, adapted their principles and adjusted to the difficulties of parliamentary rule. The English and the French, those systems commonly credited with success in this period [1860–1914] did no more.[20]

The Marxist view, summarized by Antonio Gramsci in *The Prison Notebooks*, was that the middle class had failed in its function as democratic vanguard.[21] Given Gramsci's towering intellectual influence, it is

---

[16] William Salamone, *Italian Democracy in the Making: The Political Scene in the Giolittian Era 1900–1914* (Philadelphia: University of Pennsylvania Press, 1945), 97.

[17] Frank Coppa, *Planning, Protectionism and Politics in Liberal Italy: Economic and Politics in the Giolittian Age* (Washington: Catholic Press of America, 1971).

[18] Raffaele Romanelli, *Il commando impossibile: Stato e società nell'Italia liberale* (Bologna: Il Mulino, 1988).

[19] For a review of some major works in this area, see J. A. Davis, "Remapping Italy's path to the twentieth century." *Journal of Modern History*, LXVI, 2 (1994): 291–320; See also: Raffaella Gherardi, *L'arte del compromesso. La politica della mediazione nell'Italia liberale* (Il Mulino: Bologna, 1993); Fulvio Cammarano, *Il progresso moderato. Un'opposizione liberale nella svolta dell'Italia crispina* (Il Mulino: Bologna, 1990). For some interesting reflections on intellectual ties between British and Italian historians of modern Italy, see the "Round Table: The "British" School and Italian Historiography." *Modern Italy* 22, 4 (2017), 471–483.

[20] Susan A. Ashley, *Making Liberalism Work: The Italian Experience, 1860–1914* (London: Praeger, 2003), 170.

[21] More specifically, according to Gramsci:

> The merit of an educated class, because it is their historic function, it to lead the popular masses and develop their progressive elements ... [the Italian bourgeoisie] said they were aiming at the creation of

important to mention its impact on the writing of history.[22] However, since one of the primary themes of this book has been that the middle class failed as a democratizing force pretty much everywhere in Europe, we will not pursue Gramsci's analysis of Italy further. A far more prominent school in the historiography of the period is what we can inelegantly but precisely call the non-Marxist anti-liberal view, according to which "liberal Italy was a deviant state: it had strayed from the 'normal' path of modern state development represented by the likes of Britain and France, and instead had followed an altogether different road, one that ultimately led to fascism."[23] The connection to Imperial Germany is clear and has provoked a similar, if slightly less voluminous, debate about the existence of an Italian *Sonderweg*.[24]

Foremost in this group was Salvemini, who emigrated to the United States and taught history at Harvard University. Born in the southern region of Apulia of modest means, Salvemini was a historian before joining the PSI and entering politics as one of Giolitti's most articulate and vocal opponents.[25] His mock title for Giolitti – "Minister of the Underworld" (*Il Ministro della mala vita*) – stuck from the moment he published a satirical essay in *Avanti*, the PSI's official journal, in 1910."[26] Salvemini left the PSI in 1911 and spent the rest of his political career as an independent radical, dedicated to exposing, as he put it, the "gnawing cancer of Italian democracy in the making," before he fled fascism in 1925.[27] Like Raimondo, he recognized Giolitti as a skillful

---

a modern state in Italy, and they in fact produced a bastard. They aimed at stimulating the formation of an extensive and energetic ruling class, and they did not succeed; at integrating the people into the framework of the new state, and they did not succeed. The paltry political life from 1870 to 1900, the fundamental and endemic rebelliousness of the Italian popular classes, the narrow and stunted existence of a skeptical and cowardly ruling stratum, these are all consequences of that failure.

Antonio Gramsci, *Selections from the Prison Notebooks*, ed. Q. Hoare and G. Nowell Smith (London: Lawrence and Wishart, 1971), 70.

[22] The Gramscian perspective was rich enough that it allowed Giorgio Candeloro to write an eleven-volume history of Italy that appeared over the course of three decades. Giorgio Candeloro, *Storia dell' Italia moderna*, 11 Vols. (Milan: Feltrinelli, 1956–1986).

[23] Nick Carter, "Rethinking the Italian Liberal State," 226.

[24] Paul Corner, "The Road to Fascism: An Italian *Sonderweg*?" *Contemporary European History* II, 2 (2002), 273–295. See also Lucy Riall, "Progress and Compromise in Liberal Italy." *The Historical Journal* 38, 1 (March 1995), 205–213.

[25] For a sympathetic review of Salvemini's scholarly work, see Dante Puzzo, "Gaetano Salvemini: An Historiographical Essay." *Journal of the History of Ideas* 20, 2 (April 1959), 217–235. For a general biography of Salvemini, see Charles L. Killinger, *Gaetano Salvemini: A Biography* (Ann Arbor: University of Michigan Press, 2002).

[26] The original has not been translated into English, but an Italian version has been reissued. Gaetano Salvemeni, *Il Ministro dell Mala Vita* (Bollati Boringhieri, 2021).

[27] Gaetano Salvemini, "Introduction," xii.

dictator. According to Salvemini, "Giolitti was for Mussolini what John the Baptist was for Christ: he paved his way."[28] In his analysis of the origins of fascism in Italy, "Salvemini had taken upon himself the task of indicating the connivance of the Liberal State as the key to the fascist success."[29] Other historians who broadly agree with Salvemini's analysis include Denis Mack Smith[30], Christopher Seton-Watson,[31] and, to a lesser degree, Martin Clark.[32]

As in Germany, the fascist experience in Italy complicated the historiography of the previous regime. The fascists, naturally, produced their own official histories of the period, but one must agree with Salvemini's assessment that they are too weak intellectually and too politically motivated to offer any value. More consequential are the biographies of the key participants, and specifically their own relationship to the fascist regime. For example, Croce's interpretation of fascism as a "parenthesis" in Italian history cannot really be separated from his collaboration with it. Croce was Minister of Education from June 1920 to June 1921 in what would be Giolitti's final government, and he approved of the liberal's fateful decision to include fascists in it.[33] He then supported the new electoral law of 1923 that marked a major step toward the consolidation of fascism and backed the fascists in the elections of 1924. Long after Mussolini had solidified his dictatorship, Croce held to the myth that *Il Duce* was the old regime's puppet. According to Mack Smith, Croce "told a friend in June 1926 that he was sure the Liberals could overturn Mussolini when the time was right, and that in the meantime he is our prisoner."[34] Given such dramatic miscalculations, it is hard to disagree with Smith's view that Croce's political choices colored his scholarship on the Giolittian age: "Because [Croce] wanted to forget fascism or conjure it away, he did little to explain how it had occupied and what had been wrong in pre-fascist Italy, for that would not only have seemed unpatriotic but would have meant exposing his own errors of judgment and perception."[35]

---

[28] William Salamone, *Italian Democracy*, 131–132.
[29] Roberto Vivavelli, "Introduction to *The Origins of Fascism in Italy*," x.
[30] Denis Mack Smith, *Italy: A Modern History* (Ann Arbor: University of Michigan Press, 1969).
[31] Christopher Seton-Watson, *Italy from Liberalism to Fascism* (London: 1968).
[32] Clark, *Modern Italy*.
[33] Mack Smith, "Benedetto Croce," 45.
[34] Ibid., 49.
[35] Ibid., 59.

The fascist era ironically also softened Salvemini's views on the liberal Italy he had repeatedly attacked. This was not due to any personal collaboration with the regime, for unlike Croce, Mosca, Pareto, and ultimately Giolitti, Salvemini never waivered in his opposition to fascism. Compared to Mussolini, Salvemini admits, Giolitti was a model democract: "I would have been wiser had I been more moderate in my criticism of the Giolittian system" as he was "much less reprehensible than the Italian politicians who followed him." He expressed remorse as well:

While we Italian crusaders attacked him [Giolitti] from the Left accusing him of being – as he was – a corrupter of Italian democracy in the making, others assailed him from the Right because he was too democratic for their taste. Our criticism thus did not help to direct the evolution of Italian public life toward less imperfect forms of democracy, but rather toward the victory of those militarists, nationalists, and reactionary groups who had found even Giolitti's democracy too perfect.[36]

## 7.2 COMPETITIVE OLIGARCHY: ITALY 1860–1893

One point of agreement among historians of Italy is that the unification of Italy (*the Risorgimento*) was an elite project. More specifically, it was a Piedmontese project. Although it was the most liberal of the political entities on the peninsula, Piedmont was still a constitutional monarchy with a suffrage rate of around 2 percent at the time of unification in 1860. The new Italian state was thus born with a highly restricted suffrage, as opposed to the German one where Bismarck pronounced the experiment with universal male suffrage in Prussia a success and worked it first into the constitution of the North German Confederation and then into that of united Germany (see Chapter 3). The suffrage in Italy from 1861 to 1882 was so restricted – under a hundred voters in many constituencies – that many districts resembled the "rotten boroughs" of Britain fifty years earlier (see Chapter 3). Everyone recognized the exclusive nature of the system. Count Cavour, the hero of the *Risorgimento* who could scarcely be called a democrat, lamented the fact that some deputies in the first elections had been elected on the basis of five or six votes in total.[37] Such cases were outliers, but the oligarchic nature of the system has been confirmed by subsequent research. In 1874, the median successful candidate received only 426 votes while the median constituency had a population

---

[36] Salvemini, "Introduction," xv.
[37] Smith, *Italy*, 133.

of 50,000.[38] The suffrage expansion of 1882 raised the enfranchisement rate to around 7 percent by lowering some property requirements. The literacy requirement remained, however, and it was a serious hurdle to participation as the 1882 census reported a literacy rate of only 62 percent nationally, with rates approaching 90 percent in the south.

### 7.2.1 Elite Democracy

The founders of what would become known as the "Italian School of Elitism" came of political age under this system. Gaetano Mosca, who introduced the concept of "the ruling class" into political science, derived a timeless political law from his observation of Italian politics. Summarizing his theory in 1884, Mosca explained that,

> In all societies – from societies that are very meagerly developed and have barely attained the dawnings of civiliziation, down to the most advanced and powerful societies – two classes of people appear – a class that rules and a class that is ruled. The first class, always the less numerous, performs all political functions, monopolizes power and enjoys the advantages that power brings, whereas the second, the more numerous class, is directed and controlled by the first, in a manner that is more or less legal, now more or less arbitrary and violent, and supplies the first, in appearance at least, with material means of subsistence and with the instrumentalities that are essential to the vitality of the political organism.[39]

Given such passages, it is understandable that "the Italian intellectuals came to be seen as proponents of oligarchy who celebrate the way in which liberal political institutions contain mass/popular participation."[40] Yet this was, according to Natasha Piano, due in large part to an initial misreading by Seymour Martin Lipset of their arguments. Of the three, only Mosca was against universal suffrage, and voted against the universal suffrage bill of 1912 in the Chamber of Deputies. Mosca wanted to attenuate what he saw as the "evils of parliamentarism," which he defined as "the continuous pottering, interloping, and officiousness on the part of members of the lower house."[41] His solution was to return to constitutional monarchy (his model here was Imperial Germany) and an "extensive and organic decentralization" that would transfer "many of

---

[38] Clark, *Modern Italy*, 77.
[39] Mosca, *The Ruling Class* (New York: McGraw-Hill, 1939), 50.
[40] Natasha Piano, "Revisiting Democratic Elitism: The Italian School of Elitism, American Political Science, and the Problem of Plutocracy." *Journal of Politics* 81, 2 (April 2019), 536.
[41] Mosca, *The Ruling Class*, 255.

the functions that are now exercised by bureaucracies and elective bodies to the class of public-spirited citizens."[42] Thus even in Mosca's case, his work "reads much more like an exposee of minority domination that encourages democratic renewal of political leadership from below, rather than a celebratory or resigned acceptance of elite rule."[43] Indeed, many of Mosca's criticisms are directed at the "management" of elections by the state. For example,

> It is a matter of common knowledge that the defects of parliamentary government in Europe almost all come down to improper interference with elections to central and local elective bodies by bureaucracies, acting mainly through prefects appointed by the ministries, and to equally improper interference with the bureaucracies by representatives elected to the national chambers. All this gives rise to a shameful and hypocritical traffic in reciprocal indulgences and mutual favors, which is a veritable running sore in most European countries.[44]

Vilfredo Pareto was the first social scientist to use term the "elites" widely. Until the early 1890s, Pareto was a republican democrat.[45] In 1891, he wrote about democracy that "I am not blind to its defects ... but it seems the lesser evil lies on this side." During the 1890s, however, Pareto became a critic of his own democratic government, although not of democracy in general.[46] By 1900, however, he had become an antidemocrat. His "strong hostility to democracy" was "largely a result of his own experience with a corrupt Italian regime which was run by a clique of mediocre politicians."[47] Pareto welcomed the fascist government of Mussolini, as did many other Italian intellectuals, such as Croce, and politicians, including Giolitti. He died in 1923, which was before the consolidation of the fascist regime, but was nevertheless honored by it.[48]

---

[42] Ibid., 265.
[43] Piano, "Democratic Elitism," 527.
[44] Mosca, *Ruling Class*, 265–266.
[45] According to S. E. Finer: "until he was fifty, Pareto had dedicated himself like a fanatic to tearing down the privileges of the Italian bourgeoisie. He had stood as a radical candidate against them in 1882. He had written over one hundred and sixty articles against them in the four brief years 1889–1893. His meetings had been closed down by the Italian police and he himself had become a marked man. He had given money and shelter to the Italian society refugees in 1898." S. E. Finer, "Pareto and Pluto-Democracy: The Retreat from Galapagos." *American Political Science Review* 62, 2 (June 1968), 448.
[46] Renato Cirillo, "Was Vilfredo Pareto Really a 'Precursor' to Fascism?" *American Journal of Economics and Sociology* 42, 2 (April 1983), 235–245.
[47] Ibid., 245.
[48] Pareto's correspondence reveals little engagement with fascism before the March on Rome, and Cirillo argues that the fascists appropriated Pareto after his death because "fascism needed an intellectual of the caliber of Pareto to lend prestige and credibility

Robert Michels, who coined the phrase "Iron law of oligarchy" was the clearest of the three in explicating his normative views. For him, "nothing but a serene and frank examination of the oligarchical dangers of democracy will enable us to minimize these dangers, even though they can never be entirely avoided." He viewed democracy as "the least of evils." More than either Mosca or Pareto, Michel's "pessimism is intended to motivate a kind of strategic vigilance against the plutocratic hierarchy they diagnosed as pervading liberal governments – and, more generally, strategic vigilance against the continuous threat of democracy devolving into oligarchy as a result of the consolidation of leadership."[49]

Oligarchy was not only a product of electoral rules. Indeed, one the largest checks on political participation stemmed from the policy of the Catholic Church toward the Italian state. The wars of Italian unification eviscerated the Papal states and left the Church with only Vatican City. An embittered Pope Pius IX refused to mention the state of Italy by name and referred to himself as the "prisoner in the Vatican." In 1871, he issued the *non-expedit* that threatened any Catholic who participated in Italian politics with excommunication.[50] Pope Leo XIII restated the policy in an 1886 decree of the Holy Office. In 1895, when the Italian state declared September 20 a national holiday to mark the 25th anniversary of the occupation of Rome, Leo XIII "retaliated by reaffirming the *non-expedit* in a more rigid form than ever before."[51] Thus for over thirty years, the non-expedit limited an already narrow franchise in an overwhelmingly Catholic country even further.

Contemporaries recognized the oligarchic nature of Liberal Italy. One veteran of the Risorgimento noted that,

> We brought about a revolution, which was largely the work of an intelligent, educated, and disinterested bourgeoisie ... The people were in such conditions as not to be able to participate in the revolution, and were in a sense therefore dragged along by us. But precisely because we stood alone in this effort, because we alone were intent on completing the creation of a free Italy ... we found

---

to its cause." Cirillo, 237; Finer reached a similar conclusion about Pareto's disenchantment with democracy: "His disgust with democracy was not that of the fascist who valued liberty too low, but of the lover, the outmoded individualist, who valued it too high (450)."

[49] Piano, "Democratic Elitism," 529.

[50] The policy was called the "non-expedit" because, when the question of Catholic voting was taken to the Penitentiary Tribunal in 1871, the ruling was that it was not "expedient." Interestingly, the non-expedit only applied to national politics, and Catholics were allowed to stand in local and provincial elections. Clark, *Modern Italy*, 103.

[51] Seton-Watson, *Italy from Liberalism to Fascism*, 223.

ourselves ... isolated in a closed circle and we almost came to think that our little world was the whole world, forgetting that outside our narrow circle there is a vastly numerous class, to which Italy has never given a thought....[52]

The Risorgimento veteran and Minister of Education Francesco De Sanctis decried the fact that by 1877, "We have now reached the point where there are no solidly built parties in Italy except those based on either regional differences or the personal relation of client to patron; and these are the twin plagues of Italy."[53] Over a decade later, Francisco Crispi, the Sicilian hero of the Risorgimento, elaborated on this point as follows:

Since 1878 we have no political parties in Italy ... only political men and groups, and each group, instead of comprehending an order of ideas, has been just an association of individuals whose opinions have constantly changed. This state of affairs has been actively encouraged by the government ... With the elections of 1882, the disorders of the Chamber penetrated into the country at large. The candidates did not form up in parties with definite programs, since they had no principles to defend, but were possessed only of the intention to re-enter parliament.[54]

Three years earlier, Crispi had described in detail how this system functioned. He wrote,

In parliament a kind of bilateral contract is often made: the minister gives the local population into the hands of a deputy on condition that the latter promises the ministry his vote: the prefect and the chief of police are nominated in the interests of the deputy in order to keep local interest in his favor ... There is pandemonium in parliament when an important vote comes along, as government agents run through rooms and down corridors collecting votes and promising subsidies, decorations, canals, and bridges.[55]

### 7.2.2 Trasformismo

Crispi was describing *trasformismo* – the same practice that Raimondo decried in 1913. *Trasformismo* can be defined as "the tendency of mainstream parties to converge to the center, excluding the extreme forces, as well as the ability of the politicians to change their opinions and affiliations in order to protect/promote particularistic interests, controlling the

---

[52] Berman, *Democracy and Dictatorship*, 133.
[53] Smith, *Italy*, 111.
[54] Ibid., 136.
[55] Quoted in Smith, *Italy*, 199; Although Crispi criticized *trasformismo* while out of government, he did nothing to change it while prime minister. Roberts, *Europe 1880–1945*, 179.

bureaucratic apparatus."[56] The term originated in an electoral address by Depretis in 1882, calling on his opponents to "transform" themselves and join his government.[57] An electoral deal between Depretis and Minghetti in those elections was *trasformismo*'s first manifestation.[58] As Valbruzzi describes, at its core *trasformismo* involved the systematic management of elections:

> The first step took place during the pre-electoral period, thanks to the meticulous operation of the prefects at the local level. In this respect, suffice to say that by (ab)using the local power of the prefects, the ruling elite was able to mold its parliamentary majority well in advance. The second step toward the formation of the "transformist coalition" occurred at the electoral level and took the form of "semi-coordinated electoral stand-downs," namely pre-electoral arrangements between politicians of the "liberal-conservative" camp. Finally, although this process proceeded as a never-ending vicious circle from the local level up to the central level, the third step required the formation, at the center of the party system, of a sort of "coalition of the willing" made up of all those parliamentarians willing or, in many cases, eager to trade their vote and consensus to the government in exchange for pork barrel favors.[59]

There are many points of comparison with the French Second Empire. In both cases: "The Prefect was the lynch-pin of the whole political system, the link between national and local government."[60] The Italian prefect, for example, provided names of suitable candidates for mayor. The Prefect of Caltanissetta, when submitting a list of names to Depretis (who, like nearly every Italian Prime Minister in this period also headed the Interior Ministry), wrote that his primary consideration had been to find: "a citizen who is a competent administrator, loyal to the King and devoted to the present government; my intention is to secure people who will be effective in making government candidates prevail at parliamentary elections." The job requirements look very much like those of the official Bonapartist candidates (see Chapter 4).

---

[56] Marco Valbruzzi, "*Trasformismo*, an Ugly Word for an Uglier Thing," in Erik Jones and Gianfranco Pasquino, *The Oxford Handbook of Italian Politics*, Oxford Handbooks Online, 2019, 38.

[57] Depretis declared: "We are a progressive government, and if anyone wishes to *transform* himself and become progressive, if he wishes to accept my very moderate programme, can I reject him?." Quoted in Seton-Watson, *Liberalism to Fascism*, 51.

[58] According to Valbruzzi (30) "it was the October 1882 general election, with the electoral deal struck by Depretis and Minghetti, which marked the formal inauguration of what was then called (without any negative connotation) transformism."

[59] Valbruzzi, "*Trasformismo*," 31.

[60] Clark, *Modern Italy*, 73.

It is impossible to estimate how many Italian prefects engaged in the systematic electoral fraud that had developed over the first three decades of unification. Suffice to say that most were probably somewhere between enthusiastic and reluctant participants in it. Given the low rates of participation, it is puzzling why the regime went to the trouble of engaging in such systematic fraud at all. The answer stems from *trasformismo's* requirement that the political parties deliver the votes they had promised: Even an open contest among a narrow elite contained too much uncertainty for the political elite not to manage it. In any event, election fraud was both widely documented and publicized in Liberal Italy. Pareto noted in 1891 that it had produced its own vocabulary:

It is called the *blocco* when the whole contents of the voting urn are changed, or the *pastetta* when one changes only a part of them. There is still no word for when absent people and even the dead are made to vote, though one will soon appear when this usage becomes general ... Such practices have always been endemic in southern Italy, but for some time they have begun to infect the whole country.[61]

Pareto was correct that electoral intimidation and corruption were most intense in the South. Frank Snowden's study of Apulia – the Italian region known as the "land of chronic massacres" – reveals a system of labor repressive agriculture where the state regularly intervened to quell political agitation. Snowden recounts as follows:

Violence was also employed to make campaigning impossible for the opposition ... Gangs of men were recruited by the authorities to secure the desired outcome. These men were the notorious Apulian *mazzieri*, known after the *mazza* or club that was the tool of their trade ... Electoral meetings of the opposition were broken up by the men wielding clubs, throwing stones, and firing shots. Enemy candidates and their supporters were ambushed and beaten, and their homes were stormed in the night. The opposition press disappeared from circulation.[62]

Prefects managed elections throughout the South. Snowden writes that "the municipal authorities were responsible by law for the drawing up of lists of eligible voters, the issuing of certificates which entitled them to gain access to the polls on election day, and the counting of ballots." This rendered it "an easy matter for the party in power to falsify the lists of voters, excluding opponents from the registrars and denying them

---

[61] Quoted in Smith, *Italy*, 220–221. Snowden discovers yet another term – the "ladle" – that "consisted of "ladling" additional votes into the ballot boxes. Supporters of the dominant faction were allowed to vote more than once. Emigrants abroad and even the dead dutifully cast their votes." Frank Snowden, *Violence and the Great Estates in the South of Italy* (New York: Cambridge University Press, 1986), 142.
[62] Ibid., 143.

the necessary certificates." Furthermore, "So widespread was the buying of votes that a man eligible to vote was said always to have financial resources, and was regarded almost as a man of property."[63]

Few of the politicians who united Italy were familiar with Southern Italy: The Sicilian Crispi was the exception. The first visit by an Italian prime minister to the south of his country only occurred when Giolitti did so in 1902.[64] Forty years after unification, Italy was still basically two societies. Geography allowed for only limited agricultural cultivation in the south, and the ending of tariffs following unification resulted in the virtual disappearance of its modest industrial base. Overpopulation led to the overuse of already poor soil. Thus "by the 1880s, Southern Italy was being regularly compared to Ireland," and the "Southern Question" in Italian politics was born.[65] By the turn of the century, mass emigration had become a primarily (though by no means exclusively) southern phenomenon. The illiteracy rate in Milan was 10% in 1901, but it was 43% in Naples and 60% in Benevento.[66] Regional differences were profound: The illiteracy rate in Basilicata was 75%, which was five times the rate in Piedmont (Table 7.2).[67]

Historical verdicts on the merits of *trasformismo* vary. Clark reasons that "arguably it was better that governments should 'buy off' the Southern elites, rather than simply ignore them, or repress them." After all, he continues, "this was parliament's real function in the new united Italy: to make Piedmontese rule acceptable elsewhere."[68] Salamone hardly defends the system either: "the Italian Parliament became a field of contention for factions and cliques, for camarillas and organized interests, whose skirmishes and squabbles seldom touched even the fringe of political reality." Croce could only offer a curious defense of *trasformismo* by attacking the intelligence of other historians who considered it "a sign of Italian weakness."[69] Probably the most sustained defense

---

[63] Ibid., 142
[64] Roberts, *Europe 1880–1945*, 176.
[65] Clark, *Modern Italy*, 27.
[66] Ray Domenico, *Remaking Italy in the Twentieth Century*, 10.
[67] Roberts, *Europe 1880–1945*, 176.
[68] Clark, *Modern Italy*, 66.
[69] "[A]fter 1885, "transformism" was so much an accomplished fact that it was no longer talked about, and the word itself went out of use. Nevertheless, when the name recurred it always suggested something equivocal and unworthy, a sign of Italian weakness, and the echo of this impression is to be found in the historical literature. Historians are usually professors or other simple-minded people, who are bewildered by successive changes of ministry, by the perpetual failure to realize their own hopes of a "stable government" and above all by the mutability of human affairs. The secret desire of their hearts is that things should remain as they are, and they do not consider that, if they did

TABLE 7.2 *Italian illiteracy rates in percentage by region in 1881 and 1911 (North, Central, and South)*

| Region | 1881 | 1911 |
|---|---|---|
| Piedmont (N) | 32.3 | 11.0 |
| Lombardy (N) | 37.0 | 13.4 |
| Veneto (N) | 54.1 | 25.2 |
| Liguria (N) | 44.5 | 17.0 |
| Emilia-Romagna (N) | 63.5 | 32.7 |
| Tuscany (C) | 61.9 | 37.4 |
| Umbria (C) | 73.7 | 48.6 |
| Marches (C) | 74.1 | 50.7 |
| Latium (Rome) (C) | 58.2 | 33.2 |
| Abruzzi-Molise (C) | 80.6 | 57.6 |
| Campania (S) | 75.2 | 53.7 |
| Apulia (S) | 80.1 | 59.4 |
| Basilicata (S) | 85.2 | 65.3 |
| Calabria (S) | 85.0 | 69.6 |
| Sicily (S) | 81.2 | 58.0 |
| Sardinia (S) | 79.8 | 58.0 |
| Italy | 61.9 | 37.9 |

of *trasformismo* comes from Gherardi, who recasts *trasformismo* as a genuine means of parliamentary compromise and "a practical expression of this fundamental faith in conciliation."[70] Minghetti, in particular, according to Gherardi, viewed *trasformismo* as preferable to the political extremism and violence that would emerge without it.

Gherardi's core claim that *trasformismo* constituted "the art of compromise" critical to democratic politics has been contested. Lucy Riall, for example, argues that "Gherardi relentlessly emphasizes the positive aspects [of trasformiso] but has little to say about why this process was deemed necessary." She adds that "good intentions, when expressed through manipulation of the parliamentary process, did not necessarily translate into good government."[71] Three perverse effects of *trasformismo* deserve special

---

so, there would be no history to write, or at least none of the kind which they are accustomed to write." Croce, *A History of Italy*, 13.

[70] Raffaella Gherardi, *L'arte del compromesso. La politica della mediazione nell'Italia liberale* (Bologna: Il Mulino, 1993). See also Fulvio Cammarano, *Il progresso moderato. Un'opposizione liberale nella svolta dell'Italia crispina, 1887–1892* (Bologna: Il Mulino, 1990).

[71] Lucy Riall, "Progress and Compromise in Liberal Italy." *The Historical Journal* 38, 1 (1995), 210.

mention. First, the system coopted the political opposition. Goldstein argues that "since the government always won elections through administrative manipulation and *Trasformismo* buy-offs, no deputy could ever hope to gain influence except by joining the system."[72] Contemporaries recognized the system as a "crushing machine."[73] Salvemini recounts how the opposition became demoralized and rendered ineffective by it:

> The opponents coming mostly from the North were free to protest in the Chamber of Deputies or in the press as much as they wanted. They were helpless – and hopeless. And little by little hopelessness brought "wisdom." One by one, sooner or later, they came to terms with the boss, and either they joined his flock or they carried on a mock opposition which was more useful to him than open submission (xiii)

Second, *trasformismo* paradoxically made the liberal party itself weaker. Corner argues that "as long as majorities could be formed through corruption, through the intervention of the Minister of the Interior and through electoral manipulation, and as long as the peasants did not have the vote – and this was certainly the case up until the elections of 1913 – government was not stimulated to broaden its political base and to make a play for the popular vote by entering into alliances."[74] With no incentive to organize, the liberal party became the "Great Absentee" in Italian politics.

Third, *trasformismo* increased political alienation and weakened national identity formation. The conservative Sidney Sonnino saw this as early as 1874: "The vast majority of the people, more than ninety percent of them, feel estranged from our institutions; they see themselves as subjects of the State, constrained to serve it with blood and money, but they do not feel that they form an organic, living part of it, nor do they take any interest in its existence and development."[75] Three decades later, anti-Giolittians from the political left reached a similar conclusion. Giuseppe Pressolini, the editor of the Florentine review *La Voce*, wrote in 1908, "The present democracy ... represents by now only the decline of all standards ... only the interests of the most greedy and aggressive are served ... Everything falls. Every ideal evaporates ... The disgust is overwhelming. The best no longer have any faith. The young, if they are not spineless climbers, no longer enter parties."[76]

---

[72] Goldstein, *Political Repression*, 315.
[73] Salamone, *Italian Democracy*, 23.
[74] Corner, "Italian Sonderweg," 287.
[75] Quoted in Clark, *Modern Italy*, 77.
[76] De Grand, *Hunchback's Tailor*, 161.

## 7.3 CRISIS OF THE LIBERAL STATE

Despite *trasformismo*'s "crushing effects," the liberal system of extreme franchise restrictions endured for over three decades without major challenges to it. Italy had no less than twenty-eight governments between 1860 and the beginning of 1892, but few Italians would have noted the changes as the same politicians shuffled the important positions among themselves.[77] Agostino Depretis, the leader of the Historical Left's parliamentary group, served as prime minister for most of the decade from 1876 to 1887, and as Minister of the Interior uninterruptedly from 1879 to 1887. While Marco Minghetti was the first prime minister to recognize *trasformismo* as a political tactic, it was Depretis who became its first master practitioner. During Depretis' governments, the ideological differences between the two major parties of the Right and Left were virtually eradicated. Instead, "the two in fact constituted a broad liberal party of the centre, which monopolized political and public life. Its task was the defence of the monarchy, the constitution and the unity of Italy against the subversive forces of clerical reaction and social revolution."[78] For over thirty years, the liberals succeeded in these tasks without building a party organization of any substance.

However, the decade of the 1890s was one of near permanent crisis for the liberal state. Peasant leagues in Sicily (the Fasci Siciliani) brought the island to the brink of revolution in 1893. The response of the Crispi government to the Sicilian uprising was so severe that it constituted, according to Mack Smith a "partial dictatorship."[79] Crispi appeared to have consolidated his position before Italy's defeat in Ethiopia brought his government down. The third, and in retrospect, most serious challenge to parliamentary government in Italy occurred from 1898 to 1900 when two prime ministers – the Marquis di Rudini and General Luigi Pelloux – tried to rule without parliament.

Before 1893, the major threat to the liberal state (aside from the outstanding "Roman Question") was anarchism. Andrea Costa, a former anarchist who had been driven into exile in 1877, founded the Revolutionary socialist Party of Romagna in 1881. A year later, he became the first Socialist deputy elected in Italian history. Given the slow pace of Italian industrialization, it took ten years before the Italian

---

[77] Clark, *Modern Italy*, 74.
[78] Seton-Watson, *From Liberalism to Fascism*, 50.
[79] Smith, *Italy*, 178.

Socialists held their first party congress.[80] By the second day of the 1892 Genoa party congress, there were two separate conferences occurring as the differences between radicals and moderates became apparent immediately. Nevertheless, the Italian Socialist Party had been born.

A year later, Sicily was in chaos. Although it is true that "Sicily had been in endemic revolt against government – any government – for most of the nineteenth century,"[81] the worldwide depression and a tariff war with France battered the leading Sicilian export industries of wine, fruit and sulfur in the early 1890s. Peasant leagues had existed for a long time, as had spontaneous peasant riots, but the undeniable influence of Italian socialism was novel. The *Fasci Siciliani* directed their demands not toward the Italian state, but rather toward landowners and mine owners. They were not demanding democracy so much as they were lower taxes, better working conditions, and less miserable terms in their current sharecropping and property rental leases. According to Clark, "although there were all kinds of *Fasci* – some were run by anarchists, some by local gentry, some by *mafiosi* – most were 'Socialist' in some sense, and their spread in Sicily in the early 1890s owed much to contact with North Italian workers' organizations and with Northern ideas."[82] At the same time, traditions of peasant millenarianism and cultural rifts between northern intellectuals and Sicilian peasant leaders rendered the *Fasci Siciliani* far from an organized socialist revolution.[83]

Crispi was appointed prime minister and declared the national savior. Seventy-five years old, Crispi was a member of the generation who had united Italy and had already served as prime minister from 1887 to 1891. His initial conciliatory policies toward the *Fasci* quickly gave way to repression when he proclaimed martial law on the island and sent 50,000 troops to suppress the uprisings. Under Crispi, over 1,000 people were deported without trial to nearby islands. Crispi defended his policies on

---

[80] It was Genoa because the city was celebrating the 400-year anniversary of the birth of Columbus and, crucially, rail tickets had been deeply discounted to maximize attendance.
[81] Clark, *Modern Italy*, 123.
[82] Ibid., 124.
[83] In Mack Smith's (174) assessment:

> The socialists were as little prepared for this peasant revolt as anyone else. They were mostly middle-class intellectuals who were hardly convinced yet of the need to win over the agricultural masses. Indeed, they had some reason to fear the conservatism of the *contadini* [peasants]. Naturally, they associated themselves with the Sicilian revolt once it had broken out and tried to explain it in their own terms, but Crispi was quite wrong in ascribing this outbreak to socialist initiative. Workers' groups or *fasci* had existed spontaneously in the island for some years, and they had no need of socialist doctrine or organization to make them rise in a hunger rebellion to reoccupy the communal lands which had been usurped from them.

the grounds that "pillage, arson and plunder could not be dealt with by acts of benevolence."[84] He suspended parliamentary government for six months from January to June 1895 during which time he appealed to "an eternal law above the constitution." According to his secretary/advisor Farini, during early 1895 Crispi had come to the conclusion that "parliamentary government in Italy is not possible."[85] Viewing himself as "the Italian Bismarck"[86] and drawing inspiration from Bismarck's anti-socialist laws, Crispi rushed two "emergency laws" through parliament in August 1894; the first for the "repression of anarchism" and the second for combatting "incitement to class hatred."[87] Crispi then ordered the dissolution of the PSI in October 1894 and prosecuted its leaders. The third Socialist Party Congress in Parma in 1895 had to be held clandestinely. Although Crispi's repression would ultimately backfire and hasten the development of socialist organization, it was devastating in the short term.[88]

Crispi also executed one of the largest franchise retrenchments of the period. First in Sicily, and then later throughout Italy, the government revised the electoral rolls. Crispi, with the authorization of the parliament, purged the electoral lists of supposed illiterates and thereby reduced the suffrage by over 30 percent.[89] Crispi then called elections in 1895 in which "coercion on an unprecedented scale was required" to produce a governing majority.[90] Still, Crispi had just won a majority in parliament and appeared intent on using it to further chip away at democracy.

It was ultimately only Italy's shattering defeat in Ethiopia that prevented further democratic backsliding under Crispi.[91] Italy's colonial entanglements

---

[84] Seton-Watson, *Liberalism to Fascism*, 167.
[85] Crispi added "I will not be the one to act against parliament, but my successor will be unable to govern with it." Ibid., 173.
[86] Clark, *Modern Italy*, 113.
[87] Seton-Watson, *Liberalism to Fascism*, 167.
[88] "Soon the PSI developed all the 'German' features or a modern party – individual membership cards, a network of local sections, internal electoral procedures, regular congresses. By 1897 it had over 27,000 members, and the party ran a daily newspaper, *Avanti!*; even the title was taken from the German model, *Vorwärts*." Clark, *Modern Italy*, 135.
[89] The enfranchisement rate had increased from 7.4% in 1882 to 9.8% as a result of more Italians meeting the property or educational qualifications, but Crispi rolled it back to 6.9% in 1895.
[90] Smith, *Italy*, 178.
[91] Adler notes that "had it not been for Italy's defeat at Adowa, Crispi's combination of imperialism and domestic repression might well have developed into a consolidated dictatorship." Mack Smith goes further: "had Crispi not suffered a heavy reverse in Ethiopia, he would almost certainly have managed to consolidate his partial dictatorship." There is nothing in the extant historiography that challenges either conclusion.

derived from ill-founded beliefs in the value of colonies and the delusion that all great powers needed them.[92] In 1886, Italy annexed the Port of Massawa on the Red Sea, and in 1890 formed the protectorate of Eritrea. At the same time, Italians had also begun occupying the south side of the Horn of Africa and formed a series of protectorates in what would become Somaliland. In between Eritrea and Somalia lay the independent state of Abyssinia (Ethiopia), which Italy had failed to bring under its influence. Seeking a foreign policy victory, Crispi escalated the conflict with Abyssinia, viewing it as "a simple colonial war in which the Italians could not be beaten, and which therefore did not need serious preparation."[93] So confident of victory was Crispi that he proclaimed that the name Ethiopia would disappear from the map and had new coins designed with King Umberto wearing an imperial crown to signify the new Italian empire. Instead of triumphing, the Italian army was decimated at Adowa in 1896, marking the first time a European power had been defeated on the African continent.[94] Five thousand Italians were killed and 2,000 were taken prisoner: More troops were lost at Adowa than during the Italian wars of unification.

Crispi, apparently believing that his position was still secure even after this disaster, offered his resignation to the king. To Crispi's surprise, the monarch accepted. The king then asked General Cesare Ricotti-Magnani to form a nonpolitical cabinet under the Marquis di Rudiní. Although elections still occurred and the liberal Giuseppe Zanardelli was brought into the cabinet to signal a break with Crispi's repressive course, the repression of Socialists continued apace. The state also sought to repress the other major subversive force in Italian politics: the Catholics. In September 1897, Prime Minister di Rudiní ordered prefects around the country to harass clerical associations, and the next month wrote that such groups presented a danger to public order because they often express "views contrary to the free institutions that govern us, and even in favor of the destruction of the Italian state." He appealed for prefectorial action on the grounds that "these guilty and insane statements cannot and must not be tolerated any longer."[95]

---

[92] Not all Italian statemen endorsed colonialism. Di Rudiní told the President of the Senate in early 1891 that "that African business is impossible; we might spend 50 million a year on it ... let someone else spend it, not me. I'll end up by bringing everybody home, come what may." Clark, *Modern Italy*, 122.

[93] Smith, *Italy*, 185.

[94] Technically, the Italians had already been defeated once before by the Ethiopians in the Battle of Dogali in January 1887, when 500 Italians were killed. Prime Minister Depretis resigned following this defeat.

[95] Clark, *Modern Italy*, 131.

Others pressed for even more repressive measures as they attacked the legitimacy of parliamentary democracy. The conservative Sidney Sonnino called for a return to the Statute of 1848 (The Constitution of Piedmont), by which he meant greater use of the expansive royal powers contained in Article V.[96] Sonnino wrote: "Your Majesty ... You alone are responsible for the executive power. You alone are responsible for the nomination or dismissal of Ministers, who must countersign and answer publicly for Your acts of government. The nation looks to You, and has trust in You."[97] Sonnino explained that,

The general interest of the State is not identical, day by day, with the sum of all the particular interests, individually and subjectively considered, and even less with the sum of a variable aggregation of those interests sufficient only to comprise a fleeting majority of fifty percent plus one of the political forces that represent them. In a government founded almost totally on elections, the representation of the collective and general interests is absent in the highest direction of public affairs.[98]

Sonnino's return to the constitution never materialized, but the Italian state was still only half-way through its authoritarian interlude. In the spring of 1898 food riots, sparked by a sharp increase in the price of wheat, spread up the peninsula before reaching a crescendo in Milan. The army was brought in and quashed the riots, but not before killing 80 and wounding 450 and imposing a state of martial law in four provinces. The king announced via public telegram that he was giving General Bava Beccaris, the commander of the army in Milan, the Cross of Savoy "to reward the great service which you rendered to our institutions and to civilization, and to attest to my affection and the gratitude of myself and the country."[99] Di Rudini then introduced new legislation on public order (the so-called "political provisions") that prohibited strikes in the public sector, gave the army control over railwaymen and postal workers, and further restricted press and associational freedom.[100] Thousands of people were arrested and military tribunals handed down

---

[96] Article V states "The executive power belongs to the King alone. He is the supreme head of State; he commands all the land and naval forces; he declares war, he makes treaties of peace, alliance, commerce, etc., informing parliament of them as soon as the interests of them as soon as the interests and the security of the State permit."

[97] Anonymous [S. Sonnino], "Torniamo all Statuto," in *Nuova Antologia* January 1, 1897, reproduced in B.F. Brown (ed.), S. Sonnino, *Scritti e discorsi extraparlamentari*, Vol. I (Bari: Laterza, 1972), 575–597.

[98] Ibid., 576.

[99] Quoted in Clark, *Modern Italy*, 127

[100] Ibid., 141.

draconian sentences. Giolitti and Zanardelli, who had both thus far generally supported the government, broke with it and argued that no new extraordinary legislation was necessary as the 1848 statute contained similar publishable offenses.

The new coalition of liberals, radicals, and Socialists led to the fall of Rudini and the appointment of General Luigi Pelloux.[101] A veteran of the Risorgimento who had served as Minister of War under both Giolitti and Rudini, Pelloux was appointed to the Senate in 1896. A liberal from Savoy, he initially showed no interest in enforcing the "political provisions." However, after a change to a more conservative government led to conflict with parliament and ultimately obstructionism, Pelloux announced in June 1899 that he would henceforth rule by royal decree. This would have been a rupture: "never before had anything like this been heard."[102] Farini saw the belated triumph of Sonnino here: "so now the *Statuto* is being trampled on, just as many conservatives have been demanding and wanting for so many years."[103] According to Clark: "Farini was right to be alarmed. The government was breaking all the rules of the game and exposing the Crown to danger." Parliament was ended abruptly the following week.

Pelloux was only stopped when Italy's highest court ruled his actions unconstitutional. The General tried again in March 1900 to win parliamentary sanction for a decree law that would have enabled emergency rule. The entire left (Socialists and the liberal group around Zanardelli) walked out of parliament in protest. During the period from 1894 to 1900, the PSI advocated for parliamentary sovereignty as Crispi's repression had done more than anything to convince Socialists like Turati of the value of parliamentary government. The party formed its first political alliances – with the radicals – for local elections in Milan in 1895. By 1898, they joined the Zanardelli group in a parliamentary coalition against the government. "From its birth in 1892 to 1901, the Italian Socialist party had truly been a party of Liberal action with a Socialist banner."[104]

---

[101] According to Seton-Watson, evidence from royal advisor Farini's diary indicated that the king had nearly endorsed a coup d'etat in the wake of the Milan riots:

> Under the shock of the catastrophe in Milan and in a political situation of extreme confusion, the weak and bewildered King had for a moment been tempted to depart from constitutional practice. Only at the last moment, and after half committing himself to a dissolution, did he decide to abandon Rudini. He then considered appointing a prime minister from outside parliament to govern by decree. But his advisors, notably Farini, begged him not to "leave the broad path of the constitution" and allow himself to be dragged down "the slippery slope." Their warnings were effective and the king turned on their advice to the senate. Seton-Watson, 192

[102] Smith, *Italy*, 194.
[103] Quoted in Clark, *Modern Italy*, 141.
[104] Salvemini, *Critica Sociale*, March 1, 1907.

## 7.3 Crisis of The Liberal State

The fall of Pelloux led to new elections and a resounding defeat for the government, which Clark considers a critical juncture in Italian democratization:

> Sonnino and strong government were discredited. Zanardelli and Giolitti had allied with the Extreme Left, had won a famous victory and soon came back to power pledged to more "conciliatory" policies. The lesson of the 1899–1900 rows was that governments could not govern without being attentive to parliament. Indeed it is noticeable how very "parliamentary" the battles had been. Although the "subversives" were leading the campaign, there were very few popular demonstrations, no petitions and no disorders. Men had rioted for bread in 1898; they did not riot for liberty in 1899.[105]

The liberal view of the 1890s is that parliamentary government not only survived major authoritarian reversals but also strengthened democratic practices. Croce argues that the crises of 1898–1900 were the Italian equivalent of the Dreyfus affair in France:

> When, for instance, in Italy between 1898 and 1900 the idea was conceived, and an attempt made to bring about, with the motto of a "return to the constitution," a certain reaction in the direction of the older form of government, the opposition that awoke was lively and universal. The parliament resorted to obstructionism, and the plan, dictated by the fear of movement or of too rapid movement, was thwarted, with the consequences (analogous to what at the same time, and amidst difference circumstances, happened in France) of a more resolute tendency towards liberalism.[106]

Croce continued that "Italian life after 1900 had overcome the chief obstacles in its course, and [...] flowed on for the next ten years and more, rich in both achievement and hope."[107] He concluded that "the problem of order and government ... had in fact been solved by the triumph of liberal methods, which alone could satisfy the legitimate demands put forward by the two extreme parties, neither of which possessed the power to carry them into effect."[108] Clark seems to endorse this position as well: "by 1900 the main subversive groups [Catholics and Socialists] had been 'absorbed' into the system and 'constitutionalized' – not fully, of course, but to a far greater degree than had seemed possible ten years earlier. They had even become the defenders of liberty and the Constitution."[109]

---

[105] Clark, *Modern Italy*, 142.
[106] Croce, *History of Italy*, 263.
[107] Ibid., 214.
[108] Ibid., 215.
[109] Clark, *Modern Italy*, 142.

The liberal view is broadly correct in the sense that Italy did survive an authoritarian interlude and parliamentary sovereignty emerged stronger through conflict with the executive. Sonnino signaled the conservatives' reconciliation with parliamentary democracy in an article in the *Nuova antologia* dated September 16, 1900.[110] It also true that the Socialists had become supporters of parliamentary government and universal suffrage, and Catholics were entering politics as well. Still, the exclusive franchise remained, and Crispi's purging of the electoral rolls was never reversed. Clark finds that "means tests and the literacy qualification produced such small electorates in many areas (further diminished, too, by Catholic abstentions) that the average constituency in 1900 had less than 5,000 voters."[111] The elements of competitive oligarchy remained.

## 7.4 COMPETITIVE OLIGARCHY TO COMPETITIVE AUTHORITARIANISM

"If there was a period in which Italy might have moved forward toward a more democratic form of government," writes Paul Corner "it was surely in the period between 1901 and 1914."[112] For the first time since the 1860s, the standard of living rose. Industrial production and foreign trade doubled between 1901 and 1913.[113] Giolitti inaugurated his second government after a victory over the forces of reaction. The central question in the Giolittian era was whether the practice of *trasformismo* would work on the two major political forces that challenged the ruling oligarchy. A fundamental antagonism between socialism and Catholicism opened up possibilities for Giolitti, as the Catholic leadership had concluded by the turn of the twentieth century that socialism was a greater evil than liberalism. A pastoral letter from the bishop of Verona for Lent 1901, which the clergy were meant to read in church, sounded the alarm: "Socialism is the most abject slavery, it is flagrant injustice, it is the craziest folly, it is a social crime, it is the destruction of the family and of

---

[110] De Grand, *Hunchback's Tailor*, 75.
[111] Roberts, *Europe 1880–1945*, 177.
[112] Corner, "Italian Sonderweg," 286. Corner concludes (295) that,

> the failure to form a political coalition capable of significant redistributive reform prior to 1914 was central to future developments. While this is a long way from constituting an Italian *Sonderweg* to Fascism, it may be enough to persuade us that, in the continuing battle between breach and continuity (which, it should be repeated, is *not* about inevitability), the emphasis should be placed fairly heavily on the side of continuity.

[113] Romeo, *Breve storia della grande industria in Italia* (Bologna, 1961), 82–83.

## 7.4 Competitive Oligarchy to Competitive Authoritarianism 231

public welfare, it is the self-proclaimed and inevitable enemy of religion, and it leads to anarchy."[114]

Following the first general strike in Italian history in 1904, there was a partial lifting of the non-expedit in 1904. As Adler explains: "fearful that the general strike was a harbinger of revolution," Pius X modified the conditions of the *non-expedit*, allowing Catholics to vote in those districts where a candidate of the "forces of order" was in danger of being defeated by a "subversive."[115] Salamone also notes the connection between the general strike and the lifting of the non-expedit: "the immediate cause was the general strike of September 1904, the remote cause was the Catholic and Liberal-Conservative fear of the Socialist upsurge." A 1905 Papal encyclical explained that although the non-expedit remained technically in effect, it could be lifted "to help the maintenance of the social order."[116] The non-expedit was then suspended in about 150 constituencies (out of about 500) in the general elections of March 1909, leading to the election of twenty one Catholics.[117] The lifting of the non-expedit had an immediate impact on overall voter turnout: between 1900 and 1909 it increased from 48.5% to 65.2% in Veneto, and from 52.9% to 65.9% in Lombardy.[118] In sum, Catholic incorporation (*trasformismo*) under Giolitti had gone quite far even before the Gentoloni Pact of 1913. Although the "Roman Question" still technically existed, Liberal Italy was increasingly dependent on Catholic support.[119]

The second "subversive" political force – the Socialists – proved more difficult to transform. Giolitti never succeeded in his ultimate goal of enticing Socialists into his governing coalition, but it was not from a lack

---

[114] Quoted in Clark, *Modern Italy*, 177.
[115] Franklin Adler, *Italian Industrialists from Liberalism to Fascism: The Political Development of the Industrial Bourgeoisie* (New York: Cambridge University Press, 2002), 15.
[116] Ibid., 176.
[117] "The three principal conditions for the participation of Catholics in the elections were: (1) in an electoral district of their diocese there must be a militantly anti-clerical candidate who was a member of the Popular bloc; (2) against such an anti-Clerical candidate there must be a candidate of the 'forces of order,' whether Catholic or not, who must give guarantee of not attacking religion; (3) in such an electoral district there must be great probability of victory for the anticlerical candidate should the Catholic voters abstain, while their participation would render his defeat certain (Salamone, *Italian Democracy*, 39)." The original source for the rules is: A. Schiavi, "Programmi, voti ed eletti nei comizi politici del 1909." *La Riforma Sociale* (July–August 1909), 388.
[118] Clark, *Modern Italy*, 176.
[119] The existence of the non-expedit did prevent the formation of a Catholic political party until its lifting in 1919.

of trying. As early as 1897, Giolitti had rejected the standard liberal argument that socialism represented an existential threat:

> In Italy, the Socialists, who profess with sincere conviction collectivist theories, are an insignificant minority and, as long as they abstain from violent acts, they are also harmless ... It is therefore not the collectivist theories that constitute a danger for us; rather, it is the troop of malcontents, unemployed, displaced who take the name of "Socialist" because it serves them as a flag, a rallying point, a means of effective organization.[120]

He echoed these remarks in 1901: "It is my profound conviction that socialism can be fought only on the field of liberty; the other road has been tried and you have seen the results."[121] He appeared to have generally good relations with the reformist wing of the Socialist Party. Even when the syndicalist and revolutionary wing of the party gained control in 1904 and labor militancy increased, the state remained neutral as Giolitti had promised. Following several deadly clashes between strikers and police in Sicily and Sardinia, the new socialist leaders called a general strike. This proved to be a major tactical error as Giolitti immediately called a new election in which the Socialists lost four of their 33 seats and Giolitti increased his majority further, from 296 to 339.

### 7.4.1 Giolitti's Machine

He achieved this in part through electoral manipulation. Like most Italian prime ministers, Giolitti was simultaneously the minister of the interior, which simplified the management of elections enormously. His instructions to the state's electoral machinery sound remarkably similar to those of Persigny under the French Second Empire. According to De Grand, "orders went out to the prefects in July 1904, well before the dissolution, to send [Giolitti] an estimate of the chances of the sitting deputy, possible opponents, and the forces behind each." If a Socialist or Republican victory was likely, every effort should be taken to get out the monarchist vote and to ensure that the polling places were watched over "by the monarchists of secure faith."[122] Electoral fraud was undoubtedly most intense in the south. Salvemini documented these practices at length in *Il Ministro della Mala Vita*, which was based in part on his own electoral campaign in Molfetta (Basilicata):

[120] Quoted in De Grand, *Hunchback's Tailor*, 67.
[121] Salamone, *Italian Democracy*, 47.
[122] De Grand, *Hunchback's Tailor*, 120.

## 7.4 Competitive Oligarchy to Competitive Authoritarianism   233

Under Giolitt's rule, the interference of the prefects with local government and elections reached unprecedented heights of brutality. Where the electorate was refractory to pressure and the elected mayors and town councilors refused to bow, the prefect not only dismissed them, but "managed" local and national elections. If an election had to be carried out, the police, in league with the Government supporters, enrolled the scum of the constituencies and the underworld of neighboring districts. In the last weeks before the polls, the opponents were threatened, bludgeoned, besieged in their homes. Their leaders were debarred from addressing meetings, or even thrown into prison until election day was over. Voters suspected of upholding the opposition were refused polling cards. Those favoring governmental candidates were given not only their own polling cards, but also those of opponents, emigrants, deceased voters, and were allowed to vote three, five, ten, twenty times. The Government candidates were always the winners.[123]

Given such profound differences in electoral competition in the Italian North and South, perhaps Liberal Italy is better understood as two separate political systems, with democracy advancing in the North and authoritarianism persisting in the South?[124] Salvemini appears to endorse this interpretation with his remark that "in Southern Italy elections were vitiated by pressure and violence on the part of the government, but public life was honest and decent in northern Italy."[125] Gramsci, however, argued that the Southern problem served the oligarchic interests of Northerners:

The South was reduced to a semi-colonial status as a captive market and source of savings and taxes. It was disciplined with two series of measures. The first was merciless police repression directed against every mass movement and involving periodic slaughter of peasants ... The other measures were personal favours to the class of "intellectuals" in straw hats, and took the form of jobs in the state bureaucracy, of permission to plunder local government ... In this way the social stratum that could have organized the endemic discontent of the Mezzogiorno became instead an instrument of northern policy, a private accessory to the police.[126]

Salvemini made similar points to Gramsci elsewhere, suggesting that his aforementioned quip about a liberalizing North was a one-off. More typical was his calculation that "Giolitti got from the south about 150 faithful followers, who owed to him their seats."[127] The scale of electoral

---

[123] Salvemini, "Introduction," xiii.
[124] Put another way, Italy at first appears a plausible case of subnational authoritarianism. Edward Gibson, *Boundary Control: Subnational Authoritarianism in Federal Democracies* (New York: Cambridge University Press, 2012).
[125] Salvemini, *Origins of Fascism in Italy*, 78.
[126] Quoted in Snowden, *Violence and Great Estates*, 138.
[127] Ibid., 79.

corruption in the South was common knowledge, and politicians raised the issue consistently in parliament under Giolitti. A 1910 Commission of Inquiry into the South by the government itself even confirmed Gramsci's proposition:

> The young Italian state did not succeed in creating a democracy of small landowners, of men who might have undermined the foundations of the old feudal system that had survived in fact if not in law. The new State became the slave of a new powerful group, the voting middle classes, just as the old State had been the slave of the feudal aristocracy ... usurpers who had the vote and used it to steal the land [were tolerated], with the more or less tacit complicity of the Prefects in that scandalous despoliation of the poor by the rich.[128]

### 7.4.2 The Suffrage Reform of 1912

It is remarkable that so much effort was put into the management of elections given the narrowness of the franchise. Crispi's purges of 1894 had never been undone, meaning that 1892 represented the high point of enfranchisement before the reform of 1912.[129] Giolitti was opposed to universal suffrage and had repeatedly endorsed gradualist principles in his public announcements. Addressing Parliament in 1902, he argued that "political education comes only with very long experience of public liberties. Certainly what is possible in England today was not possible a century and half ago." He continued that "when Italians had enjoyed freedom for two hundred years they would be able to indulge in such things."[130] He appeared to rule out granting the suffrage to illiterates during a parliamentary speech in March of 1908 when he said that he did "not consider calling the ignorant masses to judge the great interests of the country to be progress."[131] In 1909, Giolitti had insisted in Parliament that the expansion of the franchise, which would effectively extend the vote to the illiterate, would have to wait until Italy achieved close to universal literacy.[132] There is no reason to dispute De Grand's conclusion that "nothing in [Giolitti's] legislative record suggested that he thought universal suffrage was good policy."[133]

---

[128] Quoted in Clark, *Modern Italy*, 23.
[129] De Grand, *Hunchback's Tailor*, 164.
[130] Seton-Watson, *Liberalism to Fascism*, 254.
[131] Atti Parlamentari (AP), 22nd leg., disc., March 4, 1908, p. 19875.
[132] Piretti 2001: 552.
[133] De Grand, *Hunchback's Tailor*, 166.

It was thus surprising when Luigi Luzzati, who was Giolitti's proxy during one of his brief breaks as prime minister, introduced a bill on suffrage reform in 1911. Luzatti's proposal stopped far short of universal male suffrage (it would have increased the electorate from 2.9 million to 4.4 million) and included a provision for mandatory voting, under the theory that the landed elite and the church could harness the power of the rural masses and thereby check the organizational advantages of the Socialists in urban areas.[134] As with the Second Great Reform in Great Britain, the immediate political calculations of elites were more important than long-term predictions about the party's ability to compete. Luzzati's bill was attacked from different sides. The Socialists pressed for universal suffrage, while the Conservatives demanded guarantees on compulsory voting. Raffaele De Cesare called it "a new concession to the prejudice of the extreme parties who think they are raising the political and moral level of a people by inviting ignorant masses to participation."[135] The conservative Pietro Bertolini ultimately brought along large sections of the Giolitti block with him when he moved to suspend debate on Luzzati's suffrage reform on March 13.[136] When it became clear that Luzzati lacked the votes for his major piece of legislation, he resigned.

That Giolitti replaced Luzzati as prime minister was not shocking. Members of parliament were stunned, however, when Giolitti then proposed an electoral reform far more expansive than Luzzati's original bill. Giolitti reasoned as follows:

> I believe that today an enlargement of the franchise cannot be postponed any longer. Twenty years after the last electoral reform, a big revolution has happened in Italy, which has produced vast progress in the economic, intellectual and moral condition of the popular classes ... I don't think that an exam on how easily a man can use the 24 letters of the alphabet should decide if he has the attitude to evaluate the big issues that interest the popular classes.

This was a major turnaround from just several years earlier, and when Giolitti signaled his support for universal manhood suffrage, there was not a significant demand for it among the population – a point that some opponents of the measure raised in parliamentary debates.[137] Nor were there major signs of labor militancy: The number of strikes had

---
[134] Ibid., 164.
[135] Salamone, *Italian Democracy*, 16fn.
[136] De Grand, *Hunchback's Tailor*, 165.
[137] Piretti, 1995.

in fact been falling for several years.[138] Indeed, the PSI had been so chastened by the failed general strike of 1904 that Giolitti could reinforce his case for universal suffrage as follows: "Eight years have gone by, the country has gone ahead, the Socialist party has greatly modified its program, and Karl Marx has been relegated to the attic."[139] We will never know what else Giolitti might have added to these remarks, for as Salamone recounts "an outburst of voices, protesting or approving, broke in upon Giolitti at that point, and the sentence remained suspended forever."[140]

Giolitti had caught the Socialists off-guard, and Salvemini saw the danger immediately: "Universal suffrage from Honorable Giolitti gives us the impression of an extremely abundant dinner served at 8:00 AM, when the stomach is not ready."[141] Turati was even blunter: "I deplore that you [Giolitti] have this supreme ability to present a beautiful, a great reform in order to diminish it, to obscure it, to make it innocuous and manageable."[142] Giolitti's initiative had confused the PSI's position. At the PSI Party Congress of October 1911, Turati explained that "the extension of the suffrage was demanded and advocated by us, but it is not, today, a Socialist and proletarian conquest," adding that "the value of every reform is always proportionate to the effort it requires for its realization."[143] Conservatives like Sonnino supported universal suffrage for "It is only from universal suffrage that the government can achieve the strength to represent and protect the general interest, which is continuously endangered by the particular interests of individuals, localities and small and egoistic groups."[144] Liberals like Mosca and the influential *Corriere della Sera* held to Giolitti's previous views that the masses lacked the capacity for voting and opposed the electoral reform. Mosca used his time in parliamentary debate to explain how the introduction of illiterates would "not increase the capacity of the electoral body to understand

---

[138] Valentino Larcinese, "Enfranchisement and Representation: Evidence from the Introduction of Quasi-Universal Suffrage in Italy," Unpublished Paper, London School of Economics (2011), 13.
[139] Salamone, *Italian Democracy*, 59.
[140] Ibid.
[141] De Grand, *Hunchback's Tailor*, 165.
[142] AP, Camera, 23rd leg., May 8, 1912, p. 19177.
[143] *Resoconto stenografico del XII Congresso Nazionale del Partito Socialista Italiano: Modena*, October 15–18, 1911.
[144] S. Sonnino, "Il partito liberale e il suffragio universale," *Nuova Antologia*, s. 5 vol. 239, 305–314. My translation from Ballini (2007), 164.

## 7.4 Competitive Oligarchy to Competitive Authoritarianism 237

the big issues of national politics."[145] The bill nevertheless passed by a wide margin.

The elections of 1913 were the first to take place after the suffrage reform. There was genuine uncertainty in the outcome. In this sense, Italy was arguably never closer to meeting all the requirements of male democracy than the year before the outbreak of WWI. Parliamentary sovereignty emerged stronger after the battles of the 1890s, there were no formal counter-majoritarian institutions to speak of, and a very liberal suffrage enfranchisement had unintentionally resulted from elite competition. Is it thus wrong to consider Italy a late case of first-wave democratization: And why is Croce incorrect when he concludes that:

> In 1911 and 1912, the Liberal Government carried through a work of the highest importance in the extension of the franchise. This set a seal upon the development which had been in process in Italian political life during the past ten years, and had shown itself in the gradual granting of the demands and recognition of the needs and claims of the working classes, and at the same time in the gradual transformation of revolutionary into reforming ideals, and of the radicalism of the opposition into the moderate radicalism of the government.[146]

Again, Raimondo's laments after the 1913 remain closer to the mark. The level of repression was increased: "the election of 1913 happened in a climate of unusual violence and intimidation. The purpose of intimidation was often to ensure that poor voters stayed at home and did not exercise their right to vote, which would explain the lower turnout in swing districts."[147] Salvemini too noticed the difference between the elections of 1909 and 1913: "when, in 1913, [Giolitti] was confronted not with a mere 2,000–3,000 voters, but with 10,000 or more voters in a constituency to be 'managed,' he was forced to increase the dose of violence to ensure success."[148] There were also important details in the suffrage reform that dramatically limited its effects in the South. The law of 1911 gave the vote to male literates over twenty-one and to male illiterates over thirty or upon completion of military service. But since both literacy rates and life expectancy were low in the South, and since the army rejected a large number of men for service, Italy's most significant suffrage

---

[145] Gaetano Mosca, Parliamentary Speech of May 9, 1912. My translation from Ballini (2007), 172.
[146] Croce, *History of Italy*, 256.
[147] Larcinese, "Enfranchisement and Representation," 30.
[148] Salvemini, "Introduction," xiv.

expansion still "effectively disenfranchised the majority of the southern population."[149] De Grand finds that only about a quarter of the adult male population could vote in the southern regions of Basilicata and Calabria.[150]

And perhaps most importantly, Giolitti and the leader of the Catholic Electoral Association, along with a number of conservative candidates, made a secret pact to coordinate their campaigns. According to Larcinese, the "Gentolini Pact" offers a prime example of the efforts made by elites to neutralize the impact of democratization.[151] Salamone agrees with this assessment: "It seemed as if the Government with Giolitti at its head had made an "alliance between bad faith and the sacristy" for the sole purpose of placing a barrier in the way of the democratic parties."[152] So bitter were the recriminations in parliament that Giolitti stepped down to avoid them, even though he had once again produced a workable governing majority for himself.

There is no reason to believe that his absence would be long, for Giolitti's liberal–clerical electoral alliance had been a success. "The so-called Constitutional Liberals, of whom more than two hundred owed their election to the aid of the Catholics," notes Salamone, "seemed doubly shackled – to Giolitti's will and to Gentolini's program."[153] This new form of *trasformismo* was capable of producing a liberal majority despite the fact that there was no liberal party organization to speak of. According to Clark, "most observers assumed it [the franchise extension] would make little difference, for governments would still 'manage' elections, and the same people would still be elected."[154] Roberts also reminds us that, "even the 'liberal' reforms can be interpreted as mere tactical expedients. Elections were fought as before and Italy was ruled by the benevolent parliamentary despotism of 'this tight-rope walker,' as Mussolini called [Giolitti]."[155]

There were some contemporaries who sensed that Giolitti's emerging system of competitive authoritarianism was unstable. The socialist Labriola, for example, warned Giolitti in Parliament that:

[149] Snowden, *Violence and the Great Estates*, 138.
[150] De Grand, *Hunchback's Tailor*, 179.
[151] Larcinese, "Enfranchisement and Representation," 29.
[152] Salamone, *Italian Democracy*, 40.
[153] Salamone, 41.
[154] Clark, *Modern Italy*, 188.
[155] Roberts, *Europe 1880–1945*, 184.

## 7.4 Competitive Oligarchy to Competitive Authoritarianism 239

Your system did not create an eternal regime, Honorable President of the Council. Even this regime was mortal and contained within it the germ of its dissolution. The moment came when we saw that the Giolittian regime was undermined from all directions and those underminers were neither his followers nor adversaries in this hall ... The lucky star is extinguished, the constellation has changed, things have been turned upside down.[156]

His colleague Turati, however, seemed far less sure that Giolitti's control over the system was loosening. He admitted that:

I have been sitting in this Chamber for more than fifteen years, several of my friends have been here even longer. Well, I confess that we have never known with absolute certainty if, when the Honorable Giolitti concedes something to us that we really wanted, he does it to support us or to play us as fools.[157]

Indeed, it looked initially as if the Giolittian system had survived the cataclysmic experience of WWI. Remarking on a new Italian government, Salvemini wrote in June 1920 in a letter to Ugo Ojetti: "Here we are again at Giolitti with Sonnino."[158] Two years later, Giolitti reacted to the rise of fascism by seeking accommodation with it. According to De Grand: "Giolitti considered the new movement a political force that might be integrated into a parliamentary framework when, clearly, the Fascists had no intention of playing by the old rules."[159] Even after the consolidation of the fascist regime, Giolitti remained a member of parliament. Only four months before his death in his last speech in the Chamber of Deputies on March 16, 1928, did he break with the fascist regime by opposing its reform of Parliament. Giolitti explained that:

For an assembly to be the representation of the nation, its component must be chosen in full liberty by the electors in the electoral colleges, as Article 39 of the Statuto prescribes. However, all ability to choose is excluded because only one list can be proposed to the voters ... [which] signals the decisive departure of the Fascist regime from the regime based on the Statuto.

Perhaps the greatest charge against Giolitti is that it took him six years to arrive at this conclusion, or at least to state so publicly. It is hard not to agree with Salvemini that Giolitti paved the way in a direct sense by fundamentally misreading Mussolini. However, he was far from the only one.

[156] Quoted in De Grand, *Hunchback's Tailor*, 183.
[157] Ibid., 182.
[158] Ibid., 231.
[159] Ibid., 244.

## 7.5 PORTUGAL

Portugal was the poorest state in Western Europe on the eve of WWI. The illiteracy rate was still 75 percent in 1911, which was nearly twice the rate of Italy's and higher than even the most illiterate of Italy's southern provinces (Calabria, 70 percent).[160] A major power in the fifteenth and sixteenth centuries (the "Era of the Discoveries"), by the nineteenth century, the Portuguese state had declined to such a degree that it had nearly lost its sovereignty. Between 1807 – when the Bragança Monarchy that had ruled Portugal since 1640 fled to Brazil – and 1822 – when the monarch returned, Portugal was a de facto British protectorate. The liberal constitution of 1822 lasted for only two years before the regime was overthrown by anti-liberal revolutionaries. The reactionary 1826 constitution increased the powers of the monarch, while the 1830s were marked by civil war along with military coups. A military rebellion in 1836 led to another experiment with liberalism and the reinstatement of the 1822 constitution, but this too was fleeting. The experience was repeated in 1842 with a brief reinstatement of the liberal 1822 charter before its final displacement by the one from 1826.

### 7.5.1 Competitive Oligarchy

If the first half of the nineteenth century was marked by a high degree of both regime and constitutional volatility, by the second half, Portugal had become a consolidated competitive oligarchy. Portugal from 1842 to 1910 had one of the "most monarchical" of the existing constitutions among the constitutional monarchies of Europe.[161] According to the charter of 1826, the king could name and dismiss his prime minister and cabinet and could convoke, postpone, or dissolve the Cortes. These powers were in fact used extensively: The Portuguese monarch dissolved the lower assembly (Cortes) over thirty times between 1834 and 1910, and only nine survived their full term.[162] The system was oligarchic in addition to monarchic. The franchise reform of 1878 expanded the suffrage from 9% of the population to 14%, but a major franchise retrenchment in 1895 (on a scale similar to Crispi's in the same year) reduced it to

---

[160] R.A.H. Robinson, *Contemporary Portugal: A History* (London: George Allen and Unwin, 1979), 371.
[161] Marcello Caetano, *História Breve das Constituições Portuguesas*, 3rd ed. (Lisbon, 1971), 35.
[162] A.H. de Oliveira Marques, "Portugal." *Ocidente (Lisbon)*, 76 (June 1969), 268.

around 7%.[163] Except for a period of ten years (1885–1895), the upper house of parliament was appointed rather than elected. The ideological differences between the two major parties – the Regenerators and the Historicals (later Progressives) – were slight as they both drew from the same classes of financial and agrarian elites. The two parties "neither regenerated nor made progress,"[164] and Wheeler explains that "the chief functions of the parties, whether in times of stability or crisis, was to dispense patronage."[165] Moreover, after 1871, the two parties "rotated" in power, according to the following dynamics:

Premierships changed from one to the other party, whenever the ruling party, or an agreement between the two, or even the king thought it convenient. Reasons varied greatly from case to case: often a simple fatigue of governing brought about the change; at other times, it was the fear of some responsibility, a parliamentary debate either house of Parliament, a press campaign cleverly oriented, personal matters affecting any cabinet member, or the like.[166]

The party that called the elections won *every one* of them between 1871 and 1910. Unsurprisingly, systematic election interference was needed to ensure such results. Marques concludes that "government manipulation of local and national elections was a common practice," and no historian has contested this claim. The local caciques (local political bosses) in nineteenth-century Portugal played a similar role to the Italian prefect during elections as "local bosses" "arranged" the local vote in return for patronage. Yet the system was different from the Italy's in one major respect: *Trasformismo* was a means of doling out patronage more or less equally among two factions of a narrow elite, while *rotativismo* allowed the party in power to give up the reigns whenever it ran into difficulties and permit the new governing party to confirm this new elite pact through managed elections. According to Wheeler: "unlike parliamentary monarchy in Britain [and in Italy], where elections produced governments, in Portugal governments produced elections."[167] Both *rotativismo* and *trasformismo* were types of the mutual security guarantee that Dahl emphasized in *Polyarchy* (see Chapter 2), but neither

---

[163] Goldstein, *Political Repression*, 292.
[164] R.E. Benton, *The Downfall of a King: Dom Manuel II of Portugal* (Washington, DC: University Press of America, 1977), 31.
[165] Douglas Wheeler, *Republican Portugal: A Political History 1910–1926* (Madison: University of Wisconsin Press, 1978), 26.
[166] A.H. Oliveira Marques, *History of Portugal* (New York: Columbia University Press, 1972), 52.
[167] Wheeler, *Republican Portugal*, 27.

showed any sign of ending in universal participation or meaningful elite contestation.

As in Italy, the economic and foreign policy crises in the 1890s upended the existing oligarchic institutions in Portuguese politics. The republican revolution in Brazil in 1889 – Portugal's most important former colony – unsettled the metropolitan government which was facing a republican uprising of its own. It then antagonized its traditional protector – Great Britain – in the battle for colonial possessions in Africa. Specifically, Portugal sought to seize control of Zimbabwe to connect its colonies in Angola and Mozambique. Great Britain responded with an ultimatum – drop the Zimbabwean campaign or go to war. Portugal capitulated, and the "Ultimatum crisis" of 1890 provoked a domestic backlash as profound as that following the Italian defeat at Adowa. A failed coup by a military garrison in Oporto convinced the two major parties to rule together as a crisis government from 1890 to 1893. Then in 1894, Prime Minister Hintze Rebeiro postponed elections for that year and ruled by decree. The same year that Crispi purged the electoral roles in Italy, Rebeiro repealed the 1885 reform that had ended hereditary seats for the upper chamber. He also reduced suffrage rates by 50 percent.[168] All of these events took place during a financial crisis that forced the government to declare bankruptcy twice within the space of a decade –1892 and 1902 – and the growth of a republican movement that was willing to engage in violence to end the monarchy.

Rebeiro's democratic backsliding was not enough to rescue the system of "pseudo-parlamentarism" or to hasten the erosion of support for monarchism.[169] Wheeler recounts that "by 1906 parliament almost did not function because passionate arguments interrupted all business and obstructed legislation."[170] In 1906, King Carlos appointed Joao Franco as prime minister (Regenerators) who dismissed the legislature in 1907, suppressed the press, closed Coimbra University, and dissolved local governments headed by the opposition in Lisbon and throughout the country.[171] Franco capped his regime of "administrative dictatorship" by imposing martial law on Lisbon on January 31, 1908. The next day King Carlos and his eldest son, and heir to the throne, Prince Luis Filipe were assassinated by Republican conspirators.

---

[168] Goldstein, *Political Repression*, 292.
[169] Caetano, *História Breve*, 79–92.
[170] Wheeler, *Republican Portugal*, 43.
[171] Goldstein, *Political Repression*, 292.

## 7.5.2 Competitive Authoritarianism: The Portuguese Republic

The Republicans modeled themselves on the Republicans in France and consisted of highly educated members of the middle class. Many leaders of the Republicans taught at the University of Coimbra: out of the first 226 Republican deputies to the Constituent Assembly, 88 had attended or graduated from the same university. Following Portugal's humiliation during the ultimatum crisis, the Republicans effectively recruited from within the Portuguese navy as "many officers were impressed by republican propaganda slamming monarchical failure to win Portugal a proper place overseas."[172] Similar to the Italian Socialists, the Republicans used the 1890s to build an effective political party organization. However, in the elections of 1910, the Republicans won only 14 out of 200 seats in the Cortes as a result of election rigging "by the usual methods in rural areas."[173]

The Republicans had attempted to create a rebellion among army and naval units in 1891, 1895, 1896, and 1901. The party was also a growing electoral force, winning control of Lisbon in the elections of 1908. The obvious rigging of the elections of 1910 provided yet another opportunity to topple the ailing monarchy. Given the volatility of previous Portuguese regimes, the Portuguese republican revolution of October 4, 1910, was one of the least surprising revolutions in modern European history. Gallagher writes that "the privileged sectors of the community were not noticeably alarmed by the 1910 upheaval."[174] Still, it was an important experiment as Portugal was only the third European republic after France and Switzerland: All the rest were constitutional or absolutist monarchies of some type. The first months of the regime hardly inspired confidence that it would be democratic: "in power with no parliament as a watchdog, the Provisional Government was a virtual dictatorship."[175] The constitution of 1911 broadened the franchise, though it was still lower than the 70 percent of adult males who could vote between 1885 and 1895, and also reestablished the principle of parliamentary sovereignty. Yet in by now a familiar pattern, the franchise extensions were overturned two years later. Afonso Costa's electoral law of 1913 disenfranchised much of the working class and reduced the electorate from 850,000 to 400,000 by restricting the vote to literate males.[176] It also excluded all active-duty

---

[172] Gallagher, *Portugal*, 19.
[173] Ibid., 293.
[174] Gallagher, *Portugal*, 19.
[175] Wheeler, *Republican Portugal*, 68.
[176] Marques, *History of Portugal*, 160.

military personnel from voting. In addition, all armed-force personnel were deprived of being eligible for Congress and were also permanently excluded from positions in the civil service.[177] In sum, Costa's electoral law was a clear attempt "to undercut potential monarchist or conservative political power in elections and administration and to demilitarize Portuguese politics."[178] It did so at the expense of democracy.

Costa, "the most beloved and the most hated of Portuguese," was a student prodigy who had become a Full Professor of Law by age 28.[179] In 1900 he was elected to Parliament from Oporto and "he rapidly acquired renown as a long-winded orator and charismatic debater." Costa defended his electoral law as prime minister in parliament with the logic that "individuals who do not have clear and accurate ideas about anything, nor about any person, should not go to the urns so that it cannot be said that the republic was confirmed by sheep."[180] It was rather late in the first wave for such arguments grounded in the liberal notion of capacity: Only in Italy did a literacy requirement persist for so long. In 1913, and under a nominally republican regime, the Portuguese suffrage rate was the lowest it had been since 1860.[181]

Although he never directly said so, Costa most likely supported suffrage restrictions because he recognized that the Republicans could not win elections with wider participation given the support for both monarchism and Catholicism in the countryside. Thus, the Republicans had already made a "choice to cheat" in the elections of 1911. Those choices involved: (1) vetting all candidates by the Directorate of the Portuguese Republican Party (PRP), (2) making sure all votes cast ended up going to Republican lists, and (3) employing armed vigilantes to intimidate would-be opposition voters on election day.[182] According to Ribeiro, "the aim was not to turn the dictatorship into a regime, but to develop a regime with the dictatorship."[183] As Wheeler puts it:

The Republican leadership during the Constituent National Assembly decided not to risk another election for a first Congress, and, hence, they included in the 1911 Constitution provisions to "make" the first Congress, literally, out

---

[177] *Diário do Governo*, no. 153, August 3, 1913, pp. 2445–2451.
[178] Wheeler, *Republican Portugal*, 96.
[179] Ibid., 93.
[180] Rui Ramos, *História de Portugal*, 2nd ed. (Lisboa: Esfera dos Livros, 2010), 588.
[181] Ibid., 589.
[182] Nancy Bermeo, "Interests, Inequality, and Illusion in the Choice for Fair Elections." *Comparative Political Studies* 43, 8/9 (2010), 1126.
[183] Ribeiro, "Parliamentarianism and anti-parliamentarianism in Portugal." *Parliaments, Estates and Representation* 37, 3 (2017), 336.

of the membership of the Assembly. The arbitrary and dictatorial actions of the Republican leadership, of course, were of a piece with the nature of the Provisional Government, which had come to power through an armed insurrection and remained in power, without an election, for eleven months, passing laws and decrees without the benefit of parliament. The Constitution of 1911, therefore, was an instrument of a highly politicized environment and shaped by the power monopoly held by the Republican government.[184]

There was much debate in early Republican Portugal about whether to adopt a presidential or a parliamentary system. In the end, the latter won: parliament acquired great power, but there was no clear constitutional solution to parliamentary deadlock. Republicans debated all sorts of esoteric points in parliament, but one parliamentarian pointed out that the electoral system rendered them all trivial:

Perhaps I am uttering a heresy, but I am less concerned about a constitution than [I am] about an administrative reform and an electoral law. What I want is a republic that will not be under the rule of a class of politicians ... Without a large administrative reform, without an honest electoral law, or the independence of public functionaries, the Parliamentary Republic, like the Constitutional Monarchy, will be a lie.[185]

Most Republicans, however, did not seem interested in an "honest electoral law." Part of the issue was certainly that "the majority of Assembly delegates owed their May 1911 election victories to a combination of election-rigging by the PRP Directorate, abstention by numbers of independent and liberal monarchists, and a restricted suffrage."[186] Costa controlled the electoral machinery, and "even as early as November 1911, the question of electoral reform and the political machine of the PRP had become an issue."[187] The PRP split in 1912 not as a result over fights over ideas. As Goldstein puts it, "the politicians who dominated the new regime had no serious interest in social reform and little agreement over anything other than opposition to the monarchy and the Catholic church and the desire to gain control of power and patronage."[188] The breakup of the Republicans originated rather from fights over control of the electoral machinery. More specifically, some independent and many republican politicians resented Costa's degree of control.

[184] Wheeler, *Republican Portugal*, 78–79.
[185] Ibid., 80.
[186] Ibid., 78.
[187] Ibid., 80.
[188] Goldstein, *Political Repression*, 293.

From thereafter – and really throughout the entire history of Republican Portugal – the legitimacy of elections was contested. In November 1913, charges of election rigging by Costa led to another dissolution of parliament. The president dismissed the Costa government, although he lacked a clear constitutional basis according to the strongly parliamentary system that Republican Portugal had adopted. Rather than challenging the president's action directly, the Republicans looked toward the elections of 1915 (still with restricted suffrage for illiterates and armed forces) to return to parliament with a stronger majority. They had reason to be optimistic as Costa had appointed the district civil governors who administered the elections: "with these official loyal to the party, and with a measure of control over electoral machinery, patronage, and the voters' lists, the 1915 elections appeared to be an easy Democratic victory."[189]

Senior military officers executed a bloodless coup ("golpe de estado") under Pimenta de Castro before the elections could be held: The so-called "Movement of the Swords" of January 25, 1915.[190] The officers were supported by the republican splinter parties seeking to undermine Costa. The new government proved no more stable than the ones that preceded it. The first crisis of the new regime occurred within a month when it published its new electoral decree that granted the vote to the police and the army and set elections for June 6, 1915. The PRP controlled the government of Lisbon and much of the provinces, and Costa ordered his party members to disobey the "dictatorship" of Castro. The political standoff culminated in brief civil war from May 14 to 18, 1915 centered in Lisbon in which several hundred people were killed and over one thousand were wounded. The Republicans won both the street and political battle, and then used their electoral machine to win their largest victory yet in the elections of June 13, 1915. They immediately rushed a new bill through Congress that sought to fire all civil servants "disaffected with the [Republican] regime."[191]

Portugal entered WWI in the spring of 1916 as a competitive authoritarian regime with its combination of a large franchise and massive election rigging. The war would reshape Portuguese politics in many ways, but it led to no more domestic political stability. During its sixteen-year history (1910–1926), the Portuguese Republic had forty-five different governments. Historians of the period all agree on the high degree

---

[189] Ibid., 108.
[190] The term originated when the officers ceremoniously laid down their weapons in front of the president of the republic to signal their commitment to democracy.
[191] Wheeler, *Republican Portugal*, 125.

of political volatility within Republican Portugal, but there are major differences in emphasis.[192] Summarizing one strain of scholarship, three Portuguese specialists write that "for some historians, the First Republic was a progressive and increasingly democratic regime."[193] Since there were never free elections in Republican Portugal, the evidence for democratization is thin. More convincing is the view that the Republic was "a prolongation of the liberal and elitist regimes of the nineteenth century." Ribeiro's view that "the change of political regime in 1910 did not essentially represent a break with the monarchy's electoral practices and customs" seems more consistent with the evidence.[194] Much like Italy, Portugal transitioned from a competitive oligarchy to competitive authoritarianism very late in the first wave of democratization.

## 7.6 CONCLUSION

There were other cases in Europe where grafting liberal constitutions onto economically underdeveloped states produced similar political dynamics. Spain, like Portugal, had lost the bulk of its empire by the nineteenth century and faced constant war and domestic political instability. Between 1808 and 1880, there were eight successful revolutions or counterrevolutions.[195] During approximately the same period (1814–1874), there were also thirty-seven coup attempts, and twelve successful coups.[196] The so-called "Glorious Revolution" of 1868 followed a military revolt and led to the first attempt to establish a republic. The Constitution of 1876 was liberal but also marked a restoration in terms of a highly restrictive franchise of less than 5 percent of the population. Thereafter, Spain functioned as a competitive oligarchy through the so-called *Turno pacifico*, which involved regular transitions of power among narrow political factions and election rigging to build working majorities. It was the equivalent of the Portuguese rotativismo in nearly every respect.[197] The caciques were the central figures in election management:

---

[192] Manuel Baiôa, Paul Jorge Fernandes, and Filipe Ribeiro de Meneses. "The Political History of Twentieth Century Portugal." E-JPH, Vol. I, number 2, Winter 2003.
[193] Ibid., 5.
[194] Ribeiro, "Parliamentarianism," 337.
[195] Roberts, *Europe 1880–1945*, 168.
[196] Anthony Beevor, *The Battle for Spain* (New York: Penguin, 2006), 8.
[197] W. C. Atkinson, *A History of Spain and Portugal* (Penguin: Baltimore, 1960), 306:

> There was in fact little of substance in the conflict between the two [Spanish] parties. Each in opposition flagellated the other for the alleged abuses and betrayals of principle, each in office pursued identical tactics and a scarcely distinguishable policy. In part this rested on a genuine concern never

"Not even the leaves on the tree die without the permission of the caciques."[198] According to Roberts "this was the golden age of the *cacique*, or local boss, who organized elections and was the retail distributor of the patronage sold wholesale in Madrid."[199] So effective were they that "the government newspaper even published the 1886 election returns before the balloting occurred!"[200]

The introduction of universal male suffrage in 1890 "made small difference; the elections continued to be made by the time-honoured means of purging municipalities, cooking electoral registers, and even by polling the dead. Sometimes the votes cast were ignored and the returns filled in with figures sought suitable in Madrid. The only change was that more force had to be used as time went on."[201] As in Italy, there was little to distinguish the two major parties from one another:

One can find similar patterns in the Balkans. Between 1870 and 1914, "the two major Romanian parties, the Liberals and Conservatives, both of whom were based on the well-to-do landlords and merchants, established after 1870 a system of rotation in power essentially identical to that used in Spain and Portugal. The system was based on the highly discriminatory suffrage system of 1866 (which was imperceptibly modified in 1884), systematic election rigging, the existence of two parties whose differences were minimal compared to their tacit agreement to ignore the peasantry and uphold the status quo, and the cooperation of Prince Charles I (1866–1914, king after 1881)."[202] In turn of the century Bulgaria under Stambolov, "elections were grossly fraudulent, with troops and bands of hired thugs 'encouraging' opposition figures not to show up."[203] Greece was the most democratic Balkan state during the first wave, but it too was highly oligarchic. "No difference of principle divides one party from the other; ... the difference is of men, not measures – the sweets of office versus the cold shades of opposition."[204]

again to split the nation or incite to arms. But it conveyed also with time the impression of cynical abandonment of principle in favor of a tacit agreement to alternate in power at decent intervals and to share less the responsibilities than the spoils of office.

[198] R. W. Kern, "Spanish Caciquismo," in Kern, ed. *The Caciques* (Albuquerque: University of New Mexico Press, 1973), 45.
[199] Roberts, *Europe 1880–1945*, 68.
[200] Goldstein, *Political Repression*, 287.
[201] Roberts, *Europe 1880–1945*, 169–170.
[202] Ibid., 304.
[203] Ibid., 306.
[204] S. Victor Papacosma, *The Military in Greek Politics: The 1909 Coup D'Etat* (Kent, Ohio: Kent State University Press, 1977), 17.

## 7.6 Conclusion

Ziblatt identifies two possible solutions to conservative electoral defense. The first was to build a party of the old regime that could win elections without resorting to fraud. None of the parties in this chapter opted for this path, but rather chose an "anticompetitive strategy" that involved rigging the system in their favor. In the competitive oligarchies of northern Europe (see Chapter 6), these anticompetitive strategies took the form of counter-majoritarian institutions like plural voting or non-elected upper houses of parliament. Election fraud was a minor part of the story. In Southern and Eastern Europe, however, the management of elections was the foundation of the anticompetitive strategy, and this chapter has documented how the "new informal techniques of electoral fraud, manipulation, clientelism and corruption that *substituted* for the "old corruption" of deference and coercion" were conceived and developed.[205] In this sense, the interwar period was not so much breakdown of democracy in these states but a continuity of anti-democratic practices. In the aftermath of WWI, however, these methods would no longer work. Giolitti's attempts to "transform" the fascists as he had the Catholics, and to some extent even the Socialists, met with catastrophic results and two decades of authoritarianism. The legacy was even longer in Portugal, where Salazar inherited the role of administrative dictator from his predecessors and ruled Portugal in authoritarian fashion for nearly half a century.

[205] Ziblatt, *Conservative Parties*, 34.

# 8

# War and Democratization in Europe

The United States entered World War I (WWI) in April 1917, two months after Germany resumed unrestricted submarine warfare. In his speech to Congress asking for a declaration of war, Wilson opened with the military facts before pivoting to the ideological war aims of the United States. "The world must be made safe for democracy," Wilson implored. This was not merely rhetorical, as American foreign policy had a significant role in shaping the new democratic order. Perhaps it was because this new order was so fleeting that the democratizing effects of WWI have not been studied systematically. Indeed, in most of the literature on European democratization, the war itself is a minor factor, either accelerating preexisting democratic trends or pushing states over a final democratic threshold.

This chapter seeks to carve out a much larger place for WWI in the story of European (in addition to American and Canadian) democratization. It identifies three specific democratizing effects of the war, none of which was initially intended. The first is that the era of mass warfare and conscription had made it politically impossible to deny soldiers – even illiterate ones – the vote, and in this sense a classic theory linking conscription to franchise extensions finds considerable historical support. Yet rather than an incentive for military service, franchise extensions for all males – and for female relatives of soldiers – tended to follow rather than precede conflict. They thus appear to be more of a reward than an incentive. There were also routes to ending competitive oligarchy that were specific to the war itself: The Belgian government in exile and the Dutch government that had remained neutral both reached political compromises on "one man, one vote" (and one woman, one vote as well in the case of the Netherlands) during the last two years of the war.

The second effect of WWI was an increase in support for female suffrage among political elites. In some cases – Canada, Great Britain, and the United States – suffragettes won enough allies to enfranchise women, while in others – such as Belgium and France – their efforts would fail until the end of WWII. Still, the shift in elite opinion was consequential even in states where female suffrage failed: The French National Assembly passed a bill in 1919 on female suffrage, only to have it killed by the French Senate three years later. The defenders of the status quo were not so much Catholics but Socialists and Liberals who feared that women would vote overwhelmingly for Catholic parties.

The third democratizing effect of WWI was Woodrow Wilson's foreign policy of democracy promotion. Even if this effort was downgraded after 1919, it was nevertheless the primary reason for regime change in Germany.[1] Indirectly, it also became a cause of regime change in Sweden as well. Swedish conservatives had constructed a "Prussia of the North" and the collapse of the original model finally broke their resistance to democratization. Revolutionary threat was not a primary factor in either case of regime change, though it is true that revolutionary talk and actual revolutions internationally provided the backdrop to both. And in Germany, of course, democracy was the product of an actual revolution, not simply a threat of one, that was precipitated by loss in war.

## 8.1 WAR AND FRANCHISE EXTENSIONS

The connection between international war and domestic politics is an enduring theme in comparative politics. The literature on the connection between war and fiscal policy is particularly large.[2] The relationship of international war to democratization specifically has generated a comparatively smaller literature, although the intuition that the two are linked is certainly quite old. Max Weber wrote that: "The basis of democratization

---

[1] Wilson consistently pressed for regime change, but he neither specified the type of the new regime nor committed the US to supporting it after the November Revolution. According to Daniel Larsen, Wilson "formulated a policy of non-engagement with the newly republican Germany, and he left the German democrats to fend for themselves." Daniel Larsen, "Abandoning Democracy: Woodrow Wilson and Promoting German Democracy, 1918–1919." *Diplomatic History* 37, 3 (June 2013), 477.

[2] See, for example, Richard Titmuss, "War and Social Policy," in *Essays on "The Welfare State"* (London: Allen and Unwin, 1958); Theda Skocpol, *Protecting Soldiers and Mothers: The Political Origins of Social Policy in the United States* (Cambridge: Harvard University Press, 1992); Kenneth Sheve and David Stasavage, *Taxing the Rich* (Princeton: Princeton University Press, 2016).

is everywhere purely military in character ... Military discipline meant the triumph of democracy because the community wished and was compelled to secure the cooperation of the non-aristocratic masses and hence put arms, and along with arms political power, into their hands."[3] Stanislav Andreski made a similar point in 1954: "if the willing cooperation of the masses is militarily essential, an effort must be made to win them over, to convince them that they are fighting for themselves."[4] In a modern update of the argument, Tichi and Vindigni find that the franchise is granted "in order to provide the citizens the incentives to undertake a costly action – fighting hard in battle – which is beneficial to the elites themselves."[5] Replicating this exercise with better data, Tony Ingesson and coauthors find that it is not conscription in general, but only conscription during war that is associated with franchise extensions.[6]

### 8.1.1 Martial Origins

Recall from Chapter 7 that universal suffrage occurred around the same time as Italy's colonial war in Libya. The reform of 1911 tripled the size of the electorate and specifically gave voting rights to army vets over 21. Martin Clark identifies a causal connection between the war and the move to universal male suffrage: "In 1912, as Italy's conscript soldiers faced death in the Libyan desert, it was impossible to deny them the vote any longer."[7] Further evidence comes from the statements of contemporary politicians like Sidney Sonnino, who argued at the time that soldiers "have conquered [their right to vote] in the Tripoli battlefields: no one asked southern peasants then whether they were illiterate or not." Salvemini too claims that Italy adopted universal male suffrage because "Giolitti wanted to secure the support of the reformist Socialists to the conquest of Libya." Given such evidence, it is understandable that Przeworski concludes that: "The 1912 extension was made as part of building support for the war in Libya."

---

[3] Max Weber, *General Economic History*, 1950.
[4] Stanislaw Andrzejewski, *Military Organization and Society* (London: Routledge, 1954), 27; Both Dahl and Huntington also considered the connections between international war and democratization. See Dahl "Foreign Control," in *Polyarchy* 189–201 and Huntington, *The Third Wave*, 40.
[5] David Ticchi and Andrea Vindigni, "War and Endogenous Democracy," 2009.
[6] Tony Ingesson, Martin Lindberg, Johannes Lindvall and Jan Teorell, "The Martial Origins of Democracy: A Global Study of Military Conscription and Suffrage Extensions since the Napoleonic Wars." *Democratization* 25, 4 (2018), 633–651.
[7] Clark, *Modern Italy*, 188.

## 8.1 War and Franchise Extensions

Yet problems arise when one looks at the case with a finer lens, the most important being that the Libyan war occurred before the initial debate on the franchise extension.[8] Ever since the defeat at Adowa, "an eventual acquisition of Libya became a cardinal assumption of Italian foreign policy."[9] A public pressure campaign began long before the war itself, and it is worth noting that none of the advocates linked it with universal male suffrage. In all probability, Giolitti had decided on war by the spring of 1911. Thus the timing suggests that the franchise extension was more of a reward than an incentive.[10] Consulo reasons that the Libyan war "probably aided, if not assured, passage" of the franchise bill. "Many deputies," he continues, "thought it was unjust and impractical to deny Italians who had fought and labored for the fatherland the right to participate in the electoral process."[11] Clark explains that politicians presented both the war and the franchise extensions as symbols of national unity.[12] In any event, the war was clearly not the initial impetus for the franchise extension (see Chapter 7), and the case is consistent with Przeworski's finding that "an overwhelming number of extensions occurred after, not before, wars."

The Canadian suffrage reforms of 1917 also appear to support the "martial origins" hypothesis. Canada entered WWI on August 4, 1914, several days after the United Kingdom. Prime Minister Robert Borden promised to raise 500,000 volunteers by 1916 (in a country of only eight million), but by the end of 1916 he had only delivered 300,000 and the existing Canadian forces needed replenishing after a punishing campaign in the Battle of the Somme in July/August of 1916. The result was the "conscription crisis" that pitted English-speaking Canadians, who favored conscription to help Great Britain win the war, against French Canadians, who felt their only loyalty belonged to Canada. In advance of the federal elections of December 1917, Borden's government passed

---

[8] A secondary problem with the argument is that Luzatti's initial suffrage bill of March 1911, as the attentive reader will recall, was modest compared to the reform that emerged from parliamentary wrangling.
[9] Ronald Cunsolo, "Libya, Italian Nationalism, and the Revolt against Giolitti." *Journal of Modern History* 37, 2 (1965), 186.
[10] A third possibility is that political parties saw political advantage in enfranchising soldiers. This was most likely for conservative parties [as in Canada]. The case of Portugal in Chapter 7 shows how soldiers were disenfranchised by Republicans and the enfranchised by the political opposition several times over the course of the Portuguese Republic (1910–1926).
[11] Consulo, "Libya," 197.
[12] Clark, *Modern Italy*, 188.

three closely linked pieces of legislation in September 1917. The first – the Military Service Act – introduced conscription. The second – the Military Voters Act- – gave the vote to all Canadian soldiers as well as women serving in the armed forces, such as nurses. The third – The Wartime Elections Act – gave the vote in federal elections to the wives, widows, mothers, and sisters of soldiers serving overseas.

In this case, wartime conscription occurred simultaneously with franchise reforms. And in this case, it was not political elites *in general* that were looking to incentivize soldiers, but the Unionist party in particular. Following the split of the Liberals over the conscription question, some individual Liberal members of parliament who supported conscription joined a ruling coalition with the Conservatives from 1917 to 1920. The Laurier Liberals (1917–1921), led by former Prime Minister Sir Wilfrid Laurier, opposed conscription, along with the vast majority of Quebecois. Lyndsay Campbell reminds us that "the Conservatives' main goal was to make sure that the majority of women in the West did not vote."[13] By the summer of 1917, five states in Canada (including all of the western states) had enfranchised women for provincial elections, and there was mounting pressure to introduce female suffrage for federal elections. Fearing the electoral consequences of universal suffrage, the Unionists opted for selective female suffrage connected to male wartime service. This not only kept Liberal women from voting in the western provinces but also raised the Unionist electorate as conservative leaning households were more likely to have males who had served, or were serving, in the army or navy. Borden's Unionist government not only won the elections but also set the record for the largest percentage for any party in a federal election (Unionists 57%, Laurier Liberals 39%). The Canadian wartime reforms also provide further examples of franchise extensions and disenfranchisement occurring simultaneously, as they took the right to vote away from Canadian citizens of German, Polish, and Ukrainian origin on the specious claim that they represented fifth columnists for the German and Austro-Hungarian empires. This embittered these constituencies toward the Conservatives for decades after they were repealed.

Clearly these two cases are not enough to overturn the martial origins hypothesis. They do suggest, however, that the relevant causal mechanism is more of a reward than an incentive. The electoral reforms that followed WWI in Great Britain, Belgium, and the Netherlands demonstrate that wars can affect democratization through means other than conscription.

[13] Lyndsay Campbell, "The Wartime Elections Act and Women Voters in 1917."

These three competitive oligarchies had each created parliamentary committees on electoral reform immediately before WWI, but the outbreak of the war quickly made them moot. Only in the Netherlands, moreover, did government continue to function normally. There were no parliamentary elections held in the United Kingdom during the war, and the Belgian government worked out of a tiny enclave in northern France following the German invasion. The comparative normalcy of Dutch domestic politics during the war is also relative; the shadow of the German invasion of Belgium, and the fear that the Germans would ultimately not respect Dutch neutrality hung over the entire country for four years and certainly raised the incentives for domestic political cooperation.

### 8.1.2 Representation of the People Act

Beginning with Great Britain, the Representation of the People Act of 1918 was a direct result of wartime cooperation among the three major political parties (Labour, Liberals, and Conservatives). There is no reason to believe that anything like it would have arisen had it not been for the war, or had the war been settled quickly and decisively as each of the belligerents initially believed. Indeed, the British government proclaimed that its official policy domestically would be "business as usual" and kept up this façade for the first several years of the war. As Frederic Ogg notes in an article in the *American Political Science Review* in 1918: "It was not by choice that the ministry and the two houses turned their attention to the electoral questions while the nation was yet fighting for its life within hearing of the channel ports."[14] Politicians could not ignore the facts that the Parliament chosen in December 1910 was still in office and that the existing electoral registers were out of date and did not include millions of soldiers serving overseas. The registers, moreover, also did not take account of conscription, which the United Kingdom passed in two acts in 1916 as mounting casualties forced it to abandon "business as usual." Marwick finds that "conscription meant that first-hand experience of war was brought, not just to a couple of million volunteers and professionals, but, whether they wanted it or not, to twice as many ordinary unadventurous citizens – one in three of the adult male population."[15] It

---

[14] Frederic Ogg, "The British Representation of the People Act." *American Political Science Review* 12, 3 (August 1918), 498.
[15] Arthur Marwick, *War and Social Change in the Twentieth Century: A comparative study of Britain, France, Germany, Russia and the United States* (New York: St. Martin's Press, 1974), 61.

was inconceivable to all three political parties that an election using the same rules and registers of 1910 could be conducted immediately following an armistice whose timing no one could predict.

Following a rancorous parliamentary debate on the register of voters in late 1916, Prime Minister Asquith created a "Speakers Conference" in October composed of members from all three parties. Its goal was to recommend a consensual and modest extension of the franchise, but when it reported its recommendations to Lloyd George's government in March 1917, the radical, and to many politicians, revolutionary, nature of the bill became clear. James Bryce, for one, was against it and argued that it "revolutionizes the Constitution of this country more than any measure since the great Reform Act of 1832."[16]

Home Secretary George Cave, who introduced the bill during a parliamentary debate on May 22, 1917, had tried to anticipate such criticism. He framed the introduction of universal male suffrage as unproblematic:

The number of men to be added by the Bill, allowing something for the improvement in registration and the effect of the six months' qualification, will be about 2,000,000. As to these 2,000,000, I doubt whether there is anyone who, quite apart from any question of compromise, would desire to keep them off the register of voters. I do not believe that there is one.

Cave then reminded his audience how passionate and bitter past debates on the suffrage had been. Directly referencing the Second Great Reform (the original "leap in the dark"), he noted that:

In the old days controversies about the value of the qualifying premises, whether it should be £50 or £20 or £10, or whether it should be ascertained by rental value or by rateable value, divided parties and destroyed Governments, and the addition of 2,000,000 electors to the register would have been referred to, I have no doubt, as a leap in the dark.

Voting had become universally recognized as a right and not a privilege. Thus, Cave could legitimately claim that: "Today the proposed addition excites no emotion whatever, except a feeling of satisfaction that, by making this addition, we shall approach nearer to the ideal of representative Government, namely, to make Parliament a mirror of the nation." The major reason for the change in the political environment, according to Cave, was the war. The war had increased social solidarity and eliminated class antagonism:

---

[16] Lords, Viscount Bryce, December 17, 1917, c. 176.

War by all classes of our countrymen has brought us nearer together, has opened men's eyes, and removed misunderstandings on all sides. It has made it, I think, impossible that ever again, at all events in the lifetime of the present generation, there should be a revival of the old class feeling which was responsible for so much, and, among other things, for the exclusion for a period, of so many of our population from the class of electors. I think I need say no more to justify this extension of the franchise.[17]

The Representation of the People Act abolished property qualifications for males over 21 entirely and introduced female suffrage in the United Kingdom for women under 30 (Section 8.1.4). In a deliberate nod to wartime service, it allowed male veterans to vote at 19. The act increased the number of adults who could vote from 1/7 (1884) to 1/3 of the population. It also simplified the arcane and complicated registration requirements that were particularly important to micro-institutions of competitive oligarchy. Plural voting technically survived, but its impact was minor compared to years past. Ogg noted in 1918 that the recent reform was "more comprehensive and far-reaching than any kindred act in English history (501)." That did not mean it was universally accepted. Some conservatives wanted to restore veto power for the House of Lords in exchange for any movement on suffrage reform. Arthur Salter, for example, dismissed the Parliament Act and argued that "Our Constitution [has] been incomplete and in suspense since 1911."[18] Sir Henry Craik, speaking against the bill, argued that it was "not only a crime but criminal folly to plunge this House and the country and every constituency into an angry controversy which will turn their attention from affairs of the war."[19] The resistance to female suffrage was also significant and turned out to be the part of the act that some politicians found to be the most radical.

In the end, however, there was no diehard faction that seriously contested The Representation of the People Act as they had the Parliament Act of 1911. One reason was the toll the war took on the social class most likely to back efforts to restore veto power for the Lords, or other such oligarchy preserving measures. Lord Tennyson later recalled "dressing and packing ... in feverish haste, so anxious was I to not run any chance of missing the war."[20] The same

[17] https://parlipapers.proquest.com/parlipapers/result/pqpdocumentview?accountid=14434&groupid=96296&pgId=d2fbd368-a591-42e1-9700-1986deef1fa1#t1459.
[18] Hansard, Arthur Salter, March 28, 1917, c. 478.
[19] Hansard, Sir Henry Craik, March 28, 1917, C. 550–1.
[20] Cannadine, *Decline and Fall*, 72.

could be said for the upper class as a whole, according to the "lost generation" thesis of C. F. G. Masterman in *England after the War*. Masterman writes that:

> In the retreat from the Mons, and the first battle of Ypres, perished the flower of the British aristocracy ... In the useless slaughter of the Grenadiers on the Somme, or of the Rifle Brigade in Hooge Wood, half the great families of England, heirs of large estates and wealth, perished ... in courage and high effort, and an epic of heroic sacrifice, which will be remembered so long as England endures.

Masterman's summary is elegant and moving, but not entirely true. David Cannadine, the foremost historian of the English aristocracy, finds that four out of five notables returned home.[21] He notes that the poor also suffered as well (as they do in all wars) and that the losses were shared by all social classes. Still, even Cannadine admits that the English aristocracy's "losses were, proportionately, far greater than those of any other social group."[22] One in five of British and Irish Peers and their sons were killed in the war; the figure for the general population was one in eight. Cannadine explains why:

> The patricians were either professional soldiers or among the first men to volunteer. Most of them were junior officers below the rank of Lt. Colonel, who were rapidly posted to the front, where they shared the risks and dangers of trench life, and led their men over the top and into battle. During the first year of the war, one in seven of such officers were killed, compared with only on in seventeen of the rank and file.[23]

The British landed elite may not have been eradicated as a class, but their power was still significantly diminished: "Not since the Wars of the Roses had the English aristocracy suffered such losses as those which they endured during the Great War."[24] They were in no position to mount a political defense of oligarchic institutions like the diehards had just several years earlier, much less threaten civil war over Ireland. Even conservatives like Henry Craik from the Scottish Unionist Party conceded that "we know that after the War things will be changed, and nothing will be as before."[25]

---

[21] Cannadine, *Decline and Fall*, 82.
[22] Ibid., 83.
[23] Ibid., 83.
[24] A. Lambert, *Unquiet Souls: The Indian Summer of the British Aristocracy, 1880–1918*, 205.
[25] Hansard, Sir Henry Craik, March 28, 1917, c. 550.

### 8.1.3 Belgium and the Netherlands

That statement applied to pretty much every state involved in the war, but none more than occupied Belgium. After Germany invaded neutral Belgium in August 1914, the Belgian government fled to Le Havre in Normandy. The French state granted the Belgian state sovereignty privileges and leased it the commune of Sainte-Adresse, where 13,000 Belgian politicians, civil servants, and their families lived until the end of the war. Meanwhile, King Albert I refused to leave the country and mounted a heroic defense of the last remaining sliver of Belgian-controlled territory west of the river Yser. There was no functioning parliament, as the elected representatives were spread out across several countries and not involved in decision-making. However, Albert I was in communication with the government in Sainte-Adresse and urged it to form a national cabinet consisting of the three "pillars" of Belgian society: Catholics, Liberals, and Socialists. The Catholics were initially hesitant but relented in January 1916 and formed a national unity government.[26]

Important as this precedent was for socialist participation, this was still a government-in-exile in all but name. The German army occupied over ninety percent of Belgian territory, requisitioning food to feed its soldiers and leaving civilians to fend for themselves. To save the country from starvation, several Belgian bankers founded the *Comite National de Secours et d'Alimentation* (CNSA, "National Relief and Food Committee") in the early days of the war.[27] The CNSA became a shadow government of sorts and, critically, politicians from every party worked in it, including the Socialists.[28] Still, such cross-party cooperation in the CNSA did not ensure the demand of the Socialist and Liberals for "one man, one vote" would be fulfilled when the Belgian government reconvened in Brussels in October 1918 after the capitulation of the German army. A hardline faction of Catholics wanted to preserve plural voting, and they might well have succeeded had not Albert I, with an eye on the revolution in Germany, bypassed Catholic opposition by appointing the moderate Leon Delacroix as prime minister in another cabinet of National Union composed of six Catholics, three Liberals, and three Socialists.

---

[26] Emmanuel Gerard, "Government, Parliament, Parties (Belgium)" in *International Encyclopedia of the First World War*.
[27] This group is not to be confused with the Commission for Relief in Belgium lead by Herbert Hoover. The two groups worked together.
[28] Michael Amara, "Comite National de Secours et d'Alimentation," in *International Encyclopedia of the First World War*.

The monarch announced the immediate granting of suffrage for men over 21 without plural voting. The Liberals were against extending the vote to women, as they feared that it would be the equivalent of giving Catholic households two votes.

Turning to the Netherlands, the liberal government had appointed an all-party committee to propose electoral and school reform on November 15, 1913. In part this was a recognition of the inconclusive results of the 1913 elections, where no majority cabinet emerged. Since conservatives would not have accepted electoral reform alone, the government of Cort van der Linden (Liberals) made it clear that the two committees would report their recommendations and then seek a vote from parliament on them as a package.[29] Following the invasion of Belgium and its violation of neutrality, the Dutch government proclaimed a "God's Peace" between the political parties. In contrast to Belgium, the parliament in the Netherlands continued to function throughout the war – the government even called a snap election in 1917. In the same year, the political parties finally reached a package deal (the "Pacification of 1917") whereby the Liberals and the Socialists received universal suffrage and the Conservatives were granted state support for religious education. The 1917 reform also allowed women to stand for office (but not to vote) and removed the sex qualification from the constitution. Then in 1919 the House of Representatives passed female suffrage by a vote of 64 to 10.

The "Pacification of 1917" is a significant event in Dutch historical memory and marks the birth of consociationalism in the official narrative of democratization. Lijphart argues that "the process of accommodation was started in 1913, before the outbreak of WWI."[30] He continues that although "this international emergency enhanced the sense of urgency behind the near unanimity ... it was not the decisive factor."[31] Even if this is true, the war nevertheless had a major effect on party positions regarding suffrage. On the eve of the war, Liberals still wanted to impose literacy tests and extend the franchise to urban but not rural areas.[32] And although conscription and mass mobilization were not factors in the 1917 reform, as the Netherlands remained neutral, WWI was still a national emergency of the highest order that ultimately ended the decades-long

---

[29] Willem Verkade, *Democratic Parties of the Low Countries and Germany: Origins and Historical Developments* (Leiden: Leiden University Press, 1965), 54.
[30] Lijphart, *Politics of Accommodation*, 111.
[31] Ibid.
[32] Carstairs, *Electoral Systems*, 63.

## 8.1 War and Franchise Extensions

political standoff on electoral reform and turned the Netherlands from a fairly restrictive competitive oligarchy into a democracy.

Summarizing the examples thus far, the British case – as with the Italian (1912) and Canadian (1917) cases – provides ample evidence of politicians justifying suffrage as a reward for military service. It was not an incentive, however. It was in part an ideological change whereby elites felt they could not deny soldiers the franchise, in part a consequence of outdated electoral registers, and in part a universal acknowledgment that there needed to be changes to the entire electoral system since the election of 1910. Still, it did have something to do with conscription. However, the major suffrage reforms in Belgium and the Netherlands did not, though the former was a direct consequence of the war and the latter was at the very least an indirect one. It is not surprising that war on the magnitude of WWI would produce multiple paths to democratization. Further research would be required to demonstrate that governments-in-exile tend to democratize (Belgium), that shadow governments do as well (also Belgium), or that a credible threat of invasion forces previously deadlocked parties to negotiate (the Netherlands). At the very least, this section has demonstrated that the war was not merely the final crest of the first wave but an independent cause of democratization.

### 8.1.4 World War I and Female Suffrage

And what about women? Marwick claims that:

In the political story what is most striking in Britain, and the United States is the way in which one after another all the old leading opponents of the idea of votes for women recant, and declare that since women have played such a vital part in the national effort, of course they must be allowed to share in the politics of their country.[33]

One important convert was Prime Minister Asquith. "Some years ago," Asquith noted, "I ventured to use the expression 'Let the women work out their own salvation. Well, Sir, they have worked it out during this war.'"[34] David Lloyd George, who served as prime minister when the Act was passed, sounds much like Marwick when he recalled the following:

The Conscription Act converted the country to a realisation of the injustice of this state of things. Millions of men were forced to risk their lives for a policy

---

[33] Marwick, *War and Social Change*, 77.
[34] A. J. P. Taylor, *English History*, 94.

which they had no share in fashioning. Millions of women faced anxieties and tortures worse than death in pursuit of the same policy, and yet no woman was allowed to express any opinion as to the selection of the rulers who led them to this sacrifice. It was felt to be so unjust that in the exaltation of war, which lifted men to a higher plane of equity, this obvious wrong was redressed. Hence the greatest of all the Enfranchisement Acts, the Act of 1917 [sic!], that for the first time converted the British system of government into a democracy.[35]

### 8.1.4.1 Britain

Lloyd George is basically correct about male enfranchisement, but he appears to have forgotten, or to have strategically ignored, the strength of political opposition to female suffrage.[36] During the second reading of the bill in the House of Commons on May 22, 1917, Sir John Simon recognized the fact that nothing "would have induced a Committee of the House of Commons to agree on this contentious subject if it had not been that we were at war."[37] Sir George Cave considered female suffrage a "thorny subject" when he introduced the bill, implicitly contrasting the conflict it provoked with the consensus on universal male suffrage. Politicians advanced six major reasons for denying women the vote in the parliamentary debates: (1) a women's sphere is in the home, (2) most women were not demanding the vote, (3) it was not the right time to enfranchise 6 million inexperienced voters, as the state needed to focus on the existential tasks of winning the war and reconstructing the economy, (4) it would cripple the Conservatives, (5) it would create a new army of Labor voters, and (6) females would soon outnumber men in the electorate.

Colonel Archer-Shee, an opponent of female suffrage, combined arguments two and three in his diatribe against the bill.

As it is the women preponderate greatly over the men, and probably after the War will do so by not less than 2,000,000. Before the War I think the excess over males was nearly 1,500,000. Therefore, by giving women the vote, you give them the main political power. Then, again, women have not been asked whether they wish to have the vote at all … Hon. Members talk about women having earned the vote, but they do not want it. Why give them something they do not want? It is not a nice way of being kind to them, and I do not think that if a Referendum

---

[35] Lloyd-George, *Is it Peace?*, 182.
[36] Ogg contrasted the two major pieces of the bill that would become the Representation of the People's Act: "No strong objection was raised to the enfranchisement of the two million men … but the provisions of the act relating to women were vigorously opposed (501)."
[37] Hansard, May 22, 1917, CC 2133–2253.

were taken of the women of this country there would be anything like a majority in favour of the vote. I think there would be a majority probably against it of something like 70 per cent.[38]

And as if this were not enough, Archer-Shee also repeated the fifth argument against female suffrage, that the country focus on the war and leave such important constitutional changes until peacetime, "surely we have enough trouble at the present moment staring us in the face … Surely what this House has got to devote itself to are such questions as the U boats; secondly, the question of man-power; and thirdly, the provision of munitions; and this is no time or place to go into questions of franchise reform and redistribution."[39]

Supporters of the bill pointed out in response that the collapse of the short war illusion had rendered such "win the war first" arguments moot. As Sir John Simon put it:

The real truth is that the maxims by which we began in the early stages of the War were not suited for a subsequent period. We would not allow ourselves to dwell for a moment on any other problem whatever. That is a position you can perfectly well take up if it is going to be a war that lasts a certain number of months, but that is a position you cannot continue to hold if the War is going to last a number of years.[40]

Many politicians agreed that the war had changed the role of women in society forever. In introducing the bill, Cave asked rhetorically "whether it is possible for us … to refuse to women a voice in moulding the future of the country which their help and devoted self-sacrifice have done so much to save?"[41] One Mr. Cochrane patronizingly agreed: "Their perseverance, their energy, their adaptability, and their resources, have surpassed anything that I think anyone imagined as possible."[42] He then noted that "it is only a truism to say, I think the House will agree, that it would have been impossible to have carried on the War without them."[43] Some politicians went further and claimed that the female war effort had shattered forever the "women's place" argument. According to J. B. Watson:

The days when the extension of franchise to women can be met with a burst of ridicule are gone forever. We used to be told that women ought not to concern themselves with other than domestic affairs. We used to be told that by her

[38] Ibid.
[39] Ibid.
[40] Ibid.
[41] Ibid.
[42] Ibid.
[43] Ibid.

nature, by her position in society, she was sheltered from the buffeting and the turmoil of life. Now for nearly three years women have taken their part in affairs of the greatest moment and of the greatest consequence to this nation.[44]

Some politicians felt that the bill did not go far enough. Lord Hugh Cecil, for example, would have lowered the age limit and pointed out the stupidity of setting it at thirty:

> I greatly regret that in dealing with women's suffrage the age has been fixed at thirty years, for it seems to me the most absurd proposal ever put forward. What conceivable reason is there for saying that a woman shall have a vote after she is thirty years of age and not before? Does anybody believe that the female mind matures after that age? The Bill treats a woman's age as one might expect to see it treated in the cheapest comic papers.[45]

Responding to Lord Cecil, Sir William Bull took the floor and admitted that the age of 30 was "utterly indefensible and utterly illogical." He did, however, provide revealing details on how the committee arrived at that age:

> I found that taking the age at forty practically meant putting 3,000,000 women on the register. The next suggestion was that we should put it at thirty-five. That meant 4,500,000. It will be remembered, as I said just now, that we should be increasing the register of men by 2,000,000, from 8,000,000 to 10,000,000, and, if we adopted the age of thirty-five for women, that would be 10,000,000 men and 4,500,000 women. When the suggestion was before the Government they, for reasons of their own, considered that thirty-five would hardly do, and they reduced the age to thirty. This will put 6,000,000 women on the register. The whole of the electorate, therefore, will now be 10,000,000 men and 6,000,000 women. That is the position at the present time. I know it is utterly indefensible and utterly illogical, but a great many things utterly indefensible and utterly illogical continue for a very long time in this country, and we hope and believe that this will be a settlement of the question for many years to come.[46]

As in 1867, when politicians baldly stated their ideal property requirements for working men, fifty years later similar electoral calculations were made based on the age of women. The notion of political capacity as a prerequisite for voting for males died very hard in Great Britain, and it clearly took even longer for women. Removing the age requirement became the core goal of the woman's movement in interwar Britain. It was only in April 1928, when the voting age for women was lowered to 21 (as for males) that, according to A. J. P. Taylor, "the British electoral system reached theoretical democracy."[47]

[44] Ibid.
[45] Ibid.
[46] Ibid.
[47] Taylor, *English History*, 262.

## 8.1 War and Franchise Extensions

Would most British women have achieved the vote in 1918 had it not been for WWI? Teele makes a plausible case that the moderate wing of the suffragette movement had cooperated with the Labour party as of 1912, but she also notes the importance of the "political opening afforded by the First World War."[48] Given the strong opposition to female suffrage even after four years of total societal mobilization, it is difficult to imagine that electoral alliances on their own would have delivered British women the vote within the decade, if at all.

### 8.1.4.2 *The United States*

In the United States, the most important convert to the cause of female suffrage was President Woodrow Wilson, who argued in a 1918 speech that "We have made partners of the women in this war. Shall we admit them only to a partnership of sacrifice and suffering and toil and not to a partnership of privilege and of right?" This was in fact Wilson's first public endorsement in office of female suffrage, and his support was to prove important in the passing of the 19th Amendment. But the amendment needed to be ratified by thirty-six states to become law. This was by no means assured, as many states had recently voted against female suffrage at the state level. A Maine Pamphlet titled "The Case against Woman Suffrage" that urged the men of Maine to vote "No" in the special election of September 10, 1917 made little reference to women's role in the emerging war effort.[49] The authors' case that "Woman Suffrage is wrong in theory and bad in practice" boiled down to eight points:

1. The vote is not a question of individual "right," or what is best for the individual or for any class, but solely a question of what is best for the State.
2. The net result of Woman Suffrage wherever tried has been a loss to the State and a loss to women.
3. The vote is demanded by only a small minority of women.
4. To force the vote upon the great majority of women to satisfy a small minority would be undemocratic and unjust.
5. Men and women were created different and designed to work in different spheres for the common good – to cooperate with and supplement each other and not to compete.

---

[48] Teele, *Forging the Franchise*, 49.
[49] Maine Association Opposed to Suffrage for Women, "The Case against Woman Suffrage: the Most Important Question on the Ballot at the Special Election, September 10, 1917" (1917). *Maine History Documents*, 127. https://digitalcommons.library.umaine.edu/cgi/viewcontent.cgi?article=1125&context=mainehistory.

6. The vote would deprive a woman of her nonpartisan power, which enables her to do for the State what a man is unable to do because he is bound by political party obligations.
7. The basis of government is physical force, and the physical power to enforce the law, without which the vote is useless, is neither possible nor desirable for women.
8. Woman Suffrage is demanded by socialists and feminists as "a means to an end" – the end being "a complete social revolution."

The vote in the special election in Maine was 38,800 to 206,000 against female suffrage, making it one of the many victories of the "antis" in this period. The final battle occurred in Tennessee – where suffragettes were seeking to make it the 36th state to ratify the Nineteenth Amendment. Their movement could have conceivably stalled there had the anti-suffragettes won. A diverse coalition of anti-suffragettes – including many women – came together for a final stand. It included the journalist Ida Tarbell who wrote that while "insisting that women do the same things that men do, may make the two exteriorly more alike – it does not make them more equal. Men and women are widely apart in functions and in possibilities. They cannot be made equal by exterior devices like trousers, ballots, the study of Greek."[50] Charlotte Rowe, another prominent anti-suffragette, saw nothing less than a plot to destroy America afoot:

Under the pretense of political expediency and the fond dream of woman's emancipation from the laws of nature, suffrage leaders are working to destroy the states and enslave the American people ... The Federal suffrage amendment is a deliberate conspiracy to crush the will of the American public ... If the present legislature ratifies it will be due to the Bolshevik and socialist influences at work on them.[51]

According to Rowe: "The ultimate aim of suffrage is feminism ... Feminism is intimately and inextricably allied with Socialism and belongs to the same distorted school of thought, the same ungodly dream of irresponsible power." Finally, Rowe stressed that "Feminism is not an imaginary evil; it is a definite and logical doctrine, promulgated by the enemies of Christian civilization."[52]

The defenders of "state's rights" made similar claims about the enemies of white supremacy in the south. Senator Herschel Candler warned of the risks should female suffrage come to pass:

---

[50] Elaine Weiss, *The Woman's Hour: The Great Fight to Win the Vote* (New York: Penguin, 2018), 253.
[51] Weiss, *Woman's Hour*, 121.
[52] Ibid., 120.

Within a very few years after this amendment has passed, you will find that Congress has legislated so as to compel we people of the south to give the negro men and women their full rights at the ballot box ... Then you will find many of your counties, now dominated by the Democrats and white people, sending up negro representatives to this house.[53]

### 8.1.4.3 France

So much for the universal recognition of women as "partners" in the United States. Still, at least the US did introduce female suffrage in the immediate aftermath of the war. France – along with Belgium, Italy, and Switzerland – continued to deny the vote to women for over two decades more. It is difficult to claim that French women made any less contribution to the war effort than British women, so we must look to other sources of variation. One plausible answer is that Catholicism directly prevented female suffrage in the French case: according to Richard Evans: "the [French] feminists came up against the most persistent and intractable of their enemies, the Roman Catholic Church."[54] The official position of the Church was that "a woman is by nature fitted for homework, and it is that which is best adapted at once to preserve her modesty and to promote the good bringing up of children and the well-being of the family." Pope Benedict XV, writing in 1917, deplored the fact that many women had "abandoned the duties of the housewife, for which they were fashioned, to cast themselves recklessly into the current of life." This, he went on, "is the source of that deplorable perversion of morals, which disorder bred of war has multiplied and propagated beyond all belief."[55] The power of the Catholic Church could also explain (1) the late adoption of female suffrage in other first-wave democratizers, such as in Italy (1945) and Belgium (1948), (2) the fact that women were denied the provincial ballot in predominantly Catholic Quebec, and (3) the later adoption of female suffrage by protestant cantons in Switzerland than by Catholic ones.

Upon further inspection, however, this argument crumbles. The Republicans were in fact indistinguishable from the Catholics in their opposition to female suffrage. Republican leader and former Prime Minister Jules Simon asked rhetorically in 1892. "What is man's vocation? It is to be a good citizen. And woman's? To be a good wife and a

---

[53] Ibid., 261.
[54] Richard Evans, *The Feminists: Women's Emancipation Movements in Europe, America and Australasia 1840–1920* (London: Routledge, 1977), 124.
[55] Pope Benedict XV. "On Woman's Mission in Modern Society." *The Tablet* [London] 1 Nov. 1919: 7–8.

good mother. One is in some way called to the outside world: the other is retained for the interior."[56] Twenty-eight private bills for women's suffrage were tabled from 1870 to 1913. And it was not the Socialists or the Republicans, but the Catholic women's suffrage movement in France that "converted more women to suffragism than all other feminist groups combined."[57] The Pope also changed his position dramatically and essentially endorsed female suffrage in 1919.[58]

France appeared to be on a direct path to introducing female suffrage after the war: the National Assembly passed a suffrage bill by a vote of 329 to 95, with 104 abstentions, in May 1919. Many members of the Chamber of Deputies doubtless assumed that the measure would die in the Senate, in this case not through the veto power of an undemocratically elected upper chamber, but through democratic bicameralism. They were correct: the committee in the Senate voted 8–5 without much deliberation to reject the suffrage bill and appointed the well-known anti-suffragist Alexandre Bérard to write the report explaining its recommendation. The report immediately became known as "Berard's Fourteen Points" (a clear play on Wilson's speech) and constitutes "a landmark of French anti-suffragism, a synthesis of 150 years of arguments against political rights for women."[59] Bérard's first point was that the Chamber of Deputies vote was invalid because it had surpassed its length in office to pursue the war. The other thirteen were as follows:

2. Any legislation subversive of the established order must be thoroughly studied, and the country must first be consulted in an electoral campaign based on the issue.
3. French opinion does not approve of the change, not even in the large provincial cities; there is no trace of support in the small towns, much less in the villages.
4. The immense majority of French women, "so full of good sense," do not want the vote, and do not want to leave the home for the political arena: they know their families would suffer as a result.

---

[56] Sylvie Chaperon and Blanca Rodriguez-Ruiz. "The Difficult Struggle for Women's Political Rights in France." in *The Struggle for Female Suffrage in Europe: Voting to Become Citizens* (Leiden: Brill, 2012), 363.
[57] Steven Hause and Anne Kenney. "The Development of the Catholic Women's Suffrage Movement in France, 1896–1922." *The Catholic Historical Review* 67, 1 (1981), 11.
[58] Ibid., 27.
[59] Steven Hause and Anne Kenney, *Women's Suffrage and Social Politics in the French Third Republic* (Princeton: Princeton University Press, 1984), 237.

## 8.1 War and Franchise Extensions

5. While women did give immense service to France during the war, they did so for love of the *patrie*, not in the expectation of a reward: it would be an insult to pay them for their patriotism.
6. Women have insufficient civic education for political rights: their uninformed participation would pose a grave threat to the republic.
7. Some women do claim the vote, but they are part of "an infinitesimal minority ... a handful of incoherent feminists."
8. The assertion that women are needed in politics to secure major social reforms is contradicted by parliament's attention of twenty years to these matters: the Senate and the Chamber of Deputies do not need help in drafting legislation.
9. Feminists are beginning to "threaten an uproar in the streets, even a violent revolution like the Bolsheviks, and the Senate must not capitulate to their threats."
10. France has always guided other people toward liberty and is great enough to decide for herself, on reasoned argument and not on foreign examples, on what legislation to adopt.
11. The "Catholic mentality" of the majority of French women, combined with the hostility of the church toward the republic and liberty, means that women's suffrage would lead to clerical reaction.
12. Women's suffrage would be "a formidable leap into the unknown" that might produce a new Bonaparte, as universal suffrage did in 1848, and might thereby lead to a new Sedan.
13. Nature has given women "a different role than men ... a primordial role," to attend to the incomparable grandeur of maternity and to the family, which is the basis of French society.
14. Women are different creatures than men, filled with sentiment and tears rather than hard political reason: their hands are not for political pugilism or for holding ballots, but for kissing.

Berard summed it all up with the warning that giving women the vote would mean "sealing the Tombstone of the Republic." As Teele observes, "some of the arguments raised can seem, today, to be quintessential examples of sexism in public discourse," while others were strategic.[60] Berard had been a republican politician (radical-socialist) his entire career, and it was radicals and radical Socialists in the Senate that killed the bill in 1922. Their primary fear was that female suffrage would hand power over to

[60] Teele, *Forging the Franchise*, 146.

Catholic parties. The Chamber of Deputies put forward over forty bills related to female suffrage between 1919 and 1935, but the Senate either stifled debate on, or voted down, all of them.[61] The Popular Front government in 1936 also blocked a female suffrage bill, claiming that it was acting as the "guardian of Laïcité."[62] The situation only changed with the WWII. Charles De Gaulle, who was formerly an outspoken anti-suffragist, switched his position and the provisional assembly in Algiers extended votes to women by a vote of 51 to 16 in 1944. The most compelling hypothesis for this change is that De Gaulle had come to view communism, rather than political Catholicism, as the central threat to the republic.

- Austria
  Reform: New democratic state (1919)

- Belgium
  Reform: End of plural voting (1919)

- Canada
  Reforms:
  Universal male suffrage (1917)
  Female suffrage

- Denmark
  Reforms:
  Abolished property qualifications for upper house elections (1915)
  Female suffrage (1918)

- Finland
  Reform: New democratic state (1918)

- Germany
  Reforms:
  Acceptance of parliamentary government (1918)
  New democratic state (1919)

- Great Britain
  Reforms:
  Universal male and female franchise (1918)
  Reduction of plural voting (1918)

---

[61] Ibid., 145.
[62] Chaperon and Rodriguez-Ruiz, "Difficult Struggle," 311.

- Netherlands
    Reform: Universal male suffrage (1917)
- Sweden
    Reforms:
        Parliamentary sovereignty (1917)
        Universal suffrage (1918)
- United States
    Reform: Female suffrage (1919)

Belgium represents a second case of long-delayed female suffrage. Although some Belgian women had gained the vote in 1919, it was restricted to mothers and widows of servicemen who died in WWI, mothers and widows of citizens "shot or killed by the enemy," and female prisoners who "had been held by the enemy." In 1920, all Belgian women, with the exception of prostitutes and sex workers, received the right to vote in municipal elections. However, as in France both liberal and socialist parties calculated that women would vote for Catholic parties, and both blocked federal female suffrage bills until 1946.

## 8.2 WAR AND DEMOCRATIZATION IN GERMANY AND SWEDEN

Germany and Sweden were the two most authoritarian states in Western Europe in 1914. Sweden remained neutral during the conflict, as did Denmark, Iceland, the Netherlands, Norway, Spain, and Switzerland. Swedish conservatives, however, clearly hoped that Germany would win the war and that authoritarianism would remain intact in both states. This transnational link makes the cases worth exploring further, as does the fact that Acemoglu and Robinson include democratization in both states at the end of WWI as good fits for their threat of revolution hypothesis. Drawing on Mommsen (1981) and Gerschenkron (1943), they claim that "the final emergence of German democracy, the Weimar Republic, in 1919 was in response to the very severe threat of social disorder and revolution triggered by the collapse of the German armies on the Western Front in August 1918."[63] Regarding Sweden, they rely primarily on Collier's assessment that: "in November 1918, labor protests reached such a point as to be perceived as a revolutionary threat by Sweden's Conservative party and

---

[63] Acemoglu and Robinson, "Why did the West Extend the Franchise?" 1184–1185.

upper classes."⁶⁴ Although that is the extent of the historical evidence they provide for the two cases, their central hypothesis is plausible as there were more revolutions in Europe in 1917–1919 than at any time since 1848. The Bolshevik Revolution, moreover, revealed that communist revolution was possible anywhere in Europe. If communists could capture power in a largely agricultural society – an impossibility according to classic Marxist theory – then the chances of similar revolutions in the more industrialized societies of Germany and Sweden seemed greater than ever.

The following section looks closely at the months of August through November 1918 to assess the role of revolutionary threat in German democratization in 1918–1919. The conclusion is that it was military defeat and American foreign policy, and not revolution, that was the most important factor. In Sweden, the necessary condition for democratization was not a threat of revolution but the collapse of the Prussian system that had hitherto provided a successful model for Swedish conservatives looking to preserve the old regime.

### 8.2.1 Germany

Few historians would dispute Hans Mommsen's claim that the German population was "seized by patriotic frenzy" and that it "supported the war enthusiastically."⁶⁵ Nor would they single Germany out as unique in that respect: all nations rushed headlong into war believing that they would win a quick and decisive victory. Historians might also point out that wartime censorship existed in Great Britain and the United States, and that the German government's propaganda that victory was around the corner was the rule for the belligerent powers. Yet even if there was no German exceptionalism in limiting civil liberties and spreading misinformation to its own population, it is true that each of these elements – patriotic frenzy, support for maximalist war aims, and censorship – were magnified in wartime Germany.⁶⁶ The thesis of Werner Sombart's 1915 *Traders and Heroes: Patriotic Reflections* was that "war is the consummation of the heroic outlook, and springs from it; it is necessary in order to prevent the heroic outlook from falling prey to the forces of evil, to

---

⁶⁴ Acemoglu and Robinson, *Economic Origins*, 68; Collier, *Paths toward Democracy*, 83.
⁶⁵ Hans Mommsen, *The Rise of Fall of Weimar Germany* (Chapel Hill: University of North Carolina Press, 1996), 1.
⁶⁶ On this point, see "The Spirit if 1914 and the Ideology of the German 'Sonderweg'" in Wolfgang Mommsen, *Imperial Germany 1867–1918: Politics, Culture, and Society in an Authoritarian State* (New York: Arnold, 1990).

## 8.2 War and Democratization in Germany and Sweden 273

the narrow, abject spirit of commerce."[67] Ernst Glaser recalled a similar mood in his novel *Jahrgang 1902* (Berlin 1929):

At last life had regained an ideal significance. The great virtues of humanity ... fidelity, patriotism, readiness to die for an ideal ... were triumphing over the trading and shopkeeping spirit ... This was the providential lightning flash that would clear the air ... [There would be] a new world directed by a race of noble souls who would root out all signs of degeneracy and lead humanity back to the deserted peaks of the eternal ideas ... The war would cleanse mankind from all its impurities.[68]

There was close to universal agreement among Germans that they would triumph. There was also strong support for a political truce until this victory was achieved. Following the outbreak of war, Kaiser Wilhelm proclaimed on August 4, 1914 that "I no longer recognize parties; I recognize only Germans." Holborn interprets this as "a promise that the government would not treat any of the parties as being outside the pale, as it had done particularly with the Social Democratic party."[69] The resulting *Burgfrieden* (party truce) included a promise by socialist labor unions not to obstruct the war effort. Although the SPD achieved more influence in the Reichstag than at any other time, the Reichstag as an institution suffered from all the problems it had before the war, and only met sporadically during it.

The center of power in wartime Germany was the military, and specifically the Supreme Army Command. The German government declared a "State of Siege" that drew on a law from 1869 that empowered it to suspend any associations or public meetings and censor all publications.[70] A Prussian law of 1851, whereby district commanders of the army possessed executive power, ensured that the German military controlled local activities. The position of the *Oberste Heeresleitung* (OHL, Supreme Army Command) was first created in 1906 and filled by Helmoth von Moltke. The second OHL was Erich von Falkenhayn, the Prussian Minister of War, who replaced Moltke on September 14, 1914. Falkenhayn was in turn replaced in 1916 by the third OHL, Field Marshal Paul von Hindenburg, but the most powerful figure during this period was General Erich Ludendorff

---

[67] Werner Sombart, *Händlerund Helden. Patriotische Besinnungen* (Munich/Leipzig: Duncker& Humblot 1915), 92.
[68] Ernst Glaeser, *Jahrgang 1902* (Berlin, Gustav Kiepenheuer Verlage, 1929).
[69] Hajo Holborn, *A History of Modern Germany, 1840–1945* (New York: Knopf, 1969), 429.
[70] Ibid., 430.

(who held the title of First Quartermaster General).⁷¹ Hindenburg largely coasted on his reputation, his Bismarck-like physique, and his unflappable demeanor as Ludendorff took all the major military and political decisions.⁷² There were no serious threats to the military's hold on power, nor were there serious attempts to undermine the war effort. In fact, the support of both the home front and of every significant political party in the Reichstag for the war effort was not in question until the Supreme Army Command announced that the war was unwinnable in late September of 1918. The official organ of the SPD, *Vorwärts*, was still making appeals to its readers for war loans as late as October 27, 1918.⁷³

The stalemate on the Western Front led the Supreme Army Command to demand a resumption of unrestricted submarine warfare. When the matter was debated in the Reichstag in October of 1916, the parties of the right along, critically, with the Center Party, sponsored a resolution that effectively stripped the chancellor of any decision-making power over the issue. Craig points out the magnitude of this resolution: "In what can only be described as an act of collective irresponsibility in a matter effecting the very heart of the constitution, the principle of civilian dominance over the military, the Reichstag accepted this, and, in a very real sense, left Bethmann [the Chancellor] powerless."⁷⁴ Germany resumed unrestricted submarine warfare in February 1917 with the support of the Reichstag.

That decision, of course, brought the United States into a conflict that it had yet to frame ideologically. Secretary of State Robert Lansing wrote despairingly on March 19, 1917: "Why cannot everybody see that this is a battle of Liberty against Despotism and that liberty must win if the American idea is to survive?"⁷⁵ Wilson's address to Congress requesting a declaration of war against Germany on April 2, 1917 contained the phrase "the world must be made safe for democracy" and that "its peace must be planted upon the tested foundations of political liberty."⁷⁶ The democratization of the Central Powers only then

---

⁷¹ Martin Kitchen, *The Silent Dictatorship: The Politics of the German High Command Under Hindenburg and Ludendorff* (London: Croom Helm, 1976).
⁷² These same qualities helped Hindenburg become President of the Weimar Republic.
⁷³ Mommsen, *Imperial Germany*, 15.
⁷⁴ Craig, *Germany*, 380.
⁷⁵ Lansing, "Note on War with Germany," 9 AM, March 19, 1917.
⁷⁶ Wilson Address to a Joint Session of Congress, April 2, 1917. https://millercenter.org/the-presidency/presidential-speeches/april-2-1917-address-congress-requesting-declaration-war.

became an American – and by extension – a British, war aim. German war propaganda also cast the war a struggle between regime types. It cast German constitutional monarchy as preferable to a degenerate Western liberal democracy. As the Austrian philosopher Alois Riehl, who taught in Germany for most of his career, explained:

> We seek to defeat England, not follow England's example. The English example shows only too clearly what happens when a state is dedicated exclusively to the pursuit of commercial and industrial goals. We do not wish the state to be concerned solely with the acquisition and production of material goods. The motherland of social legislation must also remain the land of social advance and social reform.

The debate on unrestricted submarine warfare had resuscitated calls for political reform among critics of the policy, including the chancellor and the SPD, during the first half of 1917. Bethmann Hollweg declared his support for political reform in a speech to the Reichstag on February 27, 1917, which led to the establishment of an inter-party committee (*Interfraktioneller Ausschuss*) "for the examination of constitutional questions especially in regard to the structure of the representative body of the nation and its relationship to government."[77] Max Weber published an op-ed in the *Frankfurter Allgemeine Zeitung* (FAZ) dated March 28, 1917 where he argued that sacrifices in war should lead to increased political participation after it. Following American entrance into the war, the SPD partially broke the party truce by calling for reform of the Prussian electoral system in the spring of 1917. Wilhelm II's "Easter Message" of April 7, 1917, appeared to meet this demand and contained a pledge that suffrage reform would follow the war.

Holborn, however, concludes that the "emperor promised the Prussian people universal and direct, but not equal suffrage."[78] In any event, the German monarch and military soon cut off any more discussion of reform. Under pressure from Ludendorff, the Kaiser dismissed Chancellor Bethmann Hollweg and replaced him with George Michaelis, an ally of Generals Hindenburg and Ludendorff, without consulting the Reichstag. According to Mommsen, "Michaelis was an outspoken opponent of the transition to a parliamentary system of government to which the majority parties were giving little more than halfhearted support."[79] Michaelis also proved to be one of the more incompetent chancellors in Germany history, as the Supreme

---

[77] Craig, *Germany*, 381.
[78] Holborn, *Modern Germany*, 471.
[79] Mommsen, *Weimar Germany*, 5.

Command quickly realized. He was replaced with Count Georg von Hertling who was old, infirm, but the only candidate who would accept the job. By that point civilians had lost all power. Thus, when Foreign Secretary Kuhlmann suggested in front of the Reichstag that the government was seriously considering the Reichstag's peace resolution of 1917, Ludendorff went straight to the emperor and Kuhlmann was replaced with the pliable Admiral von Hintze. "In these last critical months of the war," writes Craig, "there was no authority in Germany except Ludendorff."[80]

There was also little political opposition to the war except for a faction within the SPD. Rosa Luxembourg, Karl Liebknecht, and Clara Zetkin founded the "International Group" within the SPD in August of 1914, and Liebknecht became the first member of Parliament to vote against war credits on December 21, 1915. The "International League" was renamed the Spartacus Group in 1916, leading to the expulsion of Liebknecht and others from the SPD over their opposition to the war. The end result was a split of the SPD into a pro-war faction (the Majority Social Democratic Party of Germany (MSDP)) and an anti-war faction (the Independent Social Democratic Party of Germany (USPD)) based around the Spartacus Group.

The Bolshevik Revolution of October 1917 came as welcome news to the German Supreme Command, and the Treaty of Brest-Litovsk led to tremendous territorial gains in the east for Germany. By that point Ludendorff had "succumbed to a fantastic dream of creating a great southeastern Russian state that would extend all the way to the Caucasus, of making a German Riviera on the Crimea, and of building a bridge to Central Asia in order to threaten the British position in India."[81] Such aspirations were, in fact, widespread in Germany and their apparent realization "aroused exhilaration and a new confidence in peace in Germany."[82] It appeared that victory on the Western Front was now possible before American troops began to arrive. It was, according to Craig, yet another tragic illusion: "this euphoric reaction, to which all of the parties which had voted for the Peace Resolution succumbed, with the exception of the Socialists, was to have dire results and to make the psychological effects of the ultimate defeat doubly hard when it came six months later."

It took nothing short of the *combination* of a successful allied offensive at the end of September 1918 on the Western Front (the second battle

---

[80] Craig, *Germany*, 393.
[81] Craig, *Germany*, 392.
[82] Ibid., 391.

of the Marne and the battle of the Somme), the capitulation of Bulgaria, and the collapse of the Romanian front for Ludendorff to finally seek an armistice. After having promised a breakthrough for months, Ludendorff shocked the government on September 29 by informing it that "the condition of the army demands an immediate armistice in order to avoid a catastrophe." Ludendorff had in fact notified the monarcho-military circle of the dire situation over a month earlier when he reported at the crown council of August 14, 1918, that victory on the Western Front was impossible.[83] The Reichstag was, typically, the last to learn the truth: Ludendorff would not even enter the building and sent a staff officer to the Reichstag on October 2 to inform it of the impending collapse. Wartime censorship apparently affected politicians as well as ordinary Germans, for "all of the leaders of the Reichstag parties, including the Social Democrats, were completely unprepared for such disastrous news."[84]

It is ironic that "Ludendorff's action opened the way for the introduction of parliamentary government," for he clearly detested it.[85] His calculation was twofold: first, his "sudden swing toward parliamentarization" was designed to "saddle the civilian government with responsibility for the loss of the war."[86] As Ludendorff himself put it: "I have asked his Majesty ... to bring those circles into the government to whom we mainly owe it that we are in this position. We will therefore now see these gentlemen assume ministerial posts. They are now to make the peace which *must* be made. They shall now eat the soup they have brewed for us."[87] The Kaiser agreed with Ludendorff's strategy, and the "stab in the back myth" was born.[88] Ludwig Beck, major on the general staff, repeated this argument at the end of November 1918: "At the most critical moment of the war we were assaulted from behind by a revolution that – as I now realize without the shadow of a doubt – had been thoroughly prepared beforehand."[89] As we have seen, this was a lie: the SPD and every other party in the Reichstag supported the war effort unconditionally until the end. But the lie, as Ludendorff had intended, took on a life of its own after an article in the *Neue Zurcher Zeitung* titled "Dolchstoss"

[83] Holborn, *Modern Germany*, 500.
[84] Ibid., 503.
[85] Ibid.
[86] Mommsen, *Weimar Germany*, 11.
[87] James Joll, *Europe since 1870: An International History* (New York: Harper and Row, 1973), 237.
[88] Holborn, *Modern Germany*, 503.
[89] Quoted in Mommsen, *Weimar Germany*, 19.

on December 17, 1918, solidified the narrative that would help poison Weimar democracy and abet the rise of Adolf Hitler.[90]

Ludendorff's second calculation was that a "government that would be capable of impressing the Allies by its representative character and its liberal philosophy would have the best chance of securing the best possible terms at war's end."[91] Wilson had only laid out in vague terms what an acceptable regime in Germany would look like. His Fourteen Points speech of January 8, 1918, contained less about democracy promotion than is commonly assumed. The most direct reference occurs when Wilson claims not to "presume to suggest to her [Germany] any alternation of modification of her institutions," but nonetheless continues that "it is necessary, we must frankly say, and necessary to any intelligent dealings with her on our part, that we should know whom her spokesmen speak for when they speak to us, whether for the Reichstag majority or for the military party and the men whose creed is imperial domination." Wilson amplified the message in July 1918 when he demanded, in language he would use later, that the Central Powers must destroy within them "every arbitrary power … that can disturb the peace of the world."[92] And he reiterated it in a speech on September 27, 1918, at the Metropolitan Opera House in New York City: "The German people must by this time be fully aware that we cannot accept the word of those who forced this war upon us. We do not think the same thoughts or speak the same language of agreement."[93] By late September 1918, the United States could not have made its policy of regime change any clearer.

Kaiser Wilhelm appointed Prince Max of Baden as chancellor on October 2nd to resuscitate civilian government. He was the third choice (two other candidates turned down the offer) and emerged as a consensus candidate because he was clearly within the monarcho-military circle, and therefore approved of by the Supreme Military Command, but also hailed

---

[90] A correspondent for the *Neue Zurcher Zeitung* attended two lectures by an English general and reported that he said: "the civilian population stabbed the German army to death from behind." *Neue Zurcher Zeitung* December 17, 1918, "Report on Maurice's Articles." Although it was not clear that the correspondent's summary accurately represented the general's views, the story was then picked up by the reactionary *Deutsche Tageszeitung* a day later under the headline "The Stabbed-in-the-Back German Army." See George S. Vascik and Mark R. Sadler, eds., "Did an English General Start the Myth," in *The Stab-in-the-Back-Myth and the Fall of the Weimar Republic: A History in Documents and Visual Sources* (New York: Bloomsbury Academic, 2016), 93–109.

[91] Craig, *Germany*, 397.

[92] Wilson Address to Mount Vernon, July 4, 1918, PWW, Vol. 51, 333–334.

[93] Wilson Address Opening the Campaign for the Fourth Liberty Loan, New York City, FRUS 1918, Supplement 1, The World War, Volume I.

## 8.2 War and Democratization in Germany and Sweden 279

from the historically liberal province of Baden. Prince Max had little political experience, but his slim record indicated that he was "by no means ... an unqualified advocate of parliamentarization."[94] His political views were largely irrelevant, however, as his primary task was to sound out the United States' position on peace terms. On October 6, 1918, he dispatched the first of three telegrams to Woodrow Wilson. Referencing Wilson's recent pronouncements on conditions for peace talks, Prince Max wrote:

> The German government requests that the President of the United States of America take the initiative in bringing about peace, that he inform all the belligerent states of this request, and that he invite them to send plenipotentiaries for purposes of beginning negotiations. The German government accepts as the basis for peace negotiations the program stated by the President of the United States in his speech to Congress of January 8, 1918, and in his subsequent pronouncements, particularly in his speech of September 27.
> In order to avoid further bloodshed, the German government requests the immediate conclusion of an armistice on land, at sea, and in the air.
> Signed: Max, Prince of Baden
> Chancellor[95]

#### 8.2.1.1 *The United States Demands Democratization*

Wilson's first response of October 8th inquired about the political nature of the new German government. The German government answered (second German telegram) by gesturing to the reforms already underway, including the inclusion of Social Democrats in the cabinet. In his second response (October 14), Wilson was more forceful and stressed that peace was dependent on "the destruction of every arbitrary power anywhere that can separately, secretly, and of its single choice disturb the peace of the world ... The power which has hitherto controlled the German nation is of the sort here described. It is within the choice of the German Nation to alter it."[96]

The German government replied to Wilson on October 20, 1918 (third German telegram), and argued that such reforms had already been undertaken. The telegram rebutted Wilson's claim concerning arbitrary power, noting that since Germany's "constitutional framework was a

---

[94] Holborn claims that Prince Max was perceived as follows: "To most Germans he remained a man who wanted to save too much of the old monarchical regime, if they did not even suspect him of connivance with the military authorities." Holborn, *Modern Germany*, 394.
[95] Text of the First German Note to Woodrow Wilson. https://ghdi.ghi-dc.org/sub_document.cfm?document_id=989.
[96] Quoted in Holborn, *Modern Germany*, 506.

creature of public virtue," the government of Prince Max did indeed "have the consent of the German people." The telegram pointed out that the Reichstag now possessed the power to make war and peace and that they were in the process of making the chancellor accountable to the Reichstag, although it was unclear on the specifics. Finally, it repeated the core claim that the current German government was legitimate because it was "formed in complete accord with the wishes of the presentation of the people, based on equal, universal, secret, direct franchise."[97]

The third German telegram made no mention of the future of the monarchy, nor even of the reform of the Prussian system. Wilson, who had apparently become frustrated with dealing with a collapsing authoritarian government, dispensed with all pleasantries in his third and decisive response composed on October 22 and received by Berlin on October 24. The demand for regime change could not have been clearer and "effectively put an end to monarchical government in Germany."[98] Wilson writes that:

> Significant and important as the constitutional changes seem to be which are spoken of by the German foreign secretary in his note of the 20th of October, it does not appear that the *principle of a government responsible to the German people* has yet been fully worked out, or that any guarantees either exist or are in contemplation that the alterations of principle and of practice now partially agreed upon will be permanent.[99]

Wilson continued that the proposed reforms were not enough to break the monarcho-military nexus and voiced his concerns that any democratic-seeming reforms would be short-lived if the current "masters of Germany" were not stripped of all power: "it is evident that the German people have no means of commanding the acquiescence of the military authorities of the empire in the popular will; that the power of the king of Prussia to control the policy of the empire is unimpaired; that the determination initiative still remains with those who have hitherto been masters of Germany."

Raising the stakes to the highest possible level, Wilson continued that:

> Feeling that the whole peace of the world depends now on plain speaking and straightforward action, the President deems it his duty to say, without any attempt

---

[97] *Auswärtiges* Amt to Rombeg (for McNally) and Rosen, Politisiches Archiv Auswärtiges Amt, Bonn Records, Wkg 23, geh/25.
[98] Binoy Kampmark, "'No Peace with the Hohenzollerns': American Attitudes on Political Legitimacy toward Hohenzollern Germany, 1917–1918." *Diplomatic History* 34, 5 (November 2010), 786.
[99] *Los Angeles Herald*, October 24, 1918.

## 8.2 War and Democratization in Germany and Sweden 281

to soften what may seem harsh words, that the nations of the world do not and cannot trust the word of those who have hitherto been the masters of German policy, and to point out once more that in concluding peace and attempting to undo the infinite injuries and injustice of this war, the government of *the United States cannot deal with any but veritable representatives of the German people who have been assured of a genuine constitutional standing as the real rulers of Germany.*

During the month of October, Ludendorff was still entertaining fantasies of new military victories creating more favorable peace terms that would then allow for a reassertion of military authority. Wilson's third response put an end to such hopes, though Ludendorff did not immediately grasp it. When he and Hindenburg met with the Kaiser on October 26, Ludendorff still tried to persuade the Kaiser that victory was possible. The Kaiser, a figure not known for his political skill, had to explain to Ludendorff that the Supreme Command's admission of defeat a month earlier had made it politically impossible to support the war any longer. Ludendorff resigned on the spot, but the chancellor asked Hindenburg to remain, which he did. The two generals never spoke again.

The fourth telegram of the German Government to Wilson, sent on October 27, updated the Americans on the power shift: "The President knows the far-reaching changes which have taken place and are being carried out in the German constitutional structure." It continued that "the peace negotiations are being conducted by a government of the people in whose hands rest, both actually and constitutionally, the authority to make decisions" and that "the military powers are subject to this authority." The most significant reforms in the history of Imperial Germany were passed a day later. The central amendments to the Bismarckian constitution adopted on October 28, 1918, amounted to all that the supporters of parliamentary democracy in Germany had ever wanted but never succeeded in achieving: the chancellor now needed the confidence of the Reichstag; the declaration of war and peace required consent of Federal Council and the Reichstag; and the chancellor had veto power over the appointment, promotion, and dismissal of military officers. The Supreme Command even pressured the Prussian Upper House to pass a bill on October 24, 1918, that ended the three-class suffrage system. It was, in short, "a constitutional transformation that at any other time would have transfixed the imagination of the country."[100]

This democratic transition occurred before the German Revolution of November 9th and before the threat of further revolutionary disturbances

[100] Craig, *Germany*, 397.

that plagued the early years of the Weimar republic. Acemoglu and Robinson take Mommsen's evidence for the revolutionary threat hypothesis out of context and ignore the thrust of his argument. Mommsen is clear that "it was only under the pressure of Wilson's third note that the Reichstag voted on 26 October to implement the long overdue constitutional reform."[101] Again according to Mommsen, the Kaiser's acceptance of parliamentarization "would have been virtually inconceivable without Wilson's conditions on German domestic politics."[102] Craig and Holborn both reach similar conclusions in their studies of the period. It was not the threat of revolution but American foreign policy that began the transition to democracy in Germany.

Kaiser Wilhelm spent what would turn out to be the last week of his reign entertaining various alternatives to abdication while at the military headquarters in Spa. On November 6th Ebert demanded the Kaiser's abdication while stopping short of calling for the end of the Hohenzollern dynasty. The Kaiser and his inner circle took this as an overture, and there was some discussion of appointing a regent. When this scheme collapsed, the Kaiser reverted to Ludendorff-like delusions and proposed leading his troops to Berlin and commanding a heroic counterrevolution. Quartermaster General of the German Army Wilhelm Groener regretted to inform him that: "the army will march home in good order under its leaders and commanding generals, but not under the command of Your Majesty, for it stands no longer behind your majesty." Thus ended the monarcho-military alliance that had ruled Prussia and then unified Germany for centuries. The Kaiser abdicated a day later (November 9) and fled to the Netherlands.

### 8.2.1.2 *The German Revolution*

Prince Max then called on Friedrich Ebert of the Majority Social Democrats to become chancellor. Ebert, however, had little authority outside of Berlin. The rest of the country was being run, in effect, by a combination of local workers' and soldiers' councils that had formed spontaneously to fill the vacuum left by the military's collapse. They were not, by and large, revolutionary, and the USPD had little time to exploit a potentially revolutionary situation. Summarizing decades of extensive historical research on the council movement, Mommsen notes that "for the most part, the councils were formed in the hope of healing the split

---

[101] Mommsen, *Weimar Germany*, 15.
[102] Ibid., 14.

within the Social Democratic movement."[103] Rather than calling for revolution, they provided a degree of public order in the context of mass agitation and collapsing state authority.

Before Ebert could form a government, another leading MSPD politician, Phillipp Scheideman, proclaimed the birth of the republic on November 9th from the balcony of the Reichstag building. He did this largely to preempt a similar announcement by the USPD, and in fact Karl Liebknecht announced the birth of "the free Socialist Republic of Germany" two hours later. Although the MSPD preferred an Ebert chancellorship, it recognized – and probably overestimated – the power of the USPD within the council movement. Instead of preserving some degree of continuity with the existing political system, as an Ebert chancellorship would have done, the alliance of the MSPD and the council movement decided on a new one entirely: Ebert became one of six members of the Council of People's Commissars: he joined his colleagues Scheidemann and Otto Landsberg from the MSPD and Hugo Haase, Wilhelm Dittmann, and Emil Barth (leader of the Revolutionary Shop Stewards) from the USPD. On November 10th, Groener (after consulting Hindenburg) pledged in secret to Ebert that the Supreme Command would assist in maintaining order so long as the civilian government agreed to fight bolshevism and to hold elections as early as possible.[104] Ebert outmaneuvered the three revolutionary Socialists in policy, including the crucial issue of setting elections for the National Assembly. Still, political authority between November 9, 1918, and January 19, 1919, when elections for the constituent assembly occurred, was based to a large degree from the power of the workers' and soldiers' councils. So long as that revolutionary foundation existed, the USPD continued to exert some influence and threatened the transition to parliamentary democracy. Wilson, for one, remained wary of the new German government, sending instructions to his chief advisor Colonel Edward House, who was representing the US at the pre-armistice negotiations, that there should be "no official dealings ... until a constituent assembly has been brought together." The French, who wanted to move swiftly on with armistice negotiations, ultimately prevailed, however, and democracy promotion in Weimar became a less pressing goal of American foreign policy thereafter.

In the period between the proclamation of the republic and the elections for the constituent assembly, the alliance between the MSPD and the USPD collapsed. The Spartacus Group was refounded on November

[103] Ibid., 25.
[104] This agreement became known as the Ebert-Groener Pact.

11, 1918, and the German Communist Party (KPD) was founded on December 30, 1918, at a convention of the Spartacus Group. The three representatives of the USPD withdrew from the Council of People's Representatives at the same time. The conflict turned violent on January 5, 1919, when the Spartacist uprising in Berlin was brutally repressed by the German army and demonstrated the Ebert-Groener pact in action. On January 15, 1919, members of the *Freikorps* murdered Rosa Luxembourg and Karl Liebknecht and turned the KPD and the SPD into political enemies.[105] The first several years of the Weimar Republic were marked by failed coup attempts, strikes, assassinations, and other forms of political violence. It was an inauspicious start for German democracy, and it is one of the interwar period's great ironies that what was considered the model for democratic constitutions would later provide an institutional route to power for anti-democrats. Although there were multiple factors in the collapse of Weimar democracy, the persistence of "stab in the back" lie is an essential feature in any convincing analysis. Its creator (Ludendorff) became an ultranationalist politician with little real influence during the Weimar Republic, but Hindenburg became president and handed power to Adolf Hitler, who held no stronger conviction than that the German army had been defeated at home by traitorous socialists and Jews.

### 8.2.2 Sweden in WWI

Democracy collapsed in interwar Germany, but it survived in interwar Sweden. There is no space to explain this variation here, but suffice it to say that not even the most astute observer would have predicted it in 1918. Both states entered the war as autocracies. The Swedish *Borgfred* – an agreement that political parties refrain from confrontations, such as calls for reform, during the war – was similar to the *Burgfrieden* in Germany, with the important difference being that Sweden was neutral. The *Borgfred* was in fact a large concession from the Social Democrats who, in the words of party leader Hjalmar Branting, considered Sweden "a museum of relics with regard to its constitution ... in the new era that is banging on the door."[106] Liberals too viewed Sweden as "a kind of miniature Germany up here in the north, a solid reactionary bastion

---

[105] Studies articulating some version of the argument that a divided left aided the rise of Nazism are too numerous to mention, but a good starting point remains William Sheridan Allen, *The Nazi Seizure of Power: The Experience of a Single German Town* (New York: Franklin Watts, 1965).

[106] A. K., Hjalmar Branting, April 14, 1917, 41:67.

against our neighbours" and urged Swedish conservatives to reform, a call they would resist until Germany's defeat.[107]

Swedish exports to Germany increased eightfold during the first year of the war. Several years later, as Sweden continued to export iron ore to Germany, the Entente responded by reducing exports to Sweden. The resulting food shortages in the spring of 1917 produced "hunger strikes," more calls for universal suffrage, and some isolated talk of revolution. Prime Minister Hammerskjoeld (conservatives) resigned in the summer not because of public pressure but rather because his allies in parliament had abandoned him. According to Sejersted: "it is doubtful there was a real revolutionary threat in 1917." Similarly, Ihalhainen (367) writes: "there were problems caused by the war and some extra-parliamentary calls for revolution, but no major political grouping expected one to take place in Sweden." The Social Democrats rejected all calls for direct action following food shortages; they heeded the lessons of failed general strikes in Belgium and Italy and opted for an exclusively electoral strategy. Hammarskjoeld's resignation led to elections in which the Social Democrats were the big winners and formed a governing coalition with the Liberals for the first time in Swedish history.

The most pressing question was whether the Upper House – which had not been elected by universal, direct, and equal suffrage – would recognize the new government or not. After some debate, the Upper House accepted the outcome and thereby established the principle of parliamentary sovereignty without a constitutional change and without a serious revolutionary threat. Important as the establishment of parliamentary sovereignty was in retrospect, Ihalainen cautions that "the concession could also be understood as tactical and temporary (254)." Indeed, as late as several years into the war, conservatives were still confident they could continue to preserve competitive oligarchy. A 1917 universal suffrage bill by Liberal and Social Democrats was defeated in the Upper House. In spring 1918 basic constitutional questions remained unresolved, but the most Swedish conservatives were willing to agree to was an "examination of the issue" and the formation of a toothless parliamentary committee.

Swedish conservatives were unyielding because, like German conservatives, they still believed Germany could win the war. Ihalanen's analysis of parliamentary debates shows that: "the Right counted on Germany

---

[107] Pasi Ihalainen, *The Springs of Democracy: National and Transnational Debates on Constitutional Reform in the British, German, Swedish and Finnish Parliaments, 1917–1919* (Helsinki: Finnish Literature Society, 2017), 150.

winning the war, the reform being postponed, and the need for it removed." He continues, "a decisive turn in the course of the First World War would be needed before the reform would be realised in Sweden; even then the Swedish right would remain patently reluctant and need considerable time to rethink its suspicious attitudes to the democracy and parliamentarism that was being championed by the left."[108]

After the German defeat, political reforms in Sweden closely followed those in Germany. On October 30, 1918 – two days after the adoption of parliamentary government in Germany – Swedish conservatives ended their intransigence and allowed the subject of constitutional reform to be put on the parliamentary agenda. Following the abdication of Kaiser Wilhelm on November 9, Gustav V dropped his opposition to democracy in exchange for preserving the monarchy. The king also put pressure on two conservative leaders who had opposed all reform efforts – Arvid Lindman and Ernst Trygger – to compromise. On November 14, 1918 (five days after the proclamation of the German republic), the Swedish government put forward a bill that would have immediately introduced municipal elections and postponed debate on national elections and female suffrage until the spring of 1919. The bill was then approved by a parliamentary committee on November 22, 1918. The Social Democrats rejected this compromise and there were large labor protests against it. On December 17, 1918, the Riksdag approved universal suffrage without delay.

The month of November 1918 is the most plausible moment of revolutionary threat in Sweden during WWI, and the one that Acemoglu and Robinson (2006), citing Collier (1999), refer to as the proximate cause of Swedish democratization. Neither they nor Tilton provide any further evidence for this claim, but Ihailhanen finds that the threat of revolution was indeed a prominent theme in the *Riksdag* debates of November and December 1918. Conservatives claimed that they had been forced into the reform by extraparliamentary pressure. The conservative David Pettersson objected to the "threat of revolution" to "instill an atmosphere of panic" and argued that conceding to pressure would set a dangerous precedent.[109] The Right claimed that the Swedish constitution and rule of law were under threat by extra-parliamentary pressure, casting themselves as the defenders of Swedish democracy. To them, "the entire reform appeared to be a parliamentary violation of the right of the Swedish

---

[108] Ibid., 255.
[109] A. K., David Petersson, December 17, 1918, 17:57.

## 8.2 War and Democratization in Germany and Sweden 287

people rather than an extension of them."[110] Conservatives argued the question should be put to the electorate under the old suffrage rules.

Did Swedish conservatives believe a revolution was imminent in November 1918? Or did they use the labor agitation and socialist pressure as a rhetorical weapon against reform? There is ample evidence for the second interpretation, but only circumstantial evidence for the first. According to Ihalanen, the "repeated association between the unconventional manoeuvres of a reformist government with potential revolutionary violence" and frequent suggestions that "the constitution and established parliamentary order had been violated" allowed some conservatives to "question the legitimacy of government action."[111] The frequent use of this trope explains in part why revolution and reform became linked to the reform of 1918. The governing parties increased the salience of revolutionary threat further when they claimed that nothing of the sort had occurred: "Liberal ministers concentrated on proving to The Right and their supporters ... that no threats of revolution had been used to force through the reform." The Social Democrats rejected the Bolshevik revolution as a model and feared a repeat of the Finnish Civil War, and as noted earlier, they had already ruled out an extra-parliamentary course in the spring of 1917 when the opportunity first arose. They were also one of the least revolutionary socialist parties in Europe. When the Social Democrats referred to a revolution, it "was not an open threat of revolution but was based on a strategy typical of moderate Socialists elsewhere as well: should the compromise on reform be obstructed, the moderates would not be able to prevent the radicals from proceeding to a revolution."[112] Typical was Branting's warning on December 17, 1918, during a parliamentary debate that:

Now that one sees the German Revolution, sees how it is growing in strength with this total upheaval of everything that has previously been exalted and highly esteemed there, yes, then one understands that no country which is as closely in contact with Central Europe as Sweden, owing to its location, has always been and must always be, can remain as before.[113]

While one can interpret such words as evidence of a credible threat of revolution in November 1918, one can also argue that such threat inflation was a conservative rhetorical strategy, similar to that of British

[110] Ihailanen, *Springs of Democracy*, 397.
[111] Ibid., 379.
[112] Ibid., 374.
[113] Ibid.

conservatives in 1832 (and indeed of many conservative parties during debates on suffrage reform). Even if one accepts the existence of a revolutionary threat, the primary reasons for it were international: Germany's defeat and the revolutions in Germany, Russia, and Finland. In this sense, Aidt and Jenson (2014) are closer to the mark than A and R (2006). Ihalanen finds that "all sides were persuaded to moderation by the warning example of not only Germany, but also Finland, where a failed socialist revolution had turned into the misery of prison camps (368)." Public agitation accompanied suffrage reform in Sweden in November 1918, but it is hardly clear that it was the decisive factor.

## 8.3 CONCLUSION

One conclusion is clear from the analysis of suffrage reform in wartime Sweden: it contradicts the evolutionary view of Swedish democratization. The parliamentary debates reveal how it was hardly "a purely domestic evolutionary long-term development towards representative democracy, as contemporary rightist discourse and much of later nation-state-centered historiography suggested." Rather, "its course and timing were determined essentially by international events and transnational interaction."[114] It was above all the defeat of Germany and the destruction of the Prussian model that moved the Swedish monarch and some Swedish conservatives to support democratization. Not all did, however. Hugo Hammarskjöld (cousin of Prime Minister Hjalmar Hammarskjöld, 1914–1917) admitted that: "I am no democrat and am too old to convert. I do not believe in the ability of democracy to make a people happier, and least of all in the type of democracy which is being discussed here and which is likely to soon lead to the rule by the masses."[115]

Had Germany won the war – an outcome that appeared possible as late as the spring of 1918 – there is no reason to believe that Hammarskjöld would have felt pressure to convert at all. Had Ludendorff's offensives in the west succeeded and the gains of Brest Litovsk been retained, it is also very hard to see how the monarcho-military power structure in Germany would have crumbled. Without pushing the counterfactual too far, there would have been other major implications for democracy had Germany prevailed. Belgium would not have democratized and might not even have regained its sovereignty. A decisive German victory early in the war

[114] Ibid., 373.
[115] F. K., Hugo Hammarskjöld, December 17, 1918, 10, 68–69.

(the Schlieffen Plan came close to succeeding), and before the British government was forced to introduce conscription, would have undercut the primary justification for the Representation of the People Act. In general, a German victory would have left most of Europe further from democracy than it was in July 1914.

Analyzing all episodes of democratization since 1800 ($n = 316$), Daniel Treisman finds that the overwhelming majority were not intentional (i.e., the old regime did not believe it was conceding to democratization or democracy was the unintended outcome of government policy). Autocrats make mistakes that lead to their fall, leading to a new authoritarian government or, in some cases, democratization.[116] These mistakes come in three different types, the third of which is a "major foreign policy failure that provokes foreign intervention or discredits incumbent (e.g., entering or initiating avoidable international conflict, then performing poorly)."[117] Examples of this mistake in first-wave Europe include Napoleon Bonaparte's ill-fated war against Germany in 1871, Portugal's humiliation by the British in 1890, and Italy's defeat by Ethiopia at Adowa in 1896. Overall, foreign policy mistakes account for at least 17 percent of all cases of democratization.

There was no greater foreign policy mistake for Europe than the WWI. The war was based on false ideas about the superiority of the offensive, illusions that the war would be short, and delusions that the esprit de corps of the army and the national pride of the civilian population would guarantee victory. The war was costly for the winners, indeed so costly that the United Kingdom expanded suffrage as a reward for wartime service and France nearly introduced female suffrage. The Germans committed a series of major mistakes, beginning with the invasion of neutral Belgium and continuing past the fateful bet that unrestricted submarine warfare would shift the tide of the war before the United States could begin sending troops. This is only the very beginning of a list of major mistakes that characterized the "war to end all wars." It is also fair to say that few of the democratic moments during WWI in Europe were intentional; most were unintended effects of the war.

---

[116] Daniel Treisman, "Democracy by Mistake: How the Errors of Autocrats Trigger Transitions to Freer Government." *American Political Science Review* 114, 3 (2020), 792–810.

[117] Ibid., 796.

# 9

# Conclusion

This book has argued that no European state during the first wave really conformed to any of the three master narratives of European political development during the long nineteenth century. The gradualist model of development that is entrenched in the classic and contemporary literature on European democratization overstates the magnitude of the first wave and overlooks the successful blocking efforts of the old regime. Indeed, there are so many examples of reversals, of counter-majoritarian institutions, and – above all – of the endurance of the belief that the vote was based upon capacity – that one can interpret the first wave in Europe as a successful defense of oligarchy during an age of major democratizing pressures.

Although there was a great deal of discussion about revolution from 1789 to 1914 in Western Europe, the threat of revolution rarely forced the old regime to make democratic concessions. This is consistent with Treisman's finding that the threat of revolution explains at most 5 percent of the cases of democratic transition since 1800 and his conclusion that although "unrest was common before democratization ... few episodes fit other elements of Acemoglu and Robinson's (2006) account."[1] Even if it is historically inaccurate, however, the threat of revolution hypothesis helps shift the analysis toward the growth of state coercive forces. Indeed, the modern police are the direct result of elite efforts to control and suppress would-be democratizers in Great Britain. The police in Bonapartist France became as concerned with monitoring and shaping politics as they were with preventing routine crime. That the police

---

[1] Treisman, "Democracy by Mistake," 793.

are political agents – or at least can be – is self-evident today. They have, however, been largely excluded from the literature on democratic and state development in Europe.[2]

The belief that large parts of Europe had democratized – either gradually or under threat of revolution – by the eve of WWI has itself proved remarkably resilient. One reason is that it is both comforting and intuitive to read European political development through the lens of democratic progress. This "glass half-full" view of European democratization during the first wave can be found in Polity IV, the legacy of Whig history and modernization theory, as well as in state and political party narratives. Some cases, such as the Netherlands and Sweden, are so deeply interwoven into the democratization literature as early democratizers that scholarly opinions are not likely to change quickly. But given how heavily scholars have relied on Polity IV data for theory building and testing, it would be worthwhile – and I would argue necessary – to try and reproduce such analyses using V-Dem data instead.

This book has found most support for the "special path" of authoritarian endurance during a period of economic and social modernization, with the critical proviso that it was not a specifically German story. Germany was perhaps exceptional because it combined many elements of authoritarianism – election rigging (particularly before 1901), subnational antidemocratic institutions, lack of parliamentary sovereignty, a monarcho-military alliance, etc ... – whereas other nondemocratic regimes in first-wave Europe featured only one or two of these elements.

What happens when Europeans and Americans focus on our old regime progenitors rather than our democratic forebearers? One result is that European political development appears both less exceptional and more internally varied. Another is that it provides a far better "laboratory" for studying authoritarian survival, democratic backsliding, and episodes of democratic crisis. I have pushed the argument about authoritarian resilience in this period further than most, but not nearly as far as one could: gender discrimination, systemic racism, and colonialism (both internal and external) in European political development each require books of their own. In any event, the magnitude of the first wave is still much smaller, and my central storyline has been explaining the resilience

---

[2] Exceptions include David Bayley, *The Police and Political Development in Europe* (Princeton: Princeton University Press, 1975) and Ben Ansell and Johannes Lindvall, *Inward Conquest: The Political Origins of Modern Public Services* (New York: Cambridge University Press, 2021).

of nondemocratic outcomes in an age of democratization.[3] Synthesizing the mechanisms of old regime resilience into three broad categories – ideas, institutions, and repression/cheating – we can reflect on differences and similarities with the contemporary era. Some of these mechanisms are historically bounded, but many, it turns out, are not.

## 9.1 IDEAS

The notion that voting could be restricted to those with a certain "capacity" persisted throughout the entirety of the first wave. Resources, first in the form of land, later in the form of income, were the most obvious demonstrations of this capacity, but there were many others. Age requirements, for example, were generally much higher than they are today, although lifespans were approximately half.[4] Under many electoral systems in this period, education qualified as political capacity, and high education levels meant multiple votes in Belgium and Great Britain. Literacy requirements effectively disenfranchised most southern Italians until 1912. On top of all these barriers to entry – and helping to reinforce them – was the idea that women lacked the capacity to vote. Voting restrictions based on gender persisted for two decades after the end of the first wave in two of the oldest male democracies, as well as in Belgium and Italy. In sum, it took at least a century for explicit arguments against one-person, one-vote to disappear in Western democracies.

At the same time, most, if not all, of these explicit arguments in favor of restricting suffrage to those with "capacity" are absent from contemporary democracies. That democracy is compatible with high levels of illiteracy has been demonstrated in every Indian election since independence. Fledgling democracies today regularly run elections in societies with high levels of illiteracy, and their officials defend the principle of one-person, one-vote. "The vote of an illiterate voter carries the same weight as that of the president of the Republic," according to the president of the High Independent Authority for Elections (ISIE) in Tunisia in 2017, where 16 percent of electorate were illiterate.[5] In 1970, the United States Supreme Court upheld the federal ban on literacy tests, as specified in the Voting Rights Act of 1965, in the case of *Oregon v. Mitchell*,

---

[3] Jason Brownlee, *Authoritarianism in an Age of Democratization* (New York: Cambridge University Press, 2007).
[4] The average lifespan for a British male in 1900 was 44.
[5] "Survey Reveals Illiterate Tunisians Plan to Participate in Upcoming Elections." www.ifes.org/news/survey-reveals-illiterate-tunisians-plan-participate-upcoming-elections.

*Attorney General*. In the same case, the Court also preserved the right of state and local officials to set the voting age higher than eighteen. However, so powerful was the case for lowering the voting age to 18 that Congress proposed, and three quarter of states quickly ratified, the Twenty-sixth Amendment, the first section of which reads: "the right of citizens of the United States, who are eighteen years of age or older, to vote shall not be denied or abridged by the United States or by any State on account of age."[6] The Vietnam War and the draft were the driving factors, and the slogan "Old enough to fight, old enough to vote" recalls arguments we have seen before in Italy in 1912 and debates in Great Britain preceding the Representation of the People Act (see Chapter 8). If there is any serious discussion about changing age requirements in advanced industrial democracies, it is about lowering age requirements to sixteen.[7] There is a worldwide consensus that, at least in theory, every eighteen-year-old person should have one vote.

There has been another normative change as well: whereas "democracy" was often an epithet during the first wave, most authoritarians today claim they are democrats of some kind. Old regime elites in Germany regularly pointed to the French Third Republic as an object lesson in the dangers of parliamentary democracy. Italian elites like Pareto and Mosca, who initially supported parliamentary government, came to abhor it. During WWI, the German propaganda machine pushed the idea that democracy had sapped Great Britain's national spirit and left Great Britain little more than a "nation of shopkeepers." Even those old regime elites who endorsed reforms did so while claiming that it "should never be [our] fate to live under a democracy." Today, even nondemocrats like Orbán claim they are staking out a different type of democracy – illiberal as opposed to liberal – as ideological cover for what is really Bonapartism/competitive authoritarianism.

Nor is the mass public fleeing from the idea of democracy, despite what commentators have written since Brexit and the election of Donald Trump. Early reactions to the Trump phenomenon included some startling claims about public opinion. According to Foa and Mounk, "Citizens in a number of supposedly consolidated democracies in North America and Western Europe ... have ... become more cynical about the value of democracy as a

---

[6] Section two reads: "The Congress shall have power to enforce this article by appropriate legislation."
[7] Argentina, Austria, and Croatia have all lowered the voting age to 16, Greece has lowered it to 17, and Germany now allows 16 year olds to vote in European elections (though not in federal ones).

political system, less hopeful that anything they do might influence public policy, and more willing to express support for authoritarian alternatives."[8] Their alarmism recalls similar cries about a crisis of liberal democracy during the depths of the Eurozone Crisis.[9] Bartels systematic analysis of European Social Survey data, however, tells a very different story and finds that "Europeans overall were just as trusting of politicians and parliaments, just as satisfied with the performance of their national governments, and just as sanguine about the working of democracy after the Euro-crisis as they had been before."[10] In sum, the idea that democracy has a legitimate competitor does not exist today as it had in the European past.

## 9.2 INSTITUTIONS

There are more parallels between past and present in terms of institutional strategies of preserving power. Declining political forces – or those that believe themselves to be declining – often seek to design the rules of the democratic game. Scholars have recognized how conservative forces favored counter-majoritarian institutions.[11] Boix and Ahmed focus on proportional representation in particular.[12] Ziblatt considers another type of institutional response to democratization – party organization. "When upper-class groups associated with any predemocratic *ancien regime* are able to build strong political parties, democracy evolves in a more settled fashion: when they cannot, democracy emerges, if at all, in a deeply unsettled way."[13] Neither proportional representation nor mass party organization could be considered antidemocratic as such. Indeed, a long literature argues for PR's democratic virtues, and Ziblatt demonstrates a democracy-promoting effect from conservative organizational efforts: "A strong conservative political party acts as a safeguard that does not formally 'hardwire' a reduction of the quality of democratic contestation into the structures of the political system itself."[14]

---

[8] Roberto Foa and Yascha Mounk, "The Democratic Disconnect." *Journal of Democracy* 27, 15 (2016), 15.
[9] David Art, "Why 2013 is not 1933: The Radical Right in Europe." *Current History* 112, 752 (2013), 88–93.
[10] Larry Bartels, *Democracy Erodes from the Top: Leaders, Citizens, and the Challenge of Populism in Europe* (Princeton: Princeton University Press, 2023), 145-146.
[11] Weingast, Alberts, and Warshaw, "Democratization and Countermajoritarian Institutions."
[12] Boix, *Democracy and Redistribution*; Ahmed, *Politics of Electoral System Choice*.
[13] Ziblatt, *Conservative Parties*, 363–364.
[14] Ibid., 367.

The institutions I have analyzed in this book were different: they were designed not to preserve elite influence under a democratic system but to stymie or undermine democracy itself. They were antidemocratic both in design and in practice. Some were relics, such as estate systems and nonelected upper houses of parliament, but others were newly designed counter-majoritarian institutions like plural voting and *trasformismo*. We do not find many such blatant institutional deviations from Dahlian requirements in advanced industrial democracies today. Furthermore, the micro-institutions like the arcane registration requirements of Edwardian England that raised the costs of voting through intense complication and inconvenience are pretty much absent from contemporary Europe, where the emphasis has long been on maximizing turnout through mandatory voting, voting on weekends, and lowering the voting age. The issue of restrictive citizenship laws complicates the picture, but in general access to voting is not an issue in contemporary European politics.

The same cannot be said of the contemporary United States, where state legislatures passed numerous bills targeting access to voting following the 2020 elections. Georgia's Election Integrity Act of 2021 made it illegal for anyone other than poll workers to hand out food or water within 100 feet of polling places or 25 feet within someone waiting in line. The language seems innocuous – "No person shall solicit votes in any manner or by any means or method … or participate in the giving of any money or gifts, including, but not limited to, food and drink, to an elector." And other states have similar-sounding laws that date from an era when vote buying occurred. None, however, enforces a specific ban on providing water.[15] President Joe Biden called the Georgia law "Jim Crow in the 21st Century," and added that "you don't need anything else to know that this is nothing but punitive, designed to keep people from voting."[16]

Literacy too has reemerged as an indirect tool of voter suppression in US state elections, particularly since 2020.[17] Georgia, once again, was one of several states that passed laws that limit assistance to voters who are illiterate or who struggle to read.[18] In Georgia's case, the law placed

---

[15] https://thehill.com/homenews/nexstar_media_wire/3709676-is-it-illegal-to-hand-out-water-or-food-outside-your-polling-place/.
[16] Ibid.
[17] "Low literacy voters struggle to cast ballots in the face of restrictive voting laws." www.pbs.org/newshour/show/low-literacy-voters-struggle-to-cast-ballots-in-the-face-of-restrictive-voting-laws.
[18] "The Fight Against an Age-Old Effort to Block American From Voting," September 12, 2022. Propublica.

restrictions on who can return or even touch a completed absentee ballot. Reflecting on the case of Olivia Coley-Pearson from Coffee County Georgia who has twice been charged with felonies for assisting voters, Aliyya Swaby writes:

> A lot of people that she helps are afraid to vote. They see what happened to her. And they see it as, well, if you are a city commissioner who has been criminally charged for using this legal right to help people to vote, what is going to happen to me, as someone who is not in a position of power, someone who struggles to read? Will I be criminally charged as well? Will I be getting in trouble for exercising this legal right.[19]

All this might seem like a great deal of effort to tilt a small number of votes.[20] But it is also about playing to a Republican base who believe, and who have been told by elites, that Democrats systematically rig elections. For their part, Democrats play to their base when they focus on voter suppression efforts. Although one must acknowledge that the Democrats have ample evidence for their argument while the Republicans do not, some of the renewed focus on voting rights is for internal party consumption at a specific, and very odd, juncture in American political history. Yet at the same time, the debates about the details of voting recall those preceding the Second Great Reform in 1867 in Great Britain when parties calculated their relative gains and losses based on the income levels of newly enfranchised voters. It is perhaps some small comfort that the battle for votes has come down to bottled water, drop boxes, and the other specifics of the Voting Rights Act and that the basic institutional rules of democracy are not at stake. Still, bills like the Georgia Election Integrity Act demonstrate an endless appetite for embattled political forces to try and tilt the electoral playing field through tweaking the details.

### 9.3 REPRESSION AND CHEATING

Repression of political adversaries in nineteenth-century Europe was mild by a twentieth-century standard, although quite intense by a twenty-first century one. The reader will recall that thousands of Chartists in Britain were jailed or deported. Seventy-five thousand Parisians were killed during the Paris Commune. By the turn of the century, however, there were fewer cases of mass state violence. One of the reasons, according to

---

[19] "Low Literacy voters."
[20] However, one in five Americans struggles to read, so the effects are potentially quite large.

Engels, was that "rebellion in the old style, street fighting with barricades, which decided the issue everywhere up to 1848, had become largely outdated." He continued: "Let us have no illusions about it: a real victory of insurrection over the military in street fighting, a victory as between two armies, is one of the rarest exceptions."[21] I have argued that Engel's argument could be improved by substituting the "police" for "the military" (it is not clear that Engels made a distinction between these two coercive state forces). In any event, the police were able to control the urban centers to such a degree that movements like anarcho-syndicalism in Italy had no choice but to concentrate on the countryside. This is a major difference from the last century, where the city has once again become the center of revolutionary activity and where clashes between police and demonstrators often mark decisive moments in regime transitions.[22]

The systematic election fraud found in Spain, Portugal, and Italy on the eve of WWI, and in both England and Germany for much of the nineteenth century, remains a common mechanism of tilting the playing field in contemporary competitive authoritarian regimes around the world. There are only a handful of such regimes in contemporary Europe, although more so than there were a decade ago. Elsewhere in Europe elections are run remarkably cleanly, as they are in the United States. The major difference separating the contemporary United States and Europe is that about half of Americans currently believe there is massive electoral fraud. There can be no escaping the conclusion that Donald Trump has done more than any other elite to shift public opinion in this direction.

Europe in the nineteenth and early twentieth centuries is replete with examples of elite-driven democratic backsliding. Figures like Bismarck, Giolitti, and Napoleon III, this book has demonstrated, were perpetually willing and able to hollow out any competitive institutions to remain in power. And then, from roughly 1945 to early in the twenty-first century, such practices disappeared in Western Europe and the United States. Indeed, acceptance and agreement on the democratic rules of the game acquired the status of a Durkeimian social fact among both masses and elites. That has been shattered by developments in Hungary and Poland, as Bartels argues:

---

[21] Karl Marx and Friedrich Engels. 1990. *Collected Works*, vol. 27: *Engels: 1890–95, re Europe*. Chadwell Heath: Lawrence and Wishard, 517.

[22] Mark Beissinger, *The Revolutionary City: Urbanization and the Global Transformation of Rebellion* (Princeton: Princeton University Press, 2022).

In contemporary Hungary and Poland, voters did not choose even "mildly authoritarian" regimes at the ballot box – at least not at first. Rather, they chose the only readily available alternatives to unsatisfactory incumbent governments, only to have their votes rather transparently trumped up by the winners into a "voting booth revolution" justifying "a new social contract" expanding the power of the ruling party at the expense of the courts, the media, and other political actors.[23]

Similarly, the politicization and capture of formerly neutral state and local electoral boards across the United States is not healthy for American democracy. Given the length of time it took for subnational authoritarianism in the United States to end, it is dispiriting to see renewed attempts to establish it.[24] One need not agree with a strong version of this argument – that "state governments have been leaders in democratic backsliding in the United States in recent years" – to concede that the perpetual questioning of democratic outcomes and the supercharged effort to capture formerly neutral arbiters are threatening to both democratic quality and democratic stability.[25]

\* \* \* \* \* \* \* \* \* \* \* \* \*

Having finished a long book on an unfamiliar era in which the authoritarians demonstrate a remarkable degree of agency and learning compared to their challengers, the reader might legitimately ask "and what about the democrats?" They have played a smaller role in my account of the first wave, in large part because they have received the lion's share of attention to date. Another reason is, as we have seen, that they were defeated time and again. Nearly a century divided the massacre at Peterloo, where the protestors had demanded universal equal male suffrage, to the Representation of the People's Act. The Chartists mounted three costly petition campaigns that ended in nothing. The Belgian Socialists spent two decades battling the *lois des quatres infamies* in Belgium without success, while the Swedish People's Parliaments at the turn of the twentieth century recalled the Chartist humiliations. The persistence of suffragettes in virtually every state was more impressive still, as even their erstwhile allies often proved unwilling to back them. Being a democrat – in the twenty-first century sense – was a poor and

---

[23] Larry Bartels, *Democracy Erodes from the Top* (Princeton: Princeton University Press, 2023), 214.
[24] Robert Mickey, *Paths Out of Dixie: The Democratization of Authoritarian Enclaves in America's Deep South, 1944–1972* (Princeton: Princeton University Press, 2015).
[25] Jacob Grumbach, *Laboratories against Democracy: How National Parties Transformed State Politics* (Princeton: Princeton University Press, 2022), 152.

lonely business in most of Western Europe before the First World War. Their views made them political outsiders and often the victims of state repression. We can acknowledge that this made them courageous without canonizing them.

When I began this book, I imagined that one of my major challenges would be finding contemporary relevance in a story that ends over a century ago. That turned out to be a failure of vision. As a student of European political history, I should have been able to foresee the lengths to which elites – particularly those who feel their position is declining – would go to lock in electoral advantages and create new forms of counter-majoritarian institutions. Given the breadth and variation in electoral corruption in the European past, I should have anticipated Trump's scheme to replace fake electors in seven swing states. The founding of competitive authoritarianism in the French Second Empire and its development in Imperial Germany likewise should have prepared me for the rebirth of competitive authoritarianism in Europe. And perhaps most of all, the numerous cases of democratic backsliding, democratic breakdowns, and close misses in the first wave should have made me more aware that peaceful transfers of power cannot be taken for granted. My hope is that this book has gone some small way toward reminding the reader, as the study of this period has reminded me, of both the youth of democracy in the west and of its fragility.

# Index

Page number in *italics* refers to table.

*1867: Disraeli, Gladstone and Revolution: The Passing of the second Reform Bill* (Cowling), 85

Acemoglu, Daron, 26, 48, 51, 84, 192, 200, 203, 271, 282, 290
Action Française, 169
age of reform (UK). *See also* First Reform Act (1832); Second Reform Act (1867)
  about, 16–17, 52
  and competitive oligarchy, 90
  mentioned, 14–15, 45–47, 52, 81
  slow pace of, 89
*Age of Reform 1815–1870, The* (Woodward), 46
Ahmed, Amel, 7
Aidt, Toke, 52
Albert I, 259
Alexander III, 140
*American Commonwealth, The* (Bryce), 1
Anderson, Margaret, 28, 133–136
Asquith, H. H., 164, 166–167, 170–171, 256, 261
Attwood, Thomas, 68–69, 72–73
authoritarian resilience. *See* old regime, resilience of
authoritarianism, 2, 6–7, 11–12, 20–21, 24–25, 28–29, 133–134, 291, 298. *See also* competitive authoritarianism

Baden, Max von, 279–280, 282
Bagehot, Walter, 101, 162

Balfour, Arthur James, 163, 165–167, 170–171, 173
"Barriers Against Democracy in the British Electoral System," 38
Bateman, David, 7, 24, 74
Bebel, August, 37, 146
*Before the Socialists: Studies in Labour and Politics, 1861–1881* (Harrison), 84
Benedict XV, 267, 268
Berard, Alexandre, 268–270
Berard's Fourteen Points, 268
Berchtold, Leopold von, 127
Berman, Sheri, 7, 28, 74, 132–133
Bethmann Hollweg, Theobald von, 127, 138, 146, 275
Biden, Joseph R., 295
Bielefeld school, 130–132, 146
Billault, Adolphe, 105
Birmingham Political Union (BPU), 67–70, 72–73, 75. *See also under* First Reform Act (1832), and political unions
Bismarck, Otto von, 122–126. *See also* democratization in Imperial Germany; suffrage
  about, 123–125, 131–132
  compared to Estrup, 199
  fall of, 139–141
  and Franco–Prussian War, 122–123
  legacy of, 157–158
  lessons from French Second Empire, 123–124

Bismarck, Otto von (cont.)
  mentioned, 144–145, 148, 191, 225, 297
  and suffrage, 123–126, 213
  and threat of revolution, 150
Blackbourn, David, 28, 130–132
*Blasphemous and Seditious Libels Act* (1819), 58
Blenheim Palace speech (of Bonar Law), 171
Boix, Carlos, 30–31, 200, 207, 294
Bonaparte, Louis Napoleon. *See* Napoleon III
Bonapartism, 100–101. *See also* French Second Empire
Bonapartist party, 17, 109, 120
Bonar Law, Andrew
  about, 170–171
  and Irish Home Rule, 170
  mentioned, 128, 167
  and Parliament Act (1911), 171–172
  violent rhetoric of, 171–172
Borden, Robert, 253–254
Bragança Monarchy, 240
Branting, Hjalmar, 284, 287
Brexit, 293
Bristol riots, 69–70
Brown, Gordon, 3
Brownlee, Jason, 11
Brunswick (Germany), 137
Bryce, James, 1–6
  mentioned, 9, 16
  and Representation of the People Act (1911), 256
  and suffrage, female, 18–19
Buckingham Palace Conference (1914), 1
Bülow, Bernhard von, 144–146, 151
Butterfield, Herbert, 3, 47

Campbell-Bannerman, Henry, 164
Caoutchouc Article, 185–186
capacity (to vote), 9, 19, 21, 47, 64, 82, 87, 89, 159, 236–237, 244, 256, 264, 290, 292–293. *See also* plural voting; suffrage
Caprivi, Leo von, 141–144
Carlos I, 242
"The Case against Woman Suffrage," 265
Catholic Electoral Association (of Italy), 238
Catholic Relief Act (1829), 63

Catholicism and democratization
  in Austria, 201
  in Belgium, 178, 181–182, 259–260
  in France, 36, 251, 267–271
  in Italy, 40, 205, 216, 226, 229–231, 238, 249
  in Portugal, 244–245
  in UK, 48, 63
Cato Street Conspiracy, 59. *See also* police as coercive institution, need for
causal mechanism, 22, 50
Cavaignac, Louis-Eugène, 93
Cave, George, 256
Charles X, 92
Chartist movement, 75–82. *See also* democratization in UK, police as coercive institution
  about, 7, 11
  assessments of, 75–83
  demands of, 75
  effects of, 47, 81–82, 90, 298
  end of, 80
  as justification for police, 76–77
  likelihood of success, 76–77
  and Newport Rising, 78
  and police, 82
  repression of, 15–16, 47, 75–82
  and suffrage, 57–58, 75, 80–82
  timeline of, 81
*Chartist Studies* (Briggs), 76
Christian IX, 36
coercive institution. *See* police as coercive institution; yeomanry as coercive institution
Cold War, 9
Collier, Ruth, 30–31, 158, 179, 187, 199, 203, 207, 271, 286
competitive authoritarianism, 91–126, 205–213, 230–240, 243–247. *See also* democratization in Imperial Germany; democratiation in Italy; elections; French Second Empire; suffrage
  about, 8–10, 41, 101
  in contemporary politics, 299
  and control of the press, 109
  defined, 102
  diffusion of, 95
  and elections, 126
  endurance of, 122, 134–158
  as half-way to democracy, 131–132
  mentioned, 2, 40–41, 119, 293

# Index 303

in Southern Europe, 18
stability of, 129
competitive oligarchy. *See also
under* democratization in
Belgium; democratization in
Denmark; democratization in Italy;
democratization in the Netherlands;
democratization in Sweden; first wave
(of democratization)
  about, 38–40
  defined, 8–9
  mentioned, 18, 21, 128
  and plural voting, 38, 161–162
  and voting registration systems, 257
Constitution of Piedmont (Italy), 227
Costa, Afonso, 243–246
counter-majoritarian institution, 8–10, 12, 21, 24, 29, 38, 180, 190, 193, 204, 237, 249, 290, 294–295, 299. *See also* House of Lords
County and Borough Police Act (1856), 82
Cowling, Malcolm, 85–88, 90
Craik, Henry, 257
Crispi, Francisco, 217, 223–226
Croce, Benedetto, 23–24, 205, 207, 209–210, 212–213, 215, 220, 229, 237
Curragh incident, 172–173

Dahl, Robert, 16, 21–25, 36, 38, 44–45, 48, 102, 176, 241
  axioms of, 22
Dahlian coding, 16, 30–31, 95, 207, 295
  and eighth requirement of, 36
  of European democratization, 30
Dahrendorf, Ralf, 27, 129, 131
*Daily Telegraph* affair, 145–146, 148, 156
Dangerfield, George, 46, 158
De Gaulle, Charles, 270
De Geer, Louis, 191
Delacroix, Leon, 259
democratic backsliding, 158, 175, 205, 225, 242, 291, 297–299
democratization. *See also* first wave (of democratization)
  changing authoritarian attitudes towards, 293
  and failure of liberalism prior to WWI, 298–299
  foreign policy mistakes as causes of, 288–289
  gradualism, narrative of, 21–24

  and per capita GDP, *208*
  and political parties, 294
  popular attitudes towards, 293–294
  and proportional representation, 294
  and regime types prior to WWI, 42
  Sonderweg, narrative of, 26–29
  status of, prior to WWI, 35
  and suffrage rates, *189*
  threat of revolution, 24–25
  and WWI as gateway to, 270, 288–289
democratization in Australia
  mentioned, 1, 6, 33
  and suffrage, 35
democratization in Austria, 200–202
  and socialism, 200–202
  spillover from Hungary and, 200–202
  and suffrage, 200–202
democratization in the Balkans
  and electoral manipulation, 248
  and suffrage, 248
democratization in Belgium, 178–183
  Catholicism and, 181, 182, 259–260
  and competitive oligarchy, 10–11, 18, 39, 177–178, 180, 254–255
  narratives of, 178–179
  old regime, resilience of, 177, 179–183
  and socialism, 177–183, 259–260, 298
  and Socialist Party, 179–183
  and suffrage, 39, 177, 179–183, 259–260
  and suffrage, female, 36, 182–183, 270
  and threat of revolution, 179–180
  working class role in, 179–182
  and WWI, 250
democratization in Canada
  and elections, 253–254
  mentioned, 1, 6
  and suffrage, 253–254
democratization in Denmark, 195–199
  about, 35
  and capacity (to vote), 197
  and competitive oligarchy, 197
  and myth of historical democracy, 197
  old regime, resilience of, 197–199
  partial success of, 199
  and socialism, 198
  and suffrage, 18, 35, 102, 177, 195–199
  and suffrage, female, 199
  and threat of revolution, 196
democratization in Finland, 202–203
  and socialism, 202–203
  and threat of revolution, 203

democratization in France. *See also* French Second Empire; French Second Republic
  and Bonaparte *coup d'etat*, 98
  and Catholicism, 267–268
  and competitive authoritarianism, 17
  democratic characteristics of, 95–96
  election of 1848, 93, 96
  mentioned, 1
  and socialism, 251, 269–270
  and suffrage, 36, 92, 95–96, 98
  and suffrage, female, 267–270
  timeline of, *100*
democratization in Greece
  and competitive authoritarianism, 40–41
  mentioned, 18, 32–33, 41, 248
democratization in Hapsburg Empire, 200–202
democratization in Imperial Germany, 127–158, 271–284. *See also* Wilhelm II regime
  bourgeoisie, weakness of, 130–131
  and competitive authoritarianism, 17, 40–41, 94, 128–129, 157–158
  election manipulation and, 29, 132–139, 291
  fall of Wilhelm II, 281–282
  half-way theory and, 131
  and independence of ministries, 142
  and military as check on democratization, 150–152
  old regime, resilience of, 29, 129–141, 155–156, 272
  parliamentary power, growth of, 132–133
  and socialism, 135, 140, 273, 282–284
  and Sonderweg thesis, 129
  and Sonderweg thesis, reconsidered, 129–131, 133
  "stab in the back" lie, 276–277, 283–284
  and suffrage, 9–10, 17, 29, 95, 131–132, 136, 138–140, 147, 152, 155
  and suffrage linked to WWI, 274–275
  and suffrage, female, 36–37
  and Supreme Army Command, antidemocratic ethos of, 273
  and threat of military coup, 150
  and threat of revolution, 272, 281
  and Weimar Republic, 271, 282–284
  widespread conquest, fantasies of, 275–276
  WWI, 271–284, 287–288
  WWI and US demands for regime change/democracy, 277–82
  WWI as gateway to democracy, 288
  WWI and democratic backsliding, 273–275
  WWI, loss in, 251
  and WWI, Social Democrat opposition to, 276
democratization in Italy, 205–239
  and electoral manipulation, 40
  and Catholicism, 226, 229–231, 238
  and competitive authoritarianism, 40–41, 238–239
  and competitive oligarchy, 40, 43, 205–222, 210
  and democratic backsliding, 224–29
  as dictatorship, 205–206
  and elections, 205, 207
  and electoral manipulation, 208, 214–215, 225, 232–234
  and Ethiopian disaster, 225–226
  and fascism, 212, 215, 239
  as first wave democracy, 207, 237
  gradualism, narrative of, 209–210
  historiography and, 14, 208–213
  and *Il Duce*, 212
  Liberal Italy, 207–213
  liberal narrative of, 205, 208–213
  Marxist view of, 210–211
  and North/South dichotomy, 220, 221, 233–234
  old regime, resilience of, 207, 223, 237
  and Papal non-expedit, 216, 231
  partial democracy, 206–207
  politics, character of, 206
  and renewed power of parliament, 229–230
  and *Risorgimento* (unification), 213–214, 216–217
  Sicilian revolt, repression of, 223–226
  and socialism, 205–207, 223–232, 234–236, 249
  and suffrage, 40, 205, 207, 213–214, 223, 225, 230, 234–239, 252–253
  and suffrage, female, 36
democratization in Mediterranean and Balkan states, 208
democratization in the Netherlands, 183–187, 260–261
  and capacity (to vote), 186
  and competitive oligarchy, 10–11, 18, 177, 254, 260–261

*Index* 305

and electoral reform, 260
gradualist narrative of, 183-184
gradualist narrative of, reconsidered, 184-185
old regime, resilience of, 171-187
and socialism, 186-187
and suffrage, 39, 44, 177, 184, 186-187, 260-261
and suffrage rates, 185
and WWI, 250
democratization in New Zealand
as first wave country, 6
measures of, 33
mentioned, 1
suffrage and, 34-35
democratization in Norway, 34-35, 203-204
and suffrage, 35
and suffrage, female, 35
democratization in Portugal, 240-247
and capacity (to vote), 244
and competitive authoritarianism, 40-41, 243-247
and competitive oligarchy, 43, 240-242, 247
and democratic backsliding, 242
and electoral manipulation, 208, 241-242, 245
fall of monarchy, 242
as first wave democracy, 247
old regime, resilience of, 245
Republican leadership of, 243
and suffrage, 240-242, 244, 246
democratization in Spain, 194-195
and competitive authoritarianism, 40-41
and competitive oligarchy, 247-148
and suffrage, 248
democratization in Sweden, 176-178, 187-195, 284-287
and competitive oligarchy, 177, 190, 284-285
and elections, 190, 193-194
failure of reform efforts, 195
and suffrage, female, 286
as first wave country, 4
gradualist narrative of, 187-188
gradualist narrative of, reconsidered, 187-195
historical estate suffrage system, 190-191
myth of historical democracy, 187-190

old regime, resilience of, 8, 190-195, 284-285
and socialism, 191-192, 194, 286-287
and suffrage, 39-40, 190-193
and suffrage linked to WWI, 284-288
and threat of revolution, 192, 272, 285-287
ultimate causes of, 287-288
and WWI, 251, 284-287
democratization in Switzerland
as first wave country, 6
gradualist narrative of, 22
mentioned, 1, 32, 33
and suffrage, 35, 47, 102
and suffrage, female, 37, 44, 267
democratization in UK, 45-90. *See also* First Reform Act (1832); Representation of the People Act (1918); Second Reform Act (1867)
Annual Army Act as tool of oligarchy, 172
and capacity (to vote), 256
and competitive oligarchy, 10-11, 16-17, 38-39, 45-90, 127-128, 254
and elections, 68, 166-167, 169-173
as first wave country, 3-4, 7
gradualism, narrative of, 20, 128
House of Lords, reform of, 164-168
Irish Home Rule, crisis of, 169-174
old regime, resilience of, 16-17, 52, 90, 168-169, 174-175
police as coercive institution and, 46, 53-56
as polyarchy, 22
and repression, timeline of, 60
slow pace of, 89-90
and socialism, 165
and suffrage, 7, 38, 46-47, 57, 73, 82, 84, 88-90, 128
and suffrage linked to WWI, 255
and suffrage, female, 18-19, 257, 262-265
Third Reform Act (1884) and, 127-128
and threat of revolution, 5, 46, 65-73
voting registration systems, 159-160, 295
democratization in US
and elections, 295-296
and socialism, 266
and suffrage, female, 265-267
*Demokratie und Kaisertum* (Naumann), 145-147

Depretis, Agostino, 218, 223
Derby riots, 70
Deuntzer, Johan, 36
disenfranchisement. *See* suffrage
Disraeli, Benjamin, 21, 82, 85–88
Dreyfus affair, 25, 169, 229
Dublin Police Act (1786), 54

Ebert, Friedrich, 282–283
*Economic Origins of Dictatorship and Democracy* (Acemoglu and Robinson), 5
Edward VII, 166
Edwardian Britain, 28
Edwardian crisis, 17, 158–159
Edwardian England, 1, 17, 295
Eel Revolts, 186
elections. *See also* suffrage; *and under democratization in individual countries*
  background, 9
  characteristics of in democracy, 30–31, 41, 292
  in first wave countries, 41–42
  and French Second Empire, 17
  as tool of competitive authoritarianism, 9–10, 94, 97–98, 102, 119–120, 125–126, 297
Electoral Law (1850), 7
Eley, Geoff, 28, 37, 130–132, 146
enfranchisement. *See* suffrage
Engels, Friedrich, 100, 179, 204
*England after the War* (Masterman), 258
English Civil War, 49–50, 53
Estrup, Jacob, 35, 198–199
Eulenburg, Botho, 143–145
Eulenburg, Philip, 139–140

*Fasci Siciliani*, 223–224
*Federalism and Parliamentarianism in Wilhelmine Germany* (Rauh), 157
First Reform Act (1832), 15, 16, 52, 62–75
  and French Revolution of 1830, 66–67
  and House of Lords, 68–69, 73
  and monarchical power, 167
  old regime, resilience of, 64–65
  and political unions, 67–70
  reactions to, 73–75
  and suffrage, 73–74
  and threat of revolution, 62, 65–67, 69–70, 72–73
  timeline of, 71

first wave (of democratization), 1–19
  and authoritarianism, 6, 41–42
  and capacity (to vote), 292–293
  and competitive oligarchy, 10–11
  defined, 3
  gradualism, narrative of, 15, 290
  and historiography, 13–15
  as laboratory for research, 5
  measuring, 29–34
  mentioned, 41, 288–289
  and modernization theory, 10–11
  narratives of, 3–4, 20–21, 291
  old regime, resilience of, 6–8, 16–17
  and partial democracy, 11–12
  and preservation of non-majoritarian institutions, 10
  reconsidered, 6, 15–18
  relevance of, today, 299
  and Sonderweg thesis, 291
  and suffrage, 7–8, 10, 12, 21, 23–24, 29, 34–35, 44
  and suffrage, female, 12–13, 19, 30, 36–37
  and threat of revolution, 11, 15–16, 290
  Whiggish view of, 16
  and WWI, 12
Fischer, Edmund, 37
Franchise Act (1884). *See* Third Reform Act (1884)
Francis Joseph I, 42
Franco, Joao, 242
Franco–Prussian War, 94, 122, 126
Franz Ferdinand, 127
Frederick III, 139
Free Liberals, 186
French Second Empire, 14, 100–123
  and Bonapartism, rise of, 93–94
  and competitive authoritarianism, 17, 40–41, 94–95, 100–122
  and control of the press, 109–112
  and co-optation of Republicans, 117–119
  defined, 119
  and election manipulation, 11, 102–109, 114, 126
  elections and official candidates, selection of, 102–106
  elections, prefecture system of, 103–109, 116–117, 232
  establishment of, 99–100
  explanations for persistence of, 120–122

fall of and Franco–Prussian War,
    122–123, 126
  and limits to democratization, 116
  as model for Imperial Germany, 94–95
  old regime, resilience of, 109, 119–120
  and partial democratization, 112–113
  as path to democracy, 113–116
  and police as coercive institution, 11
  and socialism, 109, 121–122
  stability of, 112–123
  and suffrage, 9–10, 17, 36, 95, 102
French Second Republic
  Bonaparte coup d'etat and, 93, 98–100
  Bonaparte election and, 92–93
  and elections, 96
  fall of, 17, 99–100
  and socialism, 95–100
  and suffrage, 7, 36, 95–98
French Third Republic, 109
  and suffrage, 36

Gentolini Pact, 206–207, 231, 238
George IV, 63
George V, 166
Georgia Election Integrity Act (2021), 295–296
German Communist Party (KPD), 284
*German Empire, The* (Wehler), 130, 157
German exceptionalism. *See* Sonderweg thesis
Germany, Wilhelmine. *See* Wilhelm II regime
Giannattasio, Nicola, 207
Giolitti, Giovanni. *See also* democratization in Italy
  about, 205
  as dictator, 211–212
  and elections manipulation, 232–234
  as enabler of fascism, 212
  mentioned, 215, 220
  and oligarchy, 230–234
  and suffrage, 234–239, 252
Gladstone, William, 82, 86–89
gradualism, theory of, 20–24. *See also under* democratization in individual countries
  critiques of, 24
  in Northern Europe, 176
  in Northern Europe, reconsidered, 176–178
  origins of, 22–23
  persistence of, 23–24

Gramsci, Antonio, 210–211, 233–234
Grand National Consolidated Trades Union, 75
Great Reform Act. *See* First Reform Act (1832)
Grevy, Jules, 119
Grey, Charles (Earl Grey), 14–15, 62, 64–65, 67, 70, 72–74, 85–86
Grey, Edward, 128
Gustav V, 194, 286

Halsbury Club, 169
Hamburg, elections in, 137
Hammarskjöld, Hugo, 288
Harrison, Royden, 84–87
Hedin, Sven, 194
Heydebrand, Ernst von, 138
Himmelfarb, Gertrude, 83–85
historiography
  of Belgium, 179
  and first wave (of democratization), 13–15
  of French Second Empire, 113
  of French Second Republic, 94
  of Imperial Germany, 129–133, 155–156
  of Italy, 208–213
  mentioned, 44
  of UK, 28, 47–52, 66
*History of England* (Macaulay), 45, 81
*History of Italy, 1871–1915* (Croce), 205, 209
Hohenlohe-Schillingfuest, Chlodwig Carl Viktor, 143–144, 152
Holstein, Duchies, 196–197
Holstein, Friedrich von, 139
House of Lords, 38–39, 161–166, 257
Hunt, Henry, 21, 57–58, 146
Huntington, Samuel, 3, 11, 29–30
Hyde Park Railing Affair, 82, 84
Hyde Park Riots, 82, 84

Independent Social Democratic Party of Germany (USPD), 276. *See also* Majority Social Democratic Party of Germany (MSPD); Social Democratic Pary (SPD) of Germany
International Group, 276
Irish Home Rule, 128, 158, 173–174
Iron Chancellor. *See* Bismarck, Otto von
*Italian Democracy in the Making* (Salamone), 209

Jacobinism, 25
*Jahrgang 1902* (Glaser), 273
Jenson, Peter, 51
July Monarchy (of France), 92, 95, 121
July Revolution (of France), 185
June Constitution (Denmark), 197–199

Kaiser Wilhelm. *See* Wilhelm II regime
Kennington Common, 80
Kreuzer, Marcus, 13, 28, 132–133, 148–149

L'Estrange, Guy, 58
Lansing, Robert, 274
Laurier Liberals, 254
Laurier, Wilfrid, 254
leap in the dark, 82–83, 256. *See also* Second Reform Act (1867)
Leninism, 25
Leo XIII, 216
Levitsky, Steven, 94, 101–102
Liebknecht, Karl, 276
Lindman, Arvid, 193–195, 286
Lloyd George, David, 164–167, 173, 256, 261–262
London Working Mens' Association (LWMA), 75
Lord Liverpool (Jenkinson, Robert Banks), 59
Lord Russell (Russell, John), 64, 76
Louis Philippe, 91–92
Lowell, A. Lawrence, 2
Lübeck (Germany), 137
Luddite movement. *See also* democratization in UK; police as coercive institution
  about, 53–54
  and coercive institutions, need for, 56–57
  mentions, 51–52
  repression of, 15–16, 53–54
Ludendorff, Erich, 273–277, 281, 284, 288
Lustick, Ian, 13, 128, 170, 174
Luxembourg, Rosa, 147, 276
Luzzati, Luigi, 234–235

Macaulay, Thomas, 24, 45, 47, 62, 65
Machiavelli, 25
Magna Carta, 3
Majority Social Democratic Party of Germany (MSDP). *See* Independent Social Democratic Party of Germany (USPD); Social Democratic Party (SPD) of Germany
*Making of the English Working Class* (Thompson), 51
Manchester Political Union, 57
Manchester yeomanry, 58
Martial Origins theory, 252–255
Marxism, 6, 14, 25, 55, 84, 87, 93, 96, 101, 179, 236
May Crisis (1832), 72
Mayer, Arno, 6
Mayne, Richard, 80
Mehnert's law, 136
Metropolitan Police, 77–78, 80
Metzsch-Reichenbach, Georg von, 136
Michaelis, George, 275
Military Service Act (1917), 254
Military Voters Act (1917), 254
Minghetti, Marco, 218, 221, 223
*Misdemeanors Act* (1819), 59
*Modern Democracies* (Bryce), 1–3, 18
modernization theory, 3, 10–11, 14, 28, 49–50, 132, 291
Montagnards, 95–96
Moore, Barrington, 49–50
Mosca, Gaetano, 209, 213–215, 236–237

Napier, Charles, 76–77
Napoleon III. *See also* French Second Empire; French Second Republic
  about, 91–93
  mentioned, 14, 17, 98
National Union of the Working Classes, 73
Nazism, 27, 129–131
Newport Rising, 78–79
*Newspaper and Stamp Duties Act* (1819), 58
Nineteenth Amendment (US), 265, 266
non-expedit, 216, 231. *See also* Catholicism and democratization; democratization in Italy
Nordic Democracy, 177, 188, 197
Nottingham riots, 70

old regime, resilience of, 6–12, 16, 127, 167. *See also* counter-majoritarian institution; elections; police as coercive institution; suffrage; *and under* democratization *in individual countries*
  and counter-majoritarian institutions, 38, 294–295
  and democratic backsliding, 297–298

and election manipulation, 204, 223
gradualism, 21–22
in Great Britain, 47
and police, as tool of, 297
and power of elites, 39
and repression, 296–297
resistance to suffrage and, 14, 38, 46
and threat of revolution, 5
as threat to democracy, 293–294
and WWI, 18, 289–292
oligarchy. *See also* competitive oligarchy
as danger to democracy, 216
and election corruption, 215–216
Ollivier, Émile, 117–119, 122
Orbán, Viktor, 293

Pacification of 1917 (Netherlands), 260
Palace Yard Speech (of Gustav V), 194–195
Pareto, Vilfredo, 213, 215–216, 219
Parliament Act (1866) of Sweden, 191
Parliament Act (1911) of UK, 39, 127–128, 158, 164–75, 257
partial democracy, 11, 112–113, 131–132
*Patterns of Government: The Major Political Systems of Europe* (Beer), 49
Peel, Robert
about, 54
mentioned, 74–75, 79
and police, establishment of, 54–55, 60–61
Peelite Principles, 61
Pelloux, Luigi, 228–229
Persigny, Duc de (Jean Gilbert Victor Fialin), 91, 103, 108–109, 117
*Persistence of the Old Regime, The* (Mayer), 6
Peterloo Massacre, 15, 16, 53, 57–59, 78, 89. *See also* police as coercive institution
Pius IX, 216
plural voting, 191. *See also* capacity (to vote); elections; suffrage
in Belgium, 40, 177, 183, 259–260, 270
and competitive oligarchy, 161–162
in Hamburg, 137
mentioned, 8, 29, 204, 249, 295
in Prussia, 138
in Saxony, 137–138
in Sweden, 39–40

in UK, 160–162, 257, 270
Plural Voting (Abolition) Bill (1892), 164
Polanyi, Karl, 10, 90
police as coercive institution. *See also under* Chartist movement; Luddite movement; old regime, resilience of; Peterloo massacre
about, 46, 78, 90
establishment of, 11, 16, 54–62, 77–78
need for, 53–59
reaction to, 61–62
as tool of old regime, 11, 186, 233, 290–291
*Political Repression in 19th Century Europe* (Goldstein), 8
*Politics of Accommodation, The* (Lijphart), 183
"The Politics of Democracy: The English Reform Act of 1867," 83
Polity IV, 20, 31, 33, 41, 43–44, 291
about, 31–34
findings of, 31–32
mentioned, 16
suffrage and, 32
vs. V-Dem, 34, 43–44
polyarchy, 21–25, 45, 176
and Polity IV, 31–34
*Polyarchy* (Dahl), 241
Poortvliet, Tak van, 186
Portuguese Republican Party (PRP), 244–246
*Practicing Democracy: Elections and Political Culture in Imperial Germany* (Anderson), 28, 133
prefecture system (France). *See under* French Second Empire, elections, prefecture system of
*Prison Notebooks, The* (Gramsci), 208–213
Prussia
army as check on democratization, 150–151
electoral system of, 137–139
old regime, resilience of, 137–139
three-class suffrage system, 29, 136–139, 149, 281
Przeworski, Adam, 15, 135, 200, 202, 207, 252–253

Raimondo, Orazio, 205–207, 237
Rasmussen, Anders Fogh, 4
Rebeiro, Hintze, 242

Reform League, 82, 85–87
Representation of the People Act (1918), 255–258, 298
and war toll on elite class, 257–258
repression as tool of old regime. *See also* Chartist movement; Luddite movement; Peterloo massacre; police as coercive institution
in French Second Empire, 101–102, 111, 117
in French Second Republic, 92, 98
in Imperial Germany, 154, 284
in Italy, 219–220, 226–228, 233, 237
mentioned, 11, 15–16, 18, 22–23, 178, 204, 292, 296, 299
in the Netherlands, 186
in Sweden, 191
in UK, 46, 52, 58–59, 60, 61, 75–82, 90
Reuss, Heinrich, 140
Ricotti-Magnani, Cesare, 226
*Risorgimento*. *See* democratization in Italy
Robinson, James 26, 47, 50, 83, 192, 200, 203, 271, 281, 290
*Rotativismo*, 208, 241, 247
Royal Irish Constabulary, 54
Rural Constabulary Act (1839), 77–78
Rustow, Dankwart, 135

Salford Yeomanry, 58
Salvemini, Gaetano, 206, 209, 211–213, 222, 233, 236–237, 239, 252
Saxony
consequences of unfair elections, 136
suffrage in, 136–137
Schleswig, Duchies, 196
Schweinitz, Hans von, 140
Second Reform Act (1867), 82–89
and capacity (to vote), 87–89
mentioned, 16, 192, 256, 296
old regime, resilience of, 17
political environment of, 86–87
and threat of revolution, 84–85
Whig view of, 83
Whig view, reconsidered, 83–85
Second Reich. *See* democratization in Imperial Germany
*Seditious Meetings Act* (1819), 58
*Seizure of Arms Act* (1819), 57
Simon, John, 262
Simon, Jules, 267
"Six Acts" (1819), 15–16, 58–59, 61

Skocpol, Theda, 24
Social Democratic Party (SPD) of Germany
mentioned, 37, 122, 127, 156, 274–275
rise of, 132
and state elections, 136–137
and suffrage, 147–148
and suffrage, female, 37
and WWI, 276–277
*Social Origins* (Moore), 50
socialism and democratization, 7, 21, 36–37. *See also under* democratization in individual countries
socialism and suffrage, 7, 21, 37
Society for the Study of Labour History, 84
Sonderweg thesis, 26–29, 128–31. *See also* democratization in Imperial Germany; first wave (of democratization)
applied to Italy, 211
mentioned, 20, 21
reconsidered, 133, 155, 157, 210, 272
Sonnino, Sidney, 222, 236, 239, 227–230
Spartacus Group, 276, 284
Staaff, Karl Albert, 194–195
Stalinism, 25
suffrage. *See also under* competitive authoritarianism; competitive oligarchy; counter-majoritarian institution; first wave (of democratization);old regime, resilience of; *and under* democratization in individual countries
as feature of authoritarianism, 133–135
historiography of, 15
modern attitudes towards, 292–293
numbers by country, 189
rates by country in 1915, 161
registration systems and, 38
as threat to democracy, 9, 47, 198
suffrage, female, 36–37. *See also* Bryce, James; first wave (of democratization); WWI and democratization; *and under* democratization in individual countries
dates of, by country, 12
Supreme Army Command, 274, 276, 278, 281, 283
*Sweden: A Modern Democracy on Ancient Foundations* (Herlitz), 189
Swiss Association for Women's Suffrage, 38

Tamworth Manifesto, 74
Third Great Reform Act. *See* Third Reform Act (1884)
Third Reform Act (1884), 39, 127–128
third wave (of democritization), 3, 11, 29
Thistlewood, Arthur, 59
threat of revolution hypothesis, 5, 11, 15, 20, 25–26, 46, 51–52, 65–66, 177, 271, 286–287. *See also under* First Reform Act (1832); first wave (of democratization); Second Reform Act (1867); *and under* democratization in individual countries
suffrage and, 25–26, 177–178, 196–197
three-class suffrage system. *See* Prussia, three-class suffrage system
Tocqueville, Alexis de, 1, 92, 96
totalitarianism, 2, 188
*Traders and Heroes: Patriotic Reflections* (Sombart), 272
*Training Prevention Act* (1819), 58
trasformismo, 217–222. *See also* democratization in Italy
defined, 217–218, 241–242
effects of, 221–222
and electoral manipulation, 218–220
justifications for, 220–221
mentioned, 40, 208, 231, 238, 295
Treaty of Brest-Litovsk, 276, 288
Trevelyan, G. M., 48, 81, 83, 209
Trump, Donald J., 293, 297
Trygger, Ernst, 286

ultimatum crisis (Portugal), 242–243
Umberto I, 226

Vandervelde, Emile, 179–183
Varieties of Democracy. *See* V-Dem
V-Dem
about, 16, 35
and clean elections, 41
and elections, 41
mentioned, 89
vs Polity IV, 20, 32–34, 41, 44, 291
Voting Rights Act (1965), 292, 295–296

Waldersee, Alfred von, 139, 152
Wartime Elections Act (1917), 254
Way, Lucan, 94, 101–102

Wehler, Hans-Ulrich, 133–134, 135, 155
Weimar Republic. *See* democratization in Imperial Germany
Wellington, Duke (Wellessley, Arthur), 56, 63–67, 72–73, 80
"Why did the West Extend the Franchise" (Acemoglu and Robinson), 5
Wilhelm II regime, 17, 129, 139–158. *See also under* democratization in Imperial Germany
abdication, 286
and *Daily Telegraph* affair, 144–145
Grand Block reform, 146–147
mentioned, 14, 28, 122, 133, 140, 146, 190
"stab in the back" lie, 277
and threat of military coup, 150–152
weakness of democratization efforts, 147–149
and WWI, 272–273, 275, 278, 280–282
Zabern affair and, 153–156
William I, 139, 185
William III, 186
William IV, 63, 71–72
Wilson, Woodrow, 274
and demand for democratization in Imperial Germany, 251, 277–81
"Women under Socialism" (Bebel), 37
Woodward, Llewellyn, 46
WWI and democratization, 250–289
and competitive oligarchy, 250
and conscription, 250, 252–255
role in democratization, 250–252
and suffrage, 12, 250, 261
and suffrage, female, 250–251, 254, 261–270, 288–289
and US policy of democracy promotion, 251
WWII, 2, 13, 182

yeomanry as coercive institution, 56–58. *See also* police as coercive institution

Zabern affair. *See* Wilhelm II regime, Zabern affair and
Zeldin, Theodore, 106, 112, 116–117
Zetkin, Clara, 276
Ziblatt, Daniel, 4, 7–8, 23–24, 175–176, 249, 294

For EU product safety concerns, contact us at Calle de José Abascal, 56–1°,
28003 Madrid, Spain or eugpsr@cambridge.org.

www.ingramcontent.com/pod-product-compliance
Ingram Content Group UK Ltd.
Pitfield, Milton Keynes, MK11 3LW, UK
UKHW041922020426
469639UK00012B/234